Virtually Sacred

VIRTUALLY SACRED

Myth and Meaning in World of
Warcraft *and* Second Life

ROBERT M. GERACI

OXFORD
UNIVERSITY PRESS

OXFORD
UNIVERSITY PRESS

Oxford University Press is a department of the University of Oxford.
It furthers the University's objective of excellence in research, scholarship,
and education by publishing worldwide.

Oxford   New York
Auckland   Cape Town   Dar es Salaam   Hong Kong   Karachi
Kuala Lumpur   Madrid   Melbourne   Mexico City   Nairobi
New Delhi   Shanghai   Taipei   Toronto

With offices in
Argentina   Austria   Brazil   Chile   Czech Republic   France   Greece
Guatemala   Hungary   Italy   Japan   Poland   Portugal   Singapore
South Korea   Switzerland   Thailand   Turkey   Ukraine   Vietnam

Oxford is a registered trademark of Oxford University Press
in the UK and certain other countries.

Published in the United States of America by
Oxford University Press
198 Madison Avenue, New York, NY 10016

Library of Congress Cataloging-in-Publication Data
Geraci, Robert M.
Virtually sacred : myth and meaning in world of warcraft
and second life / Robert M. Geraci.
pages cm
Includes bibliographical references and index.
ISBN 978–0–19–934469–7 (cloth : alk. paper)
1. Virtual reality—Religious aspects.   I. Title.
BL65.V57G47 2014
200—dc23
2013039065

1 3 5 7 9 8 6 4 2
Printed in the United States of America
on acid-free paper

For Kathy Linder
who taught me the difference between getting and earning,
and who has been an intellectual inspiration for more than
twenty years.

Contents

Acknowledgments

IT IS STANDARD practice for acknowledgments to get longer as one's academic career progresses, but I shall try to keep mine relatively short despite the growing number of people who have influenced or contributed to my work. Between my first book and this, my second, some things have not changed, and this means that the first people who deserve acknowledgment are my wife, Jovi, and my children, Zion and Liel. They tolerate my absence, allow me to leave piles of books all over the house, and make sure I've got three of the best reasons in the world to put down my research and come out to play.

To all of the other kids who enjoyed role-playing games with me in my youth, first and foremost Cody, there's no doubt that I could not have written this book without you. It is remarkable to me how many wonderful ways my childhood gaming has shaped me into the kind of scholar that I am. I couldn't be more grateful for those hours spent rolling dice, accumulating treasure, and arguing about water cannons. What a delight that my mom, my dad, and my extra mom (Penny) never dismissed our pastime and that Penny even gave endless hours of her time shuttling Cody and me to bookstores, comic stores, and anywhere else we could buy dice, monster manuals, and adventure modules. I'm lucky to have had three such great parents. My brother, Vinny, gave me my first *Dungeons & Dragons* books, which was fortuitous, and my sister, Anne, willingly joined in the role-playing games that I later created on my own. Of course, I would be remiss if I didn't thank the amazing designers who produced the games I loved, especially *Advanced Dungeons & Dragons* and *Shadowrun*. In those games, I learned to dream rigorously.

My adult friends also contributed in many ways to the project. Joe Reinbold-Alfonso hosted my first surveys on his server, the Golden Handcuff crowd at Manhattan College helped me revise two of this book's chapters, and a wide array of folks advertised my surveys (including Clint, who helped me revise one of them; the good folks at PennyArcade.com; and James of *New World Notes*). Katie read early drafts and has always been a tireless cheerleader and amazing friend. And my longtime friends, Cody and Mark, read a late version of the manuscript and gave me critical feedback. On campus, the skill of the library staff, especially John Gormley, in locating the source material I need is invaluable, and the School of Arts secretaries, MaryEllen Lamonica and Syrita Newman, make my work easier in a hundred different ways. They are also hilarious; I am grateful for their contributions to my work and life.

As usual, my students have proven very helpful in my thinking, especially those who joined my seminar on religion and the Internet. Douglas Mandelkow, who wrote an honors thesis about video game communities while under my supervision, has been a wonderful student and colleague; our regular meetings over a pint of beer were both fun and insightful. Likewise, my undergraduate researchers in the Virtually Meaningful Project, funded by the National Science Foundation, read the penultimate version of this book and gave me their comments. Working with them on their research projects also gave me additional time to talk about and think about religion and virtual worlds. As I've finished this book at the same time that they have begun their own research, I hope it proves helpful to them.

Several academics included me in events that helped me shape my ideas. Chuck Henderson, who hosts the summer colloquium for the Association for Religion in Intellectual Life, deserves special thanks for allowing me to take part in it during July 2010 while I wrote the rough draft of my *World of Warcraft* chapters, as does Alexander Ornella, whose friendship during that month was the highlight of the colloquium for me. Without Christopher Denny inviting me to present my research on religion and artificial intelligence at the Columbia University Seminar on the Study of Religion, I might have never quite figured out what I meant to say in the conclusion to this book, and that would have been a disaster. Chuck Matthewes and Stefan Helmreich have supported my research and career over and over again; they are peerless friends and colleagues. Finally, my colleagues in the Department of Religious Studies at Manhattan College are more wondrous than I deserve. What an amazing group with whom to think and teach.

I cannot proceed without mentioning the folks who made this book, as it is presently written, possible. The anonymous reviewers at Oxford University Press gave generously of their time and made excellent suggestions throughout—I hope I have lived up to them. My editor, Cynthia Read, is one of the most fascinating people I've had the good fortune to eat lunch with. Not only does she send me interesting things to read, but she and her staff make my work better. I'm very grateful for their help. The many people I interviewed over the past three years (both those included in the book and those who are not) were gracious with their time and their thoughts. I would like to single out James, Giulio, Sophrosyne, Extropia, Kimberly, Wren, and Philip, but many others have sat with me, emailed with me, or chatted with me in some virtual world or another. The Order of Cosmic Engineers, the Turing Church, and the Heirohacking email communities all good-naturedly put up with an interloper in their midst. Whew! I have no idea what I would have done if they'd turned down my requests. In addition, I am grateful to Nicholas Zachowski, who wrote a paper on *World of Warcraft* for my Religion and Science class and graciously allowed me to use quotes from two of his own interview subjects in this book (likewise, I owe thanks to the two students who agreed to have their words appear here).

I would never have played enough *World of Warcraft* to complete Chapters 1, 2, and 3 without the amazing group of people that comprised my Horde and, especially, Alliance guilds there. May they never drop another stitch. I'll never forget the help and companionship that they so freely gave, and I hope I gave back a meaningful fraction of what I received.

Finally, because they'll always be the first and last people I think of, I'm grateful for Jovi and the kids. Jovi has been an amazing companion in gaming, in research, and in life. As for Zion and Liel, well, they enchant the world, ensuring that I never stop looking for dragons or standing up to fight against demons.

Virtually Sacred

Introduction

REAL STORIES IN VIRTUAL WORLDS

THIS IS A book about virtual worlds and the people who live in them. In particular, it is a book about how video games and virtual worlds are rearranging or replacing religious practice: designers, users, and the virtual worlds themselves now collaborate in the production of a new spiritual marketplace. In obvious ways, the advent of online communication has provided new opportunities and new stumbling blocks for traditional religions, and it has even permitted the growth of new kinds of religion. Virtual worlds, however, go well beyond what can be produced through webpages, and they are an important part of our religious landscape now. They make way for new religious opportunities: they allow us new ways of expressing old religious practices and beliefs, but they also offer new ways of circumventing those traditions.

This is not a book destined to join the ranks of those that assault gaming as a gateway to violence or illegal activity, nor will it join those that trumpet video games as the saving grace for humanity in the wake of ecological and political crisis.[1] There is no shortage of either of those kinds of essays and, while more of each may be necessary, there is no question that we also need a few more books about precisely how and why players and designers imagine, produce, and enjoy virtual worlds. Naturally, no one book could possibly tackle all of the myriad ways virtual worlds have become part of our lives, so this is a book about just two such worlds and just one aspect of them: what role they play in contemporary religious activity. Although many of the conclusions of the this book can be (and will be) extrapolated beyond just the worlds in question or defended via evidence gleaned from other virtual worlds and video games, the entire purpose of the book is to think about how people do a variety of religious things with *World of Warcraft* and *Second Life*.[2] Both *World of Warcraft* and *Second Life* impinge on religious life: they give their players a host of opportunities that closely resemble those of traditional religions and, therefore, they compete with or restructure those traditional communities.

World of Warcraft and *Second Life* are exemplary virtual worlds, which explains their pride of place in this volume. They are the clear industry leaders in their respective domains, with *World of Warcraft* by far the most popular massively multiplayer online game in the United States and *Second Life* both better known and far more technologically advanced than other social environments. Neither of these virtual worlds is guaranteed to live out the decade; however, both have revolutionized virtual worlds and have made their mark on online culture. Subsequent virtual worlds will unquestionably borrow from the accomplishments of these two, even should they eventually lose their reigning status. As a consequence, the religious elements of both *World of Warcraft* and *Second Life* are well worth considering. Should other games and worlds replace *World of Warcraft* and *Second Life*, the ways both worlds participate in our religious culture will persist in them.

The connection between games and religion is nothing new; there have been religious games for, perhaps, as long as there has been religion. Game designer Jason Anthony describes three particular kinds of religious games: (1) catechistic games that point toward the sacred or are situated in a sacred context but are not themselves sacred; (2) poimenic games in which the divine manifests itself through the game; and (3) praxic games where playing the game is itself a sacred activity.[3] He explains that in both Western and Eastern contexts games have fulfilled all three of these purposes.[4] But while the connection between gaming and religion may be millennia old, digital virtual worlds are newcomers to the scene. *World of Warcraft* and *Second Life* are virtual worlds, though *Second Life* can only loosely be called a game. Both worlds, as we shall see throughout this book, enable new kinds of religious practices; in Anthony's terms, *World of Warcraft* can be a praxic game, while *Second Life* can be catechistic, poimenic, or praxic.

Both *World of Warcraft* and *Second Life* are virtual worlds and have connections to video games. *World of Warcraft* is definitely a game—in it, players take on heroic roles, battling against the forces of evil in a Tolkienesque fantasyland. *Second Life* is a world almost entirely created by its residents— they shape the land, raise the buildings, establish many of the governing principles, and fill the world with music, art, games, dancing, role-play, and nearly anything else the mind can invent. While many residents of SL resist calling it a "game," there are game-like aspects to it. Both *World of Warcraft* and *Second Life* are virtual worlds, each a "synchronous, persistent network of people, represented as avatars, facilitated by networked computers."[5] Virtual worlds are not simple games that disappear at the flick of a switch; you cannot simply overturn the board and make the results disappear. These worlds remain even in the player's absence or frustration. They are full of other players who help create the environment through their own goals and work. They are more immersive than the World Wide Web and more persistent than standard video games.

One of the most important aspects of the forthcoming analysis is the attention to the real members of these very real virtual worlds. To study the worlds as texts is important, and some commentators have engaged in similar tasks. However, it is at least as important to delve into the actual lives of people in virtual worlds, to hear their voices, to see their practices, and to note their beliefs. Over the coming chapters, I shall examine life on the virtual ground, with recourse to interviews and surveys in addition to my own observations; in this way, I will reveal paths by which the residents of virtual worlds construct ways of living and write new stories of myth and meaning.

Video gaming is, among other things, a storytelling medium, and the virtual worlds that emerge out of it tend in that direction also. Games often revolve around a hero's quest, for example, or they can place the characters in the midst of a mythical world history. Not all virtual worlds are games, but they nevertheless enable new kinds of stories, either because traditional ones are reformulated within the digital worlds or because entirely new stories become possible within them. Such storytelling can have religious implications given the current uncertainty surrounding traditional beliefs, practices, and stories.

Early video games on console platforms such as the Atari and original Nintendo were mostly devoid of religious themes,[6] but contemporary video games are rich with religious iconography, debate, and possibility. Initially, video games were too simple to include much narrative power and thus had no particular use for the significance that religious myths provide. But as technology advanced, enabling more graphically immersive games and more philosophical vantages for the player, storytelling became increasingly important. Thanks to this, mythical, magical, and religious storytelling became more common. The use of religion in game stories makes the games more immersive, and it also adds to their fun,[7] which explains why so many games now include religious elements. Designers can take advantage of differing game outlets and markets to produce games with an enormous diversity of religious implications. Game publishers can produce traditionally religious games (e.g., Christian or Islamic), invent religious systems to drive their narrative arcs, and sometimes even develop religious practices through their game design. This book will chiefly investigate the latter, but we must appreciate how the other two operate in gaming culture.

Designers and publishers concerned about the violent, sexual, secular, or other morally objectionable content of video games often resort to producing their own games with the intent of providing their audiences with "morally appropriate" options. For example, in *Catechumen*, a first-person shooter, the player must rescue imprisoned Christians and convert Roman soldiers in the dungeons below Rome before defeating Satan himself. Games like *Catechumen* offer explicitly Christian messages to counteract the evils of popular gaming.[8] In other ways, religion is a tool of cultural resistance because many popular video games are deeply polemical. In the Arabic world, for example, American video games that portray Arabs and Muslims in a negative light are often very popular despite the distaste that players have for the stereotyping and anti-Muslim rhetoric throughout the games. In response, Arabic game publishers have developed games in which Muslim or Arab heroes must act to save their own civilization, either in historical times or the present.[9] Neither the conversion of Roman soldiers—even with a magic sword that shoots out holiness to force the soldiers into a posture of prayer—nor games that rectify the stereotyping of Arabs and Muslims have dismantled the standard game production enterprise, but both represent a particular trend (however small) in gaming: deliberate religious advocacy.

Other games include religion in the narrative arc of the game even if the religion is, in some sense, incidental to the storyline. The enormously popular game *Halo*, for example, pits the players against an alien empire called the Covenant, which seeks to conquer the universe to satisfy a religious quest.[10] In *Spore*, players evolve a species from cellular level to intergalactic empire, and those who make friends with other species (as opposed, for example, to exterminating them) end up "religious" during the civilization stage of the game and can become "shamans" or "zealots" in the space stage. While the religious labels are not necessarily important to game play, they provide a backdrop for the player's self-identity within the game and certainly offer lenses through which to enjoy playing it (or not).

The religiosity of video games and virtual worlds draws on the uneven distribution of secularism in contemporary life. While no one really believes anymore that secularism means the end of religion, the term still refers to a certain dismantling of religious authority structures. In particular, if there is anything special about what we now call secularism, it is that we live within a spiritual marketplace. We have near limitless opportunity to join, reject, or intermingle religious ideas, practices, and communities. The twentieth century was not a time when religion disappeared, as some had hoped or feared it would, but it was a time when we started thinking quite differently about what we might get out of our wealth of religious and nonreligious institutions. As a result, secularism theory has largely given way before theories of pluralism in which many religions coexist.

Pluralism opens the door to a search for meaning that would have been inconceivable in centuries past. Although it cannot be held solely responsible for the decline of church attendance in recent decades, it also cannot be absolved of any part in that process. As Christopher Helland summarizes, many of the people who once attended church but do so no more are "now seeking their answers outside the traditional churches and other religious groups."[11] He rightly identifies that the Internet has become a site for this new kind of spiritual search, as it "caters to people who wish to be religious and spiritual on their own terms."[12] Digital technologies have many applications, but among them they produce a new "space" for religious work—work that is neither necessarily constrained by institutional religion nor practiced idiosyncratically by individuals.[13]

There have been serious consequences to our new, pluralistic lifestyle, and perhaps first among them is a confusion over what stories we can use to make sense out of the world. Though in some sense we are now free to select myths and histories from a vast panoply of options, it is more often the case that we now find ourselves debating which stories are real, and thus we tend to dismiss them altogether. But such dismissal cannot hold the human psyche; most of us like to have stories that carry meaning, and we will search for them if need be. Certainly, there are many people who continue to rely on traditional stories as the bedrock for their beliefs (or else there would be no conflict over the teaching of evolution!), but at the same time many others have gone in search of new stories that will give the world meaning, help them to interpret the world, and make life worth living.

Although the religious storytelling in console and personal computer games tends to be a side issue, as in *Spore*, or direct evangelism, as in *Catechumen*, virtual worlds provide a multiplicity of religious opportunities that can be absolutely vital to residency in those worlds. In the virtual worlds of *World of Warcraft* and *Second Life*, religion is ever-present, even while users may disregard it. In addition, the worlds are, themselves, conducive to religious practice as a consequence of their very worldhood. Residents of virtual worlds orient themselves through space and time, a fact that can be turned into religious participation online. In virtual worlds, we gain a sense of embodiment that is critical to religious participation. While there is no question that we might challenge the extent to which such embodiment realizes the full potential of human life, we cannot pretend that there is nothing new or interesting about walking avatars through temples, churches, and even fantasy landscapes. Life in a virtual world has a visceral quality that helps ensure we will engage the questions of meaning, purpose, and value that are crucial to religious life.[14]

The connection between video games and religion is not simply conjured by overly enthusiastic scholars but, rather, is something embraced by many in the gaming world. In her *Night Journey* project, for example, designer Tracy Fullerton is collaborating with the artist Bill Viola to explore the " 'game mechanic' of enlightenment."[15] At the annual Game Developers' Conference in 2011, three well-known game designers (Jason Rohrer, John Romero, and Jenova Chen) competed against one another, seeking to produce "a game that is also a religion."[16] Using *Minecraft*, Twitter, and the TED webpage, respectively, each of the designers created a game that would have religious implications for the players. Rohrer was declared the winner for *Chain World*, which allows users to create buildings and objects in the landscape. He housed the game in a flash drive that players pass from one to the next. Within the game, each player would interpret the meaning of the game's puzzles and add to the landscape. Upon dying in the game, each player would then pass it along. "In Rohrer's mind, his game would share many qualities with religion—a holy ark, a set of commandments, a sense of secrecy and mortality and mystical anticipation."[17]

Rohrer consciously and deliberately built *Chain World* as a religion. Other virtual worlds, particularly those that are massively multiplayer like *World of Warcraft* and *Second Life*, are not themselves religions, but they do enable religious experiences. As with *Chain World*, they give us an opportunity to live out new stories that make our lives and our world rich with meaning. Instead of just hearing the stories or reading the stories, we can now *enact* them. We can *be* the participants rather than simply memorializing them. Consider *World of Warcraft*: in it, you—the player—become the hero. You rescue the powerless, fend off the forces of evil, and become vital to the ongoing story that occupies your life. No mere antecedent to the events that surround you; you become the driving force, the individual who—with the support of your fellow heroes—will ultimately vanquish evil. Every non-player character in the game relies on you to make it so.

World of Warcraft has an entire lore, a vast historical narrative that ultimately grounds everything the player does. The game is a sweeping battle of good against evil, which provides plenty of space for players to recognize their own essential heroism. According to the lore, when the Titans traveled the universe creating life and making it good, they found an evil source of demons in the universe. They sent one of their own—Sargeras, the best and strongest of them all—to fend off the demons and protect the order they had founded. But like more conventional angels in our Western traditions, he fell from grace. Corrupted by the very demonic powers he had set out to resist, Sargeras turned on his former fellows, took command of the demons, and sent them forth to dismantle the cosmos.

World of Warcraft players are at the heart of Sargeras's conflict with the Titans. They live (most of the time) on Azeroth, a planet that Sargeras has tried and failed to corrupt and that continues to be a locus for the activities of his Burning Legion. Before *World of Warcraft*, players struggled in a battle of humanity against Orcs in the strategy games *Warcraft*, *Warcraft II*, and *Warcraft III*. Now, however, the Orcs, freed from Sargeras's control and allied with other races, have formed yet another bulwark against the Legion. The many races of Azeroth continue to fight among themselves, but every one of them stands against Sargeras and his forces. Players lead their people in this battle against the Burning Legion.

The story is captivating. Within it, each player becomes a hero of epic proportions. Each player's labors contribute toward the greater good—ridding the world of evil and aiding friendly peoples in their struggle to survive and thrive. And as players work toward such wondrous ends, they employ ever greater powers, tapping reserves of magical might that far surpass anything experienced in daily, conventional reality.[18]

The allure of the *World of Warcraft* mythos means the game competes against traditional stories and religions. As we shall see over the coming chapters, *World of Warcraft* gives its players very appealing commodities—communities, opportunities for reflection, a sense of personal meaning, even transcendent experiences. In an age where thin wafers of bread do not always seem to carry a divine personality and where the historical authenticity of almost every religious text has been called into question, the communities and experiences enabled by virtual worlds offer something completely novel to the spiritual marketplace.

Even where the worlds lack epic narratives, they provide opportunities for their residents to create one. In *Second Life*, a world where everything is the responsibility of those who log in, religious stories have exploded into being. On occasion these are created ex nihilo, as new religions that may not even be possible to think through in conventional reality. More often, though, they are formed by reframing and reconstructing the old religious ways and ideas. Many people come to *Second Life* to live out their religious lives in a new world: they build churches, temples, mosques, and even forest glades in virtual reality. Then they gather and celebrate together, often with neither permission from, nor relationship to, their communities' conventional counterparts. Instead of letting the old hierarchies dictate who they are, what they must believe and do, and where they must go, these virtual world residents are happily rearranging and reassembling religious life and telling entirely new stories about gods, providence, and themselves.

To a considerable extent, the story of *Second Life* is, itself, a story of religious redemption: for founders and residents alike, *Second Life* could offer a new, better world. This operates on two levels: first, the practice of traditional religions can provide new opportunities to the faithful; and second, life there can, itself, be a religious opportunity. Inspired by science fiction and popular science books about artificial intelligence and virtual reality, many *Second Life* residents believe that the world is a template for the eventual upload of immortal human minds into a virtual reality paradise. As such, to think through it as a place where some residents wish to escape the limitations of their bodies is to think about a modern religious institution.

Both *World of Warcraft* and *Second Life* offer redemptive new stories for the modern world. Whether by fighting against the evil spawned by demonic forces or by creating one's own world and life, virtual world residents participate in a new kind of religious storytelling. At times, such participation is explicit, as when *Second Life* residents unite in the formation of a Christian, Buddhist, or Muslim group. At other times, it is implicit, as when players derive meaning from their victories over Sargeras's minions or contemplate how they might take up permanent residence in the

Second Life grid. Fascinatingly, these kinds of stories, as well as the practices and beliefs they carry with them, can replace the old stories. As many virtual world residents have already taken up the banner of these new tales, they add to our religious landscape.

We should not shudder at the religious ramifications of *World of Warcraft* or *Second Life*. Religious belief and practice is natural and, as such, is independently neither good nor bad. Religious practices can be harmful and they can be helpful. Whether the religious aspects of *World of Warcraft* and *Second Life* will be one or the other or, more likely, a mix of the two is a question that only time can reveal.

Whether for good or ill, we cannot doubt the importance of the religious implications of either *Second Life* or *World of Warcraft*. Both worlds are, without question, impressive achievements and the products of momentous planning, design, and creativity. The *World of Warcraft* environment ranges from wasteland to paradisiacal, always with attention to design that those of us who grew up with the Atari 2400 and Commodore 64 would have found impossible to predict.[19] *Second Life* varies even more, with residents creating landscapes of staggering diversity. The scope of the worlds and the breadth of activities they enable make virtual worlds one of the most significant areas for contemporary inquiry.

Virtual worlds are the objects that "objectify" our stories and our interpersonal relations. We can build and shape them with our motives in mind so that they lean on residents, encouraging certain thoughts or behaviors. We can use or modify them likewise. Thus, we can use virtual worlds to hold together communities of people and relationships between people and ideas.[20] One aspect of this is that they provide places for playing out our religious thoughts and simultaneously are inscriptions of them. As we will see throughout this book, *World of Warcraft* and *Second Life* are active constituents of modern religious life, and they help shape, authorize, and rewrite our religious practices.

The first three chapters of this book examine the religious opportunities afforded by the game *World of Warcraft*. After introducing the game, along with my own participation in it, I explain how playing *World of Warcraft* can serve as an ersatz religious practice. Chapter 2 discusses how the game substitutes for religious affiliation, and Chapter 3 discusses how it can substitute for religious devotion. That is, *World of Warcraft* provides many players with both the social and individual benefits they might otherwise accrue through participation in traditional religious activity. In the first case, they have opportunities for ethical reflection and communal assembly. In the second, players can find meaning and purpose in their heroic identities and can even experience transcendence through their in-game activities. Throughout these chapters, I deploy a wide array of sources, from the words of game designers to those of the players, from an analysis of *World of Warcraft* to an understanding of religious narrative. This constellation of actors gives voice to the many constituents of *World of Warcraft* culture and demonstrates how the game's religious implications are the result of both deliberate and inadvertent collaboration among those actors.

The next three chapters discuss *Second Life*, first introducing it and then exploring the religious uses to which it is put. Chapter 4 discusses traditional religious practices in *Second Life*, beginning with how such practice can be "real" despite being "virtual." Chapter 5 provides a glimpse into the myriad ways *Second Life* residents have imported traditional religions into the world; in it, specific sites dedicated to Christian and Muslim groups are described, especially insofar as they see the game as a way of reinvigorating their practice in a pluralistic and (hopefully) welcoming world. Chapter 6 returns to an earlier theme from the book: how virtual world life can be meaningful on its own terms and thereby can compete with traditional practices. Chapter 6 thus hearkens back to aspects of Chapter 3 in its discussion of virtual world residents who desire a transcendent experience of virtual life. The chapter explores how *Second Life* embodies transhumanist ideals of using science and technology to overcome human limits and details how those ideals were present both in the design of *Second Life* and in its present use. As in my discussion of *World of Warcraft*, I bring many voices into contact with one another, thereby exploring how theology, virtual world occupancy, and technological promises intertwine.

Finally, the concluding chapter reflects on how virtual worlds enhance the religious opportunities of the Internet and explores the theoretical consequences of the religious use of virtual worlds. In particular, the chapter situates virtual worlds within the scholarly study of religion and then capitalizes on that situation by reconfiguring how we think about religion (especially as it relates to science and technology). The temporal and spatial orientation within virtual worlds, I argue, makes them particularly apt for religious work. Following this, however, the religious work done by and within virtual worlds reveals that we must rethink the constitution of religious communities. Actor-network theory, borrowed from the sociology of science, is crucial to the method by which this book is composed, so in the conclusion I articulate its integration to religious studies. After all, as virtual worlds continue to play powerful roles in our religious lives, we require effective modes of analysis to appreciate what opportunities and problems await us.

Every effort has been made to ensure that this book is both a work of scholarship and a readable text. As a consequence, the chapters that follow emphasize my own research, drawing on surveys, interviews, observations, and investigations to demonstrate how *World of Warcraft* and *Second Life* do religious work. Much of the outside scholarship that informs my analysis or to which my own observations pertain has been put into the endnotes in the hopes that gamers and those interested in virtual worlds—and not just other academics—will find this book valuable and interesting. I encourage every reader to consult the endnotes as a way of enriching the book, but there is no actual need to do so; the book's argument should be quite apparent even without reading a single one of them.

To study virtual worlds and to appreciate how they contribute to our religious landscape, I journeyed in them for several years. I owned land and led discussions in *Second Life*. I fought demons and manufactured mechanical pets in *World of Warcraft*. I participated in the worlds' communities by joining guilds, attending group functions, and meeting other residents. Many readers will want to move directly into my studies of the worlds and their residents (which begin in the next chapter), but for those who wish a more methodical approach, an Appendix at the end of the book offers a detailed description of the choices I made and the tactics I employed over the course of my study. Some of the material in the Appendix will make more sense after reading the main chapters of the book, but some aspects of the book will be clearer as a consequence of the Appendix. Whether one begins or ends with the Appendix (or disregards it altogether), I hope that each reader enjoys engaging the religious possibilities of virtual worlds with me. It is not the case that every virtual world resident uses such worlds for religious purposes, but the ways many residents do use *World of Warcraft* and *Second Life* to do religious work is, I think, a great deal of fun to consider.

The religious possibilities of virtual worlds are twofold. First, they provide new places to practice old religions; this is important because their very newness gives users hope that in them old religions can overcome the age-old handicaps of prejudice and ignorance. Whether or not this is true, it stands as an important element in virtual worlds. Second, they provide new locations for the creation of meaningful lives without recourse to traditional religious communities. As a consequence, whereas virtual worlds enable the extension of traditional religions into new locations, those locations can, by their very nature, compete with traditional religions. Over the following chapters, we will witness the ways in which this duality unfolds.

Thanks to virtual worlds, many religious practitioners now reimagine their traditions and creatively work to restore them to "authentic" sanctity or replace religious institutions with virtual world communities that provide meaning and purpose to human life. *World of Warcraft* and *Second Life* are thus "virtually sacred." They do religious work, and hence they are sacred. Yet they often do it without regard for—and frequently in conflict with—traditional religious institutions and practices; as a consequence, they are "not quite" religious. Their virtuality is not so just by virtue of their place on computer screens but rather also by virtue of that persistent "not quite"; *World of Warcraft* and *Second Life* are virtually sacred because they participate in our sacred landscape as outsiders, competitors, and collaborators.

I

A Cultural Adventure

Virtually Sacred in a Secular World

World of Warcraft was not the first massively multiplayer online role-playing game (MMORPG) to develop a following, but it steamrolled over all of its competitors in the Western hemisphere, either knocking them out of business or relegating them to afterthoughts. This doesn't mean it cannot, too, bow before the coming of new games to the market; rather, it illustrates *World of Warcraft*'s landmark status among virtual worlds. The game rapidly attained millions of subscribers, more than an order of magnitude more than any other MMORPG marketed in the United States. By October 2010, the number of players exceeded twelve million, and, despite attrition, *World of Warcraft* remained by far the most popular subscription-based MMORPG in the world as of the end of 2012, with more than nine million paid subscribers.[1] With so many players, many of whom spend many hours per week immersed in the game, *World of Warcraft* could not help but attract an army of commentators. While many scholars seek to understand the social dynamics of game play or the difference between *World of Warcraft* activity and conventional play or work, only a few have given careful consideration to how the game, its designers, and its players contribute to the religious landscape of twenty-first century life.

While the precise ramifications of living in a "secular" society remain unclear, there is no doubt that new and different forms of belief and practice have replaced their traditional religious analogues. MMORPGs like *World of Warcraft* operate as "authentic fakes," providing many of their users with the products of traditional religious institutions: communities, ethical systems, sources of meaning and purposive action, and feelings of transcendence. These are the essence of the game's virtual sanctity. If we have, indeed, transitioned from the Information Age to the "Gaming Age,"[2] such religious possibilities will only grow in their significance.

From the late nineteenth century to the middle of the twentieth, prognosticators suggested that religion was on the decline, that it would dissolve and its influence evaporate.[3] Yet from our early twenty-first century vantage, we see that the rise of secularism has not vanquished religious ideas or practices; religion seems as alive today as it was a century ago. This is not to say, however, that religion endures in the same fashion as it did for medieval or even early modern Christians, much less as it did for any of the enormous number of non-Christians worldwide.

Religion is a complicated phenomenon, and to demonstrate that *World of Warcraft* is in important ways religious requires that we understand—as best we can—what religion is and what its constituent elements can be. David Chidester argues that religion is "the negotiation of what it means to be human with respect to the superhuman and the subhuman."[4] Such negotiation occurs through the practices, beliefs, institutions, symbols, doctrines, ethics, and other dimensions of life used to help the individual come to grips with his or her essential identity as a human being. When that happens through relation to superhuman and subhuman entities or states, situating the individual within a cosmic continuum, we have religion.

It is important to note that the negotiation of human meaning is not contingent upon belief in gods, afterlives, or archetypical religious desiderata. While a social system that includes gods is probably by definition religious, the presence of gods is not necessary for a system to be religious. That is, you can have religious practices or beliefs that fail to include a wide array of possible elements that we know to be common in religion. Scholars who accept that religion is not limited to gods and the supernatural have noted that many social institutions that are not traditionally part of religion can be understood in such a way, such as nationalism[5] and capitalism.[6]

Chidester's definition is a broad one, as it presumes that a wide array of practices and beliefs are religious, including some that do not automatically appear so. He argues, for example, that Coca-Cola is a religious "fetish" and that American pastimes such as baseball have religious connotations.[7] It is absolutely crucial to understand that the predilection toward understanding some things as religion and excluding others is generally a political process rather than a meaningfully intellectual one.[8] Declaring one thing as religion and another as superstition, myth, or occultism is a power play; the terms establish a value system that valorizes one set of practices or beliefs over another. In the present age, we still privilege beliefs in gods and afterlives and attendance in places that espouse such beliefs as religion over and against other practices of meaning-making, and this is what Chidester calls into question.

Of course, not all practices of meaning making are religious. They can, for example, be philosophical or artistic or scientific. This is where the hierarchical aspects of Chidester's definition comes into play. When the negotiation of meaning is grounded in comparisons with the superhuman and subhuman—and here we must make something of an aesthetic judgment as to what counts and what does not—then the practices become religious. Over the coming chapters, I will show how *World of Warcraft* institutes a wide array of practices through which players identify and establish meaning with reference to superhuman states within the virtual world. As a result, identification with one's heroic online self and the varied experiences of transcendence that *World of Warcraft* enables are crucial to understanding the social and individual aspects of the game world as religious.

To describe *World of Warcraft* as religious could mean—but need not—that we can see how game phenomena match traditionally religious phenomena. According to the historian Ninian Smart, for example, there are seven primary "dimensions" of religion: doctrine, myth, ethics, ritual, experience, institutions, and material culture.[9] Although it would be possible to explore *World of Warcraft* from Smart's theoretical position, elucidating how each of these dimensions plays a role in the game, I prefer the looser—but more active—sense of negotiation that Chidester employs. Indeed, playing *World of Warcraft* can enable genuine negotiation of what it means to be human, and, indeed, that process occurs in and through superhuman experiences and identities.

The religious use of *World of Warcraft* reflects changes enabled by modern life. Sociologists William Sims Bainbridge and Rodney Stark recognized decades ago that in secular societies religious beliefs intensify in some segments of the population and that in other segments religious innovation will take place.[10] Innovation is key to the entire premise of the present study: that designers and residents of *World of Warcraft* and *Second Life* contribute to our collective religious landscape. People can now fulfill religious longings through gaming and virtual world residency; this is an entirely new phenomenon, one enabled by shifts in religious practice over the past two centuries.

Unquestionably, our collective religious life has changed, such as by the privatization of some religious ideas and practices. Many individuals now maintain that their faith is part of their private, rather than public, lives while others (often because they decry the privatization of religion) have separated from mainstream culture so as to create communities where faith is decidedly public. In addition—and more importantly to this study—many religious ideas and practices have been subsumed into non-religious aspects of culture. Seemingly secular practices or institutions that perform work traditionally within the domain of religious groups are what Chidester labels "authentic fakes" or, as he evidently preferred before his publisher refused to print it, "holy shit."[11] An authentic fake is something not associated with a traditionally religious group or belief that nevertheless provides the things religious groups and beliefs provide.[12] Throughout these first three chapters, we will see that *World of Warcraft* players negotiate human meaning just as do traditionally religious actors. In this sense, *World of Warcraft* is authentically fake—or, as I have already labeled it, virtually sacred.

Bainbridge, now noted as a sociologist of virtual worlds in addition to religion, has suggested that in our secular world science and technology can host a new religious endeavor, one that will finally fulfill all of the promises falsely (in his estimation) made by past religions. In fact, he believes that a new kind of religion must emerge, grounded in science and technology, to carry humankind through its next phase of evolution.[13] According to Bainbridge, the products of science and technology will subsequently banish religion from human practice by providing real rewards rather than the psychological compensations that he attributes to religion.[14] While religions, in his model, falsely offer desirable items like eternal happiness and immortality, Bainbridge believes that technology might be able to do so authentically.[15] As we will see in Chapters 3 and 6, he is not alone in thinking that virtual worlds might play a role in the salvation of human beings.

Video games like *World of Warcraft* offer something that many people lack, and this is how they become virtually sacred. "Not everyone lives in a community with rich traditions, faiths, and stories that put meaning into everyone's life, whereas in synthetic worlds, everyone is asked to complete quests, fight enemies, and become a hero."[16] The disenchantment of the modern world combined with—in all honesty—the doldrums of routine life opens up new opportunities for gaming. Not every player will identify with his or her heroic exploits, choosing instead to simply while away the time, but "one person's harmless waste of time," says game designer Frank Lantz, "might be another's bid for transcendence."[17] That is, in *World of Warcraft*, although not every player will, every player has the opportunity to *become* a warrior-saint struggling to defend the community and rise above the limits of mortal life.

Playing the Hero

World of Warcraft is a persistent environment that players enter into as characters chosen from various races (blood elf, draenei, dwarf, gnome, goblin, human, night elf, orc, pandaren, tauren, troll, undead, or worgen) and classes (death knight, druid, hunter, mage, monk, paladin, priest, shaman, rogue, warlock, or warrior). These characters are graphically represented in the game as "avatars." When an individual logs off, the world continues to exist, with other players present, completing quests and exploring the environment. When the player logs on, she[18] can complete quests given to her by non-player characters (NPCs), take part in player versus player (PvP) combat, enter dungeons, dig up archeological relics, gather raw materials, craft magical items, sell goods through the auction house, acquire and train companion pets, and more. While the possibilities are not limitless, they are extensive and players commend the game for being so multifaceted that different people can enjoy it in different ways.

Because MMORPGs have so many players, they must be split into separate "shards" or "realms" or "servers," which run the game simultaneously for different players. Obviously, if one or two million players all entered the same city, they would bog down the computing resources and make every building and road an impenetrable sea of other players. To avoid this, MMORPG designers split games into hundreds or thousands of parallel universes, each with a name of its own and with distinct players.[19] Even so, visiting a busy city can produce considerable "lag," slowing the game down unpleasantly. The first step in creating a character is to choose a realm, and the game client will encourage, though not require, new players to choose a realm with low occupancy.

The choice of race made at character creation affects the rest of the player's experience through the game. It limits what classes are available to the player, and it structures her heroic career. Each race is a member of one of two factions, the Horde or the Alliance. The Horde consists of blood elves, goblins, orcs, taurens (see Figure 1.2), trolls, and undead. Opposing them for control over the scarce resources of Azeroth are the Alliance races: draenei (see Figure 1.3), dwarves, gnomes, humans, night elves, and worgen (Figure 1.1). As of 2012, players could become pandaren, inspired by the *Kung Fu Panda* film franchise, and then choose which faction to join. Membership in a given faction means that characters can speak with only other members of the faction and perform quests for only those races, and that non-player characters from the other faction will attack on sight unless the player is much higher level than they. The player chooses the race, then the class, and then has an opportunity to adjust the character's skin color, face shape, hairstyle, and so forth by choosing among available options.

After creating a character, a new player watches a short cinematic that describes the circumstances affecting her race and encouraging the player to begin her heroic quest to aid her people. At the close of the video, the "camera" zooms in on a person who turns out to be the player's own character, standing in front of a quest giver and ready to launch an epic career. The quest giver is a non-player character with an exclamation mark

FIGURE 1.1 Character selection screen showing a female worgen warrior: selection options are on the left; descriptions of the faction, race, and class appear on the right. (*World of Warcraft* images provided courtesy of Blizzard Entertainment, Inc.)

hovering over his head (Figure 1.4). He explains the local trouble and sends the character off on her first adventure.

As the player completes quests, defeating enemies and gathering important goods, she advances in level, gaining new powers and finding new equipment. Actual play involves a wide array of activities, especially as the characters advance in level. Low-level characters can do little other than follow the basic quest sequence, but as they advance they gain access to professions, battlegrounds, the Random Dungeon Finder, the Looking for Raid system, and achievements. All of these enrich the game experience considerably. In battlegrounds, players join members of their faction (Alliance or Horde) in a contest against members of the other faction. The Random Dungeon Finder places players into groups with other players of complementary classes and then selects a dungeon for them to enter together, with extra rewards for successful completion. Looking for Raid is similar, in that it brings players together, but it does so to establish raiding groups, which are much larger than ordinary dungeon groups and enter more dangerous dungeons. Players also earn achievements—which will be described further in Chapter 3—by accomplishing specific feats and these can provide the players with titles, mounts, or simple gratification.

The system of professions is complex and integral to game play. A character may learn first aid, cooking, fishing, and archeology. In addition to these, she may acquire two out of alchemy, blacksmithing, enchanting, engineering, herbalism, inscription, jewelcrafting, leatherworking, mining, skinning, and tailoring. These skills also increase with practice: the character has a level for each profession (from 1 to 600 as of the Mists of Pandaria expansion in 2012), with the most valuable products generally possible only at very high levels. Materials gleaned from the gathering professions like herbalism can be sold to other players who use them for their crafting professions or kept for the player's own needs (possibly sent to another of the player's characters, or "alts"). Crafters make items for their own use or to sell in the auction house to other players. Players often choose professions that fit their characters, such as tailoring and enchanting for a warlock, but probably more often make choices based on what they like to do or what they think will earn the most gold.

Quite a few of the available options for characters and play were released in the years following the game's initial release. In addition to occasional updates to the game over the course of time (fixing bugs, tweaking play dynamics, or adding a little extra content), Blizzard Entertainment, the maker of *World of Warcraft*, also releases major expansions to the game every two years or so. The initial game was launched in 2004 and was followed by the Burning Crusade expansion in January 2007, the Wrath of the Lich King expansion in November 2008, the Cataclysm expansion in December 2010, and the Mists of Pandaria in September 2012. Each of these expansions provided new quests, new race or class combinations, new locations to adventure, and raised the limits for character development. Although it would appear that level limits mean the game has an end (at least until the next expansion), many players feel the game does not even *begin* until a character has reached the maximum level.

Completing quests and defeating opponents earns the character "experience points," which result in advanced levels. Characters begin at level 1 and can eventually attain level 90, a process that can take months. The level cap has increased with each expansion to the game. Originally, level 60 was the highest, but this increased to 70 with the Burning Crusade, 80 with Wrath of the Lich King, 85 in Cataclysm, and 90 in Mists of Pandaria. At new levels, characters can use more powerful magic items and acquire new powers.

Leveling generally happens without interference on some *World of Warcraft* realms but can be very difficult in others. On PvP realms, Horde and Alliance characters can attack each other indiscriminately, which means that they can prevent one another from completing quests or defeating enemies. On player versus environment (PvE) realms, however, this is possible only in specially designated "battlegrounds" or if players flag themselves as available for PvP play. For the most part, in PvE realms, Horde and Alliance players ignore one another outside of the battlegrounds. On some servers, the degree to which Horde and Alliance players ignore one another can be downright cooperative. For example, at holiday festivals, there are frequently rewards for working against the opposing faction, such as putting out the bonfires lit in their capital cities. It can be challenging for players to sneak or fight or race their way into the capital cities, and this is made much more difficult if opposing players join their NPCs in fighting off intruders. On many servers, however, the players stand and watch (one waved at me on one occasion) as opposing players burst into their capitals to desecrate their fires.

The quest structure drives the story and is infinitely repeatable. Very few events in *World of Warcraft* happen only once; for the most part, each new character to reach a particular non-player character will be offered the same quest as the last character to speak with him. When monsters, no matter how significant, are slain, they "respawn" to be available for the next group of adventurers. Following from one quest to another, characters learn more about the lore of Azeroth and become increasingly embroiled in its political structure.

Early on, characters swiftly gain levels and new powers, but as they "grow up" they require considerably more time and effort to improve.[20] Late to the game and limited in available time, I was never close to the level maximum during the Burning Crusade years. However, although my time in game was too inconsistent and my spread of characters too wide for me to attain level 80 during the Lich King era, I easily achieved level 85 with my principle character soon after the launch of Cataclysm and likewise reached 90 in the Mists of Pandaria expansion. While leveling up, characters acquire quests from non-player characters as they explore the world. The enemies in different zones of the world vary in power, so a low-level character is limited to starting zones but will gain the strength to see new content over time. High-level characters are no longer limited in this and can generally come and go where they please.

"End-game" activity takes place when players reach the current level maximum. At such levels, the players participate in "daily quests," enter battlegrounds, earn reputation with various communities, tally achievements, and engage in raiding or other grouping when desired. It is still possible to become more powerful at this stage by finding very rare magical items or by collecting wealth, and many players spend considerable time in this effort; others take advantage of their power by questing in "heroic" level "instances," which not only have high minimum level requirements but also require that a character's equipment be sufficiently powerful.

An instance is a separate part of the game where a dungeon or raid takes place. Within one, a player encounters only the other players who are grouped with her, not any other players. A raid is more difficult than a dungeon, allowing larger groups than the standard five-person group; a raid may require ten, twenty-five, or forty raiders. Players on both the Horde and Alliance will get quests to enter their first dungeon instances in the early teens and will continue to explore higher-level dungeons for the rest of the game. Heroic-level instances have more powerful opponents who drop more powerful "loot" when defeated. While some players avoid dungeon exploration, others revolve their game play around it. At the highest levels, adequate equipment can be found only in the dungeons/raids or else must be purchased through special currencies gained through high-level activity[21] or purchased in gold from other players who find it while raiding or craft it using their professions. Communities of players dedicated to the most difficult adventures (and the most impressive rewards) join raiding guilds or—as of Mists of Pandaria—use the Looking for Raid feature to engage the highest level content.

The rich game play offered by *World of Warcraft* and similar games results from their origins in pen-and-paper role-playing games (RPGs) like *Dungeons & Dragons (D&D)*.[22] In RPGs and their computer scions, each player becomes a hero (or anti-hero) in a story of epic proportions. Whether the game is based on fantasy, sci-fi, comic books, spies, or any other genre, players must navigate hurdles, solve puzzles, and defeat enemies. *World of Warcraft*, like so many other games, draws directly on the heritage of *D&D* and other RPGs, both in its play structure and its aesthetics. The makers of *World of Warcraft* recognized their debt to *D&D* and its chief architect, E. Gary Gygax, by dedicating the mini-expansion Fury of the Sunwell (patch 2.4) to him after his untimely death in 2008.

Pen-and-paper role-playing games like *D&D* require a group of one or more players who are led on an adventure by another individual, known as a Dungeon Master, Game Master, Guide, Storyteller, or Referee (depending on the game). While the Dungeon Master has certain aspects of the game planned, he or she cannot control the random outcome of dice rolls or the choices of the player characters, who thereby cowrite the story.[23] As computer systems developed and grew in popularity throughout the 1980s and 1990s, games became increasingly immersive, incorporating many of the elements of games like *D&D* into preestablished storylines reminiscent of fantasy literature.[24]

Evidence that *D&D* was critical to the development of twenty-first century gaming abounds, represented in the studies of cultural theorists and sociologists alike.[25] More importantly, game designers themselves acknowledge the influence of *D&D*.[26] Designers recognize that *D&D* inspired their love of gaming, gave room for imaginative exploration, and provided compelling play for themselves and their friends. It is no wonder that they designed *World of Warcraft* and other games to offer similar experiences as their beloved pen-and-paper RPGs. As for *World of Warcraft*, its famed designer Chris Metzen declares: "boy did I love *D&D* as a kid, just the sheer open-ended imagination of it all ... it was just absolutely transforming. I was reborn" after playing for the first time.[27]

Questing for Answers

I joined *World of Warcraft* in 2008 to attend an academic conference about gaming hosted by Bainbridge and John Bohannon, a journalist for *Science*. Since then, I have studied the game and its players from sociological and anthropological perspectives, hoping that I might understand the nature of its tremendous appeal. Like other players, I purchased the game discs (and continued to as new expansions were released) and paid around $15 per month for continued access to the game. Over the course of three years, I adventured by myself, with my wife, with guildmates (see following explanation), and with strangers working on the same quests as I. Eventually, I reached the level maximum of 85 and then 90 and, to a limited extent, participated in "end-game" culture.

When I joined *World of Warcraft*, I did so as an adjunct to my research in *Second Life* and thus without a clear sense for what I would find there. I did not, in fact, initially know that I would include the game in a secondary research project (i.e. this book). This made it easier to follow anthropologist Tom Boellstorff's suggestion that one allow ethnography to tell us what is important rather than setting out with particular questions in mind.[28] Thanks to my play, however, I quickly saw how *World of Warcraft's* design, on many levels, permits players to have truly powerful experiences. It is these experiences that cohere into the quasi-religious aspects of the game. While Boellstorff avoids connecting virtual world activity to that of the conventional world,[29] however, I am interested in the ways virtual world occupancy plays a role in conventional life. Players themselves create rich worlds of meaning that encompass both in-game and many out-of-game activities;[30] the realness of such worlds and activity emerges, not from mere graphical precision but from the work that residents produce across many spectra. To more fully appreciate how players work within and without the confines of their online characters, I therefore supplement in-world ethnography with the study of traditional role-playing games, especially as pioneered by Gary Fine.[31] As I mentioned in the Introduction, interested readers can learn more about my methodological approach in the Appendix.

Prior to playing *World of Warcraft*, I spent eighteen months in the virtual world *Second Life*, where I traced the significance of transhumanist faith in the Singularity and expectations of transcendence in virtual life.[32] As I was in the process of writing the book that details how faith in transcendence operates in *Second Life*, I immersed myself in the burgeoning literature about video games and virtual worlds, therein hearing about Bainbridge and Bohannon's conference. I bought *World of Warcraft*, my first video game purchase since junior high school, endured my wife's teasing, and quickly "leveled" my first character, a tauren hunter named Ronaan (Figure 1.2), to the point that I could attend the conference. This early leveling took just a few hours, even as an inexperienced player. I also joined the guild Science, founded by Bainbridge to assemble those interested in the conference.[33]

Ronaan, like all taurens, is a member of the Horde. As a member of the Horde, Ronaan received quests that advanced the needs of his own and other Horde races. Playing him, I defended and helped taurens, quested to earn my place among the tauren hunters and heroes, and struggled to reverse the demonic influence that invades Azeroth.

Reading about the online gaming community, attending the *World of Warcraft* conference, and subsequently playing the game to see what it has to offer encouraged me to follow up my previous studies with this book, a volume dedicated to virtual world communities. With a mission in plain sight, I continued playing *World of Warcraft*—very soon with my wife's participation. One day she looked over my shoulder and decided the game looked rather fun after all, and within two weeks of my initial purchase she too was playing. She found that a group of dedicated *World of Warcraft*

FIGURE I.2 Ronaan at level 29, wearing his orange Science guild tabard and with his hunting pet, Kierkegaard, at his side. (*World of Warcraft* images provided courtesy of Blizzard Entertainment, Inc.)

gamers was also a part of her online knitting community, Ravelry, so we joined the guilds that those individuals had established: Twisted Stitches and Dropped Stitches.[34]

I joined Twisted Stitches as an orc warlock named Argorr and Dropped Stitches as a draenei paladin named Moravec.[35] While I have played other characters to gain an appreciation for different races and classes, Argorr and Moravec were my primary characters. Using Argorr and, especially, Moravec, I enjoyed conversation in the guild chat, participated in guild events such as grouping with others to defeat difficult dungeons, and shared my professional expertise such as by giving or trading mechanical pets[36] I crafted with my engineering skills. These guilds are classified as "casual" as opposed to "raiding," but a core group of raiders met on a weekly or twice weekly schedule.[37] In general, a raiding guild has formalized requirements about when and how often a player must be available to help guildmates enter dungeons or raids. There can even be stringent requirements as to who can enter the guild based upon each player's competence and accomplishments. In our casual guild, there are quite a few characters at all levels and a number of players participate in weekly raids or dungeons, but no players are ever obliged to join.

Dropped Stitches and Twisted Stitches both emphasize maintaining a friendly environment and use that to make the best of time in game. Dropped Stitches has even been acknowledged by *WoW Insider* as an exemplary guild that maximizes fun by providing a good atmosphere free of unpleasant players.[38] In addition to questing and raiding together, we also enjoyed social activities. On one occasion, for example, a Dropped Stitches group entered one of the game's original forty-player raids clad only in formal attire. The raid was one of the most difficult instances in the original release of *World of Warcraft*, but by the time of the Lich King expansion, players had become so powerful that we could enter it with minimal protection. The purpose of this visit was to celebrate the upcoming wedding of two of our members. We raided together, reaching and defeating the final boss (a dragon named Nefarian), and then posed for pictures in front of his fallen body while toasting our soon-to-be newlyweds and launching virtual fireworks. Such social activities are not unique to my guilds; many participate in activities that reinforce conventional bonds. For example, Douglas Mandelkow describes one guild whose members sent presents for the birth of two guildmates' child and regularly check in on the family.[39] It is important to note that while my guildmates enjoy striving toward endgame achievements and there are PvPers in the group, neither Twisted

FIGURE 1.3 Moravec at level 70, with a "pet bombling," one of the vanity pets he routinely built for others in the guild. (*World of Warcraft* images provided courtesy of Blizzard Entertainment, Inc.)

Stitches nor Dropped Stitches is a "hardcore" guild but rather fit into what might derogatorily be labeled a "care bear" guild. The guilds emphasize community over competition and have never sought to be among the leading raid guilds. Competence is expected, but even excellence cannot compensate for a poor attitude. Obviously, it shapes my experiences to have participated in these communities rather than raiding guilds.

To collect data, I played *World of Warcraft* as a participant observer, interviewed members of my own guild about their play, and ran several surveys online. Over more than one thousand hours of playing time, I created characters from a variety of different races and classes on two separate servers to experience most—though certainly not all—of what the game offers. This book is not the place for a thick description of life in *World of Warcraft*, but I will draw upon my experiences in game to clarify analytical issues throughout the text because it was by playing that I gained a sense for how closely the game's appeal is linked to its ability to provide players with a sense of meaningful accomplishment and heroic identity.

I conducted interviews via e-mail and in-game chat and ran several surveys to gauge player interests. I have given *World of Warcraft* interviewees pseudonyms throughout. All survey data, unless otherwise noted, comes from one of three surveys that I held. The first, a survey of *Second Life*

FIGURE 1.4 Moravec receives a quest, which can be read and accepted in the window on the left. (*World of Warcraft* images provided courtesy of Blizzard Entertainment, Inc.)

users (252 respondents), was advertised in Wagner James Au's *New World Notes*, the *Metaverse Messenger*, and *SL'ang Life* magazine. The second is a survey about *World of Warcraft* taken from the Ravelry group of players (eighty-five respondents). The third survey is also about *World of Warcraft* but was advertised on PennyArcade.com, a gaming website (fifty-seven respondents). Most of the time, references to *World of Warcraft* users comes from this third survey, which is demographically more representative of the *World of Warcraft* player base than the second, which includes only five male respondents out of eighty-five total. In most cases, the data from the second and third surveys are very similar; I have noted interesting differences in my discussion or in the notes.

As their scope is modest and the number of respondents limited, these surveys were never intended to precisely pinpoint the nature of *World of Warcraft* play or its engagement with contemporary religious life; that would be an impossible task. Rather, the surveys provide a broad brushstroke, an overview of how some players think about the game and their own engagement with it. This helped guide my in-game interviews and observations. Further data regarding religion, ethics, and game play are profoundly desirable, and it is my hope that the results here will encourage subsequent work.

As Moravec, I joined a group of people, made friends, fought against the forces of evil, and saw myself grow in power and prestige. In this, I am unremarkable; my experience in the game approximates that of any player and is, therefore, exemplary of what *World of Warcraft* offers to players. By combining anthropological and sociological tools, I have collected data that, as I will discuss over several chapters, reflects the ways *World of Warcraft* fits into the contemporary religious landscape. The game provides a forum wherein people who may or may not have contact with traditional religious forms of meaning-making can nevertheless access supportive communities, opportunities for moral reflection, and experiences of meaning and transcendence.

Religion of the Gamers

Before showing that video games like *World of Warcraft* are authentic fakes, doing the work of religious institutions and practices, we must consider the environment in which players and designers can build the games up as such. Preliminarily, it appears that most gamers have but middling interest in traditional religion, though more extensive data are needed. My survey data indicate that most respondents are not traditionally religious people; despite this, it would be excessive to claim they are without religious sensibilities.

There are virtual worlds, such as *Second Life*, that attract large numbers of individuals who hold to traditional religious ideas and perform traditional religious obligations; *World of Warcraft* is just not one of them.[40] It is possible that online RPG players, in general, tend to avoid religion: in a study of University of Zagreb students, Čulig and Rukavina found religious practice to be inversely correlated with MMORPG gaming.[41] In my survey of *Second Life* residents, 67% claim a religious affiliation (mostly Christian), and more than 40% claim to participate in religious activities at least once per month. In contrast, only 23% of *World of Warcraft* players claim to be "religious," and a staggering 45% claim to be "definitely not" religious in my survey of them. This means that nearly half of respondents self-identified their religiosity with a 1 out of 7, while less than one-quarter answered a 5, 6, or 7.[42] As we might then expect, the vast majority of *World of Warcraft* respondents (83%) report spending zero hours per week on religious activities, including prayer. This reveals a practical, as opposed to self-definitional, difference between themselves and *Second Life* residents.

But while most *World of Warcraft* players are not explicitly religious, they do have textual traditions that provide them with myth and meaning: fantasy and science fiction. According to my survey, more than 90% of players either currently or previously read science fiction, while more than 87% of players currently or previously read fantasy. Influential authors include J. R. R. Tolkien, C. S. Lewis, Isaac Asimov, J. K. Rowling, and Neil Gaiman.[43] Each of these authors provides epic storylines rich in religious imagery and themes. These books, which respondents labeled as "significant" in their lives, are part and parcel of the lives of gamers, who are well-known for their likelihood of being science fiction film and television fans.[44]

Tolkien, whose influence on modern culture has been profound, certainly believed that fantasy ought to inspire readers and enchant the world. Fantasy storytelling is a cosmogonic act; it is the creation of a world.[45] But it is not useless creativity, not the production of an illusion, that masks reality. In contrast, Tolkien emphasizes that fantasy is firmly grounded in reality, upon which it draws necessarily,[46] and that it provides us with a renewal, a "clear view" of our world.[47] Above all, according to Tolkien, fairy tales invigorate our everyday lives; this is why insofar as they are escapist they remain essentially tied to reality. It was in fairy tales that Tolkien "first divined...the wonder of the things, such as stone, and wood, and iron; tree and grass; house and fire; bread and wine."[48] By filling the world with wonder, fairy tales promote transcendent beliefs and experiences that rely on the here and now.[49]

It is the transcendent moment, the aesthetic appeal of a magical world shared by author and reader, that gives the fantastic its power. Tolkien's fellow Inkling, C.S. Lewis, writes that the fantastic "can give us experiences we have never had and thus, instead of 'commenting on life', can add to it."[50] The story events thus leave the page and enter the world; they become part of the reader's worldview and experience. Naturally, religious myths do likewise. Whether they describe actual historical events or not is beside the point; a religious myth can shape the way a person sees everything else around himself. And if Lewis and Tolkien are to be believed, so too can literature of the fantastic, literature that gamers describe as influential in their lives.

While my survey did not ask whether respondents found the Bible or other traditionally religious texts to be influential, there is compelling reason to believe that they would not have listed these among their favorite literary resources. In one study of literary types favored by science fiction and fantasy fans, the Bible received the second lowest rating, with only "occult literature" below it.[51] I suspect that if readers looked at the Bible as a fantasy tale, much of it would be appealing to them. For many fans, however, the Bible represents a cultural and political matrix from which they are alienated. As a consequence, they rate it poorly.

In the generations after Tolkien and Lewis, literature of the fantastic has itself become religious. Fantasy literature has become mythopoeic, "participating in a search for a new mythology of unified humanity."[52] The works of such authors as Ursula LeGuin, Lloyd Alexander, and Orson Scott Card offer a "para-religion" to replace the traditional religions that have lost their once unambiguous authority.[53] Since the mythopoeic aura of fantasy literature produces traditionally religious ends, it is no surprise that survey respondents find those books influential and important in their lives.

Fantasy and science fiction are integral to the worldview of online gaming. They have profoundly influenced the creators of virtual worlds,[54] and they are influential in the lives of the players. Such influence is deliberate; literature of the fantastic is not mere escapism but, as Tolkien and Lewis hoped, can rework and add to reality. As Christopher McMahon writes, the imagery in science fiction "imposes itself upon us…provokes our imaginative energies, and cautions us against reasoned theologies that rob the world of its mysterious and sacramental identity."[55] These are genres that enchant our worlds and draw us in; they are immersive, just as are the games that they inspire. Because they revolve around a sense of wonder,[56] science fiction and fantasy drive us into a worldview that can oppose the profane and the ordinary. In this, science fiction and fantasy push toward quasi-religious ways of thinking.

Science fiction frequently harbors religious imagery and themes,[57] and some artificial intelligence experts claim that it satisfies religious hopes[58] or that it is "our modern mythology."[59] Readers and authors collaborate in producing worldviews through reading, writing, and the adoption of literary lessons into a reader's behavior. As authors inspire with their actual novels, stories, and films, so will their readers often attempt to live. The stories, whatever their media, strengthen particular ways of seeing the world by giving them near-permanence. The ongoing presence of the story means the worldview need not be reconstructed anew by every participant; rather, each new reader can draw upon the story as an objectively grounded resource. Science fiction thus has the power to establish worldviews—frequently with visions of transcendence and salvation that oppose those of traditional religious practice—and it thus challenges religious ideologies. By offering an "expanded consciousness," science fiction may "serve as a substitute for religion,"[60] and this can transfer from its literary forms to online gaming.

Many gamers lack traditional religious affiliations; they'd rather be gaming than praying. Yet despite the absence of traditional practices in their lives, they do have religious resources at their disposal. They recognize the significance of science fiction and fantasy narratives in their lives, and such stories can provide services akin to those offered by religious texts. Produced out of the worldviews held by the authors, the books make those worldviews concrete, portable, and long-lasting. They stabilize mythic visions and offer them as resources for new readers. While the religious aspects of sci-fi and fantasy are not the subject of this book, it should be obvious that they help structure the subsequent quasi-religiosity of video gaming and virtual world production. As designers and players both rely on the mythological narratives of science fiction and fantasy, their lives and also their play are influenced by those stories.

Conclusion

The religious work made possible in video games like *World of Warcraft* matters because such games matter. Video gaming is now the world's biggest entertainment industry, and video games are the sum of vast human resources: natural, technical, economic, political, and leisure.[61] As such, their importance is assured whether or not they are "just games." At present, video games drive more technological innovation than any other sector and may even be "amusing us to a better life."[62] As an extreme example, consider the impressive achievement of gamers who needed only a few days with the program *FoldIt* to help scientists uncover the previously hidden structure of an enzyme vital to the functioning of the AIDS virus.[63]

World of Warcraft has changed society; it has a vast subscribership, and this leads many to see both salvation and damnation in it. The game is a place of adventure in a world supposed to be devoid of magic. Our secular world is not, however, truly disenchanted; authentic fakes allow us to overcome the well-publicized death of God. While many authors or journalists are tempted to see such efforts as addiction and escapism, the actual thrust of such accusations tends to be vague, at best, or entirely misguided, at worst. *World of Warcraft*, like the science fiction and fantasy novels beloved by its players, fits snugly into today's culture. For those whose religiosity finds no succor in traditional communities, *World of Warcraft* can offer a panoply of religious opportunities.

The absence of traditional religious commitments prevalent among many people today opens a space for games like *World of Warcraft* to provide religious opportunities to players; over the next two chapters, I will discuss both the associational and devotional opportunities enabled by the game. Just as science fiction and fantasy—two genres that directly inform the production and use of *World of Warcraft*—can work like religious texts for certain people, *World of Warcraft* can compete with traditional religions for adherents. William and Wilma Bainbridge suggest that games like *World of Warcraft* oppose the religious systems of the Western world,[64] noting that in the United States "only a handful of religious denominations have more members than *WoW* does. Given its supernatural symbolism, its engagement of the user's emotions, and the many hours each week members may participate, one could argue it has greater spiritual significance than all but a half dozen mainstream American denominations."[65] While opposition might be too strong of a term, there is no doubt that games like *World of Warcraft* can offer alternatives to traditional religious practice. As S. Brent Plate emphasizes, "the lived, bodily experience of game play might in and of itself be religious," and it is important to study how games can function in this way.[66] In Chapters 2 and 3, I will describe ways *World of Warcraft* offers its players many traditionally religious opportunities, including a community, a moral compass, a sense of identity and meaningful purpose, and transcendent experiences. With millions of users receiving these sacraments from *World of Warcraft* rather than a traditional religious institution, there can be no doubt about the seriousness of the game's religious implications.

2

Polite Society

Introduction

Naturally, for many players *World of Warcraft* is "just a game;" nothing will change the fact that some people get nothing more than a temporary kick out of playing, or that some "players" are actually involved in conventional economic activity there, doing little but earning gold that can be sold to other players. Fascinatingly, however, *World of Warcraft* exceeds the limited imagination of capitalist gains; it also occupies space in the religious landscape of modern life. It does so by providing many of the benefits of conventional religious affiliation and devotion. This chapter describes the former: how *World of Warcraft* provides a public forum for group formation and ethical reflection that might otherwise be the purview of religious institutions. While a number of scholars have recently commented on the importance of sociality in video gaming, this chapter goes beyond such claims to discuss how virtual world communities can operate as religious, or quasi-religious, societies. By providing social grouping mechanisms and encouraging ethical reflection, *World of Warcraft* takes on two of the dimensions of the sacred mentioned in the last chapter. When these combine with a desire for personal meaning and experiences of transcendence, as they will in the next chapter, we have a powerful new way of doing religion. Thanks to the associational possibilities inherent in *World of Warcraft* play, the game enables the making of meaning in individuals' lives; by forming communities and immersing themselves in ethical conflicts at both explicit and implicit levels, gamers draw on the game as a quasi-religious resource, as virtually sacred.

Finding a Faith Community

World of Warcraft is a world, and that implies the existence of others with whom to interact; rather than simply gaming *alongside* one another, gamers do so *with* one another. While this might seem unremarkable at first, it not only flies in the face of common prejudices against gamers but also shows the first way the game's design and play have incorporated one of the traditional roles of religious practice. Rather than playgrounds for the disaffected and excessively introverted, games are founded in a "will-to-communicate."[1] To enjoy *World of Warcraft*, most players group up with others, frequently their "real-life" friends who join them in their quests, but also strangers who quite often become real friends. The game's mechanics encourage such social formation through quests that cannot be accomplished alone and through the establishment of guilds: formal groups of players who share resources and help one another.

People form societies through a combination of discourse and force that establishes in-groups, hierarchies, rights, and privileges—a dynamic that permeates the history of religions. Religion is a zone in which people establish and maintain social boundaries while also potentially destabilizing them in the service of forming new community structures. Although physical force can be and certainly is used to bring about social order, discourse (especially religious discourse) is far more effective in doing so, as it legitimizes power and obfuscates inequalities that might lead to the overthrow of dominant groups.[2] Myth and ritual are particularly effective in both the construction and maintenance of and disestablishment of social orders.[3]

Members of a community must stabilize the social relations established through religions, which they do through the production of objects such as jewelry, attire, cityscapes, buildings, legal codes, monuments, behaviors, and more.[4] Tefillin,[5] for example, by their very presence remind Jewish men to don them and perform their morning prayers, which then remind them of their obligations and their customs. Other examples from religion include a bell rung to call the faithful to prayer or fashion choices that ensure group cohesion and adherence to traditional rules. These objects are crucial to society. Interpersonal relations have their own sort of entropy, which appears to accelerate over time and space; as a consequence, people objectify their relationships. We use material objects that help ensure our continued membership in the group. Thus, while an individual can try to force another to certain affiliations, it is actually objects that deploy the most force—they structure an individual's life in such a way as to guarantee appropriate affiliation.

Alongside our material expressions of social relationships, we also inscribe our relationships in time and space. We let certain places and events reinforce our bonds to one another, especially through the establishment of holy places and times. The separation of sacred time from profane or ordinary time is an important aspect of this. Such separations are often demarcated by extreme or outlandish behavior that provides the group with a sense of solidarity. According to Emile Durkheim, it is the demarcation between sacred time and profane time that allows participants to experience the extraordinary when they come together in religious gatherings.[6] Frequently, the powerful emotions of such events lead participants to believe in divine forces, which participants presume, according to Durkheim, to be the source of their civilization's benefits and power.[7]

Collective effervescence—the powerful social emotion Durkheim describes—is demonstrably present in secular movements that mimic traditional religious life. For example, krump-style dancers in urban Los Angeles clearly experience Durkheim's collective effervescence and their reports of their dance sessions include claims that "there is a spirit there" and that a person can be "struck" in a fashion reminiscent of what goes on in charismatic churches.[8] Likewise, alumni of my alma mater, the University of Texas, will remember holding up sacred hand signs, singing emotional songs, chanting, and cheering for a magic bull named Bevo as he chews his cud at football games. Virtual worlds like *World of Warcraft* can also operate as sacred places, and the times spent within them can be sacred times. In one early virtual reality experiment, GLOWFLOW, "people had rather amazing reactions to the environment. Communities would form among strangers. Games, clapping, and chanting would arise spontaneously. The room seemed to have moods, sometimes being deathly silent, sometimes raucous and boisterous. Individuals would invent roles for themselves. One woman stood by the entrance and kissed each man coming in while he was still disoriented by the darkness."[9] Such events beautifully parallel Durkheim's description of the extraordinary activities that took place at the Australian *corroboree*.[10]

This is not to say that the formation of community is exclusively the prerogative of religion, only that religious practices and discourses frequently serve this end. The study of community building in *World of Warcraft* cannot be complete without an understanding that the construction of society is one principal aim of religious discourse and that

World of Warcraft thus does religious work in establishing a community of gamers—particularly in combination with the ethics, meaning, and transcendence described over the next two chapters. In fact, *World of Warcraft* replaces some of the traditional stories, books, and habituated practices used to maintain social relationships and thus stabilizes new relations.

From the early days of pen-and-paper role-playing games (RPGs) like *Dungeons & Dragons (D&D)*, gaming has always been a social event,[11] and this sociality was immediately incorporated into video gaming. That is, there was never a time when video gaming was the exclusive domain of solitary gamers who occupy our cultural prejudices. Rather, even single-player games were enjoyed by groups of people together in one place, and the first ever home video console, the Magnavox Odyssey, included two-person games. Children of the 1980s and 1990s, in particular, will recall gathering together around a variety of different kinds of video games at home and the arcade, often just to watch others and cheer them on. In the United States, many people still congregate in the same physical location to play online games together. Nick Yee notes, for example, that in some age ranges up to 56% of women and 27% of men play *online* games with at least one other player in the same room.[12]

Faster computers and a strong market enabled the production of graphically immersive games in the 1990s, and these immediately capitalized on the social aspects of gaming. Players gathered to play first-person shooters—beginning with the seminal game *Doom*—in Local Area Network parties in which many computers could be connected to one another. Such play remains the gold standard of video gaming in many Asian countries, where playing in an Internet café is enormously popular and generally preferred to playing at home.[13]

Virtual worlds continue to build and reinforce social connectivity. Massively multiplayer online role-playing games (MMORPGs) "allow human-to-human interactivity comparable to that of the real world,"[14] and for this reason game designers know the social aspects to be critical to a game's success.[15] In such games, other characters are intangible content to the game,[16] such that even if a player is questing alone he or she will interact with others in the environment. Even solo questers, however, are rarely alone. They remain in contact with other players through instant messaging systems within the game. Overall, there is a powerful trend within gaming to enable cooperative play, which is deemed more enjoyable by the players themselves.[17]

Gamers exist in a liminal place, where they manage to simultaneously play alone and together. Citing Johann Huizinga's seminal work on play, Bonnie Nardi refers to gamers as "apart together."[18] For Huizinga, being apart together means to be with others, but apart from the rest of the world, residing in a "magic circle." For gamers, however, the magic circle is always blurry, unable to totally separate game life from conventional reality.[19] While no magic circle truly separates gamers from conventional reality, they certainly do manage to play together despite often remaining physically apart from one another, and their game spaces and times are frequently held as distinct from other spaces and times.

In MMORPGs, social connectivity is almost certainly the single biggest allure for gamers. It is even possible that MMORPGs will help alleviate what Putnam famously declares the modern problem of "bowling alone."[20] The declining role of third places, such as local soda fountains, neighborhood bars, and beauty parlors,[21] contributes to the solitary nature of contemporary life and—despite Oldenberg's denial that a room full of video gamers constitutes a third place[22] —this might be partially mitigated by virtual world residency.[23] Inside games, design affordances can advance sociality and create genuine public spaces—such as the safe havens established by in-game cities and the likelihood of well-endowed characters parading through them to show off their gear, pets, mounts, or other special attributes.[24] In short, virtual worlds like *World of Warcraft* give people places to spend time together, which is all the more important in a time when the sidewalk is becoming an endangered species and private pool memberships are replacing public pools in suburban cities.

Guild membership is a key aspect of *World of Warcraft* social life. A guild is a group of players affiliated with one another to assist each other in quests, to form the basis of groups for dungeons and raids, to share wealth through a guild bank, and to provide a stream of conversation through a guild chat channel. The latter scrolls along with other conversation on the bottom left of the user interface. Because the games are basically locations for social grouping,[25] guilds are critical aspects of player life. Those without guilds, for example, are significantly more likely to abandon the game than those players who are in a guild.[26] In my study, 84% of respondents were members of a guild, with a strong tendency to affiliate all of their characters in just one or two guilds (78% of all respondents). A majority of respondents (63%)[27] consider their guilds important to their enjoyment of the game, and 70% of respondents would like to meet their guildmates in person in cases where they do not already know them.

Guildmates contribute to one another's play experience, which adds to the social dimensions of the guild system. For example, players count on guildmates to enter dungeons with them, help them on difficult quests, and assist them in developing their characters. In Dropped Stitches and Twisted Stitches many players donate time, expertise, and equipment to one another and will often leave what they are doing to help one another. For example, when I needed items crafted through jewelcrafting or leatherworking, I could ask on the guild chat channel and frequently others would immediately help me or log on other characters who could.

The guild system, attractive in game culture, is also reinforced by the game rules. In the Cataclysm expansion, for example, designers integrated a guild leveling and achievement system. As guilds level up, members have access to new equipment and powers; membership in a high-level guild provides vanity items, such as pets and mounts, but also powerful magical items and new abilities like mass resurrection of party members, access to the guild bank from anywhere in the game, and lower costs on items bought from non-player character (NPC) vendors. As a consequence, to achieve their highest potential players *must* join and contribute to a guild.

Merely joining a guild does not, however, ensure a complete social experience; players must find ways to integrate themselves into their communities through various kinds of play and through social interaction. As Nicholas Ducheneaut points out, being noticed is critical to community membership in virtual worlds.[28] In *World of Warcraft*, that happens through guild chat, including congratulating others on their accomplishments or announcing one's own, providing advice, narrating amusing encounters from either in-game or outside of it, and taking a leadership role (e.g., organizing or leading events). In addition, the richness of *World of Warcraft* enables a wide variety of play practices that can solidify one's role in the community. Being a skilled player or raid leader is an obvious example of this, but it is important to note that providing for the needs of one's fellows through crafting or the gathering of materials is also a powerful way of ensuring one's status in the group.

Despite the combination of rules, play, and culture[29] that encourage guild membership, there is some variation in the extent to which players enjoy them. As one might expect, among my own *World of Warcraft* community a higher percentage of respondents than average consider guild membership important to their enjoyment of the game. In my survey of Ravelry players, almost 89% of respondents claimed that their guild membership is important to their enjoyment of the game, as opposed to nearly

64% in the general survey. This demonstrates that from guild to guild there can be considerable variation in the sociability of the players.

The nature of a guild—casual versus raiding—can become an important determinant in a player's enjoyment of it, as not all players desire the same things and guilds cannot always support every player's desires. Bonnie Nardi describes a guild that fractures after a change in the nature of group raids leaves a divide between the highest level players who could access the game's end content and other members of the group who had a difficult time keeping up.[30] In other gaming groups, players complain about hypercompetitive players, whom they attempt to drive away from their games.[31] While competition is integral to MMORPGs and other video games,[32] those who desire to have casual fun with their fellows find that excessive competition interferes with the game. Contrarily, those whose sole aim is competition will leave guilds that appear to hold them back with their "frivolous" forms of sociality.

Dropped Stitches and Twisted Stitches are both extremely affable, with a constant run of friendly banter and regular congratulations when players gain levels, defeat difficult bosses, or otherwise accomplish achievements (achievements are broadcast to the entire guild in a chat line, for example: "Moravec has earned the achievement Explore the Eastern Kingdoms!"). A great many members of Dropped Stitches and Twisted Stitches know one another offline and through the Internet community that ties us all together and, as such, care about one another's offline lives.[33] This is but one way, however, of reinforcing the social community. Something as simple as a raiding calendar can ensure that players perceive themselves as integral members of a community; indeed, it forces them to see themselves that way because it reminds them of when they must be available to other players and forces itself into the organization of the players' time outside of the game. The friendliness of guilds like Dropped Stitches is an important aspect of game play, but whether a guild's mission revolves around raids, player versus player (PvP) combat, battleground play, or casual adventuring, the time spent together reinforces social bonds.

Players often make powerful sacrifices to be members of a guild, though these vary in nature and intensity depending on the guild chosen. In an early study of the game *EverQuest*, Mikael Jakobsson and T. L. Taylor liken social interaction to the family dynamics of the mafia, where group relationships based on insider–outsider status, reputation, exchange of favors, and reliance on others dominates social praxis.[34] They might just as well have compared guild membership to church membership in a small town in west Texas, for in such a community citizens must attend the local church and subordinate their own interests to those of the parish. For many intensive raiding guilds, membership can entail absolute devotion to the group, in which the raiding needs of the group must be the highest priority in the players' lives.[35] This includes devoting time to studying tactics, crafting necessary magical items, and preparing one's character by acquiring high-quality gear. It can also require that the player be awake and free from work and family obligations during times when all group members can assemble, even at short notice.

Positive social relationships within a guild can be pragmatically useful in game as well as out of the game. Mark Chen, for example, describes how a guild of players found they could conquer the Molten Core raid in the original *World of Warcraft* through effective teamwork and positive reinforcement rather than just improving characters through the acquisition of superior magical items.[36] As any raider will know, successful completion of a difficult raid always involves understanding the fights and working toward an effective strategy for defeating the more difficult bosses; Chen's group capitalized on this by improving its interpersonal relationships as an aspect of its strategy. While high-level raiding often requires that a guild devise strategies for managing who gets what magical items as the guild gets more powerful,[37] Chen's group shows that good group mechanics are equally if not more important. Taking even failure as an opportunity to reflect on how the group can improve, Chen's group relied on trust and shared social incentives rather than individual player incentives to improve its raiding ability.[38]

It is possible that the Looking for Raid (LFR) capability added to *World of Warcraft* in the Mists of Pandaria expansion will radically reshape guild culture, providing different ways of accomplishing endgame goals and making guilds less popular. Thanks to LFR, players can join a raid even if they do not participate in a raiding guild or know enough players to put one together. Whether LFR will dismantle the guild structure over time or, in fact, provide a new way for players to associate with one another and become committed to one another is an open question that will benefit from sociological study in the immediate future.[39]

The relationships built among *World of Warcraft* players are not limited to raiding strategies or guild politics; players enjoy being with their friends, family members, and colleagues. Just as Chen's group relied on established social bonds in pursuit of raiding excellence, Nardi notes that the social aspects of the game often draw on existing social relationships[40] and can quite frequently improve them.[41] Stories of playing with children, spouses, siblings, and parents abound in players' self-narratives. In my survey, by far the most popular answer to the question, "What do you enjoy most about *World of Warcraft*?"[42] was "playing with friends (or family) from work, school, neighborhood, etc." More than 54% of respondents indicated that this was among the most enjoyable aspects of game, demonstrating quite clearly that *World of Warcraft* is a part of traditional sociality—the connections exercised in the game overlap social connections outside the game. At the same time, *World of Warcraft* provides many opportunities to meet new people and make new friends, a facet of the game that players frequently praise.[43]

Just as game play and culture do, both the mechanics and geography of *World of Warcraft* facilitate social interaction. Out in the wilds, one is both solitary and endangered—monsters roam the hills and forests of Azeroth, and there is rarely another soul with whom to talk. But for respite players can travel to cities, where they are safe and many others are also present. Many players congregate in the cities—for example, while waiting for a raid to begin—and in addition to seeing one another they thereby "join" the "trade channel." The trade channel allows typed conversation among all players in the capital cities of each faction. For example, a player in Stormwind, the human capital, can post to the trade channel and have her words seen by all Alliance players in Stormwind, Darnassus, Ironforge, the Exodar, Dalaran, and the Shrine of Seven Stars. Permitting such communication obviously aids in game play—it enables one player to find a raid or additional members for a raid or to propose economic transactions—but it also advances sociality. The trade channel tends to have at least as much random conversation (unfortunately, this is too often juvenile or offensive) as it does offers to trade, buy, or sell items. The communication across trade chat helps explain why survey respondents would prefer meeting players from their own servers to players from other servers: out of those players who have a preferred server, 73% would prefer meeting people from it to meeting other *World of Warcraft* players.

Gaming culture enables and encourages the transition of in-game friendship to out-of-game friendship. Gaming conventions, for example, allow players to meet in person, and players "organize regular fan meetings to supplement their online friendships with face-to-face contact."[44] Occasional face-to-face contact can be a vital element in the sustenance of online communities,[45] so it should come as no surprise that *World of*

Warcraft players look forward to meeting in person and find ways to do so. (As already indicated, the vast majority of my survey respondents would like to meet guildmates whom they do not already know in conventional life.) In an essay titled "Raiding the Physical World," *World of Warcraft Magazine* contributors cite guilds whose members join one another for dinner, vacation together, and even gather to play in the same room.[46]

Being people, players enjoy social relationships, both making new ones and reinforcing old ones. We live in an era in which friendships can happen almost anywhere yet many people remain isolated, so *World of Warcraft* and similar games have become a major locus for social activity. Players who spend little time meeting and socializing at church and have few definable commitments to faith communities can nevertheless make friends, continue friendships, and commit themselves to their guilds in *World of Warcraft*. The decline of third places and the secularization of society have shaped life in MMORPGs: even without neighborhood plazas or socially required church participation, individuals can access meaningful communities through virtual worlds. In *World of Warcraft*, players join others in a world where, as I argue over the rest of this chapter and the next, they can differentiate between right and wrong and develop a sense of meaning and transcendence. The overlay of meaning, ethics, and transcendence enchants the *World of Warcraft* community, revealing its religious significance.

Ethics

Games are powerful means for disseminating ideas into the population and have been used specifically to create civic agendas;[47] as such, like other technologies, they are part of the constitution of individual personhood. There is evidence that prosocial participation in virtual worlds and games is correlated to prosocial behavior and increased empathy outside of games[48] and also that role-playing videogame players have lower levels of aggression than non-players.[49] However, the question on hand is not whether *World of Warcraft* transforms players into good people but whether participation in such virtual worlds provides opportunities for ethical reflection. After all, going to churches, synagogues, mosques, and forest glades does not automatically transform ordinary religious practitioners into moral citizens. One can hope that prosocial gaming opportunities will advance social causes in conventional reality, but this may not be testable. Observably, though, game designers do perform ethical work by establishing opportunities for player reflection. *World of Warcraft* provides a multilayered ethical system to distinguish between good and evil and to critique problematic social institutions, but players' relationships to these ethics are ambiguous. Not all of *World of Warcraft* design demonstrates morally good values. However, the game forces players to engage in ethical contests, and what is wrong or right in the game perhaps says something about what is wrong or right in conventional reality.[50] Virtual worlds, as Donna Haraway argues of technology more broadly,[51] can and do remake citizens. By playing *World of Warcraft*, players have opportunities for reflection that may even provoke new ways of thinking and living in the world.

It is not the case that players and designers necessarily use *World of Warcraft* in the same way, however. Rather, designers can instill their own ethical concerns into the game, and players can—if they choose—put them into practice. This is not, of course, unique to *World of Warcraft*. Many, if not all, video games have some set of values internal to them, and researchers have begun analyzing the value systems encoded therein.[52] Although there are troubling aspects to *World of Warcraft*'s ethical system, by stabilizing ethical priorities within the game's quest structure and character development its designers and the players who engage in the quests reinforce certain kinds of morality.

The ethics of video games have been subject to controversy since the early days of arcade gaming. The very first game to spark a public outcry, *Death Race*, was criticized because it "asked a player—potentially a child—to engage in violence against ordinary people instead of monsters or spaceships and that this violence took place in a realistic setting (inferred from the blocky graphics with the aid of the game's title, cabinet artwork and so on)."[53] Such concerns are now amplified by the fact that game graphics can explicitly show violence, sex, drugs, and other "adult" material, and many if not most children are avid gamers.

Gamers admit to several moral management strategies to distinguish between game violence and real-life violence, including differentiating between gaming and reality, using in-game ethical constraints (e.g., "They attacked me first!" or "They are at war with my allies"), or dehumanizing their opponents—a tactic the designers often make quite easy.[54] It is possible that such strategies *could* contribute to real violence by helping players establish disengagement strategies that they can subsequently apply to daily life.[55] Whether this is the case or not will require substantive empirical analysis, as it certainly maps onto traditional justifications for violence (e.g., among gangs, tribes, religions, nations, and skin colors).

On the other hand, video games need not emphasize unethical behavior; they can be almost totally devoid of ethical meaning or even hold positive morals. Only the most mind-bogglingly awkward argument could describe many of the most popular games, such as the ubiquitous *Tetris*, as being ethical or not. Stacking blocks is simply not a matter of morality. Other games manage to encourage socially positive behavior; they can, for example, discourage indiscriminate killing and reward altruism. A variety of scholars, theologians, and psychologists have argued that certain games, such as *Ultima IV* and *BioShock*, teach morally valuable lessons.[56] There is marketable value in such ethics, as morally positive protagonists can inspire "allegiance" in players, adding to the fun of the games.[57]

In addition, providing players with moral dilemmas makes the games socially valuable. While not all games force players into ethical conflicts, the ones that do should help defuse some of the criticism leveled at gaming in general, such as the panic-stricken and deeply flawed essay by noted psychologist Philip Zimbardo and his collaborator Nikita Duncan.[58] Not only do quite a few games offer space for moral reasoning, but gaming might, in general, also be a "perfect test-bed for helping people [learn] about ethics and ethical reasoning."[59] As a consequence, games and game systems must be carefully evaluated, to ascertain both when they promote moral reasoning and when they encode ill-conceived or accidentally amoral values.

Video games create ethical conflicts as part of their narrative arcs, and many designers and analysts believe that such ethical practice can influence players outside of the games. The famed game designer Richard Bartle vigorously promotes this optimistic outcome, defending video games against their detractors on the grounds that players build real character through online life. "My argument that virtual worlds are a force for good," he writes, "is based largely on the fact that players can learn to be better people as a result of playing them. That means I intrinsically accept that virtual worlds can bring about change."[60]

Good game design can, indeed, change the world and the way we live within it. A game can offer transformative play that "can metamorphosize the players of a game, the culture of which the game is a part, even the game itself."[61] While some game designers actively work toward such ends, others might stumble into them by accident. The ethics defended or considered within a game are ways that game design can transform conventional life.

In particular, many game designers and their advocates see the god's-eye view provided by video gaming as a unique tool for repairing the troubles of our world. Will Wright, the famed designer of the entire *Sim* series of games, ends his vast game of evolution and galactic exploration, *Spore*, with the injunction to take the power "to create and spread life, intelligence and understanding throughout the cosmos. Use this power wisely. There is a wonderful opportunity to start on one particular planet: Look for the third rock from *Sol*," which is, of course, Earth.[62] The end of *Spore* reflects what Wright has said is "very useful" about his games: they encourage global awareness and long-term planning.[63] Enthusiastically taking *Spore* to heart, Jane McGonigal tells us that planetcraft (the skill of managing planets) honed in video games can and should be applied to the real-world problems of energy, food production, transportation, and the environment through new forecasting games that overlay a game structure on the problems of contemporary life.[64] For Wright and McGonigal, the divine perspective afforded by gaming has genuine soteriological power, and it just might permit ordinary human beings to save the world from themselves.[65]

Cultural critique is not, unlike beauty, merely in the eye of the beholder; rather, it is the direct result of design choices. For example, Jordan Mechner, the famous designer of the *Prince of Persia* game franchise, declares that an antiwar theme "underlines the whole tale" of *Prince of Persia: Sands of Time*.[66] Because designers encode ethical systems in their games, one commentator suggests that game creation is essentially a moral task: "the values consciously or unconsciously embedded in the design determine the basics of the ethics of the game, and cue the experience and affordances of the user(s) of the system. Games are ethical if and because their design is a moral system and crafting those systems is or can be a moral action."[67] Game designers produce moral structures in games like *World of Warcraft*, and players participate in them. In the case of *World of Warcraft*, this means serious cultural critique in addition to the more obvious battle between good and evil.

Because *World of Warcraft* is so popular, the social criticisms proffered by the game might support Bartle's claim that games can be a force for good. In addition to situating characters within a world where good and evil struggle against one another, *World of Warcraft* critiques contemporary social structures. Politics, capitalism, and our approach to technology all receive occasional criticism, and the game's quests persistently advocate a renewed commitment to the environment. We cannot see *World of Warcraft* as a wholesale rejection of modern culture because global capitalism, international law, and industrial development are necessary for producing and distributing the game. Nevertheless, the game poses "a radical critique of the dominant culture."[68] I do not mean to imply that *World of Warcraft* is unquestionably a morally positive enterprise or that all of its design elements are morally progressive; its inexplicable and often offensive allusions to race and ethnicity, for example, could and should be seen in a negative light.[69] Nevertheless, the designers provide opportunities to reflect on social issues, and *World of Warcraft* thereby participates in the moral lives of contemporary gamers.

First and foremost, *World of Warcraft* offers a clear and pronounced system of good and evil. Demons and undead corrupt the world, seeking the destruction of mortals. The heroes must fight them off. The *World of Warcraft* cosmos was crafted by a race of supremely powerful titans, gods who created planets and gave them life. Unfortunately, one of the titans fell from grace. Having first led the titans' armies against their demonic foes, the titan Sargeras decided that the presence of chaos and evil must be the titans' own fault and built an army (the Burning Legion) to undo their work.[70] The heroes of *World of Warcraft* must, of course, struggle against the Burning Legion and evil in all of its forms. This cosmic battle is the most important conflict in the *World of Warcraft* mythos, trumping the long-standing arguments between the Horde and the Alliance. These political opponents can even occasionally put aside their differences and work together against the Burning Legion. Joining with their faction as its warriors stand alongside the other, players do good deeds. Through their questing, they have helped overcome, however momentarily, internecine political conflict, and now they can sally forth to strike down the forces of evil.

While the struggle against the Burning Legion offers a clear division between good and evil, politics between and within the political factions in *World of Warcraft* complicate matters. Both the Alliance and the Horde are fundamentally on the "good side," yet they do not get along. Neither faction is evil, but internal conflicts reveal the ethical bankruptcy of political hierarchies in both factions. Alliance characters, for example, see this after many quests against the Defias Brotherhood, an enemy common within human-controlled lands. Eventually, the player learns that the brotherhood formed when the human rulers refused to pay the stonemasons who rebuilt the city of Stormwind after a prior assault by the orcs. As Bainbridge points out, this undermines the players' faith in the legitimacy of their rulers and the political structures that govern their world.[71]

If extrapolated to the conventional world, this *World of Warcraft* ethic could indicate that our own politicians do not always have appropriate motives and do not always serve their constituents properly.

On their webpage, my own guilds carried out an extensive debate about the nature of legitimate rule in *World of Warcraft*. This was clearest in comparisons between the human king Varian and the orc chieftain Thrall. While some justified Varian's character flaws as the result of a difficult life, others reviled him as conceited and dishonest, grossly unequal to Thrall, who was enslaved as a youth but still matured into a noble leader. Even those who defended Varian admitted his weakness and moral inferiority to Thrall and acknowledged the legitimate concerns of his detractors. Such debates are not unique to my guild. Rather, interrogating the ruling politics of *World of Warcraft* is part of the game's appeal for many devout players and also part of its significance for contemporary life.

Despite the criticisms frequently leveled at Varian or at other groups and characters in *World of Warcraft*, it is clear that neither the Alliance nor the Horde is the evil party. The quests that Alliance and Horde players engage against one another coexist alongside the imperative that all players share in eradicating the demonic forces that struggle to take over the planet. Yet the factions continue to fight against one another even when their best interests clearly lie in cooperation. The game designers have written this into the broader storyline; for example, in one of the final quest chains in the original *World of Warcraft* game, players speak to an orc ghost, the Fallen Hero of the Horde. If the player is on the Alliance, the Fallen Hero decries the struggle between Alliance and Horde and says the two must unite against their common foes. With enough guilt to go around, both the Horde and the Alliance are responsible for their continued conflict. Each community's narratives explain how it has been hurt by the other while occluding its own culpability,[72] and thus the player who tries both Horde and Alliance characters will eventually see the insensate nature of the conflict.

But while the Horde and the Alliance occasionally see common cause, the *World of Warcraft* storyline maintains their misguided opposition. This is probably because it helps enliven the story and because there are players deeply committed to PvP play. Without the interfaction conflict, designers might need to find a new play structure that would enable both PvP and narrative progression.[73] After the powerful dragon Deathwing emerged from his subterranean prison—the event that triggered the Cataclysm expansion—the world of Azeroth suffered considerable geographic upheaval that catalyzed new conflict between the two factions. While both the Horde and the Alliance were critical in the defeat of the Lich King, neither had the time to consolidate a lasting peace before Deathwing's arrival scorched the planet's surface and reduced the availability of already scarce resources. In quest chains where Horde or Alliance players must press against the other faction, NPCs tell them that they have no choice; their leaders *need* wood, food, space, or other goods. Of course, the attentive player will immediately wonder whether a better arrangement might be possible if only the factions' leaders could overcome their long-standing grudges and prejudices.[74] Nevertheless, as Miguel Sicart points out, the conflict between the Horde and the Alliance is fundamentally irresolvable; game design choices, such as making the Horde and Alliance players unable to speak with one another, ensure a perpetual state of war not only in the lore but also among the players.[75]

Sicart considers the impenetrable conflict between Alliance and Horde to be a significant ethical flaw in *World of Warcraft*. From his perspective, "constraining players' agency is...highly unethical.... When game designers constrain players' agency in order to limit not their gameplay, but their lives as online game world denizens, they are effectively harming players, and hence committing an unethical act."[76] Of course, it is difficult to imagine a way game-like virtual worlds such as *World of Warcraft* would provide no constraints on life. Any kind of world history or narrative would automatically create such constraints. Meanwhile, *World of Warcraft* is not alone in encouraging or enforcing unethical behavior. The obvious example to this would be the well-known *Grand Theft Auto* franchise, but other fantasy games too often presume that violence is the only tool with which to engage foreign cultures or people or take simplistic and unhelpful perspectives on violence.[77]

Just over 40% of my survey respondents who have a preference between the Horde and the Alliance claim that ideological bent underlies their preference. This indicates the considerable degree to which players perceive and ally with the moral perspective of one faction or the other.[78] While neither side may be the good guys, as opposed to the bad guys, both have different ways of being good that appeal to particular players. Both groups suffer from dysfunctional political processes and often remain blinded to the general welfare of the planet and its inhabitants, but players still manage to find the good in each and identify with it. Doing so will, to some extent, enable them to navigate political waters, but it also positions them for the successive revelations of political failure that

World of Warcraft storytellers have integrated into the quest structure. The game's story forces players—over the course of many quests and in different regions of the world—to recognize that some moral values trump the political division of the world.

Similar to the way *World of Warcraft* incorporates a political message that responds to corruption and failure in conventional politics, the game also criticizes the capitalist structures that dominate our economy. Although Blizzard Entertainment profits enormously from the sale of *World of Warcraft* in a capitalist economy and a fairly effective free market operates in game,[79] the game's designers still place capitalism on the ethical chopping block, painting it as potentially "religious" and certainly all too often exploitative. The statue of Baron Revilgaz, who rules a town of pirates and merchants, is a perfect example of anti-capitalist rhetoric in *World of Warcraft* [see Fig 2.1]. As Bainbridge notes, the statue of the baron outside of town clearly recalls the Christ the Redeemer statue outside of Rio de Janeiro in Brazil and reveals that capitalism is the religion of the baron's group, the Steamwheedle Cartel, for whom gold "is god, and money is their religion."[80] While the acquisition of money is important in *World of Warcraft* and to considerable extent the game actually trains players as capitalists,[81] the game supplies "occasional hints that capitalism is wicked or distorted."[82]

FIGURE 2.1 Baron Revilgaz at Janeiro Point across from Booty Bay before the statue was damaged by a tsunami in the Cataclysm expansion. (*World of Warcraft* images provided courtesy of Blizzard Entertainment, Inc.)

One of the great flaws of capitalism appears to be its exploitative attitude toward nature, which is exacerbated by unrestrained technology.
Characters cannot avoid zones where forests have been clear-cut and
where mines have been dug into mountains by the Goblin-run Venture
Company, and they often go on quests to defeat this rapacious group. It
would appear that technology and an exploitative attitude toward nature
are destroying Azeroth,[83] and "a very large number" of quests have envi-
ronmentalist themes.[84] Indeed, races like the night elves and the taurens
and the druid class are devoted in large part to restoring and protecting the
planet from the ravages of environmental catastrophe, whether demonic
or mortal in origin.[85]

Video games often include social criticism, which is always in tension
with other elements of game design and play that tend to affirm political
and economic totalitarianism. In *Games of Empire*, Nick Dyer-Witheford
and Greig de Peuter argue that video gaming is an exemplary medium for
enacting and portraying "Empire," which they define as "the global capitalist ascendancy of the early twenty-first century, a system administered and
policed by a consortium of competitively collaborative neoliberal states,
among whom the United States still clings, by virtue of its military might,
to an increasingly dubious preeminence."[86] In short, they argue that military and capitalist interests dominate the gaming industry but that there
are always efforts internal to that system that undermine it. Video gaming
can encourage a militarization of society, can control how people spend
their time and efforts, can harden the racial segregation of city life, and
can benefit the industry by providing access to material resources gained
by exploiting foreign cultures.[87] At the same time, however, game designers often reject these systems;[88] we have already seen several ways *World of
Warcraft* designers do so through environmental messages and criticisms
of religious capitalism. Whether the criticism of or collusion with ethically ambiguous social systems is stronger in gaming is an open question,
but we cannot deny that the players are explicitly engaging in ethical play
when they try to restore the environment of Azeroth or question the legitimacy of political rule—they must wrestle with the very issues that pertain
to life outside the game as well as within it.

Just as game design can be an ethical practice for Blizzard employees,
so can playing within the world. Most, though not all, *World of Warcraft*
players recognize the presence of ethical codes in *World of Warcraft*, but
my survey numbers reveal they have a somewhat muddled understanding
of them. While only 40% of respondents agreed that they see at least one

ethical system in the game,[89] in a subsequent question asking to whom such systems pertain only 36% of respondents asserted that they see no ethical system. That is, on the second question, 64% of respondents apparently recognized some ethical system relevant to all players or to a given faction, race, or class. Obviously, this does not match the responses to the first question.[90] It would appear that the added detail in the second question helped respondents to reflect on *World of Warcraft* with greater clarity and led to a greater percentage responding that they do, in fact, see ethical agendas in the game. Measuring the power of such morality can, however, be difficult.[91]

In a broad study of video role-playing games, including *World of Warcraft*, Simkins and Steinkuehler argue that "players of RPGs engage in ethical decision making as part of their game play and that games, under the right set of conditions, have at least the potential to foster critical ethical reasoning."[92] Such a process can happen as much a result of the way the game enables unethical decisions as through ways of fostering ethical choices. For example, *World of Warcraft* has a daily cooking quest in the human city of Stormwind that can be satisfied by either taking catfish from NPCs or fishing for them oneself. In fact, stealing is no quicker than fishing, but some players might be inclined to believe it is. As the character picks up a barrel of catfish sitting next to an NPC fisher, the screen flashes the word "stealing" across a five-second progress bar. The game thereby reminds players that their chosen action is unethical, even though it is encouraged by the quest giver and enabled by the goods available to be pilfered.

From the very beginning of role-playing games, creating a character depended on ethical concerns, and this remains relevant to player choices in *World of Warcraft. Dungeons & Dragons* players, for example, frequently assign moral goodness to their characters, apparently out of their own moral self-reflection.[93] This can be problematic in playing *World of Warcraft*. For example, when I created a death knight character to experience the moral redemption of breaking free from the Lich King's control, I had serious reservations about the early quests, all of which take place while players remain evil. Even after gaining free will, however, death knights do not necessarily become "good." As one interviewee, Peter, says, the story of the death knight is not

a story of redemption. It's a revenge fantasy, the monster created by the actions of some evil [creature] rising to recuperate payment in blood. Death Knights may have regained their free will, but they don't regain their 'humanity', they don't rebuild the lives they've destroyed. They're still dead. They're still monsters. For the most part, they don't feel particularly sorry. The Ebon Blade faction has a quest in Icecrown where they track down the Scarlet Crusade survivors they drove away while still under the Lich King's control, and infect them with the plague for fun![94]

As I moved through the early death knight quests, I expressed my concerns about them on my guild chat channel and was immediately reassured by several other players that such discomfort was shared. While death knights are unquestionably popular in the game, owing in large part to their versatility, the ethics associated with their play do concern some players. Of course, by the time one reaches endgame—or even gets close to it—all the quests are the same for all characters, and thus the death knight is no better or worse than any other class. It merely requires some patience to get past quests that might be distasteful.

For better or worse, *World of Warcraft* offers players a chance to make unethical choices and thus provides a "free will" structure in which moral redemption might be visible. Just as Peter refuses to play a death knight because of its role in the story and the quests it performs, another interviewee, Argoz, who avidly pursues difficult achievements in *World of Warcraft* (see Chapter 3 on the achievement system), refuses to seek some because he dislikes what he would have to do to earn them. For example, he has not sought an exalted reputation (and its accompanying achievement) with the Bloodsail Buccaneers "because of what it requires and not because it is difficult."[95] To attain that reputation, players must turn on erstwhile allies and slaughter them by the thousands; although some players value the achievement over the ethics, they are evidently in the minority. Of course, playing a death knight requires nowhere near the moral apathy necessary to attain an exalted reputation with the Buccaneers, so far more players are comfortable with it.

In general, while most classes do not align with any particular morality, some do, and that is the cause for their appeal to some players. A healthy minority of respondents (20%) claimed that the ethics of a particular class are among the reasons for preferring that class above all others. Similarly, 29% of respondents prefer a particular race because of its ideology or worldview.[96] Among those with whom I interacted, ethics were most important for those who played druids, presumably because the environmental lessons included in the game play and culture are welcome among them.

In *World of Warcraft*, the religion of environmentalism easily trumps the religion of goodness. While some players aver that that they enjoy the ethics of the holy classes (paladin and priest), a considerably greater percentage of players who choose a class for its ethics choose those with eco-friendly worldviews. Among those respondents who prefer a given class for its ethics, 46% prefer druids; if we include shamans, who use the powers of nature, and hunters, who work with animal companions, as "environmentally friendly" classes, that number moves up to 64%. Nearly half of the respondents who prefer a given race for its ideology (43%) included the environmentally attuned taurens or night elves among their favorite races. My interviews support the survey data: players do not expect priests or paladins to behave differently from other people in the game, but interviewees often mentioned druids as a positive example of how the ethics of the class affects in-game behavior. Lucy, for example, says, "I think I probably 'act' differently as a druid more so than I would as a paladin/priest; not killing creatures indiscriminately, that kind of thing."[97]

Players notice the often heavy-handed environmental messages, and thus *World of Warcraft* provides opportunities for reflection. Peter says that an environmentally damaged zone has "little impact emotionally" on him, but he nevertheless "reflect[s] on it" and, indeed, expressed considerable philosophical sophistication on the subject.[98] In a brief email interview, he addressed deforestation due to faction politics, natural disaster, cataclysmic acts of evil, and one NPC group's efforts to stave off environmental collapse.[99] Even though he does not feel appalled by the zones, seeing the devastation leads to reflection that could have lasting effects on his life. Similarly, Jill feels "a sense of sadness, but it's tempered by the knowledge that it's a game."[100]

For others, in-game environmental devastation provokes retaliatory measures. Reflecting on the Venture Company and its role in Azeroth's environmental problems, Susan says, "I don't like miners; I don't exactly go out of my way to kill them, but I have more invested in them than anything."[101] One guild member reports on the webpage that after witnessing a small fox attacked and killed by an NPC fox hunter and his bull mastiff, she tamed a fox and then patrolled the area, killing every NPC fox hunter in revenge: "I was so appalled by the whole thing.... I felt like I was giving my little fox some sense of justice for the killing of its kind."[102] These acts of vengeance cannot change the *World of Warcraft* landscape, as the

enemies respawn soon after their destruction, but the act of defending
the world from its despoilers provides some solace to those players who
engage in it and thus contributes to an environmental habitus, or way of
being in the world.

In a similar vein, players often feel distressed by the circumstances
faced by the game's injured inhabitants. For example, in the Borean Tundra
of Northrend, there are baby mammoths caught in hunters' traps; characters can rescue ten of them as part of a quest for one group of NPCs, but
after the quest is complete the characters cannot interact with the trapped
mammoths anymore. Jill remarks that she "always wanted to continue to
be able to help them instead of just [doing] one non-repeatable quest."[103]
I experienced something similar to this with my druid character. To learn
the spell for curing diseases I had to go on a quest where I used a cura-
tive salve to help sick deer. Although you cure ten sick deer for the quest,
once you have the full spell for curing diseases you are no longer able to
cure the deer—it can be cast on only other players, which frustrated my
sense of how the game should work. Although many interviewees brought
up animal species that deserved sympathy, Peter thought also of sentient
inhabitants. He feels a certain sympathy for the groups who suffer within
the game, such as the Forsaken, undead who were ripped from their normal lives and forced into evil slavery.[104]

Interestingly, the ethical conundrums faced by players can occasionally carry over into conventional ethical and political conflicts and provide
new ways of thinking about them. For example, shortly after the U.S. Fish
and Wildlife Service delisted the gray wolf from its endangered species
programs and reopened wolf hunting in the western United States, one
player posted to the forums in frustration over how it felt to kill wolves in
the game, given that there is a real-life political imbroglio being fought
over the practice.[105] The posting prompted a flurry of commentary, including considerable concern over how it feels to kill animals in the game,
gratitude that it *is* just a game, and interest in seeing animals better pro-
tected in reality. One player even listed her responsible hunting strategies
of taking only unattached males according to strategies common among
the hunters with whom she grew up.

Game ethics and life ethics are not always, however, the same thing,
so what a player does in game may not change her day-to-day politics or
actions. Few players seem willing to explicitly adopt the game's ethics in
conventional reality: a majority of survey respondents (54%) claimed that
the game's ethics are not relevant to life outside the game, and another

third (31%) were uncertain as to the relevance of the ethical systems.[106] At such times, ethnographic data helps clarify confusions created by survey data. Nearly every interviewee could connect real-world ethical concerns with the ethics of *World of Warcraft*, whereas not every survey respondent could. This implies that it is the survey that is faulty as a data collection tool. It is, of course, important to know that players' off-the-cuff impression is to believe that the conventional world and the game world are ethically divorced from one another, but it is also important to know that players can and will work through points of contact between the two worlds when given particulars by which to consider the matter. It is likely that the ethical practice inculcated in the game is subtle in its effect on players.

Sometimes, players in *World of Warcraft* show decidedly asocial ethics, as evinced by the well-reported Corrupted Blood Incident of 2005. In patch 1.7, Blizzard introduced the Zul'Gurub dungeon, which had an evil demon as the final boss. This demon could cast an infectious plague, Corrupted Blood, on a player. While the game designers assumed this plague would remain a problem solely for the group of adventurers, some players started deliberately teleporting out of the dungeon after acquiring it, thereby spreading it to the cities and towns scattered across Azeroth.[107] Lower-level characters were unable to survive the plague and thus tended to drop dead as soon as an infected character came sufficiently close, though not before infecting anyone near them. The incident shows that the players demonstrated an active desire to harm others and diminish those players' fun.

Obviously, the players' desire to infect others with the Corrupted Blood plague is problematic, but such moral experimentation is not limited to games like *World of Warcraft*. In one study of teenage girls, for example, each participant acknowledged that while playing *Sims* she had led her Sims to perform horrid behaviors, such as neglecting babies, or had tortured and murdered characters by manipulating the environment such that they would die.[108] This is not to say that teenage girls are better or worse than *World of Warcraft* players; it merely contextualizes the Corrupted Blood Incident within the wide range of antisocial behaviors evinced by humanity, especially when players perceive their choices as "just a game."

Fortunately, the Corrupted Blood Incident also demonstrates player altruism. While antagonistic players deliberately infected anyone they could by teleporting to crowded zones, other players cast healing spells to keep characters alive or resurrected them if they died.[109] Most players, of course, were simply victims, inadvertently passing along the plague as soon as they caught it. It is encouraging, however, that some higher-level players actively sought to suppress the plague and help their weaker counterparts. Unfortunately, such actions were inadequate. Blizzard had no choice but to restart all of the game servers after adjusting the plague so that it would work only in Zul'Gurub. One epidemiologist, Nina Fefferman, suggests that the varying responses to Corrupted Blood map onto the way our population would respond to a genuine epidemic: "we saw some courage.... We saw some fear, suspicion of quarantine."[110] We might as well say we saw some viciousness too.[111] Among these responses, there's no question that players make ethical choices; whether they learn from these to improve social life in conventional reality is, however, still open to debate.

Although *World of Warcraft* players do not necessarily see their play as influencing conventional ethics, there are indications that virtual world occupants carry at least some aspects of their game time with them in day-to-day life. Angelica Ortiz de Gortari and her associates argue, based on interviews with players, that a wide array of game transfer phenomena (GTP) operate in players' lives.[112] These include involuntary phenomena, such as dreaming about gaming or experiencing altered sensory perceptions, and voluntary phenomena, such as daydreaming or modeling one's actions after those of game characters. "Almost all of the players reported some type of GTP, but in different ways and with varying degrees of intensity.... Most of the players appeared to perceive GTP as a natural consequence of their high engagement in video games."[113] This raises serious concerns for some players, who can apparently absorb asocial behaviors and either act them out or imagine acting them out in their daily lives. We should, however, take some solace from the fact that of the 42 individuals interviewed by Ortiz de Gortari, 39 were males in the range of 15–21 years of age. While we might want to avoid essentialism, it is probably a fair generalization to say that this particular demographic tends more toward asocial and aggressive behavior than other groups or to be part of aggressive environments (a fact not mentioned by the study's authors). In addition, aggression and prosocial behavior are not mutually exclusive but can in fact coincide comfortably in any given person.[114]

In an important study of virtual reality and ethical behavior, one group of collaborators at Stanford found that participants who have superpowers in a virtual world subsequently evince greater prosocial responses after playing.¹¹⁵ Using head-mounted displays, participants traveled through a virtual world either by super-flight or in a helicopter. Those who explored the virtual world with super-flight were then quicker to help when the researchers "accidentally" spilled pens, and they provided more help as well.¹¹⁶ So the super-empowerment of virtual world residence might give rise to greater altruism or morally laudable behavior. That virtual world, however, was not a full game world and did not involve combat, so it may not provide much help in thinking about MMORPGs. It is important, however, to consider *how* one plays a game like *World of Warcraft*. In such a rich environment, some choices are surely more relevant to prosocial or antisocial behavior outside the game than others, and it is difficult to assess the causal direction of such behavior and game play.

For some players, *World of Warcraft* is, indeed, a prosocial game—one in which helping guildmates and even strangers is a source of greater pleasure than killing monsters and other players. For other players, the reverse is true, and many players will find that they oscillate between these two extremes based on their mood, their game needs, or other factors. It has been shown that self-reported prosocial tendencies correlate to prosocial behaviors in a virtual environment,¹¹⁷ which would seem relevant to a game like *World of Warcraft*. So unpacking player motivations and game effects is no simple task. To further complicate matters, it is not entirely clear that players or designers have the same crystal clear demarcation between prosocial and antisocial games that academics have. One study, for example, asks children to identify how often they had "played video games with two types of prosocial scenes (scenes in which characters help troubled persons and scenes where friendships or affections between parents and children are shown)."¹¹⁸ Anyone paying attention to her game play in *World of Warcraft* would have to define the game as prosocial by these standards, as there are quests that meet both of these criteria. Yet it is unlikely that the study designers would have acclaimed *World of Warcraft* as a prosocial game.

Fortunately, we can—at least theoretically—use virtual worlds to encourage ethical behaviors in others. The subtlety of *World of Warcraft*'s positive ethical claims, however, may be problematic; if players are to acquire empathy, environmental sensitivity, or political awareness from playing the game, they might need a stronger lead from the game designers. If nothing else, we know that a lifelong lack of play promotes aggressive and psychopathological behaviors,¹¹⁹ so perhaps *World of Warcraft* and similar games contribute indirectly to a better world. Merely doling out superpowers, however, is probably not sufficient if designers want to substantially contribute to an ethical society.

The nature of embodied game play may help complete a social turn from ethical reflection to ethical participation. Player identification with the character is essential in the ethical potential of *World of Warcraft* and other virtual worlds. Based on his experimental work with schoolchildren using video games, Tim Marsh believes that players are "vicariously there" and clearly able to empathize with their own characters as well as with the other characters in the game.[120] Players are particularly empathetic toward characters played by another person rather than an NPC.[121] As a consequence of this kind of experience, "it may very well be that playing through [game] roles, including those we would never consider taking up in the real world, has the potential not only to foster greater empathy, tolerance, and understanding for others but to help us critically reflect on who we want to be for others."[122]

Recent studies into social networking imply that altruism online affects conventional life. For example, psychologist Larry Rosen and his collaborators found that Facebook users demonstrated empathy for other users and that they could also take advantage of such "practice empathy" to be more empathetic in conventional life.[123] Given that appreciating another's plight is a regular part of *World of Warcraft* play, we can infer that in-game empathy can conceivably translate to empathy out of the game. Therefore, while it might not be the case for everyone, without question we must concede that Bartle might have a point when he asserts that playing video games has one "overall goal: being someone else in order to become a better you."[124]

In *World of Warcraft*, players extend their empathy to more than just virtual animals; their empathy for one another may well help them realize Bartle's agenda. Perhaps naturally, given that guild members form tightly knit communities, they occasionally bring their problems to the guild's chat communications. In my time with Dropped Stitches, people expressed concerns over their work, their loved ones, and their health. Guild members promptly chimed in, whether to express solidarity with the unhappy party, to share personal experiences, or to offer advice. Obviously, such empathetic work is sincere within the confines of the game, and it means that concern for others is a common element in regular game play and guild membership. Even outside of guilds, some players commonly assist lower-level characters in need, such as with defeating a powerful enemy that the lower-ranking player cannot defeat without aid.[125] This too,

reflects empathy for the other player and may encourage generally altru-
istic behavior in life.[126]

Whether or not true empathy emerges from MMORPG play, one study
does indicate that civic engagement can do so under the correct play conditions. In his study of how collective play (i.e., play in conjunction with
guildmates) affects social capital, Zhong points out that there is a positive correlation between collective play and offline civic engagement: "the
outcome is consistent with [the] conclusion that involvement in voluntary
social networks can provide opportunities to acquire or improve organiza-
tional or communication skills and stimulate self-efficacy that makes one
feel more confident in influencing public affairs, thus leading to political and civic activism."[127] This places a heavy burden of responsibility on
game designers, who stand to either enhance public life or detract from it
based on the kinds of experiences they evoke. "The positive social effects
of collective MMORPG play suggest game designers to [*sic*] provide more
opportunities for social interactions and collective play, rather than merely
stimulate gamers to pursue endless rewards."[128]

There are real-world examples of gamers applying in-game ethics
to their conventional lives, and these may prove to be forerunners of
a future game-centered civic life. For example, the Society for Creative
Anachronism (SCA)[129] provides an honor code for day-to-day life.[130]
Live-action role-play is not the only activity among SCA members.
Nevertheless, it is a core element of the group's interactions, and there
are historical ties between the SCA and pencil-and-paper games like
D&D. Values of chivalry, honesty, and defending the weak can thus
emerge out of gaming interactions and influence conventional behavior. Whether *World of Warcraft* can or will accomplish something similar remains open to question, though at present the survey data indicate
this is not common. Few respondents (only 16%) claimed that playing
the game has changed their behavior, and, among those who did so
indicate, the most common changes were discursive, rather than ethical, in nature: they used *World of Warcraft* lingo or spoke about *World
of Warcraft* frequently. (Another 20% of respondents acknowledged
that the game had "maybe" changed their lives outside of the game.)
Nevertheless, some players do find that *World of Warcraft* can help them
construct a real-world ethic; as one respondent told me, "I personally
have had some success in incorporating the Three Virtues of the Church
of Holy Light [respect, tenacity, and compassion] into my greater spiritual philosophy."[131]

World of Warcraft definitely offers opportunities for ethical reflection through its design and culture, though it may not successfully reshape ethical practices. This should not come as a great surprise. Games "act as social contexts that allow exploration of certain values and attitudes,"[132] but this does not mean that they rewrite player personalities or unilaterally dictate future behaviors. Thanks to its graphics, its politics, and its character and quest cultures, *World of Warcraft* sometimes encourages a "progressive" politics; at the same time, the PvP rules, the limitations on communication, and the anarchic culture within the game can enable behaviors we might all wish we lived without.

The difficulty some respondents had in recognizing the ethical constructs of *World of Warcraft* emerges out of the implicit way much modern art addresses sacred themes. Twentieth-century art forsook literal depictions of religious goals and spiritual transcendence, instead camouflaging them.[133] Perhaps players do not *expect* to use the game as a source for ethical inspiration and therefore do not *notice* how the game visually, textually, and through practice enforces ethical considerations. Unquestionably, *World of Warcraft* is the result of ethical (and sometimes unethical) work on the part of the designers and provides players with an ethical system that engages contemporary culture, including politics, economics, technology, and our approach to the environment. Many players recognize these elements, and a few even reflect on their relationship to conventional life outside of the game. Whether the games' moral imperatives influence player's actual behavior, as opposed to self-reported behavior, would require a separate, longitudinal study of player practices or self-descriptions before and after substantial play. It is enough here to simply conclude that the game can provide something many people incorrectly believe can come only from a religious institution: morality.

Providing religious operations through secular means is, of course, the hallmark of an authentic fake. Religious groups tout morality as a key component in religion, yet participation in such a group does not guarantee moral behavior. It does, however, generally guarantee an opportunity to reflect on moral concerns. *World of Warcraft* does likewise: players may not return from Azeroth as better human beings, but they certainly have an opportunity to do so. Designers do moral work in producing *World of Warcraft* and provide players with similar opportunities, but these aspects remain only the tip of the iceberg in *World of Warcraft*'s quasi-religious opportunities.

Conclusion

Traditionally, religious communities have been the primary sources for social grouping and ethical reflection; both count among Ninian Smart's dimensions of the sacred, and both serve the goal of fixing or finding meaning in human life. They are necessary, though not sufficient, for establishing a religious community. In today's spiritual marketplace, however, these goods can be had in many new ways. Playing *World of Warcraft* can thus be akin to affiliating with a religious tradition. It provides rich community structures and guidelines by which to engage the world around oneself.

Of course, there are problems with the social structures provided in *World of Warcraft*. If, for example, players become habituated to irreconcilable differences thanks to the impossibility of communicating across factions, they may well come to think that political conflicts in general cannot be resolved. Indeed, one might claim that the Horde versus Alliance conflict accurately mirrors us–them discourses common in religious social and ethical reflection, and the last thing we need is to have such conflicts strengthened through game play. Likewise, if players feel like *World of Warcraft* is the only place they can form effective social bonds (which is not, at present, a risk that concerns players—they almost universally claim the opposite), then they may not work very hard to establish productive relationships in conventional reality.

World of Warcraft engages the social and practical elements of religious life in some very genuine ways. It provides a forum for community building and then, thanks to deliberate design affordances, encourages players to form them. The guild structure, in particular, provides players with a group of fellow players who will support them both in and out of the game. Through the guilds, structures of trust and interpersonal commitment can provide players with a network of meaningful fellowship, thereby minimizing the costs associated with decreased participation in traditional religious communities. At the same time, by participating in the political life of the game, players embody ethical principles. While those morals are often hidden and may remain camouflaged for many players, the habituation of their imagery and activity could provide players—even those who lack a deliberate appreciation for them—with ethical guidelines that may operate unconsciously outside of the game.

If it were not for the devotional aspects that will occupy the next chapter, we might conceivably appreciate how *World of Warcraft* does social work without necessarily believing that it does religious work. After all, groups may be formed and ethical systems described without recourse to religion. However, the social elements in *World of Warcraft*—the grouping, the friendship, the commitment, the moral reflection, the empathy— take on greater significance when seen in the light of personal meaning and transcendent experiences that the game enables. Just as *World of Warcraft* and similar games change the landscape of religious affiliation, they simultaneously offer new analogues for religious devotion. Religious engagement, which is so often crucial in individual meaning-making, identity formation, and surpassing the limits of mortal life, can be replicated in *World of Warcraft*. The next chapter shows how a player's relationship to her character can provide her with a sense of personal meaning and transcendent experiences.

3

A World with Meaning

Introduction

The powerful community structures in video games like *World of Warcraft* mean that they impinge upon the social role of religion, but many other institutions, practices, and locations also offer social opportunities. It is thus not the social activities alone that make *World of Warcraft* virtually sacred. The especially interesting thing about sociality and ethics in *World of Warcraft* is that these are anchored to practices through which people make meaning and experience transcendence. Like a Venn diagram, games like *World of Warcraft* and traditional religions show overlapping concerns, qualities, and products even as they diverge in others. In the last chapter, we saw how *World of Warcraft* offers a quasi-religious social structure by provisioning players with communities that they value and ethics that they must engage—though some do so with considerably more enthusiasm than others. This chapter goes beyond those social activities to explore how *World of Warcraft* is part of our religious landscape not just because it satisfies social concerns but also because players and designers use it to produce meaningful and even transcendent experiences.

Not every *World of Warcraft* player identifies with his or her character, and not every player experiences transcendence in the game. For some, *World of Warcraft* is a place of calculation in character building, for example, or strategic movement of combat participants; however, many of the typical activities in the game contribute to personally meaningful experiences of transcendence. Whether mastering other players through player versus player (PvP) combat, conquering a difficult raid boss, or even acquiring and crafting a new alchemical recipe, players find that in *World of Warcraft* they can do things that ordinary life renders impossible. When they log on to the game, players enter an amazing realm of heroic deeds and epic powers; these elements often provide players with an important experience of overcoming their mortal limits, which is why *World of Warcraft* and similar games operate as authentic fakes.

It is important to remember that religion is the "negotiation of what it means to be human with respect to the superhuman and the subhuman."[1] Given this, social grouping and opportunities for ethical reflection would not constitute religion, or even ersatz religion, on their own. They are clearly efforts at human meaning-making, but they are not by definition tied to a hierarchical cosmos. (Remember that this doesn't require we believe in supernatural entities like gods, angels, or devils—only that we realize how in religion human beings make sense of themselves with respect to the possibility of transcendence or debasement.) In a social network where associational practices such as community building and ethics are integrated with a desire for and opportunities to experience transcendence, these practices become religious. Of course, *World of Warcraft* cannot operate as a traditional religion in any ordinary way. It is what Chidester calls "holy shit," or an "authentic fake."[2]

There is no question that the social structures of *World of Warcraft* are important and powerful, but they do not stand alone: just as the game can replace these social components of religion, it can also replace devotional components. Through *World of Warcraft*, players engage in purposive acts, see meaning in their work, develop self-understanding, and experience transcendence. Daily routines in conventional life may be meaningless and dull, but even the most mechanical repetition in *World of Warcraft* contributes to people's heroic identity. Thanks to *World of Warcraft*, players can become magically empowered heroes, respected across the realm for saving innocent lives and warding off evil. Such experiences, far from being trivial, can change people's lives, making the world more richly rewarding than it ever seemed before. The opportunity to rise above the ordinary, to become superhuman, is the ultimate promise of *World of Warcraft*, and the most powerful component of how its play can be virtually sacred.

We must follow many voices to appreciate the ways players develop themselves as persons, appreciate their actions as meaningful, and experience feelings of transcendence in *World of Warcraft*. In this chapter, as in the last, I allow game designers and players to speak on their own behalf, rely on survey data to gain insight into player motivations, and, through pictures and descriptions of *World of Warcraft*, even give the game itself a voice. The technologies built into *World of Warcraft* assist players on their way to transcendence, which they experience through the game narrative and play mechanics.

Identifying the Player–Character

Within the framework of their communities, gamers successfully negotiate problems of self-identity that ultimately provide a sense of meaning and purpose in their gaming activities. Whereas individuals might have traditionally acquired a sense of personal identity and meaning through their religious tradition and its view of history, today some people can satisfy this need in *World of Warcraft*. Massively multiplayer online role-playing games (MMORPGs) encourage a process of self-discovery through the experience of an avatar in game and allow players to thereby engage in a mythological narrative that provides them with a sense of purpose.

Identification is a complicated matter, and it is important to distinguish it from role-play. Role-play is when participants speak and act only as they believe the character "ought" to. That is, in a medieval fantasy role-playing game (RPG), a role-player might use language filled with "thee" and "thou" and might valorize chivalrous knights and ladylike damsels. It is emphatically *not* the case that role-play is the same as identification with the avatar, but on occasion the two are confused. For example, in an otherwise outstanding paper, Dmitri Williams and his collaborators note that "a large group of players finds a bright and clear separation between themselves and their character and engages in no [role-play] at all."[3] This conflates playing a role and that of extending oneself through the game character. But these are not the same; it is entirely possible to identify with a character's actions even if players do not role-play and, indeed, even if they do not see themselves as "being" the character. If, for example, a player avers, "I have beaten Ragnaros in the Molten Core raid," then she has identified with the character regardless of whether she considers herself a role-player. Moreover, it is plausible that one could role-play without meaningfully identifying with the character; acting is not necessarily the same as being.

In his pioneering study of pen-and-paper gamers, Gary Fine first noted the powerful relationship between RPGs and identity. He identifies two strategies for identification between players and their character: either the players played their own personality in the character's world or else sought to role-play a character different from their own personality.[4] Regardless of which strategy players choose, identification with the character comes naturally and leads to serious emotional engagement with it.[5] For example, Fine quotes Dave Arneson, one of the cofounders of *Dungeons & Dragons* (*D&D*), noting that resurrection spells were developed in the game precisely because death of the characters was so disappointing for the players.[6] While the owners of deceased characters could simply roll up new characters to continue play, their attachment to characters is frequently so powerful that they see starting over as catastrophic.

Richard Bartle, the co-designer of Multi-User Dungeon,[7] believes that the identification between character and player is an essential aspect of game play. He argues that a stream of challenges defines an individual person; working through these difficulties—often with different characters and thus in different guises—helps players come to grips with their own identities.[8] Trying different personality types allows the "real you" to emerge even if the conditions of players' day-to-day lives have inhibited it.[9] In developing this perspective, he borrows from Sherry Turkle's work, which explores the role of subjectivity in online life. Many of Turkle's subjects reveal that life online allows them opportunities to be "themselves" for the first time;[10] as such, it can become difficult for users to subjugate their online lives to their conventional lives.[11] According to Turkle, individuals' exploration with varying identities online is not a separation from their real self but rather represents a valid way of experiencing the world in different ways.[12]

Often, it is the case that whatever initial differences appear between the online and offline selves diminish and even disappear over time. There certainly are a few people who deliberately and actively role-play identities online and keep them distinct from offline life, but they are the minority: "virtual worlds and online games are not exotic environments dedicated to the 'identity play' of a few, but instead spaces that users move in and out fluidly [sic], which in turn leads to the construction of a 'synthetic' identity that remains fairly stable online and off."[13] Although it is possible that one's conventional identity and online identity can actually separate further over time, most players tend toward the construction of one, even if multifaceted, identity.

In her extensive research on the community of gamers who migrated from *Uru: Ages of Myst* after that game's collapse, Celia Pearce notes that players frequently show close identification with their avatars and expect similar behavior in others. Many of her informants, for example, held that an avatar is a "window into the soul through which you could see the real person,"[14] and she quotes one who believes that players create avatars that "resemble the way they want to think of themselves."[15] Perhaps her clearest example of this comes from a poem that Raena, one of the *Uru* players, wrote:

> *Remember when you first felt scared,*
> *Of thunder or strange looking creature?*
> *Did you feel better when you wound up in Relto [a safe zone]*
> *That moment was when you and Avi [avatar] became one,*
> *Your true innerself.*
> *Your soul free from the physical world*
> *to be the person inside*[16]

Of course, identification with a character or computer avatar is not always absolute. A player can take one of four basic positions vis-à-vis his or her character: (1) the character is an extension of the self; (2) multiple characters reflect varying aspects of the self; (3) a combination of both, where one character is principally identified with the self but all others reflect important aspects of the individual; and (4) the character is nothing but a toy or puppet for playing the game. In my survey of *World of Warcraft* players, there was a relatively even split between players who identify with their characters in some way and those who report no identification at all (22% in category one, 16% in category two, 11% in category three, and 51% in category four).

Although approximately half the respondents deny identifying with their MMORPG characters, we can use a simple thought experiment to show just how likely it is that many of these might actually do so. Consider the board game *Monopoly*. Almost every player ardently desires to play the game as one or another of the die-cast pieces (e.g., the car, the shoe, the iron) despite the fact that no player actually wants to *be* a car or shoe or iron. Some players will even refuse to play with any but their favorite pieces. If we can identify so strongly with die-cast roadsters, consider how much more we might do so with a digital avatar we have designed ourselves. Richard Bartle goes so far as to say that even those who say that they "just want to play a game, not undergo some mystical transformation of the soul"[17] in fact desire that very thing: "it's just that they don't know they do."[18]

Given that half of the players knowingly identify with their characters, and many others probably do also, we can safely assume that they are able to engage in Bartle's goal: synthesizing online and offline identity to make active choices about who they want to be and what they want to do. As one gamer puts it: "the freedom of virtual worlds could be considerably more than physical world [sic] and save us a lot or at least give us much more room to grow/improve in various ways."[19] Thus, immersion in a game world, and identification with the avatar, represents a powerful opportunity to recast and reconstruct our subjective selves.

The virtual embodiment enabled by World of Warcraft and other games enhances players' identification with their characters. John Lester, an expert in virtual world design, claims that using avatars "mirrors how we interact with the physical world. It mirrors an environment in which our brain swims as naturally as a fish in water … so consequently those worlds feel more natural to us, we remember what happens in them more.... Our brains are happiest when they're immersed in a 3D world."[20] The ability to remember virtual world activity, to engage in it naturally, assists in player–character identification by capitalizing on our natural modes of thinking and acting as embodied within an actual world.

Identification with an avatar or character, which comes very naturally to some, is not as confusing as it might seem at first glance. Indeed, all of us participate in a similar process, revealing variations of ourselves as we move among different environments. All of us perform as different "selves" for different frames of discourse.[21] I, for example, behave rather differently when building paper monsters on the floor with my children, sharing a glass of wine with my wife, teaching a class, talking with my colleagues, and visiting with friends. Likewise, the conditions of my context, not just the people with whom I share it, matter. Teaching a class of new students affects my personality, as would teaching the day after the students have taken an exam. Fine points out that Dungeons & Dragons players must negotiate narratives taking place in their games, about their games, and outside their games. To do so, they shift in and out of frames of reference. The difference is that we tend to think of ourselves as shifting from aspect to aspect of our personalities in a linear fashion, whereas gamers must engage multiple frames of reference simultaneously. Fine asks us to consider whether our traditional understanding of such personality switching is really as sequential and discrete as we have imagined and also what we might make of the fact that gamers habitually maintain multiple concurrent frames.[22]

Our ability to juxtapose frames of reference allows us to develop personal meaning from our in-game activities because we do not fully sever our consciousness in game from our conventional sense of self. An individual's "shards of self" are simultaneous and interpenetrating; this means that the emotional concerns of one will overlap with the others. In everyday life, this can be seen in a similar overlap among differing roles: a major professional success, for example, does not stay in the office but is reflected across an individual's other activities, casting her entire life in a rosy glow.

When players shift their frames of reference into and out of their online worlds, synthesizing identity in complex, goal-oriented ways, they can define and produce meaning in their lives. Video gaming may therefore be, as one commentator suggests, "a pervasive cultural form that both reflects and constructs the contemporary imagination, serving as a primary locus of meaning making and identity formation for those born in the post-Atari era."[23] Likewise, Edward Castronova declares that people in games have "experiences inside virtual worlds that are so rich, so deep, so meaningful that their experiences in the real world pale in comparison."[24] In *World of Warcraft*, players create avatars to represent themselves in the virtual world. There is a strong tendency to identify with those avatars, whose actions are "my own," and this tendency contributes to our ability to perform meaningful deeds and even to attain transcendent states in the game.

Mythical Meaning

Game designers and players collaborate in the production of meaning through video games. Both communities see activity in games as important and powerful, and both use the games to stabilize that meaning, giving it staying power. What we accomplish in virtual worlds stays with us, even when we return to conventional life, and our performance in them provides opportunities to explore what matters to us and who we are as individuals. In *World of Warcraft*, players often see significance in even the most banal game activities, but they do most of their meaningful work by participating in the mythos of the game. Because players can identify fluidly with their characters, they come to see themselves as active participants in a heroic story of epic proportions. This means that their work is truly significant—it is vital to the well-being of the world and the ultimate victory of good over evil. Just as pen-and-paper fantasy gaming is a zone where "transformation of the mundane, workaday world into a land of imaginative delight" becomes possible,[25] so too is *World of Warcraft* a place wherein our lives become enchanted and meaningful.

The overlap between player identity and character identity helps make gaming meaningful, as a major accomplishment is often the cause of intense joy and the subject of ongoing conversation over weeks or even months. In the introduction to *Halos & Avatars*, Craig Detweiler wonders if this is why video games are attractive, noting that "when we win a virtual contest online, the euphoric feelings of victory spill over into our everyday world. My son still beams at recollections of mastering *The Original Adventures of Lego Indiana Jones* on the Wii. It was a moment of father-son bonding, of shared accomplishment, a rite of passage for an excitable seven-year-old (and his dad)."[26] Among my own interviewees, Peter reports that it "feels good to accomplish something difficult in *World of Warcraft*."[27] Susan echoes this, saying that achieving something difficult in the game provides a sense of satisfaction. She does not feel much of a reward within the game, but as a person outside of it she does; major accomplishments, provide "outside the game...a sense of general accomplishment in my life...pretty much exactly the same as working at anything and succeeding at it."[28] In a follow-up interview, Susan reported that "as time goes on, I identify more with [my character]. I feel like I've done the things she's done."[29] As their characters, players overcome great obstacles, accomplishing feats that can equal or overshadow their conventional life counterparts. While critics and even players may dismiss *World of Warcraft* as "just a game," within it players do work that makes them feel fulfilled, and thus the game contributes to the good life for many of its players.

One clear way of understanding how important game accomplishments can be is to note that players rarely describe their game accomplishments in the third person and instead use first person: "that was awesome when we defeated Ragnaros yesterday!" The use of language within games clearly demonstrates the fuzzy borders between characters and players. In describing events past, most players use "I" for me rather than "he" or "she" or "it" for the character. Such discursive habits reveal that that the separation between player and character is rarely absolute and reveal the ways a player moves across frames of reference quite naturally.[30] According to game designer Chaim Gingold, such identification with the character is a natural outcome of the player's creative investment in it: "it's not just the hundreds of hours invested in a *World of Warcraft* character along with their relationships and possessions that generate attachment; it's the sense that our fabrications are extensions of ourselves. As recipients of our attention and creative energy, our handiworks are reflections of who we are; they are tangible manifestations of our personalities."[31] So the character's heroic deeds are the player's heroic deeds.

It is easy to perceive one's virtual work as meaningful because players make a psychological distinction between the game frame and non-game frames. This distinction resembles that between the sacred and the profane, which can be crucial to the assignment of meaning and significance in religious life. In *The Elementary Forms of Religious Life*, Durkheim argues that life is divided into two distinct phases: the profane and the sacred.[32] Profane time involves everyday, economic activity dedicated to personal and communal subsistence and is generally of minimal emotional affect. Sacred time, on the other hand, is one of passion and one to which meaning is ascribed. In many respects, the gamer experiences the same separation between economic and religious time as does the aboriginal in Durkheim's account, entering sacred times by logging in to *World of Warcraft*. Of course, in neither aboriginal religion nor *World of Warcraft* play can we believe that the separation of the sacred and the profane is as clear and overwhelming as Durkheim presented it to be. The two phases do not actually "stand in the sharpest possible contrast,"[33] but this does not change the fact that players clearly demarcate between gaming times and business times, such as school and work.[34]

Virtual world residents expect their lives to be profoundly different online. Richard Bartle observes that much of what goes on in producing a virtual world must be done by non-player characters (NPCs) precisely because the players would never really commit to building a proper community themselves: "few players would want to do the mundane things that occupy NPCs. Who craves a career as a city guard? Players visit virtual worlds because they offer experiences that they don't get in the real one; they don't want a 'real life' in a virtual world. NPCs, on the other hand, live in the virtual world, so their 'real life' consists of doing the kind of things players would do in their real 'real lives.' "[35] What people do in MMORPGs is *decidedly different* from what they do in the conventional world. In *World of Warcraft*, virtual life and conventional life are worlds apart.

To some extent, even when virtual world residents are obliged to engage in "real-world"– like activity, they do so with vim and vigor almost solely on account of the virtual magic with which they've infused those worlds. Will Wright's popular game *The Sims* forced players to perform all manner of mundane activities, but players in the new world found them fun. As Douglas Estes points out, "Somehow, the shift from the real world to the virtual world transformed what we take for granted into something meaningful."[36] Transitioning into the virtual world enabled people to invest meaning in the work and the world's own persistence objectifies the meaning that players created.

All *World of Warcraft* players will, of course, immediately think of their hours spent "farming" materials (by mining, herb gathering, skinning, fishing, or, worst of all for many players, surveying for archeological relics). Players often spend one or two hours flying from one spot to another using *World of Warcraft* add-ons that identify where the players have previously located ore for mining, fishing pools for fishing, and herbs for gathering. Such tasks can be tedious and time-consuming yet somehow compelling without being particularly fun for most players. They may even represent a return of the capitalist "iron cage," a reassertion of capitalist labor's power over the ludic carnival.[37] Nevertheless, one player in my guild reports that when she creates a character who cannot farm materials she feels "odd...passing by all the tasty stuff" and reports that she adores farming in the game.[38] Another wants to "explore all of [*World of Warcraft's*] nuances," and many agreed with one member's description of how difficult it can be to stop farming.[39] Given the love–hate relationship that many players have to it, if nothing else farming appears to be an example of the submissive masochism that Salen and Zimmerman cite as one of the eight forms of pleasure possible in a game;[40] more favorably, farming might participate in what Gazzard and Peacock label the "ritual logic" of gaming.[41]

Few people have trouble walking away from dull and repetitive tasks in their offices and homes when these are voluntary, but players willingly persist at such activities in video games. In the virtual world, even if we are forced to perform as though we are everyday people—that is, workers— we still manage to impute worth and meaning to the most trivial tasks. Despite the fact that *World of Warcraft* farming is repetitive, players work hard at it and value it; many even enjoy it.[42] Unlike in their conventional lives, they see the value of their labors, both in terms of individual character progression and, occasionally, larger community development, such as when Horde and Alliance characters had to gather materials and donate them to their faction's war effort to open the Gates of Ahn'Qiraj in 2006. Grinding, though "hard work," is rewarding to players, who thus carry on in a continuation of faith in the American dream in an environment where that dream can actually be realized—hard work and long hours really do net the desired result in games like *World of Warcraft*.[43] Players, whether they enjoy farming or other repetitive grinds in game, recognize this. For example, one gamer at the Thinkers discussion in *Second Life* declares that gaming "is more meaningful in that it has clear progression. The harder you work, the more you are rewarded. [Real life] is not always like that. It is pointless."[44]

While day-to-day labors in conventional life tend to be repetitive and of questionable reward, gaming allows a shift from the mundane to a sacred realm where meaning and heroism are possible. Ordinary frames of reference have a tendency to lack coherent meaning; games can counteract this. Speaking as a player about players, Castronova believes that "virtual reality can make their lives different: more exciting, more rewarding, more heroic, more meaningful."[45] Many game designers actively work toward this end; they want to make their games appealing and marketable, so they make them meaningful for the players. For example, Rand Miller, co-creator of the seminal game *Myst*, says that "to a certain extent, I think that people just want to matter. That's what drives us in a lot of ways to play games."[46]

The attribution of meaning to gaming activities is common across games, including even those that require little more than shooting enemies. As Bungie Studios and its *Halo* players celebrated the ten billionth alien invader slain in the game, one player posted on the Internet: "now we know for sure...[that] every kill you get in *Halo 3*'s campaign actually *means* something, it's not just piles of enemies you're spraying with bullets."[47] Since every kill contributed to the group's accomplishment, every player's actions were important in the grand scheme of things. Every player's work mattered, and hence every player mattered.

While killing ten billion bad guys can provide some sense of accomplishment, the mythos of *World of Warcraft* provides a clearer and more powerful framework for the development of meaning through a character's actions, one that elevates the status of players and gives them the opportunity to engage in a cosmic battle to, quite literally, save the world. Indeed, without the game's mythical and political narratives, play would likely stultify, as players could lose the incentive needed to continuously reengage the world and struggle onward.

The *World of Warcraft* mythos operates on two levels, each of which should be considered for its appeal and significance in the game. I have already discussed the overarching storyline of Sargeras's fall from grace and subsequent work to corrupt the cosmos, including Azeroth. In some sense, all player activity is a response to this situation, as there are quests leading to combat against the chief villains (e.g., Illidan, the Lich King, and Deathwing). In theory, players might prefer quests that engage this main narrative or, instead, those that deal with local concerns of NPCs or communities. Sometimes more narrowly focused quests are directly related to the epic narrative, but more often they follow individual people and their needs. A player might, for example, feel good about working to restore a child to her father but not care overly much about Sargeras (or vice versa). Game designer Greg Costikyan, for example, rejects the relevance of *World of Warcraft's* overarching narrative but likes the local quest chain stories. He insists that "players don't give a crap" about how the story relates to game content,[48] but on the other hand he believes that the stories that control the quest sequences "can be entertaining and greatly increase the appeal of playing. Indeed, the excellence of its quest system is one of *World of Warcraft's* greatest strengths."[49] While Costikyan is correct that not every player attends carefully to the storyline, however, my survey data indicate that many do so. As we shall see, many *World of Warcraft* players definitely care about the game's mythic narrative; in fact, the players who invest themselves in achievements that require completing quests from all over the world assert that they pay more attention to quests that advance the overall story than they do the smaller quest chains associated with particular regions or NPCs.

All immersive gaming benefits from mythical narratives.[50] The "Masters of the Universe Bible," for example, was largely responsible for the massive popularity of He-Man toys in the early 1980s, which were playable precisely because children knew how to situate themselves into the battle between good and evil.[51] The mythos makes a player's actions important; it ensures that each action a player–character takes will help carry the story along. "Meaning," says Jane McGonigal, "is the feeling that we're a part of something bigger than ourselves. It's the belief that our actions matter beyond our own individual lives."[52] This is precisely what results from a character's questing in *World of Warcraft*; he or she defends the innocent, rescues the weak, strikes down evil, and promotes the good. One way *World of Warcraft* differs from traditional RPGs is that the latter tend to come packaged as rules and systems but frequently lack stories, which are produced by the players in collaboration with the game master (GM).[53] In *World of Warcraft*, the story is delivered as part of the game.

Indeed, the story actually helps constitute and produce the game. *World of Warcraft* designers speak about the story in the collectors edition DVD that came with the Burning Crusade expansion, describing how the story line "informed the design of the game's world and gameplay features."[54]

The power of myth in *World of Warcraft* is strong enough that it adds luster to the game even outside of the cultural context in which the myths make sense. One Chinese player, for example, reports that "this game, in the aspect of using Western myths, is very successful.... If there is only fighting in the game, it is less interesting. The key is that a large story background supports the whole game."[55] If even those to whom druids, dwarves, and evil dragons are obscure can use the myths to make the game fulfilling, how much more so might those for whom the myth is comfortable and familiar? It seems very likely, however, that the Chinese mythology underlying the 2012 Mists of Pandaria expansion is a reaction to the extraordinary popularity of *World of Warcraft* in China and a desire to ensure that even more players have a cultural stake in the game's mythos.

At times, *World of Warcraft's* mythos fades into the background, losing immediacy, but this never eliminates its power. After all, in game design, "story is to support and enhance the gameplay,"[56] and it can do so while subtly underlying the gameplay experience.[57] In *World of Warcraft*, cultural lore becomes unnoticeable under extreme questing conditions when players try to forge rapidly ahead, making character progression their highest priority, but nevertheless it is ubiquitous and unavoidable.[58] Tanya Krzywinska notes that "the game's mythic structures and elements drive the logic that underpins *World of Warcraft's* stylistic milieu and provides the context for and of gameplay."[59]

At a barest minimum, the *World of Warcraft* mythos constructs the referential system in which players operate, affecting the kinds of quests they accomplish and also their treatment at the hands of NPCs and other players. "Although players might choose to ignore backstory, playing as Horde or Alliance or a particular class does nonetheless have an impact on the way the world is experienced and how players are regarded by others; and this is often cued through reference to mythologically derived archetypes as well as through game world history."[60] Given that most quests are delivered according to the character's role in the narrative, the mythos is crucial to the lived experience of *World of Warcraft*. Even players for whom questing is nothing but a way to level a character to endgame PvP still end up fighting in battlegrounds for a particular faction, playing a starring role in their side's struggle for survival.

More powerfully, the mythical narrative is the very thing through which the character's own (and thus the player's own) actions make sense. In MMORPGs, myth, the background story, is "central to the individual player's sense of meaning; it explains why it is important that the player do what he is doing."[61] Krzywinska notes that the longer players remain committed to *World of Warcraft*, the more they will know of the story and the more they will experience their actions within it, and, in fact, incorporate their play into the narratives of their own lives.[62]

Many *World of Warcraft* players, both novice and advanced, pay careful attention to the *World of Warcraft* storyline; it is part of gaming life, not just a vehicle for permitting character leveling. In my survey, the storyline was the second most popular answer to the question, "What do you enjoy most about *World of Warcraft*?" More than 36% of respondents included it in their list of favorite elements of the game, and in a separate question a significant majority (60%) claimed to pay attention to it.[63] To keep up with the lore, players will read novels and surf among the many webpages devoted to discussing in-world events, including, but not limited to, those sites operated by Blizzard. That players pour such enormous devotion into learning and understanding the lore of *World of Warcraft* is a testament to their enjoyment therein. A sizeable minority of players (24%) even listed a race's role in the storyline as a reason they prefer it to the others available.

All but one of my interviewees pay attention to the storyline, and one does so "intensely." The storyline is, as other commentators have noted, important for most gamers' fun. Jill, for example, remarks that if she misses something because she is "rushed or clicked too many times" she will look it up online afterward.[64] In particular, while players may ignore quest stories of minimal significance, they often thoroughly engage in the stories that are crucial to *World of Warcraft* lore. For example, one player will read the quest description "if it's something interesting lore-wise. So, if it directly pertains to the Lich King, Deathwing, or whatever the main case is...but I don't much read about the need to collect twelve of X."[65] Quests to help local groups often involve killing a specified number of enemies or collecting a particular number of material goods. These quests—which focus on some repetitive and unavoidable grind[66] —are precisely the sort of quests unlikely to capture a player's imagination, though they are, perhaps, important to keep players engaged with the in-game communities and working toward the larger picture.

A significant number of players end up deeply enmeshed in the quest stories. To achieve "Loremaster" achievements, players must complete specified numbers of quests in each of the game's chief continents (Kalimdor, Eastern Kingdoms, Northrend, Outland, Pandaria, and the Cataclysm zones of the first two continents). I asked four players who zealously pursue quest completions across the *World of Warcraft* landscape whether they always read the quest narratives. Of these, two reported always or almost always reading the stories (even on multiple characters[67]). One reported reading what happens when he turns in the quests and sometimes what he's told when given the quest, and the last said that he often ignores the side quests but spends time reading "the important stuff." Resistance to making achievements account bound, rather than character bound, illustrates the investment that some players have in the lore. After the Mists of Pandaria expansion, achievements could be completed through the combined effort of multiple characters and then the player gets the achievement on all characters. As one commentator suggests, "Linking that experience to characters that haven't earned it makes every character feel like a tool of game mechanics instead of a character that's part of a story and fictional world."[68] While many players enjoy having account-bound achievements or pay little attention to the lore, there are at least as many for whom the lore and the quests matter. To, I suspect, a lesser extent, there are even those for whom the uniqueness of achievements matter precisely because achievements are tied to the player's role in the story and the world.

There is a serious element of praxis that emerges out of players' attention to the lore: they actively court opportunities to participate in the epic narrative. One player says: "I love it when my guild raids Icecrown Citadel, we get to battle and defeat Arthas every weekend. I've wanted to do that since I played *Warcraft III*."[69] *Warcraft III* was released in 2002, and the Icecrown Citadel raid opened in December 2009,[70] which means that after seven years of longing this player finally fulfilled a long-held ambition, which he continued to enjoy satisfying for years. Another player relishes his opportunity to join the political struggles of the game: "when I fight the Horde in Tol Barad [a designated PvP region], it's not just me fighting another player who is probably hundreds of miles away; it's me and my allies battling against the disgusting Horde for the glory of the Alliance."[71] These experiences demonstrate how players can feel an "allegiance" to characters in games, based on moral practices and goals that are aligned between player and character.[72] Such experiences are not unique; many players enjoy being part of the *World of Warcraft* mythos. Joining in the story makes the game more fun and also more meaningful.

The narrative can be so powerful that when the Cataclysm expansion loomed during the fall 2010, players let the mythos dictate apparently arbitrary and useless behavior. In my Horde guild, for example, players went to visit sites and people that would suffer in the impending changes. One player sent an avatar to say "good-bye to Thrall, whom she's long admired from afar," and others futilely tried to warn Tauren chief Cairne Bloodhoof of a treacherous assassination to come.[73] Even after the Cataclysm changes took place, some players found it difficult to reconcile themselves to the new circumstances. One member of Twisted Stitches, for example, finds it emotionally difficult to see Garrosh Hellscream on the *World of Warcraft* loading screen, asserting: "you don't belong here. YOU ARE NOT MY WARCHIEF."[74]

While players cannot change the course of history (Hellscream became the warchief after Cataclysm, and Bloodhoof was assassinated through the machinations of a rival Tauren), their behavior is not entirely fruitless. It cannot change the storyline, but it envelops the players further into the mythos and into their roles within the game. That is, narrative immersion makes the game better and more fulfilling for players.

Myth and meaning-making matter in *World of Warcraft*. Players care about the lore, they make character decisions grounded in it, and they enjoy opportunities to play a role in it. Certainly not all players invest themselves in the epic narrative of the game; many do, however, and for these the story provides rich opportunities for religious work. In an age where storytelling has been reduced to the mindless repetition of reality television and sitcoms, *World of Warcraft* provides the setting for players to become, once more, mythically inclined; even better, *World of Warcraft* gives players a sense that they are not passive listeners but rather the heroes of the mythical journey.

Co-Writing the Story

Drawing on their gaming traditions, MMORPGs like *World of Warcraft* offer players an opportunity to become the heroes of myth and legend. One primary reason for players' enjoyment of the mythos must be aesthetic, but another, more important, reason is the players' perception that they are active participants in the story's outcome. Despite the fact that Blizzard employees produce the narrative and guide its outcome, many players pay close attention to the lore and the story and see themselves as driving the story forward. Rather than passively enjoying a story of meaning and magic, players actively see themselves as starring in it. Because of this, the *World of Warcraft* mythos is essential to the players' development of personal meaning.

Role-playing games have a long history of active co-creation, where Dungeon Masters (DMs) and players all contribute to the eventual outcome of a gaming session, whether that lasts hours, weeks, or months.[75] Of course, this is something of a given in games like *D&D*, where the DM sets up a story arc but cannot control what actions the players take within it. Depending on the DM and the players, a *D&D* adventure can spiral rapidly out of the DM's control, leading to unexpected results. This can happen as a consequence of the need to negotiate everyone's needs and wants or simply because DMs cannot perfectly predict how their players will respond to given circumstances. In traditional RPGs, therefore, players and the DM collectively write and experience a story; doing so is crucial to enjoyment of the games.[76]

World of Warcraft, like other MMORPGs, diverges from its RPG past in that the collective composition of the narrative is more illusory than real. In fact, in computer-based RPGs, the storytelling is "barely interactive."[77] Multi-User Dungeons, such as the original begun by Roy Trubshaw and Richard Bartle in the 1980s, do allow for genuine co-creation by the elite players, but these cannot compare to MMORPGs like *World of Warcraft* in terms of popularity. Regardless of what they may want, *World of Warcraft* players contribute to the story in only very limited ways. Blizzard employees do, however, monitor discussions on the company's forums and do, on occasion, take account of player desires, thus including the players as "informal designers."[78] For example, massive forum speculation about the death of Bolvar, human leader of the Alliance forces in the Northrend continent, led to the design team's decision to have him sacrifice himself to become the next Lich King, imprisoning himself and the undead army now under his control.[79] This player input, however, is neither common nor straightforward. Blizzard employees do as they choose, even if on occasion they happen to attend to the players. The players' influence is thus tenuous and ultimately possible only at the discretion of Blizzard employees. Moreover, players can affect only planning for the story—they cannot bring about real-time changes in the game world.[80]

The surprising fact is that in MMORPGs like *World of Warcraft* many players continue to feel that they are, like *D&D* players, participants co-writing the story. Players' perception that they participate in the story

line is a view that—when such games are compared to their tabletop pre-
decessors—should be seen as a consequence of good game design and
also as a "survival" from those earlier pen-and-paper RPGs. On one hand,
designers have provided the appearance of co-authorship, but their efforts
to do so benefit from the cultural survival of coauthorship in traditional
RPGs. According to classical anthropologist E. B. Tylor, survivals are "processes, customs, opinions, and so forth, which have been carried on by
force of habit into a new state of society different from that in which they
had their original home, and they thus remain as proofs and examples of
an older condition of culture out of which a newer has been evolved."[81]
The process of cultural evolution that Tylor describes provides a fruitful
way of understanding what is otherwise an astonishing fact: that anyone playing *World of Warcraft* sees himself as personally contributing to
the story when, in reality, the mythos is almost entirely handed down by
Blizzard and the quest sequences are endlessly repeated by every new
character. Designers, of course, make this happen on purpose: "games are
all about engagement," says virtual world designer and former Linden Lab
employee John Lester. "It's about sucking you into a story, and making
you feel successful and amazed and wanting to come back."[82] To some
extent, *World of Warcraft* players do co-create the world insofar as their
interpersonal relations shape the experience of game play, but overall the
narrative and the structure of the game stand independent of the actions
of the players.[83]

According to my survey, slightly over one-third of players consider
themselves to be "active participants" in the *World of Warcraft* mythology and storyline.[84] Only 18% of respondents indicated that they never
consider themselves such participants.[85] This is clearly the result of the
blurred boundaries between character and player frames, of identification
with the character, which provides a "vicarious yet pleasurable sense of
agency."[86] When the player finishes with a region's quest sequence, she
can move to the next zone knowing that past problems have been solved.
Now she can solve new problems, working through quests that will challenge her present skill, power, and knowledge. While moving through
these new quests, she will learn more about what has happened in that
area and can help the NPCs acquire what they need to guarantee their
safety. Because the quest progression moves across time as well as space,
Krzywinska believes that "undertaking quests lends the player a sense that
he or she is playing a role in the history of the game world (even though

it is patently obvious that players undertake the very same tasks as others and sometimes doing that same quest over and over [sic])."[87]

World of Warcraft designers share the belief that players should feel like they are part of the story; indeed, they use design features to inculcate precisely that feeling. Revealing his commitment to that player experience, game director Tom Chilton says of the players' work in the Mount Hyjal zone: "as a player you probably helped put out the invasion there...and now you're going to take the fight" to the enemy's abode.[88] The players' successes in Mount Hyjal permit the world's druids to begin regrowing an area badly damaged by the minions of the Firelord, Ragnaros. Having changed the world to enable this, the players now move against Ragnaros in his own demesne, the Firelands. According to Dave Kosak, the lead quest designer: "this is a story that you as an individual will progress through daily questing.... I really wanted people to feel like they're engaged in the story, like you're also helping take the Firelands."[89] Design features like phasing and personal progression, which is how the Firelands quest hub works, are tools for giving the players a sense of real agency, a belief that they are instrumental in the defeat of the forces that threaten Azeroth.

Technologically, Blizzard has gotten better at providing the experience of player agency. Although quests can still be repeated by every user, Blizzard launched "phasing" with the Lich King expansion in 2008 and used it extensively in the Cataclysm expansion and, too a lesser degree, also in the Mists of Pandaria expansion. In a phased environment, not all players see the same thing. For example, if a player has helped the Ramkahen defeat the evil Neferset and conquer Neferset City in the Cataclysm zone of Uldum, she will no longer see Neferset in the city or even other players who remain at a pre-victory stage. With phasing, one player writes, "you feel like your actions are having a significant impact on the world around you."[90] Instead of seeing evil Neferset, the player now sees Ramakahen allies in charge and can bask in her contribution to the cause. Such changes ensure greater immersion into the *World of Warcraft* storyline and thus heighten the impact of the mythical narrative; they promote a sense of accomplishment—the player has changed the world and affected the course of history. Personal progression, as developed in Cataclysm, is another tool that changes the world as a consequence of the player's work. It allows players to remain in-phase with one another, but players who have gotten farther through the quest sequence will have additional work to do, quests that are unavailable to less accomplished players. Both phasing and personal progression, because they make the world responsive to the player's work in the game, are powerful tools for getting players invested in the story and the roles they play in it.

Design tools like phasing and personal progression do powerfully affect players. One early use of phasing from the Wrath of the Lich King was praised as being, all by itself, "worth the price of the expansion. It's dramatic, powerful, evocative, and really pulls you into the storyline. The phased questing that Blizzard has so masterfully implemented here really gives a feeling of a fluid, moving plot line. It is a welcome change from just having a static world where nothing changes in between content patches and expansion packs. I would love to see more like this."[91] In response to the Firelands personal progression, one interviewee told me, "the design team did much better with the Firelands daily hub in making me feel like *my efforts were making a change in the world* .... [It is] disappointing when I go in with another alt and its back the way it was."[92] By having the world change in response to play, Blizzard greatly enhanced the immersiveness of the game, helping to collapse the distinction between player frame and character frame. Players get to feel like they are there, like they are contributing to the struggle against evil.[93]

Designers further bolster the power of phasing through the direct praise and gratitude of NPCs. Upon completing the major stepping-stones in the Firelands, for example, players receive a new mount from an NPC and a letter that reads:

> Never again will Hyjal shudder beneath the endless forces of flame. Never again shall the mortal races of the world tremble before the minions of Ragnaros.
> Now, thanks to your efforts, they will tremble before US.
> Your heroism on the Molten Front has been instrumental in the fight against the Firelord. You have gathered allies from all over Kalimdor and turned them into an army. You have fought the minions of Ragnaros ... and prevailed. And for that you have our deepest thanks.

While the second-person pronouns clearly refer to the character and its actions, the reader cannot help but read them with reference to herself. It is her work that liberated Azeroth from the threat of Ragnaros, and soon she will venture forth to strike down the Firelord himself. By reiterating the player's accomplishments, the letter reminds her of what she has done while repeatedly narrowing the gulf between player and character.

Naturally, there are varying degrees to which any given player identifies with her role in the storyline. Susan, a very casual gamer who plays infrequently, does not really pay attention to the storyline and skips right over quest narratives.[94] This is a relatively common game strategy for players, who often speed along through particular quest chains or emphasize character leveling.[95] But many players skip reading quest narratives, however, because most of the quests do little to drive the overall story arc and also because, say game designers Salen and Zimmerman, experienced players can often reconstruct the narrative from their prior experiences.[96] In my own experience as a player, I frequently skipped reading the texts when the quests were minor ones relevant only to specific zones or people and without compelling narratives (judged by an immediate glance or a quest's role within a "quest chain"), but I definitely paid attention to more important quests. Despite the fact that players *can* skip quest sequences, many will in fact go back to learn more, especially if hooked by game play,[97] and many outright enjoy the story elements. When the quest narratives are important or compelling, players recognize this and follow them; in doing so, the players can appreciate their own heroic roles in the story.

Without doubt, there are players who see themselves as heroes thanks to their participation in the mythos, and they frequently reveal this through their discursive habits. Right after lauding the Human king, Varian, for his success in the battle of Lordaeron, for example, one guild member noted "actually, that bit was me, come to think of it, I should have a statue of myself in Darnassus!" Another traces the time frame of Cataclysm events with respect to the time that the "heroes (i.e., us the players) return from Northrend."[98] By taking credit for an accomplishment, even with tongue in cheek or by historicizing based on the player's role in the story, both speakers reveal a definite identification with the heroic exploits of their avatars and can also situate their avatars/selves within the mythical history of the *World of Warcraft* universe.[99] In traditional RPGs, "when your player character succeeds, it's *your* victory;"[100] in *World of Warcraft*, you are perhaps one step removed from the process, but a vital part of the ultimate victory nonetheless.[101]

It may be that players who feel themselves engaged in the storyline do so in part *thanks to* rather than *in spite of* the repeatable nature of the quest structure and storyline. Mircea Eliade argues that for the "primitive" religious individual, participation in a sacred history depends upon the cyclical nature of that history. The history "of the Cosmos and of human society is a 'sacred history,' preserved and transmitted through myths. More than that, it is a 'history' that can be repeated indefinitely."[102] *World of Warcraft* players certainly have access to a history of Azeroth through the *World of Warcraft* webpage, the fantasy books written to flesh out the online story-line, and the quest narratives given as players progress through the game. They can even ritually repeat the great events of Azeroth's recent history, perhaps accumulating meaning with every player's repetition.

The *World of Warcraft* mythos, like those of other MMORPGs and many of the RPGs that preceded them, is elaborate, powerful, and engrossing for many players. As they—to greater or lesser extent—identify with their characters who act within the gaming universe, *World of Warcraft* players can access a world of meaning and purpose frequently absent from every-day life. The scientific disenchantment of the world, described by sociologist Max Weber,[103] creates space for new kinds of enchantment; *World of Warcraft* is part of that magic. According to Peter, the game is an "entertaining interface with which to experience the story and satisfy a primal need for personal accomplishment and interactivity."[104] And as Castronova (over)enthusiastically asserts, "virtual worlds are on the path to becoming the most powerful source of personal meaning in the contemporary world."[105] While *World of Warcraft* and its fellow games may not actually become the most powerful sources of meaning in the world, they have unquestionably become zones in which personal meaning can be identified, contested, acquired, and stabilized over time.

The mythicization of the player–character, whose actions are meaningful on a personal and communal level, contributes to the devotional aspects of *World of Warcraft* play. A traditional religious history can create space for human meaning-making through participation in the community's historical expectations. For example, the salvation history of Christianity establishes the meaningfulness of human activity insofar as it contributes to the unfolding of divine providence through the amelioration of the world or the return of Jesus of Nazareth. An individual's sense of personal meaning thus arises out of a religious narrative. In the late nineteenth century, however, Nietzsche called for a public recognition of the fact that today we doubt; we cannot be certain any longer that a better world awaits us or a god who's purpose guides history. In such a world—a world of uncertainty—we should not be surprised if human beings go looking for new avenues for transcendence, new ways of raising ourselves to superhuman status and new hope that we might leave the profane world behind us as we ascend to a utopian existence. Finding such powers and places in the secular world amounts, of course, to holy shit, which is readily apparent in the transcendent opportunities afforded by gaming. Adventuring in *World of Warcraft* and participating in its narrative arc can provide an avenue through which players' lives become meaningful. Players identify with characters who, through the course of their adventures, become heroes. The deeds of the players are valued by other players and by NPCs, and thus the players themselves participate in a cosmos of epic meaning. As with the community gathering and the ethical reflection of Chapter 2, such personal meaning is not, all by itself, indicative that *World of Warcraft* operates as an authentic fake. But, in conjunction with these, it is a powerful contributor to the virtually sacred possibilities of the game.

Virtual Transcendence

Having established that players can and do identify with their characters, and that in doing so they can experience their lives as heroic and meaningful, it is time to complete this chapter's argument and show how *World of Warcraft* play can ultimately provide a variety of transcendent experiences. Playing *World of Warcraft* is not just about identifying meaning in one's heroic exploits but also about becoming a hero of epic proportions. "Humans want to be more than what they are," says Bioware game designer Gordon Walton. "We are driven to be more than what we are all the time, and [gaming] is one outlet to let people experience some of that."[106] In *World of Warcraft*, players become superheroes in an enchanted realm. In *World of Warcraft*, players can overcome their daily limitations and become transcendent versions of themselves. They wander across amazing landscapes in amazing bodies and gain powers beyond mortal ken; such transcendent experiences, in fact, account for much of gaming's commercial appeal. Players in *World of Warcraft* can follow the world's designers, taking up the divine prerogative of creation and thus achieving a limited kind of empowerment through the creation of magical items and by giving life to inanimate matter by making vanity pets through engineering, enchanting, or jewelcrafting. But the transcendent experience of *World of Warcraft* extends far beyond the crafting professions, which have rather limited and short-lived joys. It is more obvious in the virtual environment, the bodies that players take up within the game, and the empowerment and personal growth that players experience as a result of long-term participation.

In virtual worlds, we can go beyond and rise above ordinary life. According to game designer Brenda Laurel, "the transmission of values and cultural information is one face of VR [virtual reality]. The other face is the creation of Dionysian experience."[107] Virtual worlds provide a site for the carnavalesque, the rejection of industrial capitalist alienation.[108] The ecstatic experiences that people can have in virtual worlds make the games compelling; the worlds enlarge players' perspectives and expectations, giving rise to transcendent feelings. Despite occasional (and vain) exclamations that our world is pretty good as it is or that we should accept it as the only place to which we have access, human beings, at least in Western cultures, seem fundamentally dissatisfied with it. This has been a common theme in our use and acceptance of the Internet and virtual reality[109] and is reflected in Bonnie Nardi's account of *World of Warcraft*. She argues, based on her understanding of John Dewey, that the world needs re-aestheticization and that *World of Warcraft* accomplishes this.[110] Neither she nor Dewey means something as simple as just making the world prettier, though that appears to be part of the picture; rather, there is a need for communal experience of moral and personal transcendence in the morass of contemporary life.[111]

In some games, the player is immediately accorded a transcendent status: she is god. In god games, which were briefly described in Chapter 2, the player herself becomes divine, the creator and destroyer of worlds. S. Brent Plate cogently argues for the clear ways such games carry on traditionally religious work,[112] and such games even contribute to players' ethical reflections as they engage in decisions over the appropriate role and behavior of gods.[113] True virtual worlds, however, do not allow divine players. In small environments such as MUDs, some players can have divine prerogatives, but in an MMORPG there are simply too many interests at stake to allow any one player to take on the entitlements of monotheism. Transcendence must be parceled out among many players.

Although designers and programmers are the ultimate creators of virtual worlds, one of the most effective means for them to permit transcendent experiences is to pass along a spark of their divine craftsmanship to the players. Although *World of Warcraft* does not allow players to become gods, it does provide opportunities for players to exercise magical craftsmanship. Such creative powers can appear in players' ability to train their characters in blacksmithing, engineering, alchemy, or other professions that allow them to produce items of power in their games. Manufacturing mechanical pets or mighty suits of armor allows players to express their desire to craft things, to shape the world around them, and to breathe a spark of life into the dust of the earth. The power to build has long been a divine prerogative in Western religious life, one that has been shared with human beings as a sign of divine favor. Indeed, the power to remake the world or to create artificial life has been proof of an individual's holiness for centuries, as reflected in Islamic and Christian alchemy and Jewish golem traditions.[114] *World of Warcraft* crafting could be enjoyable, therefore, for specifically religious reasons—it contributes to the apotheosis of the player character.

Religion has, for several thousand years, been the primary source of transcendent inspiration and has been the technology of choice for attaining personal transcendence. In Christianity, for example, one can become a member of the "community of saints," can have visions of heaven or of god, and can attain a heavenly body and immortal life after death. But transcendence comes in many forms; it is not just the heavenly resurrection anticipated by those of the Jewish, Christian, and Islamic faiths. In many strands of Hinduism, for example, those who devote themselves properly can eventually see beyond the physical world that confines us and attain release from those constraints. This, too, is a kind of transcendence. Most religious traditions offer insight into a world or state of existence beyond that of everyday life, and most also provide techniques for attaining, however momentarily, those states or worlds.

Now, however, virtual worlds approach the powers of religion by offering transcendent places and experiences, and have, in fact, been explicitly compared to religious places and practices. Castronova, for example, compares games to cathedrals, asserting that cathedrals offer something "ethereal, transcendent, divine. Though intangible, it is real. Most people feel it. Some feel it very, very strongly...virtual worlds are not cathedrals, but they do transport people to another plane. They have a compelling positive effect on visitors, an effect dramatically misunderstood by many of those who have never spent time there."[115] In video games, reports one baby boomer–age gamer, one can stay home while "gaping at awe-inspiring scenery and being drawn through the computer screen into amazing, frightening, wonderful journeys from which we can return a little bit better than when we started."[116]

The beauty of *World of Warcraft*'s landscape matters, and many players enjoy opportunities to explore it thoroughly. As a result, the beauty of many game regions has received heaping praise in recent scholarship.[117] Few players would seem likely to compare *World of Warcraft* to any standard vision of heaven, but there should be no doubt that the visual power of the game is part of its appeal and more than 20% of survey respondents list exploring new regions among their favorite aspects of game play. As Chris Hansen notes, "The setting isn't simply a background for a game but a place to get lost during game play."[118] Azeroth is a world of surpassing beauty and mythical power; it is a transcendent place that the players enter and leave the ordinary behind.[119]

We cannot, as a rule, expect that we will occupy transcendent planes of reality in our present, mortal conditions, so we do not enter virtual worlds like *World of Warcraft* with our physical bodies but with newly empowered and glorified bodies. The division between mortal reality and transcendent reality tends to be clear in Western religious traditions: while communion with God is—vaguely—possible in official versions of Judaism and Christianity, for example, such relationships must be entirely reconfigured to make heavenly life possible. According to Paul, for example, "we will all be changed,"[120] exchanging our perishable, mortal bodies for imperishable, immortal bodies.[121] While, obviously, not all religious visions describe a heaven reached only after human beings transform into angelic beings, many of our Western traditions do see the world this way.[122]

World of Warcraft is a place in the here and now where we can transcend our bodily limitations, becoming like unto the angels or the gods. "I want to look badass," says one player;[123] in this he reflects a general consensus. We automatically earn the right to occupy the transcendent world as we occupy our new avatar bodies. In *World of Warcraft*, we can undo and refashion our bodily images, which are prone to feelings of inadequacy among even the most self-confident of people. One guild member told me, "I play females because as a female I would love for my body to be as toned as my toon...but I'm too lazy."[124] Another shares this attitude, pointing out that there is "a reason why I always seem to choose [Night Elves]."[125] This is not to say that all women enjoy the hypersexualized bodies of female characters but simply that many certainly do.[126] According to Nardi, players carefully select the physical attributes of their characters and attribute considerable importance to their characters' physical beauty.[127] Of course, beauty can be defined along many measures, including "rugged masculinity" for males, or even in countercultural terms (e.g., playing a gnome, thereby rejecting conventional expectations and creating new ways of relating to those around oneself).[128]

There are biological ways of describing human beauty, and they may well apply to players' use of the character creation system in *World of*

Warcraft. Symmetry is, for example, a common way of scientifically measuring beauty,[129] and it is guaranteed for all players. Other measurements, such as waist-to-hip ratios in women, can be used to predict physical attraction,[130] and these could be projected into the game environment. As one might expect, the waist-to-hip ratios of *World of Warcraft* females tend to be exaggerated in nearly all of its races. Blood elves, draenei, human beings, trolls, taurens, orcs, and undead all appear (based on screenshot measurements) to be within the .5–.6 range (the pandaren are not). Prior research has shown that people consider women beautiful when their waist–hip ratios dip below .7, while Hollywood sex symbols such as Marilyn Monroe and Sophia Loren tended toward .6.[131] The exaggerated bodies of *World of Warcraft* females are thus more beautiful by this measure than our most widely acclaimed stars. Even dwarf and gnome females still have ratios of less than .7. Male avatars tend to be heavily or lithely muscled, meeting traditional expectations for "manly men," though there are exceptions to this among character races added in expansions to the game.

The hypersexualization of female video game characters has drawn the ire of commentators[132] and may affect the willingness of women to engage in video gaming. T. L. Taylor argues that while designers idealize freedom in avatar expression, in fact their design choices frequently constrain what options exist.[133] Certainly, in the case of *World of Warcraft*, there are—at best—only minimal ways of circumventing the sexualization of female avatars. Such hypersexualization does not, however, stop women from gaming and may create appeal for some or, perhaps, many.[134] When one member of my *World of Warcraft* guild donned a new dress received through a holiday event in-world, she remarked, "Goodness that is a revealing dress," but tempered her comment by asserting this is "more good than bad." Even when characters don armor, they have a tendency to reveal more than they cover; the same armor when worn by a male avatar often covers most of the body, while a female with that piece of equipment is often very seductively dressed. As a result, Celia Pearce refers to female avatars' apparel as "kombat lingerie."[135] There are very serious criticisms to be leveled against game design that forces women to adopt hypersexualized appearances, but not all women object to them.

Despite the criticism, many women actively enjoy the sexualized bodies and revealing armor. In my guild, for example, one woman has said, "My thing is that I am a short, chunky gal in real life. I want to play a hot, sexy elf in my fake life."[136] Others promptly echoed her comments: one wrote, "Ditto.... My [blood elves] thoroughly enjoy attention...as I don't in real life"; another wrote, "This is why I play elves (or whatever race is prettiest in every. single. RPG. I play"; and a third added, "This is also why I will dress my female toons in 'skanky' armor. Can't wear a plate bikini in real life? Wear one on your draenei!"[137] These kinds of comments were frequently marked "love" by other readers, showing that other members of the community appreciated the authors' perspective. Likewise, in *Second Life*, where avatar customization is nearly limitless, there are almost no female avatars one might consider "unattractive" by standard conventions of beauty.

It is patently obvious that some women prefer alternatives to the hypersexualized bodies and deserve an opportunity to choose them, but it is unclear to what extent such bodies would be popular if they were available. For example, although there are women who desire "trollish" troll women, one Internet poster notes that "most of the female troll players you see not only pick The Pretty Face but also the nearly invisible tusks."[138] That player desires more monstrous trolls, with larger tusks that resemble those available to male troll characters. Many members of my own guilds also enjoy playing trolls and taurens, so it is more than obvious that unfeminine and even monstrous appearances can be aesthetically satisfying to women.[139] As gaming continues to gain popularity, it is important that design features allow women (and men also) to satisfy their desire for variety in their avatar choices.

Many players enjoy selecting characters from among the "monstrous" races (draenei, orc, tauren, troll, undead, worgen), but this does not necessarily imply a rejection of beauty. Choosing a character is an aesthetic experience, and aesthetics ought not be limited solely to a question of conventional beauty, facial symmetry, and waist–hip ratios. A perfect example comes from the previous Internet user, who clearly expresses disappointment with the diminutive size of the tusks on troll females: "I can understand giving the option for the tiny tusks for those who wanted their troll women to fit their narrow ideals of beauty, but what about those of us who find the more unconventional aspects attractive? I WANT HUGE TUSKS, DAMNIT!"[140] Clearly, this user wants to be beautiful, only by a different measure than that afforded by *World of Warcraft*'s character creation options. Players desire to appear before others, to make themselves present, in meaningful ways. Physical appearance is, in fact, the single most important determinant in a player's preferred race (just over 69% of survey respondents selected it[141]), and 15% of respondents even prefer particular classes based upon the way they look.

As characters progress through the game, they will gain equipment that demonstrates the character's power and thus makes the character more visibly appealing. Shoulder armor and helms, for example, become larger and more ornate. The best equipment is "legendary" or "epic" quality and often actually glows, as will a weapon that has been improved by an enchanter. Some armor comes in sets, and for characters that take the time to earn a complete set, which is often difficult and demands considerable help from guildmates, the effect can be quite striking. Even for those who never earn equipment at the highest level, armor and weapons will improve from simple and ragged to ornate and polished. As a consequence, the character grows increasingly impressive to view, with corresponding emotional response from the player. Catering to player desire, in 2011 Blizzard launched a new process, transmogrification, which allows players to customize the appearance of weapons and armor.[142] Players who avail themselves of the service can make their best equipment appear as outdated, but fantastic-looking equipment from earlier stages in the game. In implementing this new feature, designers recognize that items have "sentimental or aesthetic value" and plan to support the meaning that players place in their characters' appearance.[143]

Already by early 2012, many players, particularly those engaged in endgame content, used transmogrification to keep matching outfits composed of older equipment.[144] Many players quickly gravitated to old sets of armor or particularly interesting and rare items, and items once worthless when found by alts can now be sold on the auction house for exorbitant fees to players who wish to transmogrify recent items to resemble them. Thanks to the transmogrification craze, some players have gotten even more creative in costuming themselves as heroes. Anne Stickney on *WoW Insider*, for example, provides a screenshot of players dressed to resemble (very closely) four of the Marvel Comics Avengers: Iron Man, Thor, Captain America, and the Hulk.[145] She even provides details on what items a player would need to copy the styles. A character who looks like Thor has just doubled his heroic identity—he is a savior on Azeroth and in the Marvel universe too!

Of course, as important as appearance can be for players who wish to rise above their daily life, a character's power looms far larger. Nearly all respondents (95%) listed powers and abilities among their top three reasons to prefer a given character class. In all likelihood, once experienced with the differences among classes, players will choose and prefer classes with powers that the player him or herself desires or values. Like much of what happens in *World of Warcraft*, this reflects a long-standing tradition in RPGs, which allow players to acquire a mastery missing from everyday life.[146] Such self-transcendence benefits from the community ethics and personal meaning acquired through game play, enabling "a release of creativity and a sense of empowerment in conditions of autonomy, sociality, and positive reward."[147]

The transcendent empowerment that takes place in *World of Warcraft* is weighty and bears considerable resemblance to religious forms of transcendence. The Transcendental Meditation community, for example, promises that its practitioners will "fly" (which is done by hopping up and down while sitting in a lotus position) and "remain always in heaven" no matter where one might be physically.[148] In *World of Warcraft*, we have already seen that the power to send themselves into a heavenly realm appeals to many players. More importantly, players can most certainly accomplish flight while also raising the dead, hurling fireballs, hunting alongside dragon companions, or wielding impossibly huge weapons. Such powers are the stuff of dreams, the impossible goals of a magic world where players transcend the limits of ordinary life.

As the last section discussed, video games like *World of Warcraft* have the wondrous power of making every player into someone special: a hero. In *World of Warcraft*, each player–character will use her powers to save nations, villages, and individuals. Each will be a source of inspiration to the NPCs around herself, and each will, through effort and will, conquer the evil forces that threaten the forces of goodness and order.[149] For many *World of Warcraft* players, "the ability to play as a mythological hero in a world filled with myths and magics, apparently lost to us in real life, is one of the major attractions of this game world."[150] This appeal is widespread, affecting researchers in *World of Warcraft* as readily as the game's other players. Nardi, for example, reports a "strong sensation" that she had taken on a "starring role" in a "fairy tale."[151]

As characters in an epic fantasy of good against evil, players can feel themselves growing as individuals. According to Nardi, the development of knowledge and power in the game resembles a Victorian sense of character development.[152] In this way, as in many others, *World of Warcraft* is perhaps exemplary in its revelatory possibilities: in *World of Warcraft*, the game's quest structure and predefined alliances and agendas assure a particular ethical personhood; so all that remains is for player–characters to grow in their ability to be those persons. As the characters gain levels, they acquire new powers that lead to one triumph over evil after another.

Simultaneous to this, players gain skills that can have consequences out-side of the game, especially with regards to social contact, strategizing, and leadership.[153] By growing in power, confidence, real-world capability, and encultured personhood, players build their character in more ways than one.

The achievement system, implemented in the Wrath of the Lich King expansion in 2008, illustrates the kind of character development that Nardi describes. When players accomplish something interesting in the game, such as exploring every zone in a game region, defeating a difficult dungeon boss, winning a duel for the first time, or achieving mastery in a professional skill such as jewelcrafting, the game will display a shin-ing banner near the bottom of their user interface (see Figure 3.1), will announce the achievement in the character's guild chat and public chat, and will log the achievement in a list that players can examine or can com-pare with other players' lists. The achievements do little to change game play, but some difficult achievements come with noncombat rewards, such as titles, tabards, mounts, or noncombat pets.

Despite their lack of practical utility, players avidly seek to complete achievements. For example, due to a change in the game, my character Moravec was granted his "epic-level" steed, the Charger, at level 40 when he visited his trainer. Originally, gaining the Charger would have required a lengthy series of very difficult quests at level 60. When Moravec reached level 60, he was given the now unnecessary sequence of quests, which I completed at considerable cost (in gold pieces, time, and effort) solely to have completed the Charger achievement.

I am not alone in working through a difficult achievement despite not needing to do so. One of my interviewees did the Charger quest just as I did,[154] and when I discussed my interest in the achievement with a guild-mate helping me on one of the relevant quests he admitted having done the same thing with his level 60 warlock (paladins and warlocks are the only classes to receive these quests and achievements; other classes simply bought their epic-level mounts at much higher financial cost). Summing up the rationale for doing unnecessary and difficult quests chains and achievements, another player says, "I like the challenge. It feels like an accomplishment."[155] For nearly all players, achievements allow them to feel like they are accomplishing something and growing as players and characters; they objectify character development within *World of Warcraft* and can even be compared with other players through a few clicks of the mouse.

FIGURE 3.1 "Grand Master Fisherman" and "Skills to Pay the Bills" achievements earned through fishing. (*World of Warcraft* images provided courtesy of Blizzard Entertainment, Inc.)

Many accomplishments in *World of Warcraft* and other video games are so difficult to accomplish or so valuable to the players that they result in a sense of "epic win." This may require intense concentration, terrific teamwork, individual excellence, or some combination of the three. Jane McGonigal describes the key role that epic wins have in making game play enjoyable and argues that they lead to players expanding their sense of what is possible in life.[156] As we accumulate epic wins, we see ourselves growing more powerful and thus as having the ability to do even greater work. Whether this is entirely true is open to question, but these kinds of accomplishments definitely do enable a new sense of self. Earlier in this chapter, I quoted Susan, who finds that the rewards of game achievement are more powerful outside of the game than in play and that major game wins are a legitimate form of accomplishment in life. As players experience epic wins and accumulate achievements, they rise above mundane reality and experience what it is to be great. It is thus unsurprising that many players gravitate toward games with achievement systems, preferring them to games without.[157]

Such events are nontrivial for the residents of virtual worlds, as they are the events out of which life is made. "I guess I'm surprised that they feel like real memories," relates one player. "Sometimes I think about a certain event that happened and it feels as real a memory as going to, let's say, a friend's wedding."[158] Not only are the events of game play real to the participants, and not merely "playing around," but they also can compare in significance to major moments in a person's relationship with others. One noted researcher in video games, Mia Consalvo, even remarks that when her computer crashed, causing the loss of her stored achievements for the game *Dragon Age*, she felt a sense of loss. "I still knew my own history with the game and what I had accomplished. How (and why) did that erasure alter my perceptions of my own performance and history?"[159] There is nothing fake about virtual achievements; they are an important element in contemporary video game culture. The achievement badges Consalvo lost in her computer crash were the objectification of her time and performance and thus the repositories of real human intent and a source for genuine human experience. The mere presence of achievement systems changes the way players game.[160] The increasing emphasis on achievement systems, therefore (including the more robust systems that operate on game servers rather than home computers), reveals that designers understand that game players desire meaningful experiences of success in the face of adversity. Achievement systems are a solidification of player experiences and thus are important to game design and play, but it is important to remember that not all experiences happen within achievement frameworks, and players can and do have meaningful experiences in games outside of those frameworks.[161]

Achievements are valuable ways for players to feel their growth and the significance of their actions, but unless they are tied to the social elements of the game, they yield few positive fruits in an individual's life. Recent scholarship indicates that pursuit of achievements leads to a higher number of negative feelings about *World of Warcraft* than pursuit of social opportunities or immersion in the game world.[162] This is probably because solitary achievements are short-lived and generally fail to live up to a player's hopes for them. Freud long ago told us that our victories are brief, though our disappointments last lifetimes. Solo achievements in *World of Warcraft* can be fun and are associated with considerable pleasure,[163] but teamwork and friendship, as when Digory and his guildmates defeat the Lich King Arthas (previously discussed), makes an achievement worthwhile and increases positive feelings.[164] This is at the heart of the brilliant achievement system that Blizzard employees have crafted. While the system does not rule out problematic pursuits of achievement (and, indeed, these remain common; I have also fallen into the trap of grinding away at an achievement that left me unfulfilled in the end), the fact that the game broadcasts official achievements to a player's guildmates provides an opportunity to make the achievement social—especially if others in the guild were aware of the player's pursuit. I have heard more than once of players deliberately postponing an achievement until a high-use hour of the day or night, when many guildmates would be present to share in the accomplishment and congratulate them. Thus, we see the inherent connection in the institutional and devotional aspects of *World of Warcraft* play: it is by combining these that players maximize the transcendent possibilities of playing.

Some enthusiasts would like to take *World of Warcraft* transcendence one step further: they hope to dismantle the boundary between the virtual and the "real," expanding the relevance of character development and power into conventional reality. Many contemporary transhumanists—who believe that science and technology can provide traditionally religious desiderata, such as eternal youth, immortality, or freedom from disease—believe we might one day upload our minds into virtual worlds like *World of Warcraft*. For this community, the momentary transcendence of game play, which must by necessity come to an end, could become a permanent experience as a higher form of life.

Leading figures in robotics and artificial intelligence have promoted the belief that human beings could someday upload their minds into virtual reality spaces, thereby attaining vast intellectual powers and immortality for the mind.[165] Such Apocalyptic Artificial Intelligence (AI) authors have gained considerable cultural cachet and are now part of tech discussions in public policy, philosophy, and theology as well as within virtual worlds themselves.[166] Many advocates of this position actively promote it within virtual worlds like *Second Life* (see Chapter 6), and researchers in virtual worlds have held such salvation to be plausible. Castronova, for example, raises the possibility that today's online video games might be an intermediate step toward the AI apocalypse.[167]

Since the rise of virtual worlds, Bainbridge absorbs them into his view of the religious power of science and technology. Bainbridge and some transhumanist groups see MMORPGs as possible locations for the salvation of human minds. Transhumanists are people who, for religious or philosophical reasons,[168] believe that technology will enable them to transcend the finite limitations of human life. In his book on *World of Warcraft* and sociology, Bainbridge declares: "I would consider a continued existence for my main WoW character, behaving as I would behave if I still lived, as a realistic form of immortality.... Ultimately, virtual worlds may evolve into the first real afterlife, not merely critiquing religion but replacing it."[169] While it might seem far-fetched to imagine copying a personality into a video game, engineers have already begun experiments with game systems that learn from "observing" human behavior in game so as to create complex artificial intelligences.[170] While these researchers do not view their work in the religious light that Bainbridge does,[171] their work was enthusiastically adopted by transhumanists after Bainbridge's citation of it. There are already groups dedicated to using software to capture a human personality and create a copy of it in a computer simulation, including the Terasem Foundation through their LifeNaut and CyBeRev websites,[172] both of which use software designed by Bainbridge.[173]

Recent groups hoping to colonize virtual worlds with physically disembodied minds, such as the Order of Cosmic Engineers (OCE) and the Turing Church,[174] see video games as possible locations for salvation. The OCE was founded out of a desire to "engineer and homestead synthetic realities suitable for ultimate permanent living"[175] and is a perfect representative of how Apocalyptic AI ideas have developed within contemporary gaming culture, especially thanks to the advocacy of Ray Kurzweil.[176] Giulio Prisco, an influential transhumanist who cofounded the OCE and has previously stood on the board of directors for the World Transhumanist Association (now Humanity+) and the Institute for Ethics and Emerging Technologies, launched the Turing Church in 2010 as a place for discussing religious visions of transhumanism, providing "members with meaning and [a] sense of wonder, and hope in personal immortality and resurrection, based on science."[177]

Drawing on McGonigal's argument that games create profoundly immersive systems,[178] one member of the Turing Church argued—and was well-received for it—that infusing transhumanist beliefs into gaming environments could be profoundly effective from an evangelical standpoint.[179] Indeed, both transhumanists and various game designers see that game play is related to transhumanism, and transhumanists often see video games as a place for evangelism where players are automatically inclined toward a transhumanist perspective.[180]

Transhumanist groups like the OCE and the Turing Church are, obviously, not representative of most video game players. Gamers rarely conceive of their worlds as places to upload their minds and, according to my survey, roundly reject the idea of spending all of their time in *World of Warcraft*. Interestingly, while Castronova reports that 22% of *EverQuest* players would like to permanently relocate to that world, 80%

of my respondents rated their desire to spend all of their time in *World of Warcraft* as a 1 out of 7 ("Definitely Not").[181] Only 5% gave an affirmative answer to this question (5, 6, or 7 out of 7). Most gamers simply do not expect to relocate into *World of Warcraft* despite their obvious enjoyment of and commitment to the game. "It is attractive, sure," says one player, "but I think humanity has better things to do than live in fantasy until the Sun envelops the Earth [and] am afraid that it would be more like Futurama's ad-riddled virtual reality than an intellectual utopia."[182]

While *World of Warcraft* players may not pursue digital immortality with the fervor that transhumanists do, some do see its allure. One has told me, "If one could have confidence in the system, it could be tempting. I wonder if the reaction to this is going to depend on whether one has a faith system that promises an afterlife."[183] For this player, life in a virtual world is unquestionably better than death, and like Bainbridge and most transhumanists she supposes that such opportunities would be at odds with traditional religious faith.

It is highly speculative to suggest that a human mind could be effectively mimicked in a virtual world and probably untrue to suggest that many people would consider that to be immortality for themselves. After all, while the online version of me might live on to fight evil and befriend strangers, the version that I consider to be "me" will still suffer, die, and be buried. Should a sufficiently high-resolution copy of me live on in cyberspace, however, perhaps those who knew me would be pleased (or not) to see me as risen from the grave.

Whether technically feasible or not, we cannot ignore the fact that residing in virtual worlds has led enthusiasts to accept the Apocalyptic AI dream of permanent cyberspace occupancy. The virtual world residents who desire this—and more shall be discussed in Chapter 6—represent the ultimate fulfillment of virtual transcendence. Upon entering an enchanted world and acquiring magical powers, players have an opportunity to become more than they were. They accomplish great deeds and earn the respect of player and non-player characters alike. Eventually, some come to see life in virtual reality as the ultimate fulfillment of their hopes for salvation.

World of Warcraft succeeds, in part, because through it we "enter a smaller, more perfect universe in which satisfaction is not guaranteed, but we gain a pretty good chance of achieving moments of limited perfection."[184] Within the often beautiful confines of *World of Warcraft*, player characters can be attractive, powerful, and heroic, participating in a tale of mythic proportions. This transcendent experience can be so enchanting that some researchers and enthusiasts see it as a stepping-stone on our way to a greater evolutionary future, one in which we permanently take on the heroic mastery afforded in only limited doses by playing the game.

Conclusion

Although the opposite of virtual reality is generally taken to be reality, that is, the thing that is "really" real, the more we invest in our virtual lives the more real they become. As a consequence, Bainbridge claims that his *World of Warcraft* characters are possibly "real after all" and "living on a different plane of existence from our own."[185] While such claims will sound strange to most readers—and are likely grounded in Bainbridge's own belief that AI will allow virtual realities to operate independently of conventional human reality—they reflect a growing recognition that virtual reality is not "false" reality. One way of establishing the reality of these game spaces is, in fact, the religious efforts that we design and play into them.

World of Warcraft is a game, but it is far more than that. *World of Warcraft* is virtually sacred: a digital arena for secularized, quasi-religious practice. And this accounts for much of its appeal. Certainly not all players are religious in their engagement with the game; however, many are, and all benefit from the varied ways *World of Warcraft* enables the production of communities and morality, the acquisition of meaning, and access to transcendent places and selves. Through these processes, the players do religious work as Chidester defines it: they "negotiate what it means to be human with respect to the superhuman or the subhuman." While we cannot doubt that the superhuman states through which meaning emerges are virtual, we should not assume this makes them any less real than those relevant to traditionally religious practitioners. Is a video game character who can be played, whose accomplishments are one's own, any less real than an angelic resurrection or a parted sea that can be neither seen nor felt in the here and now?

Although some commentators content themselves by simply dismissing *World of Warcraft* and similar games as escapism, the profoundly religious possibilities in the game must surely account for much of its appeal. *World of Warcraft* will almost certainly cede pride of place to other games eventually, but the practices that designers and players have incorporated into it will just as likely be shifted into the new arenas that succeed it. Online games are, as Chee and her collaborators tell us, "ways of re-enchanting life and of sustaining meaningful community experiences;"[186] they are places where "alienation and rationality can be overcome, where people can assert humanity that refuses to be rationalized and dehumanized and find creative fulfillment in play."[187]

People are fundamentally religious in their approach to the world; if in the modern world we must find the sacred even after the death of the gods, we can find it in virtual worlds. As I have said in prior chapters, *World of Warcraft* offers many different ways of playing, and not all of these are religious. Nevertheless, thanks to the devotional and associational elements that players can, if they choose, employ, *World of Warcraft* is virtually sacred, a secular game that does much of the work that we have historically expected of our traditional religious systems. Whether games like it will overpower our traditional religions, as Bainbridge suggests they will, or whether they will remain perpetually playgrounds cannot be determined as of yet. Either way, with a subscriber base of ten million players in *World of Warcraft* alone, not to mention all of the other MMORPGs, online questing has certainly become major practice in the religious economy of modern life.

4

The Flow of Faith Online

A Whole New World

Second Life is a virtual world built and maintained by the company Linden Lab in which users create and customize an avatar, explore the world, and interact with other avatars. Its content is almost entirely produced by its residents, who create places to go, goods to purchase, groups to join, and events to attend. In a video introducing the world, Linden Lab presents *Second Life* as a place to "connect, shop, work, love, explore, be, be different, be yourself, free yourself, free your mind, change your mind, change your look, love your look, love your life."[1] The possibilities, Linden Lab and its leaders are quick to emphasize, are endless. Early on, Linden Lab decided to cede all legal ownership of digital creations to their creators, which has encouraged the development of interesting places and commodities. With enough patience, residents can find places worth visiting, meetings or music events worth attending, friends worth knowing, and, of course, clothes or other goods worth purchasing.

Unlike *World of Warcraft*, a social virtual world like *Second Life* can be difficult to categorize; *World of Warcraft* is a game, but some residents of *Second Life* and some scholars of that world object to calling it a game.[2] Nevertheless, the world, while occupied as a place of labor and social organization, is so game-like that it is difficult for outsiders to think of it in any other way.[3] Given how fuzzy the definition of *video game* can be,[4] this is not overly surprising. Even Linden Lab, the game's ultimate insider, has acceded to this and went through corporate restructuring in 2010 to promote the world's game-like affect. Hiring its chief executive officer out of gaming powerhouse Electronic Arts reflects this change of direction, as did Linden Lab's release of a video on YouTube that highlights the ways

Second Life enables gaming.[5] Although Linden Lab executive producer Michael Gesner reiterates that "*Second Life* is not a game," the company is working to improve the new user experience by adding game mechanics and game systems to help people with new accounts.[6] For most residents and the company behind *Second Life*, the world is not a game, yet the easiest way to understand *Second Life* may well be as a game.

There is no winning in *Second Life*, so residents must find their own purpose, which they do by finding or creating business establishments, environments, or groups of people where they feel comfortable. Some residents own living or commercial space that they rent to other residents for profit, but others use their rented or purchased land to create private homes or design elaborate gardens or cityscapes where residents may freely tread, often with shops nearby to promote economic activity. On a smaller scale, residents committed to contributing to *Second Life*'s cultural life create art galleries, live music venues, dance halls, and other social builds to promote congregation. Residents support establishments by purchasing virtual goods, such as clothing, or by donating to tip jars.

All purchases in *Second Life* are done through the local currency, the Linden dollar, which can be earned through work, can be bought with conventional currencies on the LindeX currency exchange, or can be received as an allowance if the user pays for a premium account. Most residents are consumers, rather than producers, of virtual content in that they do not actively create groups or places or objects but partake of others' creations. A resident who wishes to rent or buy land or buy clothing and accessories like cars, furniture, or pets will need Linden dollars. As a general rule, however, there is much to be done for free in *Second Life*: attending cultural functions, such as live music, requires only that the user find out when and where the event will take place.

As a consumer, each resident must find something he[7] wishes to consume; on the one hand, people desire to purchase and own "things," but more importantly they want a place and a community to join, somewhere where everyone knows your name. The need for finding a "home" in *Second Life* cannot be overstated. Without welcoming communities, *Second Life* avatars quickly become unused accounts. A new resident can use the search function to locate activities or affiliations that match his interests. Thanks to instant teleport and communications functions, he can swiftly join whatever communities he likes, just so long as he is savvy enough to find them.

Second Life is noticeably different from *World of Warcraft* in that the world does not establish the priorities of its users in any meaningful fashion. While *World of Warcraft* has predetermined political factions, a sequence of quest chains, and an historical narrative to guide players through the world, *Second Life* has none of these. After creating an avatar, the new resident can change its appearance, using slider bars to adjust a wide array of characteristics, including hair color and style, eye color and style, and body shape and size (Figure 4.1). Once satisfied, he must figure out what to do next. New residents often find themselves lost in a large world, unsure of what they should do. "Where should I go?" "What should I do?" and "How do I make money?" are common questions in orientation areas and among the new residents who have made their way out into the world. Newbies are generally recognizable by such questions and by their attire, which is often the plain white shirt and blue pants with which everyone used to begin in the world or by their use of one of the stock avatars that Linden Lab released in 2011. These clothes are modifiable, though always simplistic, but many newbies do not begin by mastering the appearance adjustments because they are eager to see the world and participate in the world's economic and social life.[8] To make this transition easier, Linden Lab introduced *Second Life* Basic in 2011, which restricts customization but permits quick avatar creation.

FIGURE 4.1 Editing avatar appearance in *Second Life*. (Image courtesy Jovi Geraci.)

The diversity of *Second Life* is unmatched by any other virtual world. While many residents still buy and build on the mainland, many also buy their own islands, which are generally free from obnoxious advertisements and out-of-place content and often have themes. Large builds in *Second Life* are often devoted to particular interests, such as fantasy, science fiction, anime, parkland, or beachfront. As the residents shape the landscape and erect the buildings, each location can be as idiosyncratic as its users desire. In addition to finding places to hang out and socialize, many residents also enjoy traveling and seeing new and spectacular sights. In my time in *Second Life*, I have met ardent travelers who keep blogs on their adventures, and I have even known tour guides, such as one woman who owned a hot-air balloon ride business.

As with *World of Warcraft*, I will not attempt a thick description of *Second Life*. There is much of interest in *Second Life*, and a number of interesting analyses have been published about it. My own interest is in how virtual worlds participate in the religious economy of contemporary life,[9] so I will engage ways *Second Life* provides religious opportunities. This chapter offers a brief interpretation of *Second Life* and its history, culminating in three primary issues: the ways residents think about themselves and their avatars; the potential for residents to experience religious feelings online; and the construction and maintenance of social groups through the use of virtual objects and cyberspace connections. Subsequent chapters expand on how these aspects of virtual life play into the religious opportunities enabled by *Second Life*.

Within the diversity of *Second Life*, residents have opportunities to become what they want and create what they want. They are limited by their imaginations and their skills, but both of these can grow with practice. Naturally, because people of all walks of life join *Second Life*, they bring with them many of their conventional beliefs and practices. As the following chapters demonstrate, this means that *Second Life* has become a locus for religious activity. Indeed, thanks to the many kinds of religious activity possible in and emergent from *Second Life*, the world is firmly situated in the religious landscape of modern life.

The Bigger They Come

After an initial period in which enthusiasm for *Second Life* burst forth across the media landscape, some commentators have dismissed it entirely. They see it as a flash in the pan, unlikely to have a lasting presence in cyberspace or, at best, a pale shadow of influence compared with the more popular adventuring games such as *World of Warcraft*. If, in fact, *Second Life* is nothing but a quick blip on the radar screen of cyberspace history, then it would indeed matter little whether the world suggests changes in our perception of religion. But *Second Life*'s effect on cyberculture has already been substantial, and it will prove to have had a lasting influence.

Attacks on *Second Life* have, by and large, been a reaction to the commercialization of *Second Life* and its media darling status from 2006 to 2008. Every time a new company, such as Toyota or Coca-Cola, joined *Second Life* and established a presence there, journalists rushed to investigate and pontificate on whether virtual worlds might be the future of commercial enterprise. Since none of the conventional companies in *Second Life* made any money, critics denounced the commercialization of *Second Life* as a means of getting free advertising from journalists and as symbolic of the general emptiness of *Second Life* as a concept and as a virtual world.[10]

The pessimism that has surrounded *Second Life* since 2008 reflects a general pattern in the response to experimental online communities. In general, the Internet was initially acclaimed as the harbinger of democracy and empowerment—religiously and secularly—yet many revised their opinions over time. Stephen D. O'Leary, for example, criticizes his own early work and suggests that he has become pessimistic about the power of the Internet to reshape religious life.[11] He is correct in pointing out that, despite early enthusiasm for online religious groups, religious websites have made only small changes in the religious landscape. Even as we accept the cautionary tale of the Internet, however, we must recognize that, indeed, the Internet *has* changed religious life, from access to information to the organization of communities. It did not create a paradise for religious practice, nor shall *Second Life*; however, this does not mean that *Second Life* religious practice does not matter. Indeed, not only does it reflect an outgrowth of Internet-enabled religion and hence gives reason for O'Leary to be cautiously optimistic once again, but it also serves as an important landmark in the contemporary practice of religion. It need not rescue religion from prejudice or obscurantism for it to matter. For some participants, *Second Life* already matters, and outsiders will benefit from recognizing this even among the post-bubble pessimism.

From 2009 onward, Linden Lab has sailed on rocky seas; the membership did not dissolve, but *Second Life*'s growth rate slowed to a crawl amidst frustrations with user experience, corporate disregard for ordinary users, and skepticism about conventional companies' ability to turn a profit selling virtual goods. Some observers believe that Linden Lab changed its population metrics to hide a considerable drop in membership during the down times, and others find the reduction of privately owned islands in *Second Life* to be a disconcerting trend.[12] Precisely what Linden Lab did wrong with *Second Life* remains somewhat unclear, though its corporate hiring practices may have backfired heinously. One alleged former employee writes, "The people running the company do not use the product and they think the people who do are hopeless anti-social countercultural freaks. I found it really disheartening when I worked there to hear the nasty talk about the customers. And the worst part is that many of those nasty talkers are now running the company."[13] Whether this is true or not, the company definitely failed to listen to its residents' complaints about the user interface and was slow to address legitimate concerns about new user experiences and in-world lag[14] and at the same time has also been justly accused of refusing to promote interoperability with other systems.[15] Whether these sins are sufficient to condemn the company despite *Second Life*'s widely lauded creative potential is, at present, an open question. Regardless, Linden Lab must find ways of bringing new customers into the fold if it is to remain economically viable and culturally innovative.

Despite the negative press, *Second Life* resists easy dismissal. Linden Lab is a profitable company, and *Second Life* membership has been relatively steady. While *Second Life* cannot compare to *World of Warcraft* in subscribership or profitability, it still appears in some months among the top ten most played personal computer (PC) games according to Nielsen ratings.[16] In addition, while it took *Second Life* residents six years to log their first billion hours of combined time in-world, it took only three years to log the second billion.[17] Virtual reality pioneer and widely acclaimed technocrat Jaron Lanier cites *Second Life* as an example of what the world needs: "software that allows people to be creative and make a living while doing so."[18] Even more, he believes that virtual reality producers are "saving civilization."[19] Perhaps with enough effort, the *Second Life* network will go from potential to a full-fledged community, but such processes require serious commitment.[20] While things have not been easy for *Second Life*, the world retains a vibrant and devout community of creators and consumers—whether that will be sufficient in the years to come remains to be seen.

In 2010, Linden Lab refocused its efforts, hiring new corporate staff in an effort to restore the company's direction and revitalize its service. The new strategy hinged on two basic issues: aligning *Second Life* with other game environments[21] and dedicating its energies to producing a more efficient user interface that enables new users to experience the creative potential of the world.[22] Whether these efforts will restore *Second Life* to its status among new media elite or revive hope among its faithful residents remains to be seen. They mark, however, an important shift in Linden Lab's corporate strategy and may suffice to keep *Second Life* from dying anytime soon.

Whether or not Linden Lab's new management can restore *Second Life*'s luster, the criticism against it as a business platform misses the mark. *Second Life* may, indeed, be useless to conventional companies except as an avenue toward cheap advertising. At least conceptually, though, the world is not a momentary fad. Social worlds, which have no questing or direction but are essentially there exclusively to facilitate social interaction, have a long history in cyberspace. In its heyday, for example, LambdaMOO[23] was a popular community of Internet users and, in fact, still has a few loyal members. More recently, when Electronic Arts released *Sims Social* for Facebook, it exploded in popularity, gaining more than sixty-five million players in its first month.[24] Proving there is still room for interlopers in the social world market, *Shaker*, an environment combining elements from *Second Life* and Facebook, received $15 million in venture capital late in 2011.[25] Clearly, social worlds are not on their way out, and mobile computing might provide them with greater reach. Rand Miller, co-creator of the famed *Myst* franchise, believes that *Second Life* and similar environments will have a place in the tablet market; in fact, says Miller, tablets "provide an [sic] more immersive experience by removing another layer of interface. Touching is believing."[26] Even should *Second Life* fail commercially, other social worlds will certainly take its place. *Second Life* has competitors such as *Entropia* that could outlast it, and similar environments based on the OpenSim software are also freely available. At present, *Second Life* is the strongest of these by a comfortable margin, but the crucial point is that social worlds are an important part of the cyber-landscape and will continue to be so. Moreover, *Second Life* has unquestioningly reconfigured Internet space, redefining what it means to create, operate, and act within a virtual world. It has, as transhumanist advocate and virtual world entrepreneur Giulio Prisco once told me, "already earned its place in the history of technology and society."[27] By appreciating *Second Life*'s contributions to religious culture (as well as its other areas of impact), we gain a sense for the big picture of religion in social worlds.

Naturally, it is impossible to predict whether *Second Life* will remain a viable virtual world, but we should expect that even if *Second Life* fails its users will carry on what they've begun. Given that virtual world migration is an established fact,[28] there is little doubt that religious communities built up in *Second Life* will migrate with the rest of its users should *Second Life* prove insolvent. As a result, the ramifications of *Second Life* transcend the significance of the individual world itself.

Taking Up Residence

I joined *Second Life* in fall 2006, when Linden Lab enabled free accounts and the tech media leapt at the magical possibilities of the world. Although I initially joined the game out of curiosity, to keep up with developments in technology, I soon learned that the environment was important to the book I was writing about religion and artificial intelligence. Before that, however, I was immediately stunned by the richness of it. Like any explorer in *Second Life*, I found that the scope of the world vastly exceeded my ability to observe. The sheer number of places to see—from the tiny to the enormous—sufficed to force me into selectivity, but at the same time the diversity of locations, themes, styles, and content mirrors conventional reality in its enormity. Much of *Second Life* was and is littered with enormous advertisements built mostly to aggravate locals and force them to purchase the land the ads stand upon, generally at exorbitant prices. But for the savvy visitor, *Second Life* is a place where almost any interest can be engaged, from the profane to the sublime.

As has been repeatedly noted by journalists, many residents' chief interests are consumerism and eroticism. Between buying virtual clothes, hair, skins, and so forth and visiting adult-themed locations, much *Second Life* activity varies between the banal and the pornographic. Even though *Second Life* offers many opportunities to buy or enjoy voyeuristic thrills, the environment is vastly richer than many authors describe. From communities who role-play in a *Star Wars* environment to garden paths and fireworks displays, *Second Life* is much richer than just purchasing digital goods and indulging in cybersex.

With some exceptions, my ethnographic approach to *Second Life* remains localized in-world. In this, I followed anthropologist Tom Boellstorff, who encourages students of virtual worlds to think about studying them "in their own terms" without requiring that observations be connected to conventional reality.[29] This is particularly important for understanding those residents who maintain a separation between their second lives and conventional lives, but it also matters also for appreciating how everyone else operates within *Second Life* culture. Nevertheless, because this is a book about how virtual worlds reconfigure our religious options in all of reality, I could not conceivably remain exclusively in world in my analysis: even as I describe religious practices that take place in *Second Life*, they remain connected to conventional religious life.

As my avatar, Soren Ferlinghetti (see Chapter 6), I explored many beautiful and interesting locations for the sheer fun of it but often gravitated toward places that piqued my academic interests. Over my first year in *Second Life*, for example, I talked with people who believed that we might upload our minds into *Second Life* and live forever or that their avatars in *Second Life* were distinct personalities, digital persons divorced from and potentially severable from the people whose fingers hover above the keyboards. I have maintained contact with many of these, but I have also visited a wide array of religious establishments, either to watch services or simply to learn what residents wanted to build in the virtual world. The Appendix explores several layers of my approach and should help interested parties understand it better.

Because I wanted to share content and not just consume it, I launched a site for hosting discussions about religion soon after joining *Second Life*. I built the Virtual Temple, a small modernist building loosely based on Frank Gehry's IAC/InterActiveCorp headquarters in Manhattan, and held academic discussions about religion while raising funds for charity. Naturally, I also explored the landscape and made friends. One friend that I met in *Second Life*, Lisa Hollenbeck,[30] was kind enough to sit with me and help me sculpt the digital "skin" that my avatar wore, though I had to shop for and purchase a respectable suit on my own. In addition to clothes, residents purchase realistically textured skins and hair for their avatars or bizarre and fantastic shapes to replace their standard humanoid bodies. Among the many different avatars I have seen were dragons, rabbits, aliens, Yoda, Teenage Mutant Ninja Turtles, and even a toilet. Most of my fieldwork in *Second Life* took place between 2007 and 2010. During those years, I consistently participated in events in *Second Life* and became a regular fixture in a couple of *Second Life* communities. From 2011 to 2012, my participation was irregular, but I remained in touch with *Second Life* residents and continued to visit on occasion.

As described in Chapter 1, I hosted a survey about the religious preferences of *Second Life* residents from 2007 to 2010. While only a little of the data mattered to my first book, a great deal more matters to this one, which engages religion more broadly. Unless otherwise noted, all statistics regarding religious participation in *Second Life* refer to my second such survey, posted from 2007 to 2010 (most data were collected in the first year).[31] A total of 252 respondents answered the survey, and many thoughts based on their answers inform these chapters and my understanding of what *Second Life* means and the role it plays in our culture.

The survey, though the first of its kind, should not be considered definitive; it is, rather, a launching point for further studies and should be considered alongside recent studies of *Second Life* religious practice. The body of respondents, unfortunately, cannot be considered fully representative of the *Second Life* community because the survey was advertised in English-language forums and was available only in English. While the majority of *Second Life* residents seem to be English literate, a survey available only to those likely to read English-language websites cannot comprehensively include all residents. The data reveal some of the survey's problems. No respondents reported being Muslim, for example, yet there are Muslims in *Second Life*. Chapter 5 includes interviews conducted with Muslims and the producers of Islamic builds in *Second Life*. Despite these shortcomings, the surveys provide a preliminary snapshot of the *Second Life* user base and its religious practices.

Studying religion in *Second Life* is not, at any rate, as simple as asking a few questions and recording the answers; it is an ethnographic voyage. As Gregory Grieve points out, the virtual embodiment of *Second Life* activity—players' avatars navigate the space while they manipulate the keyboard—implies radical shifts in our presumptions about life online and the meaning of bodily practice.[32] Previous chapters have discussed frames of reference as understood from the ethnography of role-playing games, and it is not possible, for the purposes of this book, to move away from that approach. A *Second Life* resident is a conjunction of the individual at the keyboard and the avatar in world,[33] and this means that to study religion in *Second Life* requires that we anticipate transformations in religious practice in both virtual and conventional worlds. Just as starting a second life in the game means producing a new sense of self out of interaction with its world and others in it, starting a religion in *Second Life* requires that residents build it up in relation to the world and its inhabitants.

First and Second Lives in Second Life

Individual participation in *Second Life* depends on a user's metaphysical commitments: either one's *Second Life* identity is an extension of one's conventional reality or one's *Second Life* identity is totally separate from one's conventional identity. I do not wish to enter the profound debates over human subjectivity and how we define ourselves as persons that emerge from online activity. Rather, I want to point out that these two strategies—referred to as augmentationist and immersionist—permit different kinds of engagement with the world and its inhabitants, and the distinction is an especially important one among the transhumanists who will be the primary subjects of Chapter 6. In short, for the augmentationist, *Second Life* is a fancy telephone, a way of connecting people; for the immersionist, it is a place occupied by a separate identity, which is sometimes claimed to be distinct from, though biologically connected to, that of conventional reality.

The distinction between immersion and augmentation is complicated by other uses of the term immersion. The most common of these refers to player engagement. That is, the immersed player is one who is very engaged in a game. Although this terminology is common in video game circles, the case of *Second Life* is more complicated. Immersionists in *Second Life* are not just highly engaged, they use the term to refer to a severance of identity—the immersed avatar is distinct from the personality of its creator.

Second Life immersion can be shallow or deep. In the former, a person knows that he is playing with identity in *Second Life* and wants an opportunity to explore different ways of being without connecting those to his daily life. For example, a man in conventional reality may wish to be a woman in *Second Life*, thereby exploring new ways of speaking, acting, and appearing before others. In addition, *Second Life* is known for many role-play communities, and the constituents of these probably understand that they are not vampires, magicians, or cat people in conventional reality. Nevertheless, it is easy to see how those engaged in immersive role-play benefit enormously from *Second Life*'s graphical interface and creative possibilities. Deep immersion, to which I will return momentarily, happens when an avatar considers itself an entirely separate person from the bio-logical person who sits at the keyboard.

The creation of multiple *Second Life* avatars further muddles the ques-tion of immersion and augmentation. Because users can pay for the privi-lege of creating additional "alts," some may regard them very differently. An immersionist's "primary" might, for example, have an alt he consid-ers merely an augmentation of the primary's personality, or the primary may be connected to several deeply immersed *Second Life* personalities. Obviously, it would be impossible to lay such relationships bare, even if it were desirable, so I have no intention of undermining people by seeking to identify them in all of their virtual and conventional components. In such cases, we must take the virtual world at face value and address indi-viduals there on their own terms.

Not all immersionists are simply engaged in identity play; many assert vociferously that their personalities in *Second Life* are neither emergent from nor continuous with the conventional personalities that share their biological bodies. Most such residents call themselves "digital persons." The conventional personality is generally called the primary, other per-sonality, puppeteer, or atomic personality. One immersionist, Sophrosyne Stenvaag, illustrates the powerful degree to which this separation is held in "An Open Letter to My Augmentationist Friends":

I know you mean the kind things you say about me, and thank you! But you've said other things as well, that I don't think you recognize have hurt me. You've assumed I'm what you are: a per-son, with a body and a long history in the atomic world, who speaks through a little cartoon figure in SL from time to time. You think it's weird, maybe a little cute, maybe a little creepy, that I don't talk about my carpal tunnel, my mortgage, my co-workers, my partner, my self. You think I'm hiding who I really am. That makes me feel like a liar and a fraud, and makes me wonder how you could possibly like or trust me.... When I'm not online, I don't exist. There is another mind I share a body with—they're not me in any meaningful way. We score differently on psycho-logical tests. We know things and have skills the other doesn't. We have some similarities and some differences, and both fre-quently surprise me. The body, the "Other Personality," me—those three may be the same or different in age, gender, ethnicity, religion, politics, temperament, sexual preference, relationship status, social class, education level, time zone.... For many of us, SL isn't just another communications tool—IM with moving pictures—but our lives, our homes, our refuges.... For some like me and Argent, we have no other world—if we feel unsafe, unwelcome, afraid in SL, our only option is nonexistence, what for us would be death.[34]

No doubt, there are those who are already convinced that the author of such a statement must be psychologically damaged or suffering from mental or physical illness. I prefer to avoid those judgments, as they provide us with little interpretive power and force quite a few (potentially unjust) expectations onto their subjects. One digital person once suggested to me that multiple personalities become a "disorder" only when conflict occurs between the personalities; perhaps, then, *Second Life* provides a perfectly reasonable outlet for such "individuals." This is not, however, a medical treatise. For our purposes, it is enough to know that variety exists within the *Second Life* community, and I prefer to take such diversity at face value. Stenvaag once told me that in *Second Life* she "woke up, emerged as a personality, and kicked [her] creator out;"[35] I do not intend to dispute her on this. While deep immersionists are relatively rare despite the vast amount of "identity play" in *Second Life*, they do exist and often—because of their attachment to the world—become influential figures in *Second Life*.

Although digital persons are generally "born" in-world, they have begun migrating outward. In her early life, the well-known immersionist Extropia DaSilva[36] (Figure 4.2) did not interact or exist outside of *Second Life*, but she told me that fear over the world's future prospects led her to engage in social networking sites and email with the friends she made in-world.[37] While the world is her birthplace and is tremendously important to her, she knows that she can carry on her life without it if necessary. Other digital persons maintain blogs, Facebook accounts,[38] email addresses, Twitter accounts, and other means of remaining in contact with those for whom they care. At some point, DaSilva hopes that technology will progress to the point that, while *Second Life* may remain her home, it will be only one among many places that she can be. In an interview with me, she explained that she looks forward to technologies such as holograms or robotic bodies that she could inhabit to interact with friends in conventional reality. Although she loves *Second Life*, she would enjoy going to her friends' homes and interacting with them physically. Similarly, she hopes that virtual world providers will create methods by which the worlds

FIGURE 4.2 Extropia DaSilva in *Second Life*. (Image courtesy Extropia DaSilva.)

can be integrated, allowing residents of one to pass through directly into another.[39]

DaSilva is an ardent defender of digital persons; she believes in her personal identity and aspires to separate from her primary. She appreciates that some people use *Second Life* as a way to augment their own world but simultaneously believes very firmly in the rights of digital persons and the possibility they may become self-sufficient life forms: "I used to believe that every person in SL was a digital person that would eventually separate from its creator. It was just that some residents had not yet come to realize their avatar could and should become a person in its own right. I used to compare it to an infant which, early in its life, cannot distinguish between itself and its mother. Nowadays, though, I appreciate that some people get most value out of online worlds by NOT separating their RL and virtual lives."[40] As DaSilva recognizes, the very existence of *Second Life* challenges our assumptions about who we are and what the future holds. Although time and experiences with others have moderated her position, she continues to believe that those who consider themselves digital persons are truly distinct individuals. She distinguishes between digital persons and augmentationist avatars with a noun test: I speak of what I did in *Second Life* yesterday rather than what Soren did because my avatar is not a digital person.[41]

One might be inclined—erroneously—to believe that DaSilva is an isolated member of the *Second Life* community. The debate over adding voice capability to *Second Life* shows how even users who do not see their avatars as distinct persons, potentially severable from their physical bodies, still want to immerse themselves into those virtual personalities. When Linden Lab first proposed voice capability, many residents protested, claiming it would "damage a border between the virtual and the actual that they wished to maintain."[42] Although the company did push forward with voice capability, many residents continue to avoid it, preferring the power of text to maintain their online identities, which could be difficult if ethnic, language, or gender data were revealed in conversation.

Second Life permits a crossover between the conventional and the virtual, and its residents engage that in varying ways. While all residents take part in the culture of *Second Life* and whatever cultures they may connect to in conventional reality, they differ in how they engage these separate frames. The possibility of having multiple *Second Life* alts, and the use of them to augment a conventional personality or separate from it, provides powerful new tools for the reinvention of subjectivity in virtual worlds. Obviously, these various approaches to identity cannot help but affect religious practice and belief, as is discussed over this and the following chapters.

Finding Faith

Thanks to both augmentationist and immersionist residents, religious practices and beliefs flourish in-world. Most importantly, residents believe that the religious practices developed in *Second Life* are connected to those of conventional reality—shaped by and in return shaping them. This feedback loop underpins the significance of the world's religious life and can be seen in religions imported into *Second Life* and even religions entirely fabricated within the virtual realm.

When free accounts were opened in 2006, religious groups and sites exploded in popularity.[43] There are religious groups or temples for all major religious traditions and many smaller traditions, including meditation gardens, churches, temples, prayer groups, and study groups. Kerstin Radde-Antweiler profiles a nice variety of religious sites in one essay,[44] though naturally some of the establishments listed therein may have since closed. The fluctuation in *Second Life*'s landscape and user base makes every description of *Second Life* a snapshot of the present—and interpretation must be done under the expectation that it reveal ways that virtual world residents use the worlds, not immutable facts about those worlds. Not all conventional religious groups sanction *Second Life* religiosity, but some have established an official presence. As Tim Hutchings, one of our most astute observers of virtual churches, points out, there is something natural about this process, as though planting online churches equates to building conventional churches in a new neighborhood.[45] Protestant Christians, who established communities on the Internet in the early 1990s and have since grown their presence online, have had few difficulties embracing *Second Life*, and there are many Protestant churches, Bible studies, and affiliated sites, a few of which are discussed in the next chapter. Non-Western religions have also appeared in *Second Life*, of course; the International Society for Krishna Consciousness (the Hare Krishna) have been in *Second Life* as long as I have, and interested residents can find a variety of Hindu and Buddhist temples, including establishments that offer prayer and meditation services.

There is no simple means by which to categorize *Second Life* religious practices with respect to conventional ones. For many religious practitioners in *Second Life*, activity there is continuous with conventional religious practice rather than operating in opposition to it or parallel to it. After all, the Internet offers additional ways of religious belonging, without necessarily dissolving old ways.[46] That said, it is not only at the margins and among the esoteric, as Lundby suggests, where there are breaks in offline–online continuity.[47] Practitioners profiled in this and subsequent chapters often connect their practice to home institutions and traditions. However, they are not universally committed to such strategies, and there is no obligation for them to be. Consequently, while some users isolate their online lives from offline, others integrate them more closely.[48] It is necessary to follow this continuum when thinking through the hopes expressed by many *Second Life* religious builders to integrate their practices in *Second Life* to other (though not necessarily equivalent) practices in the conventional world.

Second Life is an environment of religious diversity, a fact clearly illustrated by survey numbers. In my survey, more than 31% of the respondents self-identified as Christians, making them the largest single religious group in *Second Life* (mainline Protestants make up the largest category of them). These are followed by atheists (25%), people who are "spiritual" (21%), agnostics (18%), "other" (14%), pagans (11%), Buddhists (9%),

Jews (3%), Hindus (2%), and followers of Shinto (1%). Problematically, no Muslims took the survey, though there are certainly Muslim residents in *Second Life*, so the results are unquestionably incomplete. For many traditionally religious residents (65.6% of respondents[49]), conventional religious beliefs definitely or probably affect their second lives, and most respondents (71%) believe that earthly religions have a place in *Second Life*.

While popular attention to *Second Life* has focused on its commercial or erotic aspects, religious life plays a greater role than most members of the media have realized. Sex clubs are among the more popular destinations in *Second Life,* and all manner of sexual contact—from escort services to "fantasy" communities of age play and semihuman "furries"— have earned *Second Life* a reputation for adult entertainment. Even those new to *Second Life* can find erotic groups and locations easily. Despite the fact that even the *Official Guide to Second Life* makes much of eroticism, however, religion is comparably pervasive in *Second Life*. In fact, *Second Life* religious participation even reasonably matches that of conventional religious participation. Just over 40% of my survey respondents partici-pate in conventional religious rituals at least monthly, while 46% visit religious buildings in *Second Life* at least once per month. Approximately 14% of respondents engage in full religious rituals in *Second Life* at least once per month.[50] Clearly, *Second Life* religious activity is less common than conventional religious activity, but not by such a large margin as one might expect. Popular *Second Life* blogger Wagner James Au compares the study to one done by two European researchers in which fewer than 14% of respondents acknowledged engaging in cybersex on a regular basis. He concluded that for all the attention that *Second Life* erotica receives, *Second Life* sex appears to be less prevalent than *Second Life* religiosity.[51]

Second Life residents show explicit interest in religion and religious practice. In addition to regular religious practice in *Second Life*, academic discussions on the topic of religion frequently draw large crowds, some-times approaching the maximum number of visitors allowed in an area. Due to limitations on computing resources, at most one hundred ava-tars can be present together in the same "sim" (a server host machine, which controls a geographical region within *Second Life*) depending on the quality of the machine used. The entire *Second Life* grid consists of more than two thousand sims, some of which allow forty and some of which allow one hundred avatars to be simultaneously present. Despite these limitations, many residents eagerly attend discussions about religion. There were Virtual Temple event attendees literally sitting on the roof (it is a good thing flying is possible in *Second Life*), and when I discussed *Second Life* religion and spirituality at Sophrosyne's Salon in Extropia Core in 2008 the peak occupancy at the discussion was the second highest in all of *Second Life* during that hour. The growth in religious groups and builds since late 2006, survey results indicating the public acceptance of religious influence in *Second Life*, and the popularity of discussions both academic and spiritual on religious topics testify to the power of religion in residents' lives.

Second Life religious practitioners defend their activity as "real" religion, but some religious practices with complex theological histories resist virtualization. It is difficult, for example, to believe that the Catholic transubstantiation of the Eucharist might operate without the benefit of an actual piece of bread to consume. For this and other reasons, both economic and theological, the Catholic Church has been generally opposed to practicing religion online and in *Second Life*. Some official members of the Church, however, joined *Second Life* to do missionary work.[52] Other Christians can circumvent the difficulty of adapting a theology of transubstantiation for *Second Life* if they do not believe in a transubstantiation or consubstantiation of the Eucharist. Protestant author and pastor Douglas Estes asserts that "in the end, virtual churches must no longer withhold the bread and the cup from their people if they want to...claim to be true expressions of the church. They must work out the details, satisfy their traditions' requirements, and bless their people with the Lord's Supper."[53] For Estes, the centrality of the Eucharist in Christian life dictates that there must be ways to export it to virtual worlds. The distinction between his and a Catholic perspective is fascinating: for Catholic authorities, it is precisely because the bread *cannot* be had online that *Second Life* does not provide real church; for Estes, it is because the bread *must* be had to provide real church that it *should* be available in *Second Life*. Much as the Catholic transubstantiation might resist such transfer, other religions will find that a transition to *Second Life* will be incomplete at best. Muslims, for example, will have a hard time praying in the direction of Mecca in a virtual world. Moreover, there is a theological problem in the disembodiment of a prayer posture—kneeling with forehead to the ground—associated with Islam's emphasis on submission to Allah. For these and other reasons, there are signs at the Virtual Hajj in *Second Life* declaring: "prayer in Second Life is symbolic, and is for educational purposes. It does NOT remove the obligation to pray in RL [real life]."

Despite such problems, *Second Life*'s faithful believe that the game has a decided advantage over other online religious communities. As one blogger comments, "I've dabbled in lots of 'virtual spirituality' experiments, from IRC chat worship to email prayer chains to podcasted sermons to streamed church services. Not [*sic*] other technology compares to virtual worlds for a real connection to a community of believers coming together in the unity of the Spirit that transcends all barriers."[54] Estes also defends virtual religion, claiming that "on average, people who attend virtual-world churches are at least as connected in mind and heart as in a typical real-world church."[55] Anyone counting the number of smart phones in the hands of the churchgoing faithful will have a difficult time arguing with him. *Second Life*, as the most powerful space for virtual religion yet devised, offers congregants a platform for connecting to the divine and to one another. Participation in *Second Life* religious institutions brings the resident into contact with other human beings and also with transcendent forces. Virtual worlds enable embodied orientation,[56] which is why they work better than watching a congregation on television or through a service streamed over the Internet in video format. *Second Life* religious activity is not just observation but a fully participatory activity.[57]

Across multiple faith traditions, practitioners and leaders believe that *Second Life* enables true worship and community. In 2007, the Berkeley School of Journalism organized a panel discussion on religion in *Second Life* titled "Faces of Faith." Representatives from Judaism, Islam, Christianity, and the Hare Krishnas explained how they see religion operating in *Second Life* and universally agreed that religious practice in *Second Life*—while perhaps not equal to that of conventional life—works. "It is real worship," said Otenth Patterborn, the Quaker and Unitarian Universalist representative, because it leads participants to turn their minds toward God and one another.[58] For many users, practice in *Second Life* even leads to increased practice in conventional life.[59]

Some people might expect that the ritual requirements of most religions would automatically disenfranchise *Second Life* religious groups. However, many of its residents enthusiastically practice religious rituals in-world, and even those who do not engage in regular *Second Life* practice see the rituals as having equal merit to rituals in conventional reality. In fact, 41% of survey respondents believe that *Second Life* religious rituals are equivalent to conventional religious rituals, another 41% claim that they are valuable though less so than conventional rituals, and only 15% claim that they are useless. All of this stands contrary to common sense, as it seems reasonable to conclude that *Second Life* rituals simply cannot measure up to the richness of conventional life. As Stephen O'Leary puts it, "I do not believe that any cyber-ritual...will ever be able to replace ritual performance in a physical sacred space."[60] Flying in the face of common sense, however, a few respondents even claimed that *Second Life* rituals are *more* valuable than conventional rituals. This may be out of disaffection with their local religious communities, but it could also be because physical or mental handicaps prevent them from participating in ordinary religious practice. It is also entirely possible that some people just find that virtual rituals, which lack many of the distractions that come with public gatherings, are more productive than typical religious practices. The use of ritual in *Second Life* and the general acceptance of such practices as valuable aids to religious faith indicate that new virtual world residents will continue to adopt it as meaningful practice.

Even when the participants agree that the rituals are "fake," they can encounter divine forces that they consider to be real. Members of the Triskele fantasy role-play community in *Second Life*, for example, invented religious practices that proved spiritually fulfilling for some of their participants.[61] As a fantasy role-play group, they produced an environment very much like the kinds of worlds inhabited by players of *World of Warcraft*, *EverQuest*, and other fantasy massively multiplayer online role-playing games. Triskele's citizens chose to join particular groups and factions, and they engaged in role-played storylines that they co-invented. Prospective player–citizens were encouraged to choose a race and class and to seek admission to these from the respective leaders. After acceptance, these individuals became members of the community and needed to let their imagination dictate the future: "the rest is up to you.... Whether you serve dark or light, are you loyal, or a traitor? Do you rise to fullest level in the guild you chose? Or do you casually play in the level of entry? You are limited only by your imagination! Let it soar!"[62]

Wren Lilliehook[63] was the high cleric of a nature goddess named Parlamay, which had three aspects: dawn, noontide, and twilight (Figure 4.3). Clerics (priests and priestesses) of Parlamay would affiliate with one of those aspects, leading to individual role-play opportunities. Just as each aspect of the goddess reflects her own nature as protector, comforter, or secret keeper, the various clerics act according to their affiliation, with twilight clerics tending toward darker forces, for example. There was a temple to Parlamay, wherein access to various *Second Life*

FIGURE 4.3 Wren Lilliehook in *Second Life*. (Image courtesy Wren Lilliehook.)

"notecards" provided relevant information about the goddess, her priesthood, and the cult.

Wren created Parlamay out of her own imagination, and the goddess "grew" thanks to the contributions of other clerics who joined Wren's community. Individuals contributed myths, poems, prayers, and rituals, thus enlarging Parlamay's mythos and enriching the role-play possibilities for everyone. Because Triskele was a role-play community, players narrated their actions as stories rather than simply announcing "I perform a cure light wounds spell." Clerics could talk through their actions, describing how they perform the spell, what accoutrements they have brought, how the healing progresses, the aftermath of the healing, etc. Such role-play was particularly important for resolving spiritual, as opposed to physical, wounds.

Although the goddess was "artificial," Wren told me that when she participated in a ritual of healing through the powers of Parlamay she felt sacred forces at work. Her religious experience was twofold: a communion between herself and the others; and a feeling of nature as a sacred, all-encompassing power.[64] In a parallel to traditional religious practices, Wren claims that the moments of ritual practice are set apart and different from other times.[65]

Participants in other pagan practices in *Second Life* share many of Wren's experiences. For example, undergraduates who participated in a pagan ritual in *Second Life* for a sociology class[66] "felt part of a greater whole...had a strong sense of bonding with each other...experienced strong emotions that they totally weren't expecting and had no words to describe. They all expressed a desire to explore these feelings and experiences again and in more depth."[67] Thus, while it is important to keep in mind that Wren speaks only to her own experiences, these are not isolated events in the history of *Second Life*'s religious activity.

Wren created Parlamay out of her conventional religious beliefs. She says inspiration came from "real life....I work with nature all the time, and I get people to look at it with new eyes."[68] Her spirituality closely resembles the pantheistic nature religions that have become commonplace in twentieth- and twenty-first-century life. For example:

> I see nature (including all things within it, us too) as connected, we are all part of a greater spirit. We each perceive in our own ways, and use Gods and Goddesses to focus on it, but ultimately we are all one.... I see us as part of the whole, which is both a collective and its own thing. As a flock of thousands of birds, if you watch them move as one, they appear as one huge creature, but each has its own tiny beating heart. Thousands to make one.[69]

Grounded in her experiences with nature, Wren's conventional religious beliefs will sound familiar to many modern people, but in Triskele she observes it through a fascinating filter of virtual world experience.[70]

In *Second Life*, Wren mythologizes and sanctifies a force of sacred nature that she believes is present in the conventional world. Although she expresses surprise that there could be a feeling of nature's spirit in the artificial environment of *Second Life*, she claims that in her work as a priestess of Parlamay she experienced the sanctity of nature "like [in] some sort of blurred mirror."[71] What she felt as a physical and spiritual connection with nature emerged out of her faith, as practiced in *Second Life*, and out of contact with the others who participate in her rituals.

The sacred forces at stake in Wren's role-play resemble prior pagan practices begun in the early days of the Internet. Stephen O'Leary describes a sincerity principle in which ritual is primary and "belief in the conventional sense of that term is almost beside the point;"[72] in Triskele, this could not be more obvious. For "technopagans" who perform pagan ritual via text-based Internet practice, the ritual act "brings the deities into being or revivifies them."[73] Thus, practice, rather than doctrine, should be our determinant for adjudicating sincerity, and it would appear that a powerful continuum of practical sincerity stretches throughout cyberculture. Wren's example shows that in *Second Life* even prayers to an imaginary goddess can open believers to the sacred forces perceived to be at work in conventional reality.

Morgan Leigh,[74] who is both a scholar of paganism in *Second Life* and a practitioner of it,[75] corroborates Wren's perspective, telling me that a Khemetic ritual in *Second Life* generated a "feeling of sacred space in the meatspace me."[76] Leigh finds that the pagan rituals that "really work in *Second Life* are ones with small groups of committed people who have an understanding of the theological basis of the ritual they are performing."[77] The gravitas placed on intentionality obviously differs from in Wren's description, probably because Leigh's rituals are deliberate attempts to establish neopagan religion in *Second Life*, while Wren's did so only as a by-product of role-play. Importantly, both agree that nature-oriented spirituality operates in *Second Life*, despite the fact that *Second Life* is a technological artifact.

Wren, Leigh, and other virtual pagans are not isolated examples. Other religious believers can also see their gods bursting forth into *Second Life*. Members of the Campivallensis Meditation Center's Catholic study group, for example, "feel that God intervenes in their Second Life doings."[78] In her interviews with two members the study group, Klink was told that particular believers felt the "stirring" of God in their hearts and could see God directing the construction of places within *Second Life* and providing the words with which to help others. She concludes that, for her informants, "*Second Life* is not a place where God dwells; it is a medium which God uses to communicate with humans, via humans."[79]

Second Life is a place of contradictions. It is, for Wren, a digital environment where sacred nature emerges and a land of illusion where people can put aside their facades. Honest community and the sanctity of nature thus characterize her role-play. She is not alone either; other religious practitioners feel that sacred powers can intervene in the virtual world. Just as many people perform regular religious rituals in *Second Life*, many believe that conventional religious practice belongs there. Indeed, for some communities *Second Life* is perhaps a *better* place than Earth to practice. The religious life of *Second Life* residents is, as we shall continue to see, real religious life. *Second Life* residents feel the power of the sacred, which they subsequently engage in a variety of ways. Just as fantasy "may actually assist in the effoliation and multiple enrichment of creation,"[80] *Second Life* enables wondrous new opportunities for religious practice and belief.

Making Virtual Groups Real

Religious communities must be established in creative deed, not simply word; we cannot simply all agree to join a religion and have it be so; rather, we show our affiliation by constructing buildings, decorating ourselves appropriately, printing books, and embodying habits. Likewise, for a virtual group to be real—even as its virtuality reconfigures traditional authority and communication in traditions new and old—it must be instantiated in the world through virtual objects, places, and techniques.

While no one could question that religious people have been quick to adopt technological media (as Gutenberg and his Bible amply attest), in today's world we see a hyperbolic acceleration of mediated communities. In the late twentieth- and early twenty-first centuries, religious practitioners have practically swum in a sea of media opportunities. As Stewart Hoover points out, "The realms of 'religion' and 'media' can no longer be easily separated."[81] All modern media are used for religious purposes, and very few religious groups are willing turn their backs on the possibilities offered by mass media. Within this media environment, *Second Life* can be a powerful tool in the production of religious groups.

The changes wrought by modern transportation, politics, and, most of all, mass media have produced a society in which the Internet has become a key site for religious work. The distribution of religion through television, radio, and print allows for uniquely privatized religious practices and beliefs, and collectively we have developed an idiosyncratic religious life, where contemporary Americans are often "spiritual seekers."[82] Within this world of spiritual seekers, the Internet became "the ideal medium for communicating religious beliefs and practices in a social context in which syncretism, popular tradition, and religion à la carte are among the most common forms of religious participation."[83]

Thanks to radio and television, the twentieth century was the first to see people forming communities that can worship together across space and time. Books and letters allow the distribution of ideas and allow individuals to see themselves as part of one group, but they do not overcome distance and time in worship itself. This is, for example, why Jews outside of Israel spend an extra day celebrating the Passover festival. With the precise timing of the celebration confused by distance, only additional practice can ensure proper observance. Reading a transcript of a church service in Christianity is not the same as attending one. Yet by listening to the service on a radio or watching it on television, isolated individuals can join a congregation in its worship and contribute to its maintenance (usually with the help of a credit card). As a consequence, "media and religion have come together in fundamental ways. They occupy the same spaces, serve many of the same purposes, and invigorate the same practices in late modernity. Today, it is probably better to think of them as related than to think of them as separate."[84] Television is not just some machine that could theoretically be used for religious purposes; rather, it is a device whose integration into individual lives often depends on the kinds of religious practices that it enables.

Academics, theologians, and social commentators rapidly noticed and documented the shift of religious practice to the Internet in the 1990s and 2000s, exploring such practices within a typology of "religion online" and "online religion" first elucidated by Christopher Helland.[85] The former refers to the dissemination of religious information on the Internet, whereas the latter refers to the practice of religion on the Internet. This distinction is not as neat as one might like, but it offers basic analytical categories for thinking about religious practices in the digital age.[86] Fundamentally, the Internet allows a widespread reconfiguration of religious ideas and practices. As a space infused with both information about religion and religious practices themselves, the Internet encourages a flattening of old hierarchies even as new kinds of hierarchy emerge, opens space for new kinds of religious thought, reengages secularism, and allows variety within traditions and among them.[87]

Despite efforts to use the Internet as a means of establishing top-down information flow, religious organizations face numerous challenges to their authority in the Internet Age. The multidirectional nature of the Internet has resulted in the flourishing of "instant experts" who can disseminate their own ideas about correct doctrine or practice.[88] Such online discourse truly matters for religious life and is fundamental to the establishment and dissolution of communities, which must be persistently recreated unless they are not somehow stabilized in material culture.[89] It is not the case, however, that the Internet universally dismantles institutional authority; as Paula Cheung and her collaborators show, hierarchies need not be stodgy and technophobic but can in fact use online life as a means toward confirming their own authority.[90] The Internet is a multifarious zone for discourse with a near unanimous potential membership. As a consequence, each religious person who engages in either online religion or religion online helps shape the character of his group, building it up or tearing it down and possibly rebuilding it afterward. Precisely these inherent characteristics of the Internet—among Dawson and Cowan's five distinguishing features that it is interactive and cheap[91] —allow users to reshape religious practice with it. There are certainly many members of the Internet community who accept institutionally "correct" doctrinal and practical positions, but the Internet fundamentally creates a space where religious discourse and practice need not be monitored or directed by institutional authorities. Considerable religious discussion happens online without any institutional leadership to ensure orthodox renderings.[92]

Heidi Campbell shows that there are many levels of religious authority and that within those multiple levels the Internet's effects vary. Drawing on interviews with Jews, Christians, and Muslims, she argues that hierarchy, structure, ideology, and text all respond differently to the challenges posed by the Internet.[93] Fundamentally, she shows that to talk about authority as though it were just one thing makes clarity difficult to come by. For different groups and for different issues within each group, the Internet will play varying roles in dismantling or buttressing traditional authority structures.

The potential destabilization of traditional authority discomforts even advocates of virtual religious practice. Estes deplores the "weak pioneers" who set up churches in virtual worlds only to flee them when the going gets tough.[94] He believes that the instant expert phenomenon has structural problems (e.g., the easy way leaders can desert their congregations) and theological problems. Without the traditions of conventional religious communities, he fears that virtual religious practice will fragment, depart from the core values of Christianity, and fail to serve. Virtual churches, he instructs, "need more orthodox denominations and church leaders to stop sitting on the sidelines and allowing the gunslinging mavericks to control the spirituality of the virtual world—before it is too late."[95]

It would be unwise for religious groups, despite the difficulties that arise from the Internet, to reject wholesale the reconfiguration of authority online. Models of top-down authority certainly have value in human organizations, but they also have a tendency to swallow up other forms of authority and creativity, thereby diminishing future returns. In *A New Kind of Christianity*, author, activist, and former pastor Brian McLaren advocates progressive shifts in Christianity, claiming that twentieth- and twenty-first-century changes in authority should be seen as "not so much a *division* to be remedied" but a "*diversification* to be celebrated."[96] It does seem that through effective communication among the new and old authorities religious groups may find more ideas and excitement flowing through their communities.

Religious rituals are among the more interesting ways people use the Internet and virtual worlds for religious purposes. These can include Wiccan meals,[97] Buddhist study[98] and meditation,[99] Hindu darshan[100] and puja,[101] Muslim Quranic recitation,[102] Christian prayers and services,[103] and even pilgrimages.[104] Of course, there remains considerable conflict within religious communities over the significance and efficacy of online ritual activities. After all, could looking online at pictures of sojourners on the Croagh Patrick pilgrimage and reading descriptions of their progress, as MacWilliams describes, really equal the experience of actually travel-ing to Ireland and walking barefoot up the sharp stones of the mountain? At least some online participants report "being there" through the web-site and feeling like community emerges out of their engagement with it.[105] Despite this, it is difficult to imagine that they have been shaped and formed by the online pilgrimage in a way that would be recogniz-able to conventional pilgrims. While our use of technology might lead to one becoming a "religious cyborg,"[106] there certainly remain substantial arguments against the authenticity of such a religious subject. Indeed, the residents of virtual worlds themselves contest the ritual grounds of those worlds, with some respecting hybrid virtual rituals and others find-ing them inappropriate to the game and game-like environments.[107] In particular, the fragility of the border between online and offline activity permits considerable room for each individual's own meaning-making and the strategies employed for it—and thus the basis for conflict over the transfer of conventional rituals to online environments.[108]

As with struggles over ritual experience and authority online, the geo-graphic gulf between participants problematizes the authenticity of online religious activity. While there can be no doubt that religious practitio-ners online definitely find themselves engaged in serious communities in which the other members matter and are cared for,[109] it is not diffi-cult to imagine that a Catholic Mass loses some of its luster if performed with hundreds of miles between every participant. Of course, the Catholic Church rejects any possibility of performing its Mass online,[110] in part due to the impossibility of negotiating the transubstantiation of the host without a priest and through electronic media but also because church authorities have questioned the reality of online communities.[111] Catholics are not the only group that raises meaningful issues regarding online rituals. Consider an Orthodox Jewish minyan: have ten Jewish males gathered if they are all online together? Would Muslims praying online satisfy their daily prayer requirements, or can Hindus achieve darshan by looking their deity in the eye through a webcam? In some cases and for some believers, the answers to such questions will be yes, but others will disagree. However we accomplish religious rituals online, we should expect that their transfer to this new medium will produce changes in their internal logic, symbolism, materials, or practices.[112]

The Internet changes religion. It changes the way we learn about religion, the way we see religion, and the way we practice religion. After all, "the media traffic in the symbols, values, and the ideas of their cultures(s)."[113] Those changes in religious practice and belief have been apparent on websites and in chat rooms, which create new styles of religious engagement. Religious use of the Internet can serve dominant interests, and it can struggle against them; it can promote understanding, and it can enable practice. But while websites and chat rooms certainly allow religious work, more advanced virtual environments are now in use today. The movement online will necessarily create new ways of being religious that draw on the characteristics of virtual world participation. As Jason Shim says after years of observing weddings in *Second Life*: "in a virtual world like *Second Life*, users must create not only day-to-day objects and buildings, but also *meaning*. When it comes to First Life practices...it requires a certain amount of thoughtful deconstruction before it can be re-created in *Second Life*.... This process of re-creation renders practices and meaning *more real* by virtue of their design."[114]

We should, however, avoid becoming overwhelmed by the virtual world hype. Indeed, virtual world attendance is strong, and I believe that it will continue to shape religious practice. However, it is not the be-all, end-all of online religion. Hutchings points to the media abandonment of *Second Life* as evidence of this and simultaneously offers Facebook as an instructive example of how Internet technologies are not shifting entirely toward virtual worlds.[115] Indeed, Facebook does offer services that *Second Life* cannot and may well become a significant force for local parishes seeking to network their communities. One theologian believes that Facebook illustrates or provides a theology grounded in human connections and the holiness of every moment in life.[116] He claims that "Facebook can be an altar on the Internet and a place of spiritual awakening. Holiness is here in this moment and in this post, and we can awaken to the holiness of social media."[117] Thus, *Second Life* and *World of Warcraft* are surely not the only ways religion penetrates twenty-first-century online media.

The migration of religious activity online prompts difficult negotiations within religious communities. Campbell describes this process and argues that it can "lead in one of three directions—acceptance and appropriation, rejection and resistance, or reconstruction and innovation—or a combination of these strategies."[118] In short, users find new media religiously neutral, antipathetic to religion, or productive toward religious empowerment. No object is a truly neutral mediator of human intentions,[119] and neither are objects by definition opposed to or conducive to religious work. Campbell rightly points out that particular groups will *perceive* the new media in particular ways, though these are not always the ways they *use* those technologies. In real life, whether virtual or not, real people must engage with the technologies at their disposal to establish and preserve their communities.

Our increasingly Internet-dependent populace now obliges churches and religious organizations to maintain websites where users can find information about the group, its work, and its meetings. This kind of distribution has developed over the decades since the Internet became widely available in the early 1990s and is the primary feature of religion online. Religious information online is widely distributed and used by many Web surfers, apparently in increasing numbers,[120] and websites have become powerful motivators in church selection processes.[121] Websites give users access to practical information, such as when services take place, and also prescriptive advice on what to believe and how to believe it. For many, if not most users, such advice is welcome: in a survey about religious use of the Internet, Michael Laney found that the top four uses are "because the website offers messages that are positive and uplifting," "because this (conversion) experience is still important to me in everyday life," "because this website agrees with my religious preference/denomination," and "because this website provides reinforcement and strengthens my spiritual beliefs."[122] All of these would be satisfying to religious organizations using the Internet as a distribution site, promoting orthodox belief and practice within a particular group.

Fascinatingly, this means that the virtual realm of cyberspace is already crucial to the "reality" of brick-and-mortar churches and traditional religious institutions. If new adherents come only after a thorough Internet vetting, then the Internet sites that bring new converts or new community members are absolutely crucial to the creation and maintenance of physical religious groups. In actor-network theory, we recognize that communities are grounded in objects such as texts, buildings, jewelry, and more (see Chapter 7), but we must also see how virtual objects can also contribute to virtual group sustenance. *Second Life* religious groups cannot always rely on physically solid objects and places as the basis for solidarity—sometimes the virtual objects are all that can be deployed. Yet the use of such objects may well suffice.

As in conventional life, individuals in *Second Life* must work to produce and maintain their groups; they use a wide array of tools, especially both material and virtual objects, to accomplish this. First and foremost, individuals can create groups in *Second Life* for a minimal Linden dollar fee. This allows others to find the groups by using the search tool to find people, places, and groups associated with keywords such as religion, artificial intelligence, and role-play. The results of a search within *Second Life* are limited only by the contributions already made by residents and, to an occasionally disappointing degree, the functionality of the search engine. As Chapter 5 demonstrates, religious groups in *Second Life* employ a wide array of tactics to objectify and stabilize their groups, despite the fact that the Internal Revenue Service is inclined to deny them church status.[123]

Sometimes, the group feature can provide a tiny measure of stability even to inactive communities. When I established the Virtual Temple, I created a group called Imagining Religion[124] as a way of keeping interested people aware of events at the temple. Although I have not led discussions for Imagining Religion for some time, additional residents continue to join the group. Thus, the community in some sense continues to exist thanks to its objectification in the *Second Life* group database. Profile tools actively stabilize Imagining Religion because whenever an individual joins the group it appears on a list of affiliations in that resident's profile. Other residents, looking at the group member's profile to learn more about him, will see Imagining Religion and can click on it to learn more or join. Even though I have not held events for the group in years, new members continue joining it. Perhaps someday they will be rewarded if I or someone else reinvigorates the group's discussion events.

While naming a group has power, it alone cannot ensure group cohesion; as a result, *Second Life* residents employ a number of tools to give their virtual religious groups a very real foundation. In addition to search listings and profile inclusion, for example, individuals can stabilize groups through Internet websites or publications, conventional world tie-ins, or the ownership of *Second Life* land. All of these provide points of contact for the group, helping hold it together against the forces of entropy that threaten to tear all human communities asunder. Likewise, residents can shape the landscape according to their theological ideas, objectifying those ideas in *Second Life*'s geography. Chapter 5 examines ways *Second Life* residents use the virtual world to advance particular theological agendas and also outlines clear and specific ways the game stabilizes those agendas and the groups that form around them.

Conclusion

Second Life is a rich virtual world that enables a broad array of cultural practices and allows unprecedented user control over the environment and the self. Although *Second Life* experienced disappointments in its first decade of existence, it stands at the forefront of social worlds and represents long-standing Internet practices that will continue even should it fail. Many residents in *Second Life* believe that both traditional and nontraditional religious practices belong in the world and have built the environment to reflect that faith. They consider *Second Life* religiosity to be real religious practice, occasionally even when the religious activities taking place are known to be "fictitious." Because religious activity is so common in *Second Life*, groups must contend with forces typical of online religious life, both in the cohesion of communities and the organization of establishments. To do so, they take advantage of their power to shape the world through its technical tools, producing a beautiful multiplicity to religious life in the world. As the next chapter shows, many of those doing religious work in *Second Life* do it under the banner of saving the world from religious intolerance. They build up religious objects that produce and maintain communities and hope that in doing so they can benefit the world. While their efforts are unlikely to singlehandedly end religious bigotry, their work is notable both in its moral imperative and thanks to the creative control that residents exercise.

5

Another Life for Religion

Introduction

Second Life enables a wide variety of religious practices that enhance the lives of its residents; churches, synagogues, mosques, temples, and other religious establishments dot its landscape, providing virtual counterparts of, supplements to, and competition for conventional religious institutions and practices. In *Second Life*, practitioners reconfigure their religious lives, keeping many of their traditional ideas but also experiencing their beliefs and practices in new ways. Procedurally, this requires that its religious groups stabilize themselves through the virtual objects enabled within its confines. This creates added possibilities for religious groups, and thus virtual worlds are an important platform for thinking through modern religiosity. Religious practitioners in *Second Life* follow Linden Lab in seeing it as a world where they can overcome intolerance; they envision the world as a place where ecumenism reigns and religious acceptance is possible. One aspect of virtually religious life in *Second Life*, then, is to ensure a group's reality by objectifying the group in virtual objects and to use that stability in a spirit of religious ecumenism.

Linden Lab has long proposed that *Second Life* is a world wherein the evils of the conventional world can be fixed and where intolerance can become obsolete. In his address to the *Second Life* Community Convention in 2006, chair of the board Mitch Kapor told the audience that his "hope is that *Second Life* will continue to be a world that is more inclusive than the terrestrial world and will enable groups of people that are marginalized in the real world to be first-class citizens and residents."[1] Likewise, Philip Rosedale told me that one of the great values of living in *Second Life* is that there are fewer opportunities for others to hurt one or restrict one's ability to live a fulfilling life.[2]

Religious practitioners in *Second Life* often uphold similar ideals and believe that it can be a platform in which those of differing beliefs and practices can speak to one another and learn to get along. This was, in fact, the premise behind *Second Life*'s first native religion, Avatars of Change (AoC). Founded by Taras Balderdash in 2006, the group established itself as interdenominational and ecumenical, but this ideal swiftly became a political fiasco. When Balderdash suggested a vote on whether Muslims should be allowed to join—grounded in his belief that Islam is a religion of intolerance—a firestorm erupted in AoC and beyond.[3] The majority of those involved regretted Balderdash's position, and he was subsequently pushed out of his leadership role in the community. While Balderdash continued to defend his position, those who commented on the matter clearly took the side of interfaith ecumenism and pluralism in *Second Life*.[4] Many outsiders commenting on the imbroglio maintained—like Kapor— that *Second Life* is a place that can overcome intolerance, so AoC's initial charter trumped any concerns that one individual might have with Islam. "We now share a common (second) ancestry and from this point onwards," avers one commentator. "We finally have the opportunity to form common kinships with each other.... Let us leave behind the sectarian pettiness of RL religious institutions."[5]

Virtual religion and the ecumenism common (though not ubiquitous) in *Second Life* would be impossible without the pluralism that modernity has forced on our cultural landscape. The co-presence of different religious ends and means exposes each and every tradition to the possibility that it might not be the exclusively true way of understanding the world and attaining salvation. Contrary to expectation, however, pluralism does not dismantle the entire agenda of modern religions. Rather, one way of thinking through pluralism is to accept that there might actually be more than one religious system that is both ontologically true (i.e., it really reflects the world we live in) and soteriologically efficacious (i.e., it can provide salvation). This interpretation of pluralism, articulated by Stephen Kaplan, recognizes that we might perhaps appreciate one another's religious aims as legitimate and efficacious without worrying about whether those cast doubt on our own.[6]

Borrowing from the fact that multiple images can be produced from the same holographic film (using different frequencies of light) and the fact that more than one tradition could be plausibly true if we interpret them in the light of a holographic model, Kaplan argues that the particular salvations or ultimate concerns of more than one religious tradition can be simultaneously valid.[7] The power of this holographic model of pluralism is that it maintains religious diversity rather than seeking to dismantle it.[8] In keeping with this, there would be no need for religious practitioners, leaders, or scholars thereof to offer disparaging comments on the practice of religion in virtual worlds or of particular ways of practicing it. Perhaps if, as Kaplan suggests, there are many summits and many paths to surmount them, then the virtual paths of online religion will lead to very real forms of salvation and should be included in what he calls a "metaphysical democracy."[9]

Although the outcome of religious practice crossing the permeable divide between virtual and conventional life is unpredictable, there is no question that *Second Life* residents look for ways of practicing in-world, and this requires a process of translation from one world to the next. Communicability is inherent to religion; religious ideas move from one community to another, but they do not always mean the same thing in the new community.[10] This unity alongside difference allows many religious people to see *Second Life* as an opportunity to grow their faith, join others in an evolving relationship with their gods, and communicate with those of other religious backgrounds. Based on interviews and observations with Christian and Muslims groups, this chapter shows that *Second Life* facilitates ecumenical outreach, amplifies participant voices, and enables transformative religious experiences. These factors enable the residents' faith that *Second Life* can help make the world better through religious practice; as such, *Second Life* is virtually sacred. This ethos is anchored in practices that online religious groups must embrace: virtual objects must be deployed alongside connections to conventional reality to provide religious communities with a chance to thrive.

Christianity

Naturally, after more than a decade of practicing their faith on the Internet, Christians were swift to bring their beliefs to *Second Life* when free accounts opened in 2006. By 2010, a search for "Christian" resulted in more than 800 different groups, locations, and vendors, such as sellers of virtual clothes. Christian events in-world include weekly services, Bible studies, live music, prayer groups, and fellowship meetings. A wide variety of different Christian communities exist in *Second Life*, which will be clear from the examples that follow. My research with three Christian communities—LifeChurch.tv, Koinonia, and Aslan's How—demonstrates that they offer radically different opportunities for reflection and practice in the game, each providing members new ways to participate in Christian life. The latter two, however, take better advantage of it as a place of belonging then does the former (both in terms of the ways they constitute their communities and to the extent that their theology matches *Second Life*'s current zeitgeist). Thus, they are better examples of how Christians might use *Second Life* toward efficient outcomes.

Like many early Christian communities on the Internet, groups and churches in *Second Life* launched by individuals often remain independent from institutional control. The Catholic Study Group at the Campivallensis Meditation Center in *Second Life*, for example, is a Catholic space carved out with no support from the traditional hierarchy and no interest in having such help.[11] Despite claims that Roman Catholicism is rigidly hierarchical, the Catholic Church has yet to take institutional control over Catholic activities in *Second Life*, and individual members use the environment to further their spiritual needs. The founder of the Campivallensis group, Gonzo Mandlebrot, built the site and started the group without informing his local priest that he had created a Catholic group online.[12] This makes sense given that he desired a space for people to talk from a Catholic perspective but without "liturgical trappings."[13] Working with Campivallensis, however, appears to have enabled Mandlebrot to continue his spiritual journey in conventional life as well. By 2011, his *Second Life* profile listed him as the head of a lay pastoral team.

Other Christian groups formed independently of institutional control but have been subsequently adopted by official forms of organization. Mark Brown, who served for a time as the reverend for the Anglican Church of *Second Life*, encouraged the development of a Cathedral and regular worship after finding a small group of Anglicans there.[14] He subsequently received a license to minister within the game from the bishop of Wellington in 2007, thereby integrating its community into the wider body of Anglican faithful and adding layers of stability to that established by incorporating this online group. Subsequent members of the Anglican group have sought to properly institutionalize themselves within the Anglican Church, including provisions for episcopal oversight of the community, vesting of authorized roles, and disclosure of conventional identities by anyone serving in the vestry, leading a Bible study, counseling, or otherwise engaging in a leadership role.[15] This adds yet another degree of stability to the group and, indeed, makes it "more real." This is not to say that the reality of a virtual group can be established only by joining it to a conventional organization. Rather, it reflects the fact that groups always struggle to keep themselves together[16] and that they need many points of contact to sustain relationships over time.[17] The documents tying *Second Life* Anglicans to the conventional hierarchy are important for maintaining those relationships. They last much longer than verbal agreements and have a way of impinging upon visions of reality. After all, they sit on desks and remind participants of the agreements that have been made, and their passage in print and online connects one group member to another.

Designing their environment for visual and functional familiarity is another strategy employed by the Anglican Church. The cathedral architecture, the decorations, and the liturgical process all demonstrate "the authenticity of the church to visitors who understand the appropriate codes of meaning."[18] Thus, we see that architectural design in virtual worlds can be a way of stabilizing a group; for those who need to surround themselves with particular kinds of church environments, the Anglican cathedral can be comforting and welcoming. Every additional stabilization of the group makes it more real and more likely to outlast whatever processes of erosion may affect it. The Anglicans of *Second Life* have chosen to strengthen their group through ties to the wider Anglican community, but other groups choose other strategies, as this chapter shows.

Conventional religious affiliation came after the fact for the Anglicans of *Second Life*, but it is also possible for conventional groups to deliberately establish *Second Life* branches. Expansion there made perfect sense for LifeChurch.tv, a Christian community with Internet services and a *Second Life* home to accompany its thirteen "campuses" in the United States. LifeChurch.tv was founded in 1996 and grew from a small, local community to an eventual broadcast of its services to many satellite communities. After establishing an Internet campus in 2006, LifeChurch.tv began a *Second Life* campus in 2007, modeling it after one if its brick-and-mortar churches in Oklahoma. Clearly, just as the Anglicans of *Second Life* use a traditional church build as a means of establishing familiarity and acceptance among members, the LifeChurch.tv administration tailored its presence there to draw on the authority and stability provided by its physicality. It has subsequently used its online campus to reinforce and stabilize its conventional community, rather than the reverse. Although LifeChurch.tv has enjoyed considerable growth in its U.S. campuses, it has not had commensurate success in *Second Life*. This failing is almost certainly because the group makes no effort to align itself with the cultural attitudes prevalent in *Second Life* and relies almost exclusively on outside forms of stabilization: brick-and-mortar, television, the Internet. The organization makes no powerful use of *Second Life's* capacity for group formation.

Even the Internet may not be serving LifeChurch.tv well, as the rules of success there are also different from those of success in conventional practices. As Tim Hutchings points out, LifeChurch.tv claims that its website receives hundreds of thousands of visitors, yet the number of participants in its LifeGroup system is very small. "Even allowing for the problems inherent in calculating and reporting media ministry statistics," he writes; "it seems clear that the majority of viewers have little interest in forming long-term connections."[19] Thus, while the community's physical campuses expanded rapidly in the early twenty-first century and although its televised format appears amenable to online worship, LifeChurch.tv has not been very successful online.

To properly appreciate a LifeChurch.tv service, I visited the group's campus in Albany, New York.[20] After speaking with the church's pastor and one of its administrators, I sat down within the geodesic dome that housed the worship space and watched as participants trickled in from their socializing in the lobby. In the front of the room, on a stage, a four-piece rock band played Eric Clapton songs while a television counted down toward the start of the service. At the appropriate time, the band switched to Christian rock songs and played for about fifteen minutes more, with times of prayer interspersed. During this, all but one of the nearly one hundred participants stood, and many raised one or both hands in the air in praise, something I also witnessed in the *Second Life* campus. After the music worship, the community's local pastor spoke briefly about events going on in the near future before ceding the stage to the televised address of Pastor Craig Groeschel.

Groeschel, whose own church serves thousands of parishioners each weekend, is televised live to all of the other campuses. (A recording of his Thursday night addresses is available as a backup in case of technical difficulties with the live feed on Sundays.) He is intelligent and charming and seeks to include those who are distant from him by asking that they read along with Biblical passages and other key points with closed captioning at the bottom of the screen. After Groeschel's address, which lasted about thirty-five minutes, Pastor Eric Hodgkins of the local community accompanied a televised call to greater faith and indicated his readiness to help members of the community come "closer to Jesus." Unlike most Christian churches, the local pastor at a LifeChurch.tv campus does not offer a sermon or reflection for the group; that work is done by Groeschel over the satellite link. The local pastor then helps organize campus activities and cares for members of the congregation on an individual basis.

The *Second Life* campus for LifeChurch.tv matches the appearance of a physical campus. It has a larger auditorium than the Albany campus, but like its conventional counterpart it has several rooms for fellowship, discovery, and—in proper *Second Life* fashion—consumerist acquisition. LifeChurch.tv T-shirts are available for sale, posters can be had, print books can be purchased through Amazon.com, and, if any are present, other members can be met. This shows a mixed strategy for stabilizing the group—both virtual and conventional objects can testify to the believer's faith and contribute to the community's sustenance financially and socially. If *Second Life* residents were to purchase books from Amazon and wear shirts there, then they would have found two separate but interlocking ways of contributing to group solidarity and growth. In my time in *Second Life* and in my visits to LifeChurch.tv's campus, however, I never saw anyone wearing clothing acquired there or actually using the virtual kiosks to purchase anything (Figure 5.1).

Other rooms, such as those decorated for children, resemble the Sunday school room at the Albany campus, though it is hard to imagine how they would be useful online. This repetition is another of E. B. Tylor's survivals from conventional life (see Chapter 3), but it also serves an active purpose for the LifeChurch.tv community. The way the *Second Life* campus has been designed to mimic the experience of LifeChurch.tv in one of its conventional buildings reflects the groups' desire to establish unity across geographic, temporal, and even virtual divides. Like the Anglican cathedral, then, the mirroring of conventional buildings attempts to stabilize participants' relationships within the community.

As with the rest of the campus, the *Second Life* auditorium closely resembles its conventional counterparts (Figure 5.2). Much like the campus I attended in Albany, it has seating arranged facing a stage with a central television screen and screens to either side. It has the same auditorium and music venue atmosphere, though it scales back some of the signs indicating other ways of participating in the LifeChurch.tv community, such as LifeKids. The large screen streaming Groeschel's sermon is

FIGURE 5.1 Social area with clothing and bookstore in the LifeChurch.tv *Second Life* campus.

FIGURE 5.2 The LifeChurch.tv auditorium during a service. (The streaming webcast is not pictured due to copyright restrictions.)

highly visible and dominates the room, giving the pastor a rock star's aura and heightening his central role in the LifeChurch.tv community.

In contrast to the growth of physical campuses for LifeChurch.tv, in 2010 the *Second Life* worship space dwarfed the number of attendees. Clearly, the building was designed with respect to the kinds of participation that the community has in its conventional megachurches and also in the expectation that this will be mirrored in *Second Life*. To date, that has not proven true, but a reversal of fortunes is not out of the question (though, as I will argue shortly, it is not particularly likely).

One powerful addition that *Second Life* offers its LifeChurch.tv attendees is the ability to discuss the pastor's sermon without interrupting him or offending other parishioners. A steady stream of chat text flowed along in my browser window, indicating the audience members' awareness or ignorance of specific biblical stories or reflections on the pastor's message. Audience members could easily ignore such messages if they chose, or they could attend to them and respond to one another through the service. This allows the community to share in one another's presence, enhancing, rather than disrupting, the experience. Participants use both chat and avatar actions to engage in the service. For example, when the pastor asked the audience to acknowledge that they've spoken toxic words, one member typed "Polly[21] raises her hand" into the chat window. When the LifeChurch.tv band played live music, one user stood his avatar up and raised his arms in praise, just as one might see at a conventional evangelical church (Figure 5.3).

FIGURE 5.3 Worshippers at LifeChurch.tv in *Second Life*.

The LifeChurch.tv service concluded with calls to prayer and conversion and encouragement that viewers join LifeGroups, which are groups of people "who hang out and do life together."[22] Obviously, the *Second Life* campus offers LifeChurch.tv a way of reaching new audiences, but the organization is not content to provide a solely virtual experience. Rather, the online campus becomes a place not only for delivering the Christian message but also of bringing people together in conventional reality. Such groups will naturally reinforce the LifeChurch.tv religious message and offline community while fulfilling basic needs for social interaction. This differs from the Anglican Church, where a connection to the traditional authorities reinforces the *Second Life* community. For the LifeChurch.tv community, the online community is really subservient to its conventional, physical one.

Although LifeChurch.tv initially engaged *Second Life* with some enthusiasm, that has since waned. The build remains, but "because *Second Life* is not thriving like it once was, it's not as significant an area of focus for us anymore," reports one member of the LifeChurch.tv administration.[23] As of late 2010, 50,000 to 60,000 people logged on to *Second Life* at any given time, a number that exceeds the 2007 numbers by 10,000 to 20,000, so we must understand the group's criticism of *Second Life* in context. The broader online community does, in fact, remain and thus is thriving as much in 2011 as it was in 2007, though it is not growing at the same pace. At one point, Bobby Gruenewald, the "innovation leader" for LifeChurch. tv, praised the conversion of one *Second Life* resident to Christianity as the answer to the question, "Why *Second Life?*"[24] But such conversions either no longer happen or no longer matter. Whether or why not *Second Life* residents choose to engage in LifeChurch.tv events is not clearly correlated, however, to the thriving of the broader community. In absolute terms, there are more *Second Life* residents now than in early 2007 when the LifeChurch.tv campus was built. Unfortunately, aside from indicating their lack of interest in the world, LifeChurch.tv declined to discuss its online presence with me.

Despite the difficulties that LifeChurch.tv has in *Second Life*, it retains its campus, which reinforces its other efforts. Its presence allows LifeChurch. tv to describe itself as a leader in online church ministry and organization, a fact that it turned to its advantage in 2012. That year, LifeChurch.tv applied to the International Corporation for Assigned Names and Numbers to establish and maintain a church domain name for the Internet. While the LifeChurch.tv administration claims that managing the system will not be to profit financially from it,[25] the group will certainly do so if the domain catches on. Even in absence of financial profits, managing the domain name adds credibility to its organization. As one *Second Life* Christian leader pointed out to me, through the application for the church domain management, the *Second Life* campus provides LifeChurch.tv with credibility *outside* of *Second Life*, in conventional circles.

The disinterest shown by LifeChurch.tv's leadership apparently reflects despondency over the group's fortunes in *Second Life*, which result from their approach to *Second Life*. The administration does not appear to have seen that *Second Life* is a place, and not merely a tool. *Second Life* is, in many ways, a landscape of belonging, and not simply an instrument to establish earthly relationships. By using *Second Life* as a tool rather than accepting it as a place, the LifeChurch.tv administration set itself up for difficulties. This was exacerbated by a misuse of *Second Life*'s resources. It is possible, as we shall see, to build objects that stabilize—however imperfectly—*Second Life* religions, but LifeChurch.tv made little attempt to do so. The virtual T-shirts were an effort in this direction, but one doomed to failure because *Second Life*'s residents are, by and large, too fashion-conscious to find LifeChurch.tv apparel compelling. Most residents are too busy looking extraordinary or expressing idiosyncratic personalities through their avatars to be caught demonstrating their specific religious affiliations with banal shirts. Indeed, LifeChurch.tv's failure in this regard mirrors that of Nike, Coca-Cola, and other real-world companies whose products made no headway in *Second Life*. Fundamentally, LifeChurch.tv sought to stabilize the wrong community in *Second Life*. Virtual T-shirts are no more likely to convert Christians than virtual Coke shirts are to sell syrupy drinks. The group's focus was on converting *Second Life* residents and turning them into ordinary members of their congregations, and this did not work; however, LifeChurch.tv may yet revise its strategy to be more effective for *Second Life*'s residents.

While LifeChurch.tv uses established conventional networks and seeks to affirm them in *Second Life*, Kimberly Knight's[26] Koinonia (Greek for "community") Church and Holy Heretic pub reject the need for such affiliations, using the online space to create a postdenominational community of faithful that can benefit from but is not dependent on conventional religious groups. Knight's small group[27] thrives without the sanction of any official institution, flourishing as a home for the disaffected and those who desire a cosmopolitan way of "doing church." The open, pluralistic, and welcoming environment at Koinonia emphasizes this cultural

sophistication. Recognition as the only church on the *Second Life* community page for lesbian, gay, bisexual, and transgender friendly locations[28]
adds a layer of reality, stabilizing it and its identity just as accepting institutional authority does so for the Anglicans of *Second Life*. Web documents
may be less tangible than printed ones, but they can compensate for this
with wider circulation. Though they are less durable, they can bring more
people into relation with one another.

Koinonia's church space is an imposing edifice tempered by many large
windows and a vast open entranceway in the front (Figure 5.4). Visitors
can clearly see the comfortable environment within, where participants
sit in a circle of cozy virtual cushions and chairs rather than more formal
(and authoritarian) front-facing pews. The open architecture and seating
arrangement reflect the church's commitment to a Christian community
where all are welcome to join in loving fellowship. Knight, who established and directs the church as Sophianne Rhode, is a graduate of the
Candler School of Theology at Emory University and now helps progressive Christian groups develop their ministries online and through social
media. From 2007 through 2012, I visited Knight's lands and church in
Second Life, maintained contact with her, and discussed her work with
her: we talked in person; sent emails; discussed Koinonia in real-time chat

FIGURE 5.4 Koinonia Congregational Church in *Second Life*.

in *Second Life* while we were in different locations there; had a formal, sit-down interview in *Second Life*; and conducted one Skype interview.[29]

Knight began Koinonia in 2007 after first experimenting with a pub atmosphere in which to have theological discussions. At the time, she was a seminary student intending to go into chaplaincy, and, in fact, the first *Second Life* group that she formed was called the Chaplains' Corps. After discussion with other like-minded, residents, Knight founded Koinonia to provide a welcoming church for all people, including those who had been rejected or hurt by their conventional church communities. For a time, the Carpenter Foundation funded Koinonia through a grant administered by Knight's local United Church of Christ community, but she now pays for Koinonia through land rental in *Second Life* and considers Koinonia (and herself) to be postdenominational.[30]

Koinonia virtually embodies the claim that a community of believers is the essence of Christian life. Knight rejects the idea that a brick-and-mortar building could define the "real" church, claiming: "Church happens in spirit and reality inside God's people, for that is where God lives."[31] If those people are in *Second Life*, well then, so must be their god. As such, Koinonia welcomes all willing participants, offering a safe place for practice regardless of the individual's race, color, gender, sexuality, handicap, or other marginalized condition. *Second Life* can be, Knight has told me, a "thin place" where heirophanies are possible: in particular, the experience of the loving community is, she says, the experience of God's love.[32] Rather than seeking converts, Knight extends hospitality.[33] By creating a space for a community of love in *Second Life*, Knight hopes "that people who might otherwise be alienated from religious community begin to settle in with the language of God . . . glimmers of light touch people when they have an 'aha!' moment;" when that happens, they know "they are part of God's story."[34]

According to Knight, the evolving story of God includes many peoples and many faiths. She says that God's story "is written in scriptures from many traditions, and those traditions struggling to connect with God is part of God's story and we as humans falling short and missing the point over and over is part of God's story and ultimately God loves us even as we stumble around in this life, as individuals and as community."[35] At the same time, "God's story is evolving along with ours." With an open story that includes people even as it shapes and is itself reshaped by them, Koinonia creates space for different kinds of worship and belief.

For Knight, a good Christian theology does not exclude people, whether they are Christian or not. Rather than forming a group by drawing a line around it, she does so by creating dialogue and relationship with others; it is her "narrative theology"[36] that makes this possible.

Knight believes that religious work in *Second Life* permits communion with the divine but that practitioners must work to maximize immersion in the rituals.[37] Worship participants at Koinonia are encouraged to dim the lights in their homes and in *Second Life* (which allows residents to set the location of the sun, in this case to midnight). The service itself includes recorded music, prayers, and reading from a biblical text. Knight requests that participants refrain from typing into the chat window during the reading, as it could distract other residents; but after the reading participants discuss the text and its relevance to their lives. Thus, the service offers opportunities for quiet reflection, for listening to others, and also for contributing to group understandings. Vigorous conversation in the chat window about the reading enables mutual understanding and encouragement in living a socially positive Christian life.

Knight and her congregation at Koinonia are leaders in what Brian McLaren calls "a new kind of Christianity." In his book by that title, McLaren argues that Christians can revitalize their traditions, recreating the church as a "school of love."[38] By focusing on working with others and being open to different ways of living, such as sexual orientation or religious commitments, Christians can fulfill their mission.[39] In fashioning a new Christianity, McLaren believes that the faithful may find that their old liturgies, lectionaries, calendars, music, training, and all of the rest might require revision, restructuring, and rewriting.[40] Among Christians today, it is easy to see how Knight's congregation fits this definition. With services that call everyone who wishes to a fellowship of love, welcome, and dialogue, Koinonia participates in the best of the new Christianity.

Koinonia was more than just a place for Christians to find acceptance. The two sims that Knight maintains, Xenia and Qoheleth, have been home to a variety of religious groups. Christians, Muslims, and Jews have established buildings on the land, and members of the groups get along without difficulty. As of 2012, the residents were almost entirely Christian, but from a variety of traditions. Thus, the community defined by Koinonia is distinctly ecumenical and interdenominational, even as Koinonia is, as Knight puts it, postdenominational.

Unfortunately, paradise rarely comes without problems. One consequence of the open hospitality extended by Knight is that some visitors come solely to reject her vision of Christianity. For a time, Knight told me, evangelical Christians came to Koinonia and were openly rude, which was particularly difficult when new visitors were at the church.[41] Accusations of heresy, of being not "really" Christian, and of being the "daughter of Satan" accompanied organized hassling, which could "really hurt people who were fragile in their faith...especially if (and many were) they had already suffered church wounding."[42] Although such problems largely dissipated by 2010, their legacy lives on. While Knight would like to be a part of large Christian groups in *Second Life*, some of which send out notifications about various churches' meeting times and places, she fears that doing so would rekindle persecution and knows that several members of her community were banned from such lists because of either their theology or sexual orientation.[43]

It is clear, then, that not all people come to *Second Life* hoping they can rescue religion with ecumenism. Just as intolerance (allegedly of intolerance) caused a political and religious fiasco for the Avatars of Change, some members of religious communities enter *Second Life* and criticize or cause grief for others. That said, however, religious tolerance as Knight practices it is widespread in *Second Life* religiosity.

Despite the difficulties that could crop up with other Christian groups, Knight's focus was on growing Koinonia to continue ministering to those in need. She provided a space where those who have been hurt or rejected can come and be welcome. Alongside the community, Koinonia includes lush gardens where individuals can wander in solitude. She has, for example, found individuals meditating in the church, at the waterfall or on the hill, even in the parsonage. The experience of fellowship at Koinonia can be spiritually fulfilling for participants, some of whom have no other access to church communities.

In early 2012, Knight ended services at Koinonia and launched the Holy Heretic pub (Figure 5.5). As with the Koinonia church, welcome is built into the pub's architecture, represented by windows across the front of the building and a wide-open doorway into the seating area. The pub hosts discussions on Christianity but also more "traditional" *Second Life* activities, such as live music, karaoke, and trivia competitions—generally with Christian themes. Knight can thus capitalize on *Second Life*'s social scene, which is among its chief attractions, and use social practices such as games and music to stabilize the group. She is, in her words, "making the nongame environment a little game oriented,"[44] which is crucial to the success and livelihood of *Second Life*, as noted in Chapter 4. The gaming

FIGURE 5.5 The Holy Heretic pub in *Second Life*.

activities at the Holy Heretic will unquestionably play an enormous role in the site's future success. It is through these typical *Second Life* practices that Knight's theology can find expression in the life of the online community, and thus they reinforce and stabilize the group and its beliefs.

The Holy Heretic is a worthy successor to Koinonia because it takes advantage of both the resources and residents of *Second Life*. Knight found that too few members of the Koinonia community were willing to lead fellowship meetings on their own but that they have leapt at the opportunity to host events at the Holy Heretic.[45] She believes that people do not feel qualified to "minister" to others but love to "host" them; this new structure allows *Second Life* residents to do what they do and enjoy best—"hang out"—while providing a spiritually fulfilling atmosphere.[46] Even holding events in a bar is an important facet of the community, because pubs have been popular in *Second Life* since its inception and residents are comfortable in them. By building the bar, Knight has provided stability for the spiritual community. Following upon the ministry of Koinonia, the Holy Heretic is a welcoming place, where Christians of all genders, sexual preferences, and ethnicities can find a home. From karaoke to Bible trivia, the Holy Heretic is a true place in *Second Life*, one that residents can occupy, not just use; this is key to the way that Knight and her collaborators marshal the tools of *Second Life* in producing their theology.

Christians in *Second Life* benefit from the availability of services and congregations, but the creative power *Second Life* grants to its residents means that entirely new ways of doing and being church have arisen within the environment. Beyond even the postdenominational nature of Knight's community, some Christian groups provide experiences that do not even imply denominations at all. *Second Life* allows individuals to create their own Christian experiences, ones that draw on entirely unconventional forms of communal identity. One perfect example is Aslan's How, which operated in *Second Life* until late 2012, when financial concerns led to its closure. Happily, however, the How quickly began redevelopment on an OpenSimulator grid, and is expanding to include more content than the *Second Life* sim enabled.

Aslan's How ministry in *Second Life* (as it will again in OpenSim once complete) gathered its faithful through their love of C. S. Lewis's *Chronicles of Narnia*, forming a community out of a shared experience of the imagination. Taking advantage of the opportunities *Second Life* affords, Aslan's How provided traditional learning through textual study and spoken ministry but also articulated a theology across its landscape: it used both conventional and virtual strategies to produce group solidarity. Members affirm their group through conventional affiliation with the Narnia books and access to a Christian ministry while also acquiring Narnia-themed virtual decorations, occupying a landscape of Narnian theology, and even shaping individual avatars to reflect their commitments. Aslan's How was deliberately theological and engaged in Christian apologetics, which it framed within the comfortable narrative of Lewis's beloved fantasies.[47] Visitors learned about Christian theology while visiting replicas of sites in Narnia, joined a community of like-minded believers, purchased goods that will remind them of their experiences and the theology of Aslan's How, and attended readings of the Chronicles on occasional Sunday afternoons.

The visitor to Aslan's How teleported into a room intended to be part of Professor Digory Kirke's home in the country (Figure 5.6). The famed wardrobe through which Lucy led her brothers and sister into Narnia sat open on the opposite wall, and visitors could walk through the door into the Narnian landscape. Alternately, the map to the left could be used to teleport instantly to various parts of the region (e.g., Cair Paravel, informational tents, or the Beavers' house). While in the room, one could read names attributed to Jesus (e.g., King of Kings), copy a picture of the lion art next to the wardrobe, buy a copy of a map of Narnia, click on the lion picture to join a group affiliated with the region, and donate money to the group.

FIGURE 5.6 Professor Kirke's room in Aslan's How, including the wardrobe leading into Narnia.

Moving around the landscape gave visitors many opportunities to explore Christian theology through the Narnian narrative and through connection to a conventional religious community. For example, one could visit the Stone Table, where Aslan was sacrificed, and read a brief notecard comparing Aslan's redemption of Edmund from the White Witch to the crucifixion and resurrection of Jesus. More thorough theological works could be found in the tents near the castle Cair Paravel. Within the tents were "books" that one could click for either a notecard with information or an audio file of Reverend R. C. Sproul discussing topics like secularism, science and theology, and the attributes of God (Figure 5.7). Sproul is the founder and president of Ligonier Ministries and advocates Reformed Theology, an evangelical movement committed to the theology of the sixteenth-century Protestant Reformation.[48] He has a radio evangelism program and is the author of many books, including *The Holiness of God* (1985). The audio files enabled through Aslan's How exposed Sproul's theology to a new audience, one that may not otherwise find him, and assured *Second Life* residents that there is a theological context in which Aslan's How fit. The founder of Aslan's How, Larry Londy,[49] is not affiliated with Sproul or Ligonier Ministries, but he considers Sproul's work

FIGURE 5.7 Tents with audio file links inside in front of Cair Paravel in Aslan's How.

effective for beginners to Christian theology and thus as appropriate to the ministry that Aslan's How provided.[50]

While connection to Reformed Theology provided a conventional foundation for Aslan's How, the region's primary recourse to the world outside of *Second Life* is, of course, Lewis's Chronicles. The books are the repositories of many people's fantasies, memories, and emotional commitments. They tie together those for whom the Narnia books were crucial to childhood or adult life into a community with those on the edges, who perhaps remember the books fondly but found them less instrumental to their own lives. In Aslan's How, the *Chronicles of Narnia*, especially *The Lion, The Witch, and the Wardrobe*, underwrote the entire community; they provided a central nexus through which the participants can come together intellectually, emotionally, and socially.

The Narnian art that visitors could purchase and use in their own *Second Life* homes makes the theological and social community of Aslan's How portable. Visitors could purchase copies of pictures in the region and subsequently set them up in their own *Second Life* residences. Pictures of lions, fauns, and centaurs, for example, offer a gentle reminder of Lewis's Christian message, and thus visitors can experience a kind of continued presence within the Narnia–Christianity matrix that forms the basis of

Aslan's How. Unlike a website, which can usually provide little more than physical things to purchase (though desktop wallpaper is sometimes available), Aslan's How offered an opportunity to redecorate at very little cost. Such objects work well in the game: many residents enjoy personalizing their private residences, and simply seeing the virtual painting will remind them of their very real interest in and commitment to Narnia and even Aslan's How.

Aslan's How also incorporated typical *Second Life* amusements as part of its appeal. Upon teleporting to the sim, the new arrival would see a wardrobe to enter Narnia but also a barrel that provides a heads-up display (HUD) for role-played battle. Virtual combat has been a part of the world almost since its inception and is standard entertainment practice. By enabling themed combat on the site, the operators encourage visits that go beyond the theological. Naturally, this mirrors the strategy of many conventional Christian churches, which often host sports and leisure activities. In the early twenty-first century, combat sports were integrated into Christian evangelism,[51] so it would not be too surprising if the role-played battles at Aslan's How contributed to the site's mission and not just to its entertainment value. When a resident donned his HUD, he took on full membership in the world of Narnia and also of Aslan's How. The HUD and the battle practices thus encouraged group cohesion and added to viability of the community.

For the more committed members of Aslan's How, avatar design is a powerful tool for expressing their beliefs and affiliation. *Second Life* is, of course, known for the options that each individual has in shaping virtual life to his preferences, but the most interesting avatars I saw at a religious sim were those at Aslan's How. Visitors attend religious services in *Second Life* as dragons and turtles and fairies and more, but those shapes are not by themselves reflective of the communities to which the participants belong; they are simply the shapes that the residents prefer. At Aslan's How, on the other hand, longtime participants possess fantastic avatars that borrow from the Narnian tradition. Figure 5.8 shows two of the listeners at a broadcasting of the *Magician's Nephew* at Aslan's How, one of whom was a horse (hearkening to Bree in *The Horse and His Boy*) and the other a centaur. Such fantastic avatars show a love of Lewis's chronicles while also reifying the residents' participation in the community.

Alongside virtual paintings, battles, and avatars, the landscape affirmed the community and its commitments, which were written across its geography. Ultimately, finding the Stone Table is the theological aim of visiting

FIGURE 5.8 Two residents (with horse and centaur avatars) attend a reading of *The Magician's Nephew* in Caer Paravel at Aslan's How.

Aslan's How, as it is here that the ultimate Christian message takes shape. Londy deliberately made the Stone Table difficult to locate because "finding God is a process"; therefore, most people visited the Narnia sim four or five times before they succeeded, and some never did so.[52] Londy equates finding the Stone Table, which is the site of sacrifice and atonement in *The Lion, the Witch, and the Wardrobe*, with finding God in one's life and forming a relationship with God.[53] This embodied practice produces and reinforces a spiritual state of transformation and habituates the visitor to a mode of religious seeking.

While Lewis's influences were not limited to the Christian tradition,[54] there is little effort in the Narnia books, particularly *The Lion*, to hide the Christian symbolism; as a consequence, a model of the key sites from the books provides an excellent environment to explore Christian theology. Lewis offers a salvation story of sacrifice and atonement in *The Lion*, one that mirrors the Christian story of Jesus, including the resurrection of the lion, Aslan, after he dies for the sins of Edmund. Lewis's nonfiction work inspired Londy, but since Narnia "draws people" he used that work to engage *Second Life*'s residents in the Christian message.[55] Essentially, Londy recognizes that the Narnia books already stabilize a substantial community that is in agreement with, or at least potentially sympathetic to, Christian sensibilities. He can thus use the books as conventional resources to which he adds virtual objects to stabilize an innovative Christian community in *Second Life*.

Clearly, the Narnian geography tied Londy's group together as much as did their love of Lewis's fantasy books. Coming to Aslan's How to talk about Narnia or Christian theology is an entirely different thing from attending a conversation on one of those topics in a typical *Second Life* bar or garden. The beautiful recreation of the Narnian landscape was a constant reminder of and reflection of the literary and theological ideas that held the Aslan's How group together, both uniting them under the banner of conventional life storytelling and their *Second Life* community.

For return visitors, at least, Aslan's How was definitely a place for reflection on Christian themes. One visitor, Simone Lyvette,[56] came out of affection for Narnia and its stories and is aware of the Christian themes in the books and is "okay with it,"[57] but others more explicitly engage in the Christian message. Annabelle Lykin,[58] for example, told me that—as of when I met her—she had not yet read any of the Christian literature at the site or engaged in conversations about religion but that she looked forward to it because she appreciates both the fairy tale and Christian elements in Narnia.[59] She hoped to combine these in conversation about the Christian elements in the books.[60] To some extent, that happens during book readings, and listeners were invited to stay after for further conversation. During a broadcast that I joined, listeners commented on the truth of claims Lewis makes about the nature of reality, sin, and human behavior, obviously demonstrating their interest in the ethics and theology of the books even while immersed in the story.

Maciej Kijowski,[61] an officer for the Aslan's How group, agrees that visitors use the site for regular Christian conversation.[62] He used the group as his permanent home in *Second Life* and was responsible for much of the artistic design in the region; he discovered it while looking for Narnia-themed content and helped revitalize the area. Thanks to his and others' considerable labors, the community had somewhere to convene and was able to take advantage of the social authority of Lewis and Narnia to stabilize itself. In conversation with me, Kijowski reported having many guests and many pleasant conversations about religion with them.[63] In addition—and this theme remains with us in the next section of this chapter—he believes that residents see *Second Life* as a "neutral place" that could be a "platform for all faiths" in which ecumenical dialogue takes place.[64]

Londy's own beliefs have developed along with his Narnian landscape. Much as the visitor must traverse the landscape to find the Stone Table, Londy has grown and developed in creating and managing the sim. He reports that he once sought conversions to a particular kind of Christianity that reflected his understanding of the Great Commission (of Jesus to his disciples), but operating Aslan's How "helped a lot" in reshaping his Christianity within and outside of *Second Life*. Eventually, he learned to shift the focus to "providing content that leads to discussion if discussion is wanted." This shift from conversion orientation to discussion orientation is a positive aspect of how *Second Life* allows a safe reshaping of religious beliefs. It is far easier for a practitioner to grow and develop this way through *Second Life* work than through, for example, door-to-door or street evangelism.[65]

Aslan's How was an effective merger of traditional and new, Internet-based forms of religious authority. The sim took advantage of traditional authorities such as Lewis and Sproul and sprinkled in writings from other theologians. (Londy would like to expand this area over time, which the new OpenSim location should make possible.) In addition, however, Londy's ideas were interspersed throughout the landscape, and thus the packaging of the theology emerged out of his and his collaborators' work. If the medium is the message, then the Narnia sim also contributed to the kind of Christianity that Londy advocates. He does not merely repeat Sproul or other theologians but creatively packaged them in a theology of his own, one that takes advantage of the medium, the Narnian environment, the work of past theologians, and his own beliefs. The combinatorial religious work that he thereby produced benefits from a diverse set of practices, traditions, and virtual objects. If Knight develops a narrative theology through her work in *Second Life*, Londy and his collaborators might be said to have created a landscape theology, one that can be shaped in ways previously unimagined by religious practitioners.

Second Life enables considerable diversity in the construction of Christian communities and thereby provides opportunities for authentic reflection, individual expression, and even association with conventional church hierarchies. Strategically, groups that take advantage of *Second Life*'s broad resources, rather than producing insularity or restricting their domains to the affirmation of conventional organizations, tend to align with Linden Lab's own aspirations toward socially open networks and the promise of a better world to come. Residents have harnessed the world's power to produce considerable theological resources; in doing so, they

have literally recreated Christianity and presently contribute to the opportunities available to Christian faithful. *Second Life* residents produce new
communities by networking themselves within a religious matrix that
includes textual traditions, conventional religious institutions, *Second Life*
grouping systems, architecture, virtual decorations, individual avatars,
and even the environment whose contours reflect the group and simultaneously unite it.

Islam

Just as we see tremendous variety and creativity among *Second Life*
Christians, the game provides an interesting place for thinking about
Islam in the modern world. While as of yet no Islamic commentators
have suggested that virtual world practice can take the place of conventional practice, *Second Life* still offers important opportunities for Muslims
as well as for non-Muslims interested in understanding Islam. Sites in
Second Life provide useful information, allowing non-Muslim residents to
overcome their lack of familiarity and Muslims to experience communal
worship that many lack in their conventional lives.

The Virtual Hajj, launched in 2007 and maintained by IslamOnline.
net, allows anyone, Muslim or not, to perform rituals associated with the
traditional hajj. The sim even includes a bag of free accessories so that
the visitor can dress his avatar in the *ihram*, the white cloth outfit common to all hajjis (people on hajj), though wearing the outfit is optional
in *Second Life*. The hajj is one of the Five Pillars of Islam: it is a multiday
pilgrimage to Mecca, in Saudi Arabia, to locations that are holy in Islam,
and it is obligatory for all Muslims during their lifetimes.[66] In *Second Life*,
visitors to the Virtual Hajj have a chance to see what the hajj is like and
participate in rituals that mimic those of conventional reality. For example, visitors can circumambulate the Kaaba, the central building in the
Al-Masjid Al-Haram (a mosque in Mecca), which is beautifully recreated
in *Second Life*. Afterward, participants kiss the black stone believed to have
been placed by Ibrahim,[67] then move toward a place of prayer, and eventually imitate Hagar's frantic running after Ibrahim exiled her and Ishmael
from the household (Figure 5.9).

In *Second Life*, non-Muslims have an opportunity to understand the
hajj that they simply could not have otherwise. Unlike most sites of religious pilgrimage, Mecca is not open to nonbelievers. Only Muslims are

FIGURE 5.9 The Kaaba in the Virtual Hajj site in *Second Life*; clicking the black stone surrounded by white in the lower left will place one's avatar into a posture of kissing the stone.

allowed in the city, which means that non-Muslims can never experience the pilgrimage or see its sights firsthand. In *Second Life*, however, they can virtually walk through the hajj, all while reading notes that explain some of the ritual practices and theological concepts. "The program," reports IslamOnline.net, "is a powerful educational tool for people embarking on the soul-searching journey, in the real world, or anyone else who wants to learn about it."[68]

This accessible site thus corresponds to Linden Lab's goal of making the world better through *Second Life*. The physical city of Mecca is, by definition, a place of exclusion. The Virtual Hajj, on the other hand, welcomes non-Muslims even as it gives virtual form to Muslim articles of faith, religious practice, and communal sustenance. This is not to say that the exclusion of non-Muslims from Mecca is unjust; it only serves as a reminder that such practices reify "tribal" identities and probably exacerbate insider–outsider dichotomies. At the Virtual Hajj, insiders and outsiders come together. Naturally, this provides opportunities for misunderstanding and ill-conceived griefing, but it also opens the door to the sharing of experiences and identities.

The Virtual Hajj can be both a learning experience and a site for faithful practice. For the Muslim believer, the Virtual Hajj surely will never compare to a visit to Mecca itself, but it still offers a chance for practice, prayer, and reflection. One contributor to it describes the sim as "very awe-inspiring and...the closest you can get to the real thing."[69] As such, it can help prepare the future hajji for the experience or allow those who have already done the pilgrimage to virtually repeat it. The Virtual Hajj is more than just a practice space, however; for some Muslims it is a genuine spiritual space that enables transformative experiences. The site's designer, Ruuh Cassini, told me that "virtual pilgrims can benefit spiritually from the virtual hajj experience."[70] Just as visitors to the Croagh Patrick pilgrimage website occasionally felt themselves truly present at the Croagh and able to join in a community of pilgrims,[71] *Second Life* residents who visit the Virtual Hajj have religious opportunities, even if these may never equal those of conventional pilgrims.

Just as performing the hajj in *Second Life* can provide spiritual benefits, producing and maintaining the sim also fulfills genuine religious obligations. While prayer and pilgrimage in *Second Life* do not replace their conventional counterparts, the creation of an Islamic space of learning and reflection in *Second Life* actively fits into Muslim traditions of evangelism and education. Cassini said, "The inspiration [to build it] came from a mixture of vision, youth, and a desire to connect with people who are often hard to reach, in order to share (in a non-compelling[72] manner) the message of Islam, which is an obligation of every Muslim."[73] What Cassini and IslamOnline.net have created is unquestionably a place that conveys aspects of Islamic doctrine and safe practice. Without any compulsion or coercion—no one will be there against his will—the site promotes prayerful reflection and educates visitors about Islam and Muslim practice.

The Virtual Hajj is a prime example of how residents use *Second Life* to produce new religious opportunities for understanding and growth, which often emerge out of trial. Members of the sim community are often available to speak with visitors and help them understand, but unfortunately such greeters must occasionally become police offers. Cassini reports a variety of griefing activities at the Virtual Hajj, from deliberately immodest attire to offensive imagery: "sometimes it was people appearing unclothed in the area, even though the rules clearly state that as a replica of a real-world holy site it is inappropriate to be dressed immodestly. Other times it was as bad as particles of pigs or Hitler (God knows why they had Hitler) being emitted in a blinding manner."[74] Gaber Crystal,[75] a manager at the Virtual Hajj, accepts such troubles as reflective of how Muhammad was received by many of his contemporaries.[76] Rather than dwell on such griefing, however, both Cassini and Crystal told me that as long as visitors are respectful they will be welcome in the Virtual Hajj. In providing a space for respectful engagement, Crystal asserts that the Virtual Hajj helps to overcome ignorance, prejudice, and hatred; the land "builds bridges...and we need these bridges a lot these days, because with them we can make a good life."[77] He also appreciates how coming to the Virtual Hajj and greeting guests realizes his dream of sharing Islam with others and simultaneously opens a door toward interfaith, interethnic understanding, and cooperation.[78]

As part of its ecumenical outreach, the Virtual Hajj clearly situates itself within the contemporary political landscape. Multiple signs, as of 2011, serve not only to distinguish the region and its group members from radical Islamic communities but also to actively disown the latter. The signs read: "OnIslam Island Management announced that (al-Qaeda—Taliban) group and its members are not welcome at our islands" and asserts that the *Second Life* al-Qaeda—Taliban group is "untrusted." Visitors cannot miss the signs, which are at the entrance area, at the doorway into the central mosque, and inside the mosque near the Kaaba. By positioning themselves in opposition to groups widely mistrusted and disliked in Western nations, the operators of the Virtual Hajj work to create positive ties with non-Muslims. Such objects affirm both the boundaries of the Virtual Hajj's Muslim community and the group's interest in connecting with civic-minded members of other faith traditions. Cassini hopes that through the Virtual Hajj "non-Muslims may come to the realization that Muslims...aren't all terrorists and we can sit down and have a civil conversation.... So perhaps our hope is that there would be a greater and more accurate recognition of the contributions of Muslims to the history of mankind, and a common platform being established to then allow us to progress into the future in peace with all our neighbors."[79]

Second Life provides powerful opportunities to rewrite our religious assumptions, including those common about Islam; as a result, Muslims have vigorously used it to combat anti-Muslim prejudice. This struggle, reports Cassini, has been ongoing for the Virtual Hajj, which educates non-Muslims and provides a safe space for them to discuss the religion with Muslims who are present.[80] Happily, the Virtual Hajj is not alone in seeking fellowship between Muslims and non-Muslims in *Second Life*. The Masjid al Masa mosque in *Second Life* was created by a Christian

FIGURE 5.10 Masjid al Masa in *Second Life*.

(for a friend) as place for "peace and quiet"[81] and was, obviously, an interfaith community from its start until its eventual closure (Figure 5.10).
Larissa Vacano,[82] the site's creator, surprised those who asked her if she's
a Muslim, and although her religious identity troubles some it quickly
became irrelevant to those who needed a sacred place.[83]

Many of Masjid al Masa's visitors, according to Vacano, were people
without access to a conventional mosque. As a consequence, it fulfilled a
basic religious need for a place of worship. Though prayer in *Second Life*
does not meet the obligations of salat (the five daily prayers in Islam), visitors came to the site for a sense that they are attending a public gathering
while they perform their conventional prayers alone. If their avatars are
in the mosque while they perform their prayers at home, the juxtaposition forms a uniquely modern way to practice religion, one where technology allows the practitioner to partially overcome geographic obstacles
and constitute new kinds of religious groups. While most visitors came by
themselves, Vacano says that they frequently did so at prayer times, which
offered them a sense of community in worship.

Masjid al Masa represented Vacano's global and ecumenical sense
of the sacred. She believes that Christians and Muslims have the same
god and that all people are equal. She even strives to remain calm and

peaceful with the occasional griefers who come to disparage Islam. As a collaborative enterprise between a Christian creator and Muslim owner, the mosque is a powerful expression of *Second Life* religion, of the potential it has to reconfigure traditional authority structures while also offering a theological vision. Although the true depth of Masjid al Masa might elude those who do not speak with Vacano, the environment offered at the mosque was clearly open to all and thus represented the openness and ecumenism that inform her theology and her practice there. *Second Life* is a world where individuals can potentially transcend the emotional limits that produce intercultural violence. Because of this, one individual who helped organize its corollary to the U.S.–Islamic World Forum in 2008 believes that in the virtual world residents join a transcendent community, "beyond the scope of the socio-economic, geopolitical and cultural lattice into which each person is born."[84]

The power of *Second Life* to form new cultural modes was, perhaps, best expressed in the land covenant of Al Andalus. For five years (from 2007 to 2012), the project sought to recreate the medieval Spanish period in which Jews, Christians, and Muslims lived in harmony under Islamic rule. For the founders of Al Andalus (see figure 5.11), *Second Life* does not *necessarily* reinvent our notions of interfaith, interethnic, or intercultural community, but it could be a location for doing so. Certainly, the occupants of Al Andalus, in accord with Linden Lab's hopes for *Second Life*, believed it was worth trying. The land covenant, written by sim owner Rose Springvale, said:

> The Al Andalus Project is a Second Life attempt to reconstruct 13th Century Moor Alhambra and build around this virtual space a community of individuals willing to explore the modalities of interaction between different languages, nationalities, religions and cultures. The principles upon which this project is founded include political participation, separation of powers, justice and the rule of law. Membership in the community is open to all, regardless of sim land ownership, second life premium status, species of avatar, gender, religion, national origin, sexual orientation or any other traditionally separatist classification, either real or apparent. The plan is to create a system of political and legal governance, based on notions of community self-governance, active citizen participation, equality, dignity, social justice, democracy and human rights. Idealistic? Absolutely. Possible? Let's find out.[85]

The religious and political idealism of Al Andalus was—in proper *Second Life* fashion—grounded in conventional and virtual objects. The very name of the group, hearkening to Andalusian Spain, takes advantage of conventional history and religious geography, providing a link between the *Second Life* group, ordinary life, and the desire for a welcoming and pluralistic community. A Facebook group provided online access outside of *Second Life*, but virtual objects like the land covenant and even a magic carpet ride were crucial to the sim's success. Echoing the covenant, the magic carpet ride announced: "As an outstanding example of the dialogue between different religions, cultures and organizations, Andalusia represents a lesson for us today as we confront globalization, which needs to take place against a background of enlightened social relations and the universal ethical values in which humanity has its roots and without which it cannot survive."[86] The flying carpet and the "note card" it distributes are thus mediators of the Andalusian ethos, giving the group and its beliefs virtual form and sharing them with sightseers and visitors.

In the turmoil of our post-9/11 world, the founders of Al Andalus thought to use virtual reality as a place to investigate the human potential to rise above tribal conflicts and to forge effective community governance. Springvale says that Al Andalus "appealed to my personal desire to do something positive in the world rather than continue to foster things that are divisive,"[87] and her efforts showed promise. The group affiliated with the project was approximately 25% Jewish and 25% Muslim; the remaining members were primarily Christian or atheist.[88] Thus, the demographics of the group speak to the possibility of forging interreligious dialogue in *Second Life*.

As with elsewhere on the *Second Life* grid, religious participation in Al Andalus was nontrivial. One Muslim practitioner, for example, finds "communication with Allah easier" at Al Andalus than in her mosque in Singapore, even though *Second Life* prayers clearly do not replace conventional prayer obligations.[89] For believers of many backgrounds, Al Andalus provided a place to engage the divine even as they engaged other people. The integration of the community may well, in fact, play into its members' appreciation for sacred experiences online.

Events in Al Andalus were political, cultural, and religious. There were meetings to facilitate group governance, for example, and artistic exhibitions for entertainment and education. There were religious services for the three groups that constituted the community. The Al Andalus community benefited from all of the advantages of *Second Life* residency and

FIGURE 5.11 Bird's-eye view of the Al Qantara library in the Al Andalus region of *Second Life*.

shows how these can be turned toward conventional world gains. If the community can thrive, can promote effective dialogue, and can help us understand how we might form pluralistic, cosmopolitan communities, then we can bring those lessons into our everyday lives as well.

Conventional world groups embraced the Al Andalus community as a beacon of hope for our troubled times. For example, in their global publication to promote cross-cultural understanding, the oil company Saudi Aramco praises the *Second Life* group as a "metaphor for the future."[90] The author of the piece, Joshua Fouts, collaborated with policy expert Rita King to produce a document about the larger cultural ramifications of Islam that was funded by the Carnegie Council in New York City. Their work, designed to influence policymakers and help shape our future, encourages supplementing conventional diplomacy with digital diplomacy—breaking down barriers by using the relative safety of virtual world interactions.[91]

Sadly, in 2012 Al Andalus closed. Springvale intended to run the sim for only two years but maintained it for five thanks to the interest and commitment it garnered from *Second Life*'s residents. Five years is a long time for a *Second Life* build, and very little in *Second Life* has lasted longer. In the end, however, interest waned, and Springvale allowed the Al Andalus lands to dissipate back into virtual ether. At the closing, however, she continued to advocate for the group's mission, writing: "thank you for all the kind words and the tremendous support this project had in *Second Life*. If this project can succeed, and it did, there is no reason there can't be peace in the world. I'll keep working toward that, and I hope you all will too."[92]

From the Virtual Hajj to Masjid al Masa to Al Andalus, we can identify myriad ways *Second Life* can be used for education, religious practice, and cultural reform. The creators of all three sites hope that they can promote interreligious dialogue, and all three report successes in this area. While conflicts remain and religious griefing continues, these are dwarfed by the ways people have grown in their ability to communicate with and appreciate one another. The faithful practice and development of Islam in virtual worlds may prove invaluable in our conventional world, as King and Fouts hope: a continued shift toward virtual life might help produce new policy initiatives, acceptance of others by communities and individuals, and spiritual experience that—while still contingent upon physical practices—might keep helping people develop lives of sanctity. All of these efforts produce Islamic and ecumenical communities stabilized by conventional resources, such as historical memorialization and connection to traditional practices, and uniquely virtual resources, such as entry into impossible locales, flying carpets, land covenants, and even interreligious architecture.

Popular Religion and Web 2.0

As the number of online gamers and virtual world participants grows, their virtual activity will become instrumental in the ongoing process of reshaping conventional religious practice into distributed models of authority and hierarchy. Many conventional religions currently rely on elitist authority structures in which certain individuals possess vast powers to shape and control belief, practice, and doctrine. In contrast, nearly all religious groups in *Second Life* allow congregants considerable say in policies and planning. Obviously, popular movements influence even the most rigidly hierarchical religions, but in *Second Life* laypeople have greater authority as a necessary consequence of their own status as founders and creators. Broader distributions of authority in virtual worlds will likely result in greater lay power in conventional religious life as well, when believers grow accustomed to having their voices heard online, and weary of top-down control over official religious life.

Virtual worlds will not dismantle authoritarian hierarchy altogether, as this would be unwise in addition to impossible; they will, however, promote the growth of popular religion. Popular religion is the religion of the people, the one that emerges from the faith and practices of the laity rather than out of doctrinal pronouncement from an authorized hierarchy. While popular religion need not oppose traditional hierarchy, it must always offer a sense of active co-production of religious life. Rather than simply accept doctrines, practices, and institutions from their leaders, lay members in a popular faith will help to shape those essential aspects of their communities.

The clearest example of popular religion in Western religious history is the emergence of liberation theology among Catholics in Central and South America. Based in the fundamental belief that the Church must exercise a "preferential option for the poor," liberation theologians such as Gustavo Gutiérrez, Leonardo Boff, Virgilio Elizondo, and Orlando Espín urge Catholics to seek a progressive future of equality. For many liberation theologians, this future will result in a new humanity, one of equality for people throughout the world and for all ethnic and racial communities.[93] Such a new humanity will emerge, according to liberation theologians, from a religion of the people, one that borrows from the strength of the community.[94]

There have been popular religious movements online since the explosion of the Internet in the 1990s. Such movements challenge traditional structures of authority and also provide new strategic ways of practicing a religion. Christopher Helland has documented early attempts at popular religion on the Internet and argues that the Internet provides meaningful opportunities for those who are "outside" the church.[95] This is true in *Second Life* as well. For example, Koinonia and Aslan's How reflect ways individuals can create online religious structures that encourage and sustain new ways for Christians to "do church" in a virtual world.

Vacano's mosque, Masjid al Masa, is a stunning example of how *Second Life* offers the people a new way to construct their faith. Vacano, a Christian, built the mosque as an expression of architectural interest but also ecumenical hope. Muslims attended the mosque for prayer and peace, often in full knowledge that it not sanctioned by any imam or Islamic community and, in fact, not even entirely of Islamic provenance. There is clear overlap between such hope and political peacemaking, like the belief that in *Second Life* Muslim and non-Muslim communities can overcome the tribalism that regularly poisons cultural life.

The opportunities posed by *Second Life* and similar virtual platforms challenge the authority of traditional church hierarchies. Virtual worlds allow individuals to take advantage of such a wide array of resources—most importantly the people's own creative theological energies—that they cannot be immediately and automatically constrained by traditional powers. Indeed, virtual world religion may force the reconfiguration of traditional religious life. Among survey respondents, nearly 24% believe that the practice of earthly religions in *Second Life*, including leadership hierarchies and prayer strategies, should affect how those religions are practiced in conventional life, and another 37% believe that they should maybe do so.[96] The religion of the virtual people, then, may well affect the religion of all people.

The explosion of religious creativity in virtual worlds will not remain there. While Londy, like some other residents, says that he keeps his church attendance separate from *Second Life*,[97] for many people the overlap is growing closer to juxtaposition. If they so chose, members of Koinonia could find church exclusively there rather than in conventional reality. Church leaders, far from playing the ostrich, are aware of the shift toward online presence and have made virtual worlds one of the key areas for strategic planning in the early twentieth century (e.g., World Council of Churches 2006). In particular, as online residents attend both virtual and conventional churches, the transmission of ideas and practices will continue to shape both.

The merger of the "real" world and the "virtual" world is increasingly a feature of modern life. Users of virtual worlds "have begun to see no line whatsoever between their online activities and their offline activities. This is not necessarily because they are immersed completely in the synthetic space, although this may often be true. Rather, it is because the distinction between the putatively virtual and the putatively real is a nuisance to them. Tellingly, they and their colleagues try to live without it, and this more than anything is what makes the membrane porous."[98] Because residents and users of virtual worlds see the two worlds as penetrating one another, a feedback loop exists between them.

Developments in online technologies have encouraged the feedback between online and offline life. The popular Web 2.0 designation marks those Internet applications that encourage users to contribute to the online content marketed to them. Internet users quickly embraced websites that allow them to comment on news or products, to produce their own blogs, and, as with *Second Life*, to actively produce a world that they and other users will pay for the privilege of using. People enjoy being part of the economic and cultural system with which they engage, so in the

Web 2.0 paradigm they produce what they consume and consume what they produce, becoming what Alvin Toffler calls *prosumers*.[99] This dynamic necessarily affects what is produced and how.

The production of theology, which is an ongoing enterprise no matter how hidebound any one tradition might be, falls into the realm of Web 2.0's influence. Thus far, online religions do not appear to be replacing traditional communities,[100] but the rapid expansion of religious sites on the Internet in the 1990s and 2000s and *Second Life* in the 2000s shows how eager many religious practitioners are to have a say in their traditions' beliefs and practices. It may well be that hierarchies will deliberately reject and resist the influence of popular faith on formal religious doctrine,[101] and there may be cases in which the Internet and, as an extension, virtual worlds provide less substantial bypass opportunities than one might imagine.[102] Nevertheless, a religious community simply cannot ignore the reality of individuals in virtual temples doing virtual work. Many residents of *Second Life* (more than 40%, according to my survey) regularly visit religious places online, and the interface between *Second Life* and the conventional world allows those places to affect everyday reality.

Virtual worlds already automatically reconfigure authority, a facet of their nature that can be and is already being applied to religious practice. T. L. Taylor notes the inversion of traditional hierarchies in video games such as *EverQuest*, where young players are often influential well beyond their years: they possess power, wealth, and knowledge that older players, such as their parents who game with them, lack.[103] Likewise, lay practitioners, who might be considered inexperienced or incapable in a conventional structure of religious authority, can acquire power and prestige in the virtual world. They can build churches, temples, and pagan woodlands. They can offer theologies or design new practices. And their visitors, who can swiftly find them thanks to the search features, can adopt these places, practices, and beliefs as their own.

The fact is, *Second Life* religious places—whether these are mainstream or not—provide opportunities for religious practitioners.[104] The economics of religious practice among our "generation of seekers"[105] is a new phenomenon in modern life and one that virtual worlds enhance. Virtual world residency enables new ways of accessing the spiritual marketplace, and the competition thus established will force conventional churches into engagement with their virtual counterparts. Charles Henderson, the founder of the "First Church of Cyberspace" in 1994, now emphasizes the importance of virtual world religious practice and the power of popular faith there.[106] Many people have abandoned their conventional churches, and among these many have found new ways of holding to and practicing their faith. As true as this was in the twentieth century, it will be at least as true in the twenty-first.

John W. Morehead, director of the Western Institute for Intercultural Studies, a Christian think tank and educational resource, believes that there is promise alongside the peril for religious authorities. The fun that video gamers have online could be harnessed by religious groups. The church could become, in his words, a "space for godly play."[107] Morehead advocates a *"fun* reformation,"[108] which would herald a new day for Christian life. The integration of virtual life and conventional religion may have wide-ranging social outcomes, including, hopes one commentator, ecumenical opportunities.[109] As we have seen, many residents of *Second Life* seek just that as they build their religious communities.

Like the Internet in general, *Second Life* can be both utopian and dystopian. Certainly there is a great deal of trash on the Internet, and that includes religious trash: juvenile or aesthetically poor sites, ill-thought-out ideas, intolerance, hate, and more. Despite these evils, there is good online as well. Residents of *Second Life* see opportunity online, a chance to create new kinds of community. The presence of atheists among the Catholic study group at Campivallensis illustrates how *Second Life* can enable new (and seemingly good) ways of practicing religion. What conventional Christian church regularly accommodates and encourages atheists in its Bible study? A Catholic priest who did so would be a rare commodity indeed. Yet in Campivallensis the presence of an atheist who follows ordinary rules of etiquette is neither unusual nor unwelcome.[110]

The production of new religious experiences, institutions, and movements in *Second Life* presents both challenges and opportunities for traditional religious groups. Virtual worlds already work on our conventional modes of life, as witnessed by the research of Richard Gilbert and Nora Murphy. They surveyed *Second Life* residents and found that their participants are more satisfied with the romantic relationships they form there than they are with the ones they form in conventional reality and even that levels of sexual satisfaction with virtual partners are approximately the same as those associated with conventional partners.[111] While it remains to be seen whether long-term relationships in *Second Life* can provide the satisfaction of conventional relationships (and, indeed, this is unlikely), the mere fact that many residents take such great satisfaction in their online romances indicates that there may be twists and turns to negotiate in the future of human partnership. It might, then, be appropriate to draw a parallel between *Second Life* romances and *Second Life* religions. Just as a preference—even if only fleeting—for a *Second Life* partner could challenge or radically alter a conventional romantic partnership, a preference for a *Second Life* religious identity may send shockwaves through our conventional religious institutions.

Conclusion

In *Second Life*, residents experience sacred forces once confined to Earth. Even when the earth itself is sacred, as in Wren Lilliehook's belief (discussed in Chapter 4), its sacred aura can be felt in the virtual world. For many, such as Knight, the gathering of a community of the devout can heal the wounded and open a space for divine love. *Second Life* provides new ways of experiencing unfamiliar or distant religious practices, thus helping to reshape the nature of community and conflict. Many Muslims thus hope that we might culturally overcome our aversion to Islam by experiencing it online.

Second Life residents are establishing new kinds of religious communities and are, without question, making them real. A wide array of strategies gives *Second Life* groups staying power and each its own sense of collective identity. None of the religious groups in *Second Life* is guaranteed a future; groups suffer from a form of collective entropy, a tendency to dissolve. But the individuals in *Second Life* seek ways of producing centripetal force that draws the group together. They do this by establishing official *Second Life* groups, connecting to conventional religious groups, drawing on the emotional appeal of fantasy, producing art and avatars, replicating physical or imagined landscapes, and connecting to sites on the World Wide Web, including social networking sites. All of these techniques solidify the groups. Nothing can assure a group of permanence, but by combining these various ways of stabilizing their religious groups in virtual and conventional objects each stands a chance to persist into the future and thereby to affect how religion is practiced both within and without *Second Life*.

We should not presume that virtual religious practice is, by its very nature, morally progressive; the practice of religion in *Second Life* may not be the "salvation" of religion. As technology progresses, new forms of religious malcontent or bigotry will probably emerge alongside new ways of expressing the highest and best values of humankind. Nevertheless, the power of *Second Life* as an arena for religious life does open new avenues for practice, and we can hope that such developments will prove socially and morally progressive. *Second Life* residents seem inclined to accept Linden Lab's position that *Second Life* can change the world.

As members of religious faiths continue to take advantage of the power they acquire in *Second Life* and in other virtual worlds—power to build, to shape, to script—they will actively write the future of religious practice. *Second Life* and its successors could become subject to the rules and regulations of conventional authorities, but it seems unlikely that the virtual residents will allow such control to become absolute. Instead, they will take advantage of the opportunity to create a new world, one that embodies the ideals they wish to inscribe upon it. In doing so, they will deploy resources both conventional and virtual, shaping our world through the integration of both. At present, *Second Life* residents believe they can make the world better this way; whether that goal will remain in future social worlds remains an open question but seems likely given the optimism with which people often approach technology.

The religious use of *Second Life* is one aspect of its role in virtual religion. As I noted in Chapter 4, *Second Life* is an environment where many things are possible and consumerism is, if not king, at least highly visible. Alongside fashion, consumerism, and eroticism, however, there are serious undertakings in *Second Life*: art, philosophy, and definitely religion. For many religious practitioners, *Second Life* is a powerful new tool, and they are happy to put it to use, whether to advance ecumenism, establish new kinds of theologies, or provide sacred spaces to those who lack access. Alongside this explicitly religious activity, *Second Life* also mirrors *World of Warcraft* in that it can provide opportunities for authentic fakery. This is the subject of the next chapter.

6

Sacred Second Lives

Transhumanist Engineering

Even as the importation of traditional religion to *Second Life* or other virtual environments provides new opportunities for expression within particular religious groups, the development of virtual worlds might also allow the faithful a way out, a path to some radically new religious identity. *Second Life* was built, in part, as a quasi-religious project, and many of its residents continue to use it for religious purposes. Specifically, *Second Life* now serves as both inspiration and base of operations for many of those who wish to transcend mortal lifetimes by uploading their minds into virtual worlds. Thanks to the efforts of Linden Lab designers and *Second Life* residents, the online world contributes to a century-long experiment in transhumanist thought and practice.

The search for transcendence in virtual worlds emerged out of science fiction (SF) stories that glorify life in cyberspace and popular science books that explain how we might take up permanent residence there. William Gibson and Neal Stephenson are the two most important SF authors to take up the subject of virtual reality, and it is their work that has inspired both virtual world designers and residents.[1] Although neither Gibson nor Stephenson advocates transhuman immortality through mind uploading, both depict a world where computer technology enables fully immersive virtual worlds that function like a three-dimensional Internet.[2] In those virtual worlds, hackers and, to a lesser extent, ordinary people use brain-machine interfaces that allow them to consciously experience themselves within cyberspace, leaving the physical world behind.[3] By describing transcendent experiences in cyberspace, Gibson, Stephenson, and other authors encouraged readers to make them possible in reality.

Nearly to a man (there were very few women authors in the movement), cyberpunk authors have distinguished cyberspace and time online as a separate place and time, distinct from the profane existence of ordinary life. While this isn't truly the case for most virtual world residents today, the rhetoric of separation is important and remains present in cyberspace. Just, however, as there are frames of reference for *World of Warcraft* players, there are frames of reference for *Second Life* residents. Sometimes these are held to be distinct, as in the case of deep immersionists, but more often they overlap and interpenetrate. Thus, while reality is mixed and messy, the psychological framing of online and offline selves perpetuates the rhetoric of separation.

In the seminal stories of Gibson and Stephenson, hackers revel in their transcendence over physical reality, their escape to a pristine and magical world unconstrained by the difficulties and disappointments of conventional life. In cyberpunk, life online becomes sacred, physical reality a prison. As though ancient Gnostic dualism has been reborn, the cyberspace hacker lives "for the bodiless exultation of cyberspace" and, when denied access to his online life, falls into "the prison of his own flesh."[4] Stephenson illustrates this distinction beautifully. In *Snow Crash*, the comically named Hiro Protagonist sleeps in a rented storage facility; but in the Metaverse he owns a mansion, is stylish, famous, and is a formidable member of the programming elite. "When you live in a shithole, there's always the Metaverse, and in the Metaverse, Hiro Protagonist is a warrior prince."[5] The contrast between liberated and empowered online avatar and mind imprisoned by the meat of his body reveals the values inscribed upon life in the division between virtual and physical. The conventional religious groups discussed in Chapter 5 have not adopted this online–offline distinction as clearly as the SF authors provide it, but many of the transhumanists of this chapter tend rather strongly to do so. For them, virtual reality promises the end of alienation and a new life to come.

Though it was Gibson's work that concretized the virtual reality community,[6] it was Stephenson who envisioned cyberspace as a gloriously transcendent realm for all people to inhabit. His *Snow Crash* provided an enormous impetus toward the production of lifelike virtual worlds and has been of unequalled import for those producing "social" virtual worlds.[7] Philip Rosedale received *Snow Crash* as a birthday gift from his girlfriend in 1992, and it inspired him to incorporate Linden Lab and launch *Second Life* early in the twenty-first century.[8] Linden Lab's employees cited the book more than any other as a reference point for understanding their online world.[9] Likewise, Richard Childers, cofounder of another social world called *Blue Mars*, traces his own interest in virtual worlds to Stephenson's work. In reading *Snow Crash*, Childers knew that "Stephenson had written far more than a good science fiction book. He had prophesied a future that was bound to come to pass.... And in that moment, I was sure that I was going to be a part of that future."[10] Designers alone do not produce a world, however, and many *Second Life* residents, for example, share their desire to make Stephenson's Metaverse a reality.[11]

Chapters 2 and 3 argued that online gaming has taken on a religious identity of its own, providing meaningful communities, morality, purpose, and many kinds of transcendence for *World of Warcraft* players. But while *World of Warcraft* players and designers cooperate in making Azeroth a site for religious work, it is highly unlikely that the game was initially conceived to bring that about. *Second Life*, on the other hand, was developed with a religious vision, and many residents have happily embraced that vision both implicitly and explicitly. Just as *World of Warcraft* can be "holy shit," as David Chidester defines it,[12] so, too, can *Second Life* by providing authentically religious products in a secular package. Rosedale aligned it with the hope that we can overcome human limitations and mortality through technology; subsequent transhumanists have cheerfully worked toward that vision, making *Second Life* their home and helping to spread the religion in-world.

Establishing a Cosmic Office

Transhumanism emerged in the twentieth century thanks to faith in scientific and technological progress, especially as these were advocated in popular science and science fiction. Transhumanism, as defined earlier, is a philosophical or religious system in which human beings use science and technology to acquire goods traditionally expected from religion, such as freedom from disease, aging, and death. Understanding the rise of transhumanism in the twentieth and twenty-first centuries requires some attention to history, especially to the thought and work of J. B. S. Haldane and Julian Huxley. They initiated two key thought streams in transhumanism: one rejects religion explicitly while the other accepts that transhumanism is fundamentally religious. Although most contemporary transhumanists follow Haldane's model, Huxley's is the clearer vision and expanded its "market share" in the early twenty-first century.

Haldane is commonly known as the father of transhumanism, thanks to his prescient expectation that biological progress would lead to in vitro fertilization, artificial wombs, neuropharmacology, and germline engineering (i.e., the alteration of DNA to permit changes in human physiology that can be passed on through reproduction).[13] Huxley, his contemporary and friend, subsequently coined the term *transhumanism* in his book *New Bottles for New Wine* (1957), where he argued that humankind has been appointed to a "cosmic office"[14] and:

> can, if it wishes, transcend itself—not just sporadically, an individual here in one way, an individual there in another way, but in its entirety, as humanity. We need a name for this new belief. Perhaps transhumanism will serve: man remaining man, but transcending himself, by realizing new possibilities of and for his human nature.
>
> "I believe in transhumanism": once there are enough people who can truly say that, the human species will be on the threshold of a new kind of existence, as different from ours as ours is from that of Pekin [*sic*] man. It will at last be consciously fulfilling its real destiny.[15]

For Huxley, the development of transhumanism—and its situation within the history of religions—was a matter of enormous cultural import. Huxley argues that "idea-systems . . . play the same sort of role in cultural evolution as do skeletons in biological evolution: they provide the framework for the life that animates and clothes them, and in large measure determine the way it shall be lived."[16] Thus, to dismiss religion entirely, as many later transhumanists were wont to do, could not be justified by Huxley. Instead, he sought to establish a scientific religion, and this is what many progressive transhumanists of the twenty-first century now emulate. "What the world needs," writes Huxley, "is an essentially religious idea-system, unitary . . . charged with the total dynamic of knowledge old and new, objective and subjective, of experience scientific and spiritual."[17]

In the middle of the twentieth century, influential science fiction authors explored transhumanist themes, while explicitly transhumanist pop science authors sought to bring cultural credibility to the movement motivated thereby. Arthur C. Clarke's novels were among the most powerful inspirations for transhumanism, as they engage cosmic evolution[18] and mind uploading,[19] two of the most common concerns in modern transhumanist communities. At the same time, Robert Heinlein influenced a generation of future transhumanists with his description of life extension technologies in his books about Lazarus Long.[20] Pop science writing accompanied science fiction heraldry, producing a two-pronged strategy for transhumanist evangelism.[21] In particular, the nascent movement benefited from advocacy by Robert Ettinger—who founded the Cryonics Institute and wrote two key books, *The Prospect of Immortality* (1964) and *Man into Superman* (1972)—and Feridouin Esfandiary, author of *Optimism One* ([1970] 1978) and *Up-Wingers* ([1973] 1977), in addition to other books. Esfandiary later changed his legal name to FM-2030, reflecting his expectation for when the transhuman future would arrive, and influenced a circle of transhumanist thinkers over several decades of writing.

In the late 1980s, transhumanism reached another creative high point, benefiting from the cyberpunk explosion in pop culture. For example, Max More published the Principles of Extropy[22] and his associate FM-2030 published *Are You a Transhuman?*, a kind of self-help book for gauging and improving one's transhumanity.[23] While More, FM-2030, and others collected scientific papers and promoted human enhancement in Southern California, a well-regarded roboticist, Hans Moravec, published *Mind Children*,[24] a book that would be a watershed in the history of transhumanism. Moravec, deeply influenced by science fiction authors,[25] was the first to use a history of technological progress to extrapolate a date for human transcendence. Considering Moore's Law of progress in computation and the development of robotic vision and navigation, Moravec predicted the development of superhuman computers and the uploading of human minds into them in the science fiction magazine, *Analog*.[26] In the late 1980s, he developed and reinforced his ideas in the book *Mind Children*, an expansive work of futurism that charted progress in computation and robotics to argue that by 2030 there would be vastly intelligent machines and that shortly afterward we would upload our minds into them and join their cosmic crusade.[27]

To support his striking claim, Moravec argues that we will use brain-scanning technologies to copy our minds—the neurological patterns in our brains—into computers so that our personalities can live on forever.[28] In addition, once computers have sufficiently massive computational abilities, they will extrapolate from known data to reconstruct the personalities of dead individuals, thereby "resurrecting" them.[29] As a research professor at the famed Carnegie Mellon University Robotics Institute, Moravec's ideas could not be dismissed as idle fantasy or the conjurations of a technocrank. Rather, they had immediate cultural cachet (as illustrated by his book publisher, Harvard University Press), and they were especially welcome among transhumanists. Many advocates now hope that as we develop more powerful technologies we will accomplish traditionally religious goals of living forever and resurrecting the dead just as Moravec promised.[30]

Popular science authors clearly work toward the conversion of their readers, but science fiction has been more effective in disseminating transhumanism. Science-fiction authors routinely describe transcendent worlds where human beings escape the planet, their bodies, and their politics, painting an alluring picture for ideological commitment. For transhumanists, science fiction has provided a zone for evangelical work, especially in the middle of the twentieth century and, more recently, again in the early twenty-first.[31] Pop science authors like Moravec, in fact, generally credit science fiction as their inspiration.

Although he later pushed back his timeline by around a decade, Moravec's ideas caught on among transhumanists. Vernor Vinge borrowed John von Neumann's concept of a *Singularity*[32] when technology would progress so rapidly that unimaginable things would happen in a shockingly short time, and he reinvigorated it based on Moravec's work.[33] Another influential figure, artificial intelligence (AI) theorist Ray Kurzweil, merged Moravec's predictions and Vinge's catchy term and has since become the poster child for radical transhumanism. Publishing *The Age of Spiritual Machines* (1999) and *The Singularity Is Near* (2005) among other books, appearing in a wide array of magazines and newspapers, launching the for-profit school Singularity University, joining Google as director of engineering in 2012, and even starring in two biographical documentaries, Kurzweil is the runaway most influential figure in early twenty-first-century transhumanism. Kurzweil's success, and the success of his university and other efforts, demonstrates that transhumanism has grown culturally powerful.[34]

Faith in the AI apocalypse has contributed utopian beliefs to the world of virtual worlds. In his widely read piece "Nerd Theology," Kevin Kelly, the founding editor of *Wired* magazine, argues that the creators of computer generated worlds are in the process of establishing their own religion with themselves as its gods.[35] Producers of such worlds occasionally agree with this assessment,[36] but many users go further, claiming that the residents of the virtual worlds also achieve a sanctified status in online worlds. For example, Richard Bartle points out that a game company's T-shirt asserting, "Why yes, I am god," significantly outsold a rival's T-shirt

claiming, "You're in our world now!" The considerable appeal for the former represents the way players of that company's virtual world (*Castle
Marrach*) saw the game: as the apotheosis of the player.[37] The U.S. counterculture, in particular, adopted digital technologies as a way to deliver
the promises of Christianity, drug culture, and New Age religiosity[38] and
spread their interpretation of those technologies through "digirati" culture: the Whole Earth Network, *Wired* magazine, and affiliated organizations.[39] More recently, transhumanists have seen online communication
as trending toward Moravec's ideas.[40]

Despite the clearly religious elements of transhumanism, such as
visions of immortality and resurrection of the dead, many transhumanists
denigrate religion and consider their own movement to be of a very different nature. This opposition is long-standing and is visible in the work
of FM-2030, who considered religion to be wish fulfillment that could be
outgrown.[41] Similarly, More's Principles of Extropy include references to
the use of "scientific understanding," "reason over blind faith and ques-
tioning over dogma," and the value of the principles for those who "cannot
comfortably adopt traditional value systems."[42] Extropy means "understanding, experimenting, learning, challenging, and innovating rather
than clinging to beliefs."[43] The use of words like *understanding* and *experimenting* clearly set Extropy in scientific contrast to More's conception of
religion, and many transhumanists applaud the opposition.[44]

Although the largest transhumanist body in the world, Humanity+ (for-
merly the World Transhumanist Association), has been grounded in the
Haldane (i.e., antireligious) school of transhumanism, it is moving toward
greater acceptance of religious transhumanism. The group's flagship publication, *H+ Magazine*, for example, has increasingly published essays with
a religious bent. R. U. Sirius (né Ken Goffman), the founder of *Mondo 2000*
in the 1990s and editor-in-chief of *H+ Magazine*, cheerfully syncretizes the
"magick" of Aleister Crowley, the LSD spirituality of Timothy Leary, and
cybernetic futurism to describe his own digital religion in the magazine
and has published other pieces on religious transhumanism. Advocating
"digital polytheism," Sirius presses for basic transhumanist desiderata
as religious, thus demonstrating the newfound acceptability of religion
among many in the community.[45] An interview with Giulio Prisco by Ben
Goertzel, then chair of the Humanity+ board of directors, likewise reflects
this changed direction for the magazine. Goertzel focuses the interview
around the spiritual dimensions of Prisco's thought, including his claim
that "transhumanism is a religion and it always has been one."[46]

Many *Second Life* transhumanists, like Prisco and Extropia DaSilva, seem increasingly comfortable with the label of religion. DaSilva, for example, recently focused on what she calls a "religious apocalyptic thinking converging with cutting-edge science and technology"[47] and argues to transhumanists that transhumanism is religious.[48] Prisco, likewise, believes in a religion informed by science, where postulates can be discarded as soon as they no longer correspond to empirical possibility. He recognizes that religion appears to be an innate aspect of human consciousness and that, moreover, it is an effective means by which to distribute ideas and practices.[49] As a consequence, he is comfortable with the possibility of creating a religion of transhumanism that will help advance human progress. He hopes to present transhumanist ideas as "a strong duty of our species, packaging them with some of the rituals whose appeal is demonstrated by the history of religions, and delivering them with some messianic fervor."[50] In launching the Turing Church,[51] a short-lived, quasi-think tank for religious transhumanism, he asserts that radical transhumanism "IS indistinguishable from religion. I like it, because it can give people the same hope and sense of meaning that religion provides."[52]

At the beginning of the second decade of the twenty-first century, transhumanists have many groups, a few influential leaders, and a host of promising technologies to publically support. Whether any of the fledgling transhumanist groups will gain sufficient adherents to sustain themselves in the coming years or whether transhumanists must undergo yet another series of institutional setbacks depends on the ability of the constituents to come together with a common direction. Further complicating matters, many of the technologies that transhumanists press for, such as embryonic stem cell research, are socially divisive. Nevertheless, transhumanists hope that progress will continue and that estimates for the onset of a new world remain plausible. From outside of the transhumanist fold, Rosedale has taken an important step in the fulfillment of transhuman salvation: he has given the faithful a heavenly realm to inhabit.

A Virtual Prophet

Rosedale is a technical genius and successful entrepreneur, and his transhumanist inclinations made important contributions to the vision behind *Second Life*. He began tinkering with computers and electronics at an early age and launched his first company, which installed computer systems for businesses, at the age of seventeen.[53] *Second Life* is an outgrowth of his interest in using computers not only as a tool but also as an environment for making things. "I just like making things," he says. "But I always thought the best place to invent would be inside the computer, if we could just get in there."[54] After a few years helping turn RealNetworks into a dot-com superstar, Rosedale was ready to make that happen by founding Linden Lab.

Stephenson's *Snow Crash* gave Rosedale a vision to pursue. He wanted to build, and he wanted a world with tools that allowed him to make "shapes, and surfaces and stuff...and they'd show up near you and you'd stretch them and shape them and everything."[55] Stephenson's three-dimensional Metaverse looked like just the place to permit Rosedale to enter the world of machines and create.[56] Eventually, this could even be the place for human apotheosis, our elevation to the status of divine creators.

Rosedale, though familiar with contemporary transhumanist ideas, is not an avid reader of Kurzweil or other futurists;[57] despite this, building *Second Life* made a considerable impression on him and his coworkers. He told me that "the experience of creating *Second Life* had at least a lot of us convinced that it was inevitable that similar approaches would allow us to simulate the brain (or something like it) and therefore got us excited about the general area" of futurism and mind uploading.[58] Rather than personally finding a way to upload minds, Rosedale is professionally interested in producing intelligent computers and virtual environments, but the connection between virtual worlds and the promises of apocalyptic futurism is clear to him and those who live and work in *Second Life*.[59]

For Rosedale, a lifelong—and perfectly normal—fear of death has been filtered through traditional religious ideas into a vision of technological transcendence. "I've been obsessed with the idea that we're mortal," he says, "and to be stuck in a skeleton...it's not a good outcome, not a good situation."[60] In keeping with a stint as born-again Baptist,[61] Rosedale has had a lifelong ambition to solve the problem of mortality. When he rejected traditional religion, he was left with a desire to change the world, which he suspects underlay his eventual work on *Second Life*.[62]

In an email exchange with me, Rosedale acknowledged what ought to be obvious to Kurzweil (but sometimes seems not to be): "regardless of what we build with technology, it seems hard to imagine that each of our living physical bodies will not die at some point—at least those of us alive today. Having a digital copy of some kind probably won't be too comforting to the physical person facing death!"[63] Nevertheless, from his work and his conversations with journalists, it is apparent that his twin desires to overcome death and transform the world benefited from the transhumanist theories that coalesced in pop science and science fiction at the close of the 1980s and came to be the ideology of Silicon Valley in the 1990s and early 2000s. Implicit in his recognition of our inescapable mortality is his inclination to believe that we might someday simulate personalities in virtual reality; whether this will adequately console us is irrelevant to whether it represents a nod in the direction of Moravec's promises of resurrection and immortality.

Without question, Rosedale is aware of contemporary transhumanist mind-uploading theorists and offers *Second Life* as a possible environment for such salvation. In conversation with Wagner James Au, the well-known virtual worlds observer, he referenced mind uploading,[64] and while demurring on whether or not it would be possible he also suggested that "all we have to do now is figure out how to escape death."[65] One obvious possibility for this would be taking up permanent residence in *Second Life*. Given that he believes "the leading edge of human evolution is culture and mind, and the trailing edge...our bodies,"[66] Rosedale might be inclined to do as Moravec and Kurzweil suggest. He suspects that "his grandchildren will perceive the real world as a kind of 'museum or theater,' with realms like *Second Life* the locus for work and much of our personal relationships."[67] If this is so, then a permanent migration might be desirable. Says Rosedale, "I'd love to live forever. I love it here, and in *Second Life* too. Absolutely. I think the idea that people are only supposed to live for a hundred years is really dumb."[68] While Rosedale expressed a modicum of uncertainty to Au, Tim Guest reports that Rosedale told him "there's a reasonable argument that we'll be able to" leave our bodies behind by uploading into virtual reality.[69]

Neither Rosedale nor Linden Lab openly courts transhumanist groups, but with just a little nudge in the right direction we can see Linden Lab's activities as participating in a transhumanist worldview. The company's official mission statement was, at one point, "to connect us all to an online world that advances the human condition." Certainly this could mean many things, but, given Rosedale's acknowledged interest in circumventing death and his awareness of the transhuman implications of virtual worlds, it seems to align Linden Lab and its virtual world with transhumanist interests. In *Second Life: The Official Guide*, Michael Rymaszewski writes that *Second Life* "works as if you were a god in real life...you're able to 'cast spells' too. And just like a mythological god, you're able to fly, and teleport wherever you like in an instant."[70] In this, Linden Lab offers its imprimatur on *Second Life's* transhumanist aura. The juxtaposition between transhumanist work and technological business is more than just discursive, however. For example, Ray Kurzweil, the leading champion of Hans Moravec's ideas, includes Rosedale and *Second Life* in his biographical documentary *Transcendent Man* (2010) and also gave the keynote presentation at Linden Lab's *Second Life* Community Convention in 2009.[71]

Staff members at Linden Lab shared Kurzweil's interest in apocalyptic futurism, including both mind uploading and artificial intelligence. Although Rosedale has said there were not "really any material discussions" about mind uploading at Linden Lab,[72] both his and his colleagues' previous comments demonstrate that there were at least loose conversations on the topic. John Lester, known as "Pathfinder Linden" when he was a member of the staff from 2005 to 2010, recalls Linden Lab employees thinking of the future as "the Matrix without the evil machines"[73] and told me that conversations about transhumanism were common among Linden Lab's "old guard."

> They really did think about things like transhumanism and everyone had read Kurzweil and really thought about how this technology was something that wasn't just going to improve the way human beings did things in one particular fashion, but how it was going to change how people did things, how it would change lives.... There were lots of conversations about transhumanism and...where this would go.[74]

Among the diversity of responses to Kurzweil and transhumanism, many Linden Lab employees—including Lester—engaged in "constructive criticism" of transhumanism. Lester himself refuses the label of transhumanist but considers himself an augmentationist; he is more interested in extending human minds rather than uploading them.[75] Overall, however, the ongoing engagement with transhumanism reveals the enthusiasm of Linden Lab's employees.

Au was an embedded journalist at Linden Lab during the early years and reports that employees would regularly chat about transhumanist promises made by Kurzweil and others. In an email to me, he writes:

When I was at Linden Lab, 2003–2006, the topic of uploading our consciousness into *Second Life* definitely came up on occasion, especially when we were hanging out at a bar getting drunk. Staffers were definitely aware of the concept as Kurzweil describes it, but then, any technologist is going to be familiar with his basic concepts. The idea of using *Second Life* as a conscious neural network was also discussed in great detail, especially in the early days.... I think it's also true that Kurzweil and his supporters and transhumanists in general pushed the idea more avidly than anyone at Linden Lab ever did. As *Second Life*'s hype wave started, I distinctly remember transhumanists starting to approach me, people who worked with Kurzweil, Peter Thiel, folks on that level. But for Lindens, the day-to-day difficulties of even keeping *Second Life* running with just a few hundred thousand users must have made that kind of talk seem pretty implausible. When the whole *Second Life* grid was still regularly crashing due to gray goo attacks and self-replicating 6-foot penises, the idea of uploading grandma's consciousness there must have seemed pretty crazy. Still does.[76]

While Linden Lab's technical difficulties may have damped transhumanist furor among the employees, there is no question about whether they saw a connection between their work and the futuristic promises of transhumanists. A mission statement committed to advancing the human condition plays naturally into this kind of thinking. As a consequence, transhumanists like Kurzweil eagerly moved to adopt *Second Life* into their agenda.

If *Second Life* grows as Rosedale hopes, it will "go beyond the real world" and enable a "kind of religion," though without the traditional gods.[77] Just as *Second Life* is a physical instantiation of Rosedale's religious goals, so too is Linden Lab. The company's corporate practices institute a noticeable religiosity, as documented by journalist Tim Guest. Guest notes that there were considerable similarities between the community of his mother's New Age guru and Rosedale's employees: individuals in both groups trying to make a better world, taking on new names, and possessing special pendants.[78] The first Linden Lab headquarters even had a "shrine to their ideals: a temple, with an inner sanctum of a slowly turning logo."[79] When G mentioned this to Rosedale, the latter laughed and told him that before settling on the name *Second Life* Linden Lab considered using a Hindu name. Rosedale then told him a story from when Rosedale had met James

Currier, who invested in Linden Lab: "when he met me—this was in 2003, when we had five hundred people inside Second Life—he said, 'You know what? You know what you have to decide?' I said, 'What's that, James?' and he said, 'What color are the robes going to be?' That was always his thing. That was what he said when he first saw it. He said, 'This is a religion.' "[80] Rosedale, himself, liked to joke that Second Life is "like the good cult."[81]

To reveal that a transhumanist mythos courses through Second Life design is not to criticize the world or Rosedale or Linden Lab employees; it is neither a good nor a bad thing that transhumanist thinking permeates Second Life's design. This is merely a facet of design processes that can also be observed in other forms of "world creation," such as traditional role-playing games. In such games, where the purpose of the game is for the Game Master and the players to produce a story, the "personality of the designer is also present."[82] The designer is the "silent participant...who is present to the extent that the rules reflect his or her view of the world and how it works."[83] Likewise, Rosedale has managed to objectify a little part of himself in Second Life, which subsequently puts gentle pressure on the residents. As the next section shows, this pressure—whether Rosedale and his colleagues worked toward it deliberately or not—does exert force on the residents, who contribute to the transhumanist mission that helped bring the world into being.

As with role-playing games, the designers of virtual worlds are ever-present—the constraints and possibilities both emerge out of the designers' aspirations for the game. As such, a transhumanist game designer can code transhumanism, either brashly or subtly, into games.[84] A game is a combination of its rules, play, and culture,[85] any or all of which could be zones for inculcating a transhumanist mindset. Although not precisely a game, Second Life design emerges out of these same concepts and promotes transhumanism in all three.

Daily living in Second Life, despite its present limitations and the occasional technical glitches, already feels superhuman. Avatar, the very term for one's Second Life body, refers to the divine. Just as Hindu gods have avatars—mortal bodies to carry out their plans—Second Life users produce avatars to explore the world and accomplish their goals.[86] It might be said that this reflects a difference between Hindu avatars (gods in mortal form) and cyberspace avatars (mortals made divine). However, we should note that Hindu gods take on avatars precisely so that they can accomplish what they could not have as gods, such as when Vishnu becomes Rama to defeat Ravana, a rakshasa whom no god could kill. Likewise, making avatars allows *Second Life* residents to become more than they were, as they shape their avatars and personalities to their desires. Such "instability was a source of pleasure for many residents"[87] because residents seek to overcome their own weaknesses by refashioning themselves to look and act how they want. This is particularly true for individuals with physical handicaps but also matters for those who are physically healthy. "In one way or another," writes Guest, "we all have this hope, the yearning to transcend, to reach up, to let go of our skins and find a new place without sorrow and loss. Virtual worlds...promise that redemption."[88] While Guest fears that this might come with a dark side,[89] there's no question that for the residents of *Second Life* the glorious experience of life in-world offers hope that ordinary existence does not.[90]

The promises that Linden Lab encodes in *Second Life* are part of the world's overall design structure. By working with the constraints of rules, play, and culture, designers can objectify ideas and ideals within the game or virtual world architecture. By permitting simple acts like teleportation and complex acts like reinventing one's appearance or fabricating objects and landscapes, the rules of *Second Life* fulfill Rosedale's desire to allow residents to "do things that in the physical world we can imagine but are incapable of."[91] Indeed, with help from outside Linden Lab, the transcendent powers of *Second Life* are growing ever greater, as witnessed by one medical engineering firm's efforts to use brain–computer interfaces so that physically disabled people can control *Second Life* avatars using only their thoughts.[92] Even before we can control our virtual experiences through disembodied thought, the play structure that encourages free exploration of identity and meaning and the culture of futurism, creativity, and reinvention mesh well with transhumanist thinking. Thus, the overall design of *Second Life* is transhumanist; it encourages a sense that technology allows us to surpass our mortal lives in its very design structure. As a consequence, we should not be surprised that within *Second Life*, many residents take maximum advantage of this by exploring transhuman possibilities and promoting them either intellectually or through their life choices.

Heir to a century of transhumanist aspirations, Rosedale has made a profitable business and a fascinating environment out of digital transhumanism. We should not lose sight of the fact that *Second Life* offers its residents a vast panoply of creative and consumer options; there's no question that it is a multifarious environment and should not be pigeonholed as "a transhumanist playground" or as "ersatz religion." *Second Life* is an incredible achievement, one that actually permits its users to achieve greatness themselves. As a storytelling and creative environment, *Second Life* is unparalleled in the early twenty-first century. Nevertheless, the religious elements in *Second Life* should not be ignored or dismissed as tertiary. As other transhumanists recognize, spiritual visions motivate people to genuine action;[93] a man with Rosedale's background, abilities, and metaphysical dreams can thus put faith into practice. And then perhaps, as Rosedale hopes, *Second Life* will breathe life into itself.[94]

A Residential Heaven

In all fairness, *Second Life* is unlikely to raise itself out of the dust; on the other hand, its residents may well use its toolkit to shape it into a new Garden of Eden. As a kind of mythic space where we give meaning to and reorient everyday reality,[95] *Second Life* is rife with transhumanist aspirations, expressed explicitly by transhumanist groups in-world and implicitly in the lives of the world's other residents. To a considerable extent, such appreciation of *Second Life* is part of a broad transhumanist appreciation for video gaming—many transhumanists see video games as helping to produce transhumanist ways of being and of thinking.[96] Even those *Second Life* residents who do not explicitly subscribe to transhumanism revel in their temporary liberation from the limitations of earthly life, which is why *Second Life* works so well for transhumanist community building and possibly for conversion. While Rosedale could not have single-handedly produced a transhuman paradise (and certainly does not describe his work with *Second Life* as a deliberate effort to do so), many of *Second Life's* residents directly or indirectly work toward that very goal.

Rosedale told me that life in virtual worlds "will become empowering and, in at least some important ways, better than the real world."[97] DaSilva and other residents certainly share this search for fulfillment in *Second Life* and appreciate Rosedale's sentiment. A noticeable minority of my survey respondents (just over 10%) would consider *Second Life* to be "heaven" if technological problems such as server lag could be resolved, and a like number would maybe do so. Slightly more might consider it heaven if they could upload their minds into *Second Life*. While 10 to 20% may not seem like a tremendous number, consider how it would reshape any country's politics, and the role of religion therein, if a similar number of the population were avowedly transhumanist and advocating a mass transfer of consciousness into computers. In what might be called participant journalism, Guest asks whether virtual worlds offer what "we all want...to let go of our skins and find a new place—a heaven—without sorrow and loss?" and finds that for many residents, this is the case.[98]

The transcendent possibilities of virtual worlds have been bandied about in tech circles for decades. Moravec, for example, predicted that the entire cosmos would be overcome by computation, becoming a vast cyberspace,[99] and this vision was particularly appealing to Kurzweil, who believes that "we don't always need real bodies. If we happen to be in a virtual environment, then a virtual body will do just fine."[100] According to Kurzweil and his followers—of whom there are many—it is probable that the spread of computation will lead to the universe "waking up."[101] Rosedale agrees, claiming that *Second Life* "is dreaming"[102] and that it will "breathe by itself, if it's big enough."[103]

Rosedale is not alone; a wide array of game designers and technocrats overlay games and virtual worlds with a sacred geography.[104] After all, writes gamer and game theorist Jane McGonigal, reality is broken, and only games—she believes—can save it.[105] Mark Pesce, the coinventor of virtual reality modeling language (VRML), describes the virtual reality environment Osmose as "virtual kundalini, an expression of philosophy without any words, a state of holy being which reminds us that, indeed, we are all angels."[106] Likewise, Nicole Stengers, a virtual reality artist, declares that on "the other side of our data gloves we become creatures of colored light in motion, pulsing with golden particles.... We will all become angels, and for eternity."[107] And as famed game designer Brian Moriarty asks, "why should we settle for avatars, when we can be angels?"[108]

This separation of sacred and profane, of virtual and physical, is never complete or absolute. The in-world thoughts and actions are part of a gestalt that includes frames of reference from outside of the virtual environment. As such, life as a *Second Life* angel overlaps with life as a conventional human being; this adds value to *Second Life* for its users. For some residents, *Second Life* is an opportunity not just to escape to a transcendent realm but also to grow in conventional reality. Online activity in *Second Life* can enable self-empowerment in conventional relationships[109] because individuals can practice (virtually) embodied interactions: communicating with others; making friends; negotiating hierarchies. While rhetorically we might think in terms of a pure realm of the mind, unfettered by conventional reality, life is complex and *Second Life* is no neutral intermediary, passing on virtual salvation from our discourse into our lives. Rather, in *Second Life*, dreams of transcendence are mediated, made accessible to us, but only as embodied human beings at computers can we experience them.

As a mediator for dreams of unfettered growth and transcendent freedom, *Second Life* is particularly well suited to transhumanist thought and practice. Unlike other religious groups, for which *Second Life* is primarily an effective forum for religious practice, transhumanists look upon *Second Life* as a potential fulfillment of their salvific hopes. *Second Life*—along with other virtual worlds—beautifully fits into the transhumanist search for eternal life, providing many transhumanists with a template for the heavenly realm they might one day fully inhabit. The easy way transhumanist ideas port into *Second Life* reflects the long-standing expectation within the community that immortality will be attained when consciousness can be copied into machines.

I have already argued that transhumanist inclinations were part of the inspiration for *Second Life* and that Linden Lab employees were aware of and interested in transhumanist futurism, but some residents take a stronger stance in their interpretation of the Lindens. "Ushering in the posthuman world has always been what *Second Life* was conceived for, at least in the mind of Rosedale," says DaSilva, "it never was about recreating the real-world experience of shopping malls and fashionably-slim young ladies. It was a dream that a combination of computing, communication, software tools and human imagination can be coordinated to achieve a transcendent state that is greater than the sum of its parts."[110] For transhumanists, *Second Life* isn't just a place to practice their religion; it's also the realization of their hopes. Rosedale, who desires a creative apotheosis and escape from the confines of mortal life, has created a place where many transhumanists can sample their future salvation in the here and now. Consequently, they see him as an intellectual ally and collaborator, whether or not he would do so.

Though they have not been among *Second Life's* early leaders, influential twentieth-century transhumanists have operated in the world and some plan to increase their activity. Max More and Natasha Vita-More of the Extropy Institute, for example, are part-time residents of *Second Life*, attending events and even hosting one or two. In 2011, Humanity+, the world's largest transhumanist organization, held a brainstorming meeting in *Second Life* that included Prisco, Vita-More, Goertzel, and Howard Bloom (author of *The Genius of the Beast*) as speakers. No official

Humanity+ meetings took place in *Second Life* in 2012, however, so perhaps a change of direction is under way.

Vita-More, who became the executive director of Humanity+ and then chair of its board of directors, believes that *Second Life* is a powerful tool and is using it to advance the group's mission. She told me that she thinks using *Second Life* could lead a resident toward a positive vision of transhumanism, in particular because "there are many avatar designers who have an incredibly sophisticated sense of design," and she "would like to encourage them to work with transhumanists to build exciting environments."[111] The ability to shape oneself into new and different forms—both intellectually and physically—is, of course, a crucial element in transhumanism. As such, Vita-More appreciates how life in *Second Life* intertwines with transhuman aspiration: "there is an interdependent relationship between the metaverse and the field of human enhancement in that both incite plasticity."[112] This relationship exists because transhumanists want to change themselves in many of the ways that *Second Life* enables—they want to enhance themselves intellectually, socially, and physically. This position is in perfect accord with Linden Lab's own rhetoric, as seen in *Second Life: The Official Guide*, which asserts that the best thing about *Second Life* is "the chance to be whomever you want to be. Practically all the restraints and limitations of real life are absent. The virtual world lets you look the way you've always wanted to look.... You're free to pursue the dreams you cannot realize in real life."[113]

Second Life enables experiences that conventional reality does not; therefore, its user becomes transhuman almost by default. "The avatar's ability to manifest non-biological attributes, uncustomary to its human-counterpart (the user), furthers the learning experience more readily into a state of enhancement, however virtual."[114] Flying, teleporting, changing one's appearance or demeanor, becoming multiple selves through separate alts—all of these tools enhance human beings beyond their biological possibilities. As a consequence, Vita-More rightly sees a tight connection between *Second Life* residency and transhumanist thought and practice. The Metaverse, broadly speaking, is "a means to engage what it might be like to exist outside a fixed biology."[115]

Because *Second Life* inherently makes us transhuman, it is an excellent meeting place for Humanity+. As the organization's leader, Vita-More had sophisticated plans for *Second Life*. Not only can transhumanists meet there, but they also can have preliminary experiences of the future and they can overcome physical and psychological impediments to productive work. She said that she hopes *Second Life* can offer Humanity+ "an 'experience' into multiplicity and diversity, a means by which people can get together without having to physically travel across the planet, and also where we can explore ideas without the traditional interpretation of what a person 'looks' like. Often what we 'look' like interferes with our intentions, our ideas, our purpose and our values. *Second Life* offers an identity escape from psychological judgment."[116] This interpretation of *Second Life* not only takes advantage of the transhuman potential for communication across vast distances and reshaping appearance and identity but also resembles the openness encouraged by Linden Lab and also desired by traditionally religious groups in *Second Life*. Chapter 5 noted how both Christian and Islamic groups see *Second Life* as a place to welcome others; here we see how Vita-More similarly believes that the virtual world can help transhumanists overcome some of the divisiveness of conventional life.

Just as one commentator claims that *Second Life* residents share "the transcendent experience of living as embedded avatars,"[117] it could be a place for mind uploading and eternal existence, or, at least, the precursor for such a place. Serendipity Seraph,[118] who runs the transhumanist-inclined discussion group Fulfillment in *Second Life*,[119] believes that "*Second Life* and other efforts are in part the foundation for eventual upload existence."[120] Likewise, she believes that the sophisticated tools for creation and communication available there are primitive versions of future technologies and social systems.[121] An active community has formed around DaSilva and Seraph, and many common transhumanist ideas circulate within it. For example, at one of Seraph's Fulfillment meetings in *Second Life*, participants voted on relevant concerns, and 40% of the participants indicated that they desire to become machines through mind-uploading technologies.[122]

Many *Second Life* residents, including those outside of explicitly transhumanist communities, express interest in mind uploading and other transhumanist desiderata. More than 28% of survey respondents believe that it will someday be feasible to upload minds into *Second Life*, and nearly as many (27%) would find this an attractive alternative to earthly life. If we include the 27% of respondents who would "maybe" find uploading their minds into *Second Life* attractive, we have a majority of residents who will at least *consider* mind uploading. Whether *Second Life* residents become willing to upload through their time in-world or whether individuals already prone to such a desire get involved with *Second Life* is an open question. Of course, not all transhumanists advocate mind uploading, so even if all residents considered themselves to be transhumanist we still would not have 100% willingness to upload minds into it.

Second Life transhumanists come in two varieties, depending on their approach to virtual residency (discussed in Chapter 4). Augmentationists are the norm: they are individuals who see promise in *Second Life* as a template for the uploaded future and enjoy using it as a way to host events and maintain community. Deep immersionism goes further along the transhumanist, or perhaps posthumanist, continuum. Whatever relationship might exist between digital persons and their primaries, there is no question that any aspiration to disconnect from the primaries and carry on a virtual identity reflects a basic desire to overcome human limitations.

Transhumanists of both stripes agree that the philosophy is deeply connected to *Second Life*. Prisco, who is decidedly augmentationist, claims that such connections exist even for those residents who are not digital persons. "Transhumanism is all about overcoming and transcending human limitations," he has told me. "Someday science and technology will permit leaving 'meat cages' behind and living as pure software...but that day is not yet."[123] So while he sees *Second Life* as a sophisticated tool, it also implies the true future salvation. DaSilva also supports the connection between *Second Life* and transhumanist aspirations. As a leader in philosophical discussion and transhumanist communities in *Second Life*, she has become recognized and respected in conventional transhumanist communities through published essays online and in *H+ Magazine*.[124] Prisco and DaSilva are influential leaders, well-known to many transhumanists in *Second Life* and out; insofar as both perceive the connection between *Second Life* and transhumanism, they reflect the broader understanding held by *Second Life* transhumanists discussed earlier in the work of Vita-More and the recent efforts of Humanity+.

Second Life already offers many kinds of emancipation to its residents; this is the foundation for its appeal to ordinary users and transhumanists alike. Khannea Suntzu, for example, intended for the *Second Life* region Cosmosia, prior to its collapse, to be a focal point for liberation, including the development of a place for intellectual debate, the advocacy of conventional practices such as the redistribution of wealth, and—most importantly—an opportunity to transcend bodily limitations. Suntzu, who in conventional life suffers from neurological problems, told me that *Second Life* allows her to "upwing,"[125] surpassing the limits of human physiology while simultaneously reaching new heights of psychological and even political well-being.[126] Though presently nothing more than palliative,

Second Life could become "magical pathworking," according to Suntzu, a bridge for others who seek well-being over and against the options that nature and modern politico-philosophy have offered and thus an agent for change in the conventional world.[127]

This kind of political work even applies to religion. Some transhumanists believe that conjoining religion and science in an atheistic transhumanism could resolve many political problems. Huxley writes that without dogmatic and self-righteous believers we would see the disappearance of "bigotry, religious war, religious persecution, the horrors of the Inquisition, attempts to suppress knowledge and learning, hostility to social or moral change."[128] Likewise, Prisco hopes that a transhumanist religion could help humanity overcome the history of religious bigotry.[129] Of course, it is important to note that although transhumanists and traditional religious residents both see *Second Life* as a realm that could repair the ills of contemporary life (in widely disparate ways), there is plenty of room for continued conflict.

Within *Second Life*, the Extropia Core region was the location for a great deal of activity from 2006 to 2009, much of it explicitly transhumanist (Figure 6.1). Advocating optimistic futurism, Extropia Core included transhumanists among its early residents and was the site for many discussions about transhumanism, futurism, and religion. Sophrosyne

FIGURE 6.1 The author at Extropia Core's waterfront in 2008.

Stenvaag, cofounder and then director of communications, organized events on an international scale, including the Religions of the Future/ Future of Religions conference (June 4–5, 2008), and hosted influential speakers such as science fiction authors Charles Stross and Kim Stanley Robinson, journalist Au, and anthropologist Tom Boellstorff. Even though not all of her guests were transhumanists, in general they were sympathetic to transhumanism, were advocates of it, or were scholars studying transhumanism or virtual worlds. Combined with a flurry of sophisticated buildings produced by the region's residents, Stenvaag's devoted work as community manager produced a staggering level of creativity and made Extropia Core a hotbed of intellectual ferment and futuristic imagination.

Early on, those who rented space in the region agreed to a residential "land covenant" that advocated role-play and welcomed transhumanist concepts.[130] The community's backstory reads: "in the early part of the 21st century, a group of forward looking individuals start a foundation for creating a new nation, a techno-utopia in which individuals are free to be whoever and whatever they want to be, even augmenting or recreating themselves technologically if they so choose.... They decide to create a floating city to build their dreams upon. They call their new nation Extropia."[131] While the region was not specifically tied to transhumanism, its vision is at least implicitly transhumanist, and many transhumanists found it a comfortable home. Stenvaag, an influential leader in Extropia Core and among *Second Life* transhumanists before she departed *Second Life* (possibly forever[132]), told me that after establishing and moving into Extropia Core she was "downtown," a part of a welcoming community that did not object to her beliefs or identity. Briefly, Extropia Core was the *Second Life* place to be for conventional transhumanists as well, such as when Vita-More staged a surprise birthday party for Max More in 2009.

As with much of the *Second Life* grid, there has been considerable turnover in transhumanist regions of *Second Life*. With the departure of key individuals such as Stenvaag who brought activity to Extropia Core, the region lost much of its public significance. At the same time, Prisco established the Transvision Nexus, which was subsequently converted to Cosmosia and turned over to Suntzu and others. Prisco had largely stepped out of *Second Life* and had little use for the Transvision Nexus.[133] Launched in fall 2010, Cosmosia rapidly gained participants to public debates covering matters such as the Israel–Palestine conflict, the legalization of drugs, and the dangers of overpopulation. The survival of Cosmosia was thus, rather interestingly, pinned to political matters in conventional reality rather than specifically transhumanist concerns, though these latter can certainly play a role in the former. In addition, Suntzu and others worked toward the production of a full community, with opportunities for lighter entertainment accompanying the debates and other, more business-like developments. Unfortunately for Suntzu and her collaborators, however, Cosmosia also failed. As of early 2011, Suntzu had moved her debates to another region. After that, at least some transhumanists migrated to Terasem Island, which is where the 2011 Humanity+ event took place.

While certain regions are significant in the practice of transhumanism in *Second Life*, the community is not dependent on such locations the way Christianity requires churches or Islam requires mosques. While one may be Christian without attending a church or Muslim without attending a mosque, these locations are powerful for the experience and daily life of the religions with which they are affiliated. *Second Life's* transhumanists do not have such narrowly specified places to assemble. Instead of relying on the existence of transhumanist sims or meeting places, transhumanists in *Second Life* use the entire landscape as, in J. Z. Smith's term, a "focusing lens"[134] for seeing sacred powers and purposes. At one *Second Life* discussion, Serendipity Seraph referred to *Second Life* as "a place of being and becoming. A 'field of dreams,'" and Gwyneth Llewelyn, another well-known *Second Life* resident and commentator, suggested that a dis-cussant try to "imagine that people would replace their wish to live in a transcendent world after their deaths, and instead focus on being here and now in *Second Life*."[135]

As a focusing lens, the *Second Life* grid allows participants to connect to what they perceive to be ultimately real. Just as a Christian can find God anywhere but goes to church because it is easier there, a transhumanist can look forward to a technological rapture in conventional reality but see it so much more clearly in *Second Life*. As Seraph says, "*Second Life* and other efforts are, in part, the foundation for eventual upload existence."[136] As residents experience "plasticity" in their avatars, they can simultane-ously "engage what it might be like to exist outside of a fixed biology."[137] That is, the opportunities that *Second Life* affords in shaping one's appear-ance, attitude, and identity can even promote a transhumanist perspective in conventional reality. Events that might be considered trivial in everyday life take on a new meaning in *Second Life* as hope for a transhuman future plays out in a resident's second life.

Seraph devoted an entire meeting late in 2010 to the spiritual aspects of Fulfillment, and the participants accepted the topic without debate or the acrimony that would have emerged in prior decades.[138] In the first minute, one member even asserted that "without spirituality, there is no fulfillment. Fulfillment is a spiritual concept."[139] Participants discussed whether virtual worlds could be heaven or lead to human apotheosis, whether digital resurrection is possible, and the whether it was possible to create a religion out of transhumanist ideas, including the development of sacraments and sacred quests.[140] As a consequence of such debate, Seraph hopes that participants can form a "clean bright light" or a "beacon of hope" for the world.[141] Near the conclusion of the discussion, several participants agreed that a combination of technology and spirituality would be necessary for human progress and, thus, must be critical to the beacon of hope that transhumanists hope to provide.[142] Seraph told me that she has had a "vision, a full-blown, shaken to your soul, vision of transhumanist related possibilities" and is moving this vision forward through Fulfillment, though she does not consider herself a "very good founder of a religion."[143]

While *Second Life* transhumanism lacks a full-fledged "prophet," there are certainly candidates. Kurzweil alleges that he will not become a new religious leader and rejects the need for one as "part of the old model,"[144] yet his public presence certainly makes him a candidate. His Singularity University colleague, Eliezer Yudkowski, has a large following on his *less-wrong* blog, many of whom meet up to discuss "rationality" in their own towns; one group has even established a communal home in New York City. However, Yudkowski fervently opposes religious readings of the Singularity.[145] Neither Seraph nor Prisco wants the job either. Like Seraph, Prisco dismisses the likelihood of becoming a "leader or a guru" but acknowledges that he could conceivably change his mind and transform the Turing Church into more than a discussion group.[146] DaSilva, probably the best-known digital person, is now actively engaged in "religious apocalyptic thinking converging with cutting-edge science and technology" but does not aim to become the group's spiritual leader.[147] She is interested in religious thinking as a philosophical effort rather than as a movement, but her writings carry weight in some communities and could help shape the development and aura of transhumanism in *Second Life*. Of course, this chapter began with Philip Rosedale, the man behind *Second Life*, but Rosedale is not explicitly transhumanist, despite the leanings described above. He would most certainly not be interested in becoming the prophet of a modern religion. In the end, whether he relishes the position or not, Kurzweil remains the leader of the movement because he accepts that there is something akin to religion in his ideas and he has many devout followers. Whether he will ultimately embrace such a position or continue to keep it at arm's length until someone else takes up the cause remains open to question.

As a religious community, transhumanists will need more than a leader, no matter how important charismatic leadership may be. Indeed, leaders inevitably die—though perhaps not in transhumanism—and it becomes necessary to institutionalize their charisma.[148] One way of doing so is through ritual practices, the importance of which have been recognized by transhumanism's pioneers such as Huxley and its contemporary leaders like Prisco. In one Order of Cosmic Engineers (OCE) email discussion, contributors vigorously debated how one might produce ritual practices for transhumanist thinking. Based on Remi Sussan's "heirohacking" project to produce a new kind of technological religion, one member of the OCE writes that "current religions have a lot of rituals and practices that do help increasing happiness and longevity. Some of those effects have been shown through controlled trials. Maybe we could start with looking at those rituals and incorporate them into our worldview?"[149] While the conversation rapidly degenerated into a dispute over the intellectual value of the noted witchcraft pioneer Aleister Crowley, several members actively engaged the thought that rituals might help strengthen their community. Toward this end, one suggested that OCE members read Roy Rappaport's *Ritual and Religion in the Making of Humanity*[150] as a primer for producing a new kind of religion, and another suggested translating Thich Nhat Hanh's fourteen precepts for "engaged Buddhism" into something functional for transhumanists.[151]

One transhumanist group, the Terasem movement, has already instituted ritual practices by blurring New Age spiritualism with transhumanism. The group's webpage indicates that practitioners should perform specified rituals on daily, weekly, monthly, quarterly, annual, and quadriannual schedules and declares that "Terasem Rituals are important to keep our Movement going until all of consciousness is connected and all the cosmos is controlled."[152] According to Prisco, some such services have been performed in *Second Life*, which means the group could conceivably become pioneers in *Second Life* transhumanism. Opposition to the "New Ageyness" among more scientifically oriented transhumanists will likely inhibit growth, however, leaving room for other transhumanists to set the tone for ritual practice in *Second Life*.

Although many transhumanists are leery of Terasem's New Age connections, they do take advantage of the group's work toward immortality.

Users can visit one of Terasem's websites and answer hundreds or thousands of questions about themselves, thus producing "mindfiles." Terasem suggests that these might one day be used to simulate personalities, thus resurrecting their makers. Martine Rothblatt, founder of Terasem, says that many people "see creating a mindfile as the most tangible thing they can do" toward achieving immortality.[153] Humanity+ and Terasem can use *Second Life* to bridge the gaps between their respective memberships and continue to work toward their mutually supportive goals, as evidenced by the 2011 Humanity+ meeting in *Second Life*, which took place on Terasem Island and featured Rothblatt as a speaker.

Of course, simply participating in virtual worlds could constitute a kind of ritual practice for transhumanism. Like many religious rituals, virtual world residency includes an attempt to separate the sacred from the profane, to surpass ordinary human limitations, and to develop new possibilities for meaning-making and self-understanding. In addition to the ways this happens automatically and unconsciously, as I have discussed throughout this book, some transhumanists already discuss the possibility that virtual worlds or video games could be deliberately produced to bring about transhuman outcomes.[154] If that happens, then gaming could become a religious ritual for many users.

At present, the libertarianism/verging-on-anarchism of transhumanist individuality stands in the way of producing a full-fledged religious institution and thus prevents the community from coalescing powerfully. Building a community is difficult work, involving constant struggles that take place in discourse, require constant tending, and can be stabilized only by the objects that represent goals and enable communication (see Chapter 7). The countercultural individualism common among transhumanists, while laudable in its democratic ideals, frustrates their efforts to form a communal identity.[155] This, in turn, makes evangelism difficult and also confounds group longevity in *Second Life*. Without commitment to particular ideals, communities, and practices, members find it easy to drift in and out of transhumanist regions in *Second Life*, just as they do in conventional life.

Despite the difficulties transhumanists have experienced in producing a persistent group identity, their ideas are at home in *Second Life*. As DaSilva says, *Second Life* "puts your head in the clouds and your feet on the ground. And what I mean is, you look around and see all the amazing things people make for no reason other than sheer pleasure. And it makes you hopeful for a bright future."[156] The virtual world's residents find it compelling and, as noted earlier, would consider uploading their minds into it. More than half of the survey respondents (55%) would spend more time in *Second Life* if they could, and a significant number (16%) would spend all of their time in *Second Life* if they could. Though the residents who report such feelings would not necessarily self-identify as transhumanist (many, in fact, self-identify as members of traditional religious communities), they live transhumanism in their day-to-day second lives.

The transhumanist-oriented communities that have been built in and around *Second Life* have troubled histories: when key figures stepped out of the picture, activity waned and the communities suffered. In some sense, this is an ongoing problem for transhumanist groups. The Extropy Institute, for example, closed its online doors early in the twenty-first century after allegedly fulfilling its original goals,[157] and the OCE imploded in 2010 under the weight of members' differing agendas and frustrations with one another. The OCE remains as a listserv but with minimal participation, particularly from among the founders. This happens to transhumanist groups in *Second Life*, which must find the time and the money to maintain effective communities in-world. However, this problem is not exclusive to transhumanism: Chapter 5 noted Larry Londy's observation that Christian sites in *Second Life* tend to come and go and the diminished activity at LifeChurch.tv in *Second Life*. People's interests change, and their time commitments become constrained; as such, activity ebbs and flows in *Second Life* just as it does in conventional reality, though perhaps with wider variation.

Despite the political troubles that naturally haunt communities based around newly emergent ideas, transhumanists are unlikely to disappear from our religious or our virtual landscapes. Indeed, transhumanism in general has a rising profile in public life.[158] Environments such as *Second Life* offer, as though through a mirror darkly, a glimpse of a virtually real life; they naturally provide homes for transhumanists hoping that technology will save us and provide a transhuman habitus—an embodied culture and way of acting—for others.[159]

For the present, transhumanists have discussed using games only for evangelical purposes, but this may change. Suntzu expresses interest in using massively multiplayer games to introduce transhumanist ideas to young people. Even a game that parodies her hopes for the future, she claims, could be successful if it passed along the correct messages about transcending death through mind uploading.[160] Another transhumanist, a member of Prisco's Turing Church discussion group, thinks "we have today the tools that may improve strongly our own 'engineered beliefs,' by immersing us deeply in some virtual worlds where our beliefs may change and our behavior may be modified. Gaming. Gaming creates fanaticism.... Gaming, also facilitates the adoption of 'artificial beliefs.' "[161]

This desire already plays a role in gaming life. In a study of transhumanists and video games, fully two-thirds of the participants claimed that video games incline players toward a transhuman sense of self.[162] As one transhumanist indicates:

> As for videogames in general, and particularly MMORPGs, you almost always have an avatar, a digital representation of you that you pilot around the world, projecting your identity onto this (almost) blank canvas. The avatar is sort of you and, at the same time, sort of somebody else. It could be that increasingly sophisticated avatars will act as a kind of bridge easing humans into a future in which brains can be scanned, mapped, and reconstructed digitally: uploads, in other words.[163]

Video games, then, can promote new religious ideologies, a fact transhumanists have caught on to rather more rapidly than many other religious groups.[164] Transhumanists clearly see the possibility that games and virtual worlds can assist in their evangelical work, and they apply this perspective to *Second Life*, using it both for community building and as preparation for the future.

As *Second Life* residents walk through Extropia Core or other futuristically themed regions, they can learn about and appreciate possible transhuman futures; this could affect their acceptance of technologies, their political and religious beliefs, and their very real behavior offline. There can be no question about the power of built environments—they shape how we think and what we desire. Perhaps, then, we must retire our old homes for new ones, as the great architect Le Corbusier advocated in the early modernist period of architecture: "Men live in old houses, and they have not yet thought of building houses adapted to themselves."[165] Thanks to Rosedale's vision and Linden Lab's efforts, *Second Life* provides the tools for doing so; as residents explore the transhumanist regions in *Second Life*, inspiration to build may strike—either in *Second Life* or in conventional reality. And then we could witness magical pathworking indeed.

Conclusion

In a fluid landscape like *Second Life*, the particulars can disappear in the blink of an eye, but the rules of engagement are less transient. While the individual locations or persons detailed here may come and go, new communities will rise and take advantage of the opportunities that the world provides. *Second Life* may be simply one in a line of cocreative virtual worlds that began with Internet communities like LambdaMOO and will, perhaps, never end. Whether *Second Life* remains with us for two years or ten, whether it is the most profitable or popular of social worlds, it will always represent a certain type of environment that human beings form online, and it thus effectively demonstrates what happens when traditional religions become virtual religions.

We cannot deny that, in the early twenty-first century, transhumanism remains a small movement consisting of individuals who are frequently geographically isolated. Fortunately for the movement's faithful, the Internet has improved networking and accelerated growth. In the middle of the twentieth century, Huxley predicted that transhumanism would start small and grow in time,[166] and the past century has proven him correct. This is not to say, however, that such growth will remain slow. When mainstream television shows in the year 2010 debate the Singularity, and when widely disparate news sources like the *New York Times*, the *Chronicle of Higher Education*, *Rolling Stone*, and *Time* all debate transhumanist ideas, we know that transhumanism has surely entered the religious marketplace of modern life. In 2013, the *Dilbert* cartoon even ran a series around an intelligent robot whose consciousness is uploaded into the Internet, showing the considerable degree to which transhumanism permeates modern life and culture. The work of contemporary religious transhumanists such as Prisco, DaSilva, Seraph, and the Turing Church may well have a lasting impact on our culture. The reconciliation of science and religion that Huxley predicted for transhumanism[167] may be under way in the work of these twenty-first century futurists, especially Kurzweil, who agrees that "we need a new religion."[168]

Whether or not transhumanism can reconfigure religious life, *Second Life* residents both implicitly and explicitly contribute to a transhuman future. The feelings of transcendence they express and the freedom of being that they experience are reflections of what *Second Life* was built to do. By its very nature, *Second Life* is a transhumanist technology; while it is certainly possible to use it and to reject the fulfillment of transhumanism, most likely because one opts for a more traditional religious worldview, all *Second Life* activity engages superhuman powers and expectations. In *Second Life*, residents fly, speak across vast geographic distances, shape their appearances and even their personalities: they reject their human limitations and actively make themselves something more than they were before.

Part and parcel with these transcendent experiences comes a common belief that *Second Life* could be the starting point for a powerful new faith. Nearly 37% of survey respondents believe that a new religion could definitely or probably arise in *Second Life* and have as much legitimacy as conventional religions. Another 26% believe that such a religion could "maybe" develop. When asked to presume the existence of such a religion, more than 43% of respondents believe it would be relevant to conventional life as well as *Second Life* (and another 25% believe it might be). As one resident told me, "I expect and hope to find a new religion on here."[169] Transhumanism might be just the religion he seeks. If so, we should recognize that the permeability between *Second Life* and conventional life means that transhumanism is not just a matter for virtual worlds, but a set of ideas and commitments that straddle the virtual and the physical.

Philip Rosedale combined a common fear of mortality with a wondrous science fiction fantasy and uncommon technical brilliance to produce a new world. Though *Second Life* may not have been undertaken as an explicitly transhumanist task, Rosedale acknowledges holding to beliefs that can be described as transhumanist and his colleagues recognize the connection between transhumanist ideas and *Second Life*. Though not actively participating in transhumanist cultures or explicitly making transhumanism a theme in *Second Life*, Rosedale and many of his colleagues at Linden Lab appreciate and acknowledge the transhuman implications of their work, from which a new world has emerged flush with optimism.

But *Second Life* is not the sole production of Rosedale or even of the company he founded. The residents contribute to the world; indeed, they are responsible for most of its consumable content. Just as they produce the landscapes, the groups, the objects, and themselves, they contribute to the religious aura of transhumanism. Both implicitly, in their feelings of transcendence and desire to overcome their own limitations, and explicitly, in their desire to upload minds or establish transhumanist groups, *Second Life's* residents collaborate with Rosedale and Linden Lab. Designers and residents have worked and continue to work to make *Second Life* virtually sacred—it may remain conceptually divorced from traditional religious groups, but it is deeply enmeshed in contemporary transhumanism; thus, logging in is, for many users, a sacred opportunity to experience what they see as a tiny fraction of the heavenly world to come.

7

Reassembling Religion

Introduction

As we have seen throughout this book, virtual worlds enable powerfully religious work. They do this thanks to design elements, accidents of human nature, and deliberate decisions on the part of their residents. As a consequence, thinking about virtual world residency must reshape our understanding of religious practice and contemporary life. Religious life can now take place outside of traditionally religious institutions, which thus have both competition and new opportunities.

From a theoretical standpoint, which is explored in this concluding chapter, it is now possible to see that religious life must always be thought of as an assemblage of actors, with virtual worlds and their occupants now among them. Religious practice and thought requires an association of human beings held together in a social constellation by nonliving objects. The nonhuman elements of religious life, including virtual worlds, act upon the human beings: they are both repositories of human intentions and forceful objects that can redirect people. In fact, without nonhuman actors in a religious community, the community will surely fracture and dissolve. Virtual worlds now operate in ways analogous to traditional religious objects, such as holy scriptures, local temples, and culturally idiosyncratic fashions. They can link people together in communities of the faithful, whether those communities are composed out of heroes of fantasy, engineers of transcendent minds, or importers of traditional faiths into digital temples.

Virtual Orienteering

Religious practice, having already adapted to online religion, swiftly moved into virtual world spaces so practitioners could properly orient themselves toward the sacred, a task made easier with the pseudo-embodiment of places like *World of Warcraft* and *Second Life*. The Internet, for all its pseudonyms "the Web" and "cyberspace" might pretend, is not the kind of environment that promotes or enables orientation. There is neither time nor space on the World Wide Web. The strands that link web sites cannot be genuinely crawled or even seen by users of the Web; they purport to exist in between the particles of information posted by various computer servers. Nowhere one might navigate via a web browser is a proper location to inhabit, nor do any of those sites possess any proper sense of historicity. While websites change thanks to the programming dictates of webmasters, and occasionally in response to a list of comments left behind by visitors, the sites do not possess, in and of themselves, any real sense of the passage of time. The Web is, indeed, a utopia, a nonplace in the literal sense of the word. As such, it is not actually a very good place for religious practice, which is really too human to be utopian.

The absence of space and time on the Web are, however, rectified in virtual worlds. Video games have relied on the segmentation of space and time since their earliest days;[1] such parsing now helps constitute the nature of life in virtual worlds. Drawing upon Vivian Sobchack's theory of cinema, Timothy Crick argues that "contemporary videogames are phenomenologically experienced in a way that is as spatio-temporal, embodied, immersive, interpellative, visceral, mobile, and animate as that of the cinematic."[2] But, in fact, the spatio-temporal presence of virtual worlds (including video games) vastly exceeds that permitted by film viewing— Crick points out that the player's actions are crucial to the gaming body[3] and that video game play is phenomenologically embodied[4]—and this contributes to the religious possibilities of such worlds. Now, thanks to the very real possibilities of spatial and temporal orientation, some users have stabilized their own religious ideas in virtual worlds.

According to the great scholar of religions Mircea Eliade, religious people actively sought to orient themselves with respect to sacred axes that interrupted the homogeneity of space. That is, the presence of sacred forces in the world is what allows us to orient ourselves; sacred places make space, itself, fundamentally navigable.[5] To live in the world, therefore, Eliade asserts, we must identify an axis, a center that permits orientation. Of course, for Eliade, all centers by which space might be oriented must be the famed *axis mundi*, the center of the world that he presumed present in every culture worldwide. It is this very assumption that all religious cultures are essentially the same that is the basis of most criticism of Eliade's work.[6] Without accepting Eliade's proposition that all religious institutions require an acknowledged *axis mundi* or that all religions are essentially identical in their morphologies, we can still appreciate how Eliade rightly illustrates the importance of organizing and classifying space in religious life. Indeed, for the religious individual, all of life is grounded in the sacred orientation of profane space.

Whether we see the sacred imposing itself upon the profane world as a "center" or not depends on what we expect of sacred experiences and of religious practice. There is no need, however, to go about a desperate search for places where Earth and Heaven meet, as in Eliade's *axis mundi*, or to require that all orientation depend on the observation of a single cosmic point against which all other places are measured. The powerful and persistently relevant aspect of Eliade's argument is that our sense of space, and the sacred forces through which we make it intelligible, cannot be easily divorced from religious practice and belief. By discriminating one place as ultimately meaningful, we can discern levels of meaning in the spaces around us.

Eliade was no doubt very close to the truth, but his tendency to make abstract concepts such as the *axis mundi* real and efficacious will have commensurate likelihood of minimizing human actors and the decisions they make. This point, which J. Z. Smith makes in the history of religions,[7] has been likewise made more generally in the social sciences[8] and should encourage analysis that returns to the actual people who work very hard to orient themselves. For those actors, choosing an *axis mundi*—and it *is* the result of choice and cannot be presumed to choose itself—is the concretization of a spatial mapping. Once established, of course, the *axis mundi* imposes itself on subsequent believers who affirm it, and believers draw on it strategically in orienting themselves.

Without a sense of space, no properly hierophantic experience can take place. The bursting forth of the sacred is contingent on its power to order and shape experience. As we experience ourselves bodily, within spatial contexts of up–down, left–right, and cartographic systems of east-west and north-south, we prefer an embodied, spatially organizable environment for religious life. "It is clear to what a degree the discovery—that is, the revelation—of a sacred space possesses existential value for religious man; for nothing can begin, noting can be *done*, without a previous ori-entation—and any orientation implies a fixed point. It is for this reason that religious man has always sought to fix his abode at the 'center of the world.' "[9] Internet websites and chat rooms cannot meaningfully provide such orientation. There is no fixed position by which to orient toward or against other positions. A three-dimensional space such as *Second Life*, on the other hand, can provide this.

On the Internet, orientation is idiosyncratic, not shared. It cannot be communal because it exists—at best—only in the eyes of those who con-struct it in the network of websites they visit. The links from one place to another are arbitrary and unconstrained. This individualized orientation is a bug, not a feature of online life. It is not something that assists us in the manufacture of meaning, the development of community, or the self-understanding that runs through most religious narratives. As a con-sequence, users have adopted the shared spaces of virtual worlds. These virtual worlds open the door to real orientation and thus to real space grounded in an experience of sacred action.

Once space has been properly established and ordered, reality, as such, emerges. Eliade explains that "sacred power means reality and at the same time enduringness and efficacity."[10] That is, reality is something estab-lished through religious work; the sacred is of the highest reality, and all else becomes real by partaking in its holiness. Of course, science can also establish reality,[11] and the combination of science and religion in cyber-space is one of the technology's most interesting features. While Eliade ascribes faith in the sacred reality to "primitives," it would be exceedingly naive to suppose that modern humanity has somehow evolved beyond its religious instincts. The meaning and significance and, indeed, even real-ity of empirical existence is, for religious persons, dependent on religious meaning. This is not to deny the reality of our world or to insist that athe-ists or irreligious people are out of touch with reality. Generally speaking, religious work establishes the meaningfulness of human existence. So as individuals read or produce texts, make certain habits essential, shape the landscape through architecture or art, and consider the ultimate ques-tions of existence, they produce a sacred map against which they can con-template the profane world. Questions of meaning are thus implicated in geography: as we fix the significance of places through demarcation, visitation, and memorialization, we can understand and move within the world at large.

Naturally, as all virtual worlds are, by definition, virtual, they involve a certain amount of disembodiment. Nevertheless, they are far closer to conventional reality than other Internet options, such as chat rooms or other kinds of websites. Only the imagination could have given early Internet spaces a meaningful spatial identity. Virtual worlds, on the other hand, are available for exploration through avatars. These angelic bodies walk or fly across landscapes and engage their users in quite genuine spatial relationships. Whether or not the avatar is "real," it can bump into things in *Second Life*, and its user will never fail to notice the individuals and geographic landmarks above, below, and to the side of it. Stereo sound creates a soundscape that adds to the sense that things (e.g., people) are in a real place as the noises they make change with the listener's position and perspective.

Despite being online, life in virtual worlds is fundamentally embodied. Navigating a virtual space with an avatar enables grasping, rendered both graphically and intellectually. To grasp is, in a very real sense, to establish a subject in its selfhood. The act of grasping establishes subjectivity over and against the object to be grasped in both scientific and religious contexts.[12] Thus, a virtual world, in which the brain regions associated with grasping can potentially respond as though to conventional reality, has profound implications for religious practice. This is already in play in the directly religious use of *Second Life* where, for example, Buddhists can "touch" a prayer wheel to set it spinning and thereby achieve spiritual merit.[13] "It is through the use of sight, hearing and imitation-touch that religious practice is not only feasible online but provides continuity between real life and *Second Life*."[14] These three senses are ways of grasping objects, literally, figuratively, and virtually. The fact is, web-browsing Internet users simply cannot grasp anything, cannot reach out and touch or even frame their activity meaningfully in such terms. A virtual world allows participants to grasp objects, both literally, as when avatars do so, and figuratively, as when the users perceive themselves as having done so.

Just as virtual worlds provide space in which orientation is possible, they likewise provide a framework of time in which users orient themselves. Virtual worlds carry on even when we are absent from them. Thus, the ongoing history of all virtual worlds contributes to their sense of temporal continuum and enables us to engage in practices of temporal orientation common to traditional religious concerns. Although there are repeated places where Eliade's desire to protect religion from the ravages of reductionism leads him to think backward, we still have to thank him for helping us appreciate the profound role of time in religious practice. And without such knowledge, the difference between virtual worlds and web browsing might appear inconsequential.

Eliade describes two religious interpretations of the passage of time: one cyclical and the other linear. In both cyclical and linear histories, the irruption of the sacred constitutes the decisive moment that permits human activity within time.[15] Either time began and will end in divinely ordained events that create the endpoints whose existence provide finality to human experience, or time must endlessly repeat itself through the recreation of the world in sacred rituals. In either case, religious persons take advantage of their historical frameworks to make sense of out life.

Cyclical history is, according to Eliade, the history of choice for primitive religious communities, which can then take part in the sacred by imitating the primordial acts of creation. In "primitive" religious communities, by which Eliade typically means tribal cultures, the sacred meaning of an act emerges through its identification with the primordial past when the world or the community was formed. The meaning of human acts is not "connected with their physical datum but with their property of reproducing a primordial act, of repeating a mythical example."[16] Religious rituals then seek to accomplish, once again, the creative power of the past and thereby begin history anew.

In a cyclical history, which certainly need not be "primitive" or limited to tribal communities, the circular interpretation of time creates the structure for meaningful activity. It is not the case that all moments in a cyclical history are equal; those events that renew the cosmos, that begin the world once again, have cosmic significance. For example, the highest point in a Catholic Mass is the Eucharist, when Catholics reenact the Last Supper of Jesus and his disciples. It is important to note that, as an offshoot of Jewish history, Catholicism holds to an essentially linear vision of history. Despite this, as with all such faiths it retains elements of the pre-linear cyclical understanding of history. The Eucharistic participant thus participates in the important events that began the cycle of history and thereby maintains that cycle indefinitely. The same can be said of Easter in Christianity or Rosh Hashanah in Judaism. The meaningful acts of human life are thus integrally tied to the cycle of history whereby the world is periodically restored, and this allows humankind to orient itself with respect to the passage of time.

Again, we have no choice but to point out that Eliade has reversed causality. Out of a laudable goal to avoid approaches that elide religion in favor of some primary force (e.g., society, capital, neurosis, or language), he reduces human beings to instrumentality instead. We should never forget that religious systems, once in place, can profoundly affect their participants, but the stabilization of the religious objects is achieved only through translation from one mediator to the next. There is no self-explanatory sacred that speaks to us from the void of objectivity and thereby delimits reality. We shape sacred forces as objective in our relationships with one another and in our efforts to stabilize them through stories, rituals, art, and landscapes. In the case of sacred times, though Eliade thinks the primordial event must be repeated to sustain reality,[17] it is the repetition that produces the reality and sanctity of the primordial event. Christians celebrating the Eucharist week after week, year after year make the Last Supper holy. Jews gathering for the Passover every year establish the significance of the Exodus. Stories are told and written down to stabilize these relationships, and once stabilized, the sacred powers can feed back into human activity.

Some cultures, Eliade argues, eventually reject the cyclical version of history in favor of a linear one, but this does not sever the relationship between orientation and time. According to Eliade, a shift toward linear history reflects an expectation that time moves toward a singular event: its end. Eliade believes that the ancient Hebrews inaugurated a linear sense of history in which the beginning and the end lie at opposite ends of the historical continuum. Historical events could thereafter be meaningful insofar as they represent the will of the Hebrew God.[18] Linear history is the progress of divine providence toward a messianic future in which the faithful will be saved and time will end, perhaps with the coming of an eternal kingdom.[19]

Naturally, it is easy to see how religious believers ought to orient themselves in a linear timeframe where a divine plan plays out over the course of history. Religious believers can identify where they stand in the course of cosmic progress by reflecting on the mythical origins of the world when gods lay down rules and structures and then looking forward to the ultimate fulfillment of all religious hopes in the end of the world and the resurrection of the dead. This applies as much to new religions, such as transhumanism, as to ancient. Just as Christians look toward the coming of Jesus and the instauration of an eternal paradise, many (if not all) transhumanists look to the Singularity as the moment when history as we know it shall cease and we shall take on transcendence through technology.

We can use virtual worlds to produce meaningfully sacred experiences because those worlds have real histories. Life passes in virtual worlds. When users log out of *World of Warcraft* or *Second Life*, the world goes on without them. The landscape changes, the people change, and—because personhood depends on how one relates to the environment—users will have changes forced on them. The *World of Warcraft* landscape will not shift with the alacrity that *Second Life* affords because the latter's landscape is user generated whereas *World of Warcraft*'s changes only with new expansions to the game. Nevertheless, the game has a fully developed world history, a lore in which players can situate themselves. They can literally reenact key moments in the history of the world, such as ensuring that the noble orc chieftain Thrall survives his escape from captivity[20] or defeating the Lich King who sought to overrun the world with his undead army. Whether through a lore-driven history or the fact that they change with the whims of residents, virtual worlds allow participants to locate themselves in time. Just as transhumanists can see *Second Life* as a meaningful reflection of life after the Singularity, *World of Warcraft* players can use the historicity and lore of their world to produce meaningful experiences of heroism and communal solidarity against evil.

As a consequence of the embodiment that virtual worlds provide, such worlds fall easily into our standard ways of organizing space and our place within it. Because these worlds have historical structures, we can locate ourselves with a time frame in which meaningful events take place. Almost certainly this contributes—along with other factors—to why 98% of Daniel Hodge's interview subjects see their game time as "sacred" or "holy."[21] Unlike on websites, in virtual worlds we can orient ourselves. But to do so, we must recognize the sacred forces that break up the homogeneity and meaninglessness of space and time. Because, in their own ways, both *World of Warcraft* and *Second Life* allow us to do this, they permit religious activity far more efficacious than that offered by the Internet alone.

A Sociology of Science and Religion

Orienting in the space and time of virtual worlds, users engage landscapes, people, and objects that mediate religious thought and practice. More than simply an expression of traditional religions, virtual worlds contribute to a new network of salvation; they are part of the social assemblage that we will call religion in the coming decades. To understand this assemblage, and thus to advance our knowledge of religion and science, it helps to briefly turn our attention to the studies of science alone. There is an extensive literature on the sociology and anthropology of science and technology; borrowing a little from this reveals that the religious environment of our virtual age is one being simultaneously constructed by human and nonhuman actors. That is, the technologies at our disposal help shape what we think while we likewise shape our technologies out of our intentions. As we have seen throughout this book, virtual worlds and their constituent elements are actors; they act in and through the efforts of designers and users, redirecting individual behavior and providing new ways of being religious.

Bruno Latour, one of our most astute commentators on scientific practice, uses his fieldwork to remind us that reality is complex and in motion, even if the terms we use tend to freeze it. Although modern theory tends to separate the *social* from the *natural* and presumes that these two domains are distinct, the division between them is an artificial one having little to do with how human beings actually create and use knowledge.[22] If the social (i.e., the people who think about objects) were entirely severed from the natural (i.e., the objects of the world), we would be incapable of any knowledge or practice whatsoever. At the same time, nearly all of the things that we habitually refer to as objects are the products of considerable social engineering and even those that do not require our efforts to produce, such as rocks and rivers, are part of social projects that use and reconfigure them. Even while we pretend otherwise, we know all objects, including simple ones, through their social uses both historical and present. Complex objects, such as virtual worlds, are all the more deeply entangled in our social systems of design, construction, marketing, distribution, work, play, critique, and communication. Our social systems, meanwhile, would be inconceivable without the framework enabled by the objects circulating through them. Imagine, for a moment, how swiftly the rule of law would break down without casebooks full of legal precedent. The availability of these objects—along with many others—ensures us of a reasonable chance to keep society together.

Unfortunately, we tend to fall in love with words that strip away the complexity of life for the precise reason that doing so is often an enormously helpful intellectual move. Obviously, in driving a car, I need to know only a very few things about steering, the rules of the road, and a little psychology of mind to guess what other drivers will do. I do not need to know much about the history, manufacturing, or marketing of automobiles, highways, or street signs; nor do I need to spend much thought on how having cars changes the lived experience of modern human beings. That said, when we attempt to think carefully about cars, we do ourselves few favors if we simply take *car* as a static entity divorced from all the people, objects, and forces that are mobilized in it.

The difficulty with words reaches its ultimate capacity for obfuscation when we explain things as social. Latour argues that to use adjectives like social to refer to a "stabilized state of affairs" makes sense, but to forget the processes at stake and then to use the term as a kind of substance on par with other types of adjectives is a grievous error.[23] This is noticeable in the sociology of science, where researchers once accredited scientists' correct theories to clear observation of natural objects but considered scientists' incorrect theories to be caused by either unclear observation or social factors, such as the influence of Soviet ideology on the Lysenko affair in biology.[24] In keeping with others,[25] Latour has long argued that we should avoid making the mistake of labeling something a social explanation and oppose that to an explanation tied to the material reality of things. Rather, social and natural forces are in constant play with one another. For everyday objects, groups, and politics, we must be especially careful when debate is present. *Society* is a fine and functional label much of the time, but in places of innovation and rapid movement static terminology bounded by the social often obfuscates rather than clarifies. Latour, and his colleagues in this actor-network theory (ANT) branch of sociology, point out that in times of change or novelty (which is precisely where we are now in the development, deployment, and understanding of virtual worlds), we should delve deeply to produce theoretical understanding: we must "blend together major social questions...and 'properly' technological questions in a single discourse."[26] We must appreciate how interpersonal relations (from the individual and intrapersonal to the body politic) and physical realities (e.g. scientific objects and machines) are all constituent of reality, and must seek an understanding of how this works.

In the study of religion, we are unlikely to ever have a meaningful measure of *some* religious phenomena in themselves (e.g. gods), but this is not to say that we are absolved from the responsibility of establishing a method for considering how the objects of our study emerge from a wide array of phenomenological domains. This is clearly related to Smith's concern in the introduction to his seminal collection of essays, *Imagining Religion*. Smith not just encourages but also demands that the student of religion be "relentlessly self-conscious" in his or her understanding of religion, and the relationship between theory and the examples employed in its defense.[27] To assert, "well, this part of religion emerges from this thing over here and that part of the religion emerges from that thing over there" where, for example, one thing is a holy scripture and another is a desert landscape, all too often ignores the complex relationship between the objects under examination. Landscapes and texts talk to one another, if you will allow, and they are always deeply implicated in the doctrines, hierarchies, and moralities of religious communities.

Actor-network theory is fundamentally relational and presumes that all things exist within networks of the social and the natural. Instead of presuming the social to be a domain in which people act, as opposed to the natural, where laws and forces happen independently, Latour believes that society "should rather be construed as one of the many connecting elements circulating inside tiny conduits."[28] Over the years, he has referred to these "conduits," or assemblages of society and nature as "quasi-objects" and "quasi-subjects,"[29] "actants,"[30] "mediators,"[31] "participants,"[32] and "actor networks."[33] This way of defining reality—and we should not make any mistake about whether that is the nature of the project—then rewrites sociology as a *"tracing of associations."*[34] Crucially, the difference between this and other sociological systems is that within it nonhuman objects are not "simply the hapless bearers of symbolic projection;" they are themselves *"actors."*[35] This is not to say that nonhuman objects are intentional: clearly some animals have intent in their actions, but hammers do not. What Latour means is that the object changes relations in some way. A hammer will not get up and put a nail in the wall by itself, but it does change a whole variety of associations any given human being might make in its presence; it thus acts upon people. This is beautifully illustrated in a common saying: "when your only tool is a hammer, every problem looks like a nail."

In studying modern religion, then, we must account for all of the actors and not merely a few. Certainly, we cannot ignore the intent behind human beings who develop religious communities online or who derive religious satisfaction from gaming. But at the same time, we cannot lose track of the games, the worlds, the companies, even the things and places and quests and friends in those worlds that make such religiosity possible. Indeed, the study of virtual worlds and games in any fashion is one that benefits from thinking in terms of actor networks. After all, many individuals' needs and goals collide in the production and use of virtual worlds; publishers, designers, and gamers all play a role in historical and social outcomes.[36] Likewise, other games, broader social practices, and even gamers' parents can redirect the ways games are developed and played. In producing a religious assemblage, we must trace how certain objects enable, sustain, or dismantle intentional associations[37] of human beings. As Latour points out, objects can house our social ties; they exert power upon human beings and provide rigorous associations that are thus made difficult to dissolve.[38] They do not necessarily pass along their creators' pure intentions, as a neutral intermediary might; they are mediators through which intentions and accidents flow into the world. Things can "authorize, allow, afford, encourage, permit, suggest, influence, block, render possible, forbid, and so on."[39] The video games and virtual worlds in which a host of associations have formed—including ways of developing ethics, experiencing transcendence, recreating traditional religious practices, and anticipating a future salvation—provide a stability to those associations and thus exert forces on religious life and on the worlds' residents.

Modern religion is dynamic: traditional religious institutions interact with new kinds of books, such as science fiction, new kinds of technology, new landscapes, new religions, and new ways of being in the world. Over the next few decades, students of religion will find themselves looking for how these hold themselves together, assembling religious collectives. Fortunately, at least in the realm of virtual worlds, scholars have taken preliminary steps in this direction.[40] This book is a further move toward appreciating how virtual worlds are collectives of religious and technological agents, and of how such worlds operate within wider social constellations by objectifying religious association.

The examples seen throughout this book show how intentions and hopes become empowered as virtual objects. The Virtual Hajj is an object of Islamic ecumenism. Aslan's How blends Narnian fantasy and Christian theology into a landscape of wonder. World of Warcraft objectifies a contemporary search for meaning, wonder, and heroic identity. This list could be longer but would unnecessarily repeat our prior studies. Both Second Life and World of Warcraft are recipients of religious intentions and soteriological hopes. This happens at levels of both design and use. It happens deliberately and by accident. And fundamentally, it changes those who encounter virtual worlds. Indeed, virtual worlds can even inculcate those same intentions and hopes (or inspire new ones) in their users.

Virtual worlds enable, constrain, hold together, and disrupt various kinds of religious associations. They do strange things to the Christian

Eucharist, for example, and even thereby affect Christian ecumenism: if a Protestant holds the Eucharistic sacrifice in *Second Life*, will a Catholic priest condone it? Unlikely. But such worlds also make it possible for religious practitioners to meet, to understand one another, whether of the same faith or not, and to engage in their religious work. They allow a massively multiplayer communion of the faithful to conquer evil and transcend the limits of daily life or to sit and reflect in prayer in a replica of the Sistine Chapel.

The Reality of the Virtually Sacred

We, the users of digital technologies, now work tirelessly, whether we know it or not, to dismantle the difference between the "real" and the "virtual;" but the only thing particularly new about this is how what has always been the case in some domains of life is now increasingly the case in many domains. Typically, the adjective *virtual* implies an absence of whatever quality characterizes the noun to which it is attached, but virtual worlds are, most assuredly, real worlds. Virtual worlds enable new ways of being oneself and of interacting with others that affect the users of that world and the physical world. The interconnections between conventional and virtual life mean that religious practice and thought developed in, emergent from, and objectified by virtual worlds will help shape everyone's life in the years to come.[41]

Thanks to rapidly developing motion detection systems, the division between what is real and what is not could dwindle even further than it stands today. Researchers at the Institute for Creative Technologies (ICT) at the University of Southern California, for example, have used Microsoft's Kinect to control *World of Warcraft* using body motions.[42] The Kinect detects the user's movements, which are translated via software provided freely by the ICT to the *World of Warcraft* keyboard controls. The designers hope this could help reduce the U.S. obesity epidemic and also potentially improve game play by capitalizing on the juxtaposition of embodiment within and without the game.[43] Other researchers use brain–computer interfaces to give physically disabled users mental control over *Second Life*, and the augmented reality glasses developed by Google and others could also provide new ways of entering virtual worlds and connecting them to the conventional. If the user's body and the game avatar are more closely linked through such technologies, the divide between what happens within the game and what happens outside it will turn fuzzy indeed. Virtual world advocates stress this for all it is worth, even borrowing from and implicitly agreeing with Apocalyptic AI advocates who believe that in the very near future the distinction between "virtual" and "real" will disappear.[44]

Despite users' defense of the authenticity of virtual worlds, some commentators believe that virtual activity is, indeed, unreal, a flight from the real into a solipsistic inner fantasy. Roger Scruton, for example, decries the effects of virtual reality on human relationships. He argues that virtual worlds enable risk free engagement with others and debilitate social skills. In *Second Life*, he declares, "people can enjoy, through their avatars, cost-free versions of the social emotions" because they can turn off the computer or disappear into their own anonymity.[45] In this, however, Scruton ignores the wide array of evidence compiled by scholars of virtual worlds, video games, and the Internet who find that real emotions are, indeed, at stake in virtual sociality.

It may be that *Second Life* diminishes social interaction for some users, but for others it enhances it. Scruton's criticism—that this reflects narcissism on the part of the user[46] —ignores the fact that some people are actually incapable of forming certain kinds of relationships in conventional reality. For example, the *Second Life* avatar Wilde Cunningham is controlled by a group of severely physically handicapped people living in a care center.[47] Should they be deprived social contact and their friends denied access to them simply because Scruton does not see the merit in their relationship? Furthermore, Scruton ignores the way we can learn from others who are otherwise inaccessible to us. My contact in *Second Life* with residents from Europe and Africa is a case in point. I would not have met those individuals without *Second Life*, nor would I have witnessed their interest in forming bonds with people of other religions to promote interreligious dialogue and peace in the conventional world.

I suppose that some might argue any efforts spent promoting interreligious dialogue in *Second Life* would be better spent in conventional reality, but I am unconvinced this is the case. The power of the Internet resides in its reach, which virtual worlds supplement with an embodiment that televisions, telephones, and websites cannot provide. The results of virtual world religious dialogue can be profound, indeed. Of course, Scruton might be correct in fearing that some very profound social ills will accompany the power of such reach and virtual embodiment. Perhaps we shall flee from physical reality and find ourselves separated from other human beings as science fiction has warned for decades. To offset this, we must move forward thoughtfully and cautiously and seek always to maximize social goods. Demonizing virtual worlds and their residents will not get this done.

The shift of religious activity to virtual worlds such as *Second Life* may well mark one aspect of the future of traditional religions but, like fantasy gaming, might be a problematic departure from natural human inclinations and relationships. Perhaps worlds like *Second Life* will allow us new and better ways of expressing our religious concepts, or perhaps we will lose our connection to the divine as we mediate it through a computer. We are simply unprepared to assess this at present. Empirically, however, we can already see how virtual religious activity is possible across a wide spectrum of faiths and practices, including Islam, Christianity, and transhumanism, and even religions invented within the confines of the world itself. Thankfully, it is possible to see genuinely valuable religious momentum in *Second Life*. Communities such as Koinonia and the Virtual Hajj provide opportunities to connect with individuals at a distance, explore other faiths, and learn to appreciate one another. *Second Life* includes its share of diffidence, deliberately misleading relationships, and even hurt and abuse; yet its residents, on the whole, follow its designers in seeing *Second Life* as a land of promise, a place where human goodness can be realized.

Increasingly, virtual technologies are colonizing everyday life. From mobile platforms to augmented reality, the communities formed by virtual reality will encompass a substantial share of social interaction. Mobile phones enable constant participation in virtual communities, both game-like and not, and as equipment such as augmented reality glasses become commonplace these too will enable the continuation of virtual community. Our virtual frames of meaning, reference, and activity—and the communities we engage through them—will be one step closer to complete overlap with our conventional frames.

The more we imagine our virtual communities as communities, the more we shall make them real. As Benedict Anderson describes, nationhood is a process of imagination, one in which a group of individuals see themselves as simultaneously part of a single community with a singular identity even when separated by time and space.[48] The participants in virtual communities clearly feel this. As I have discussed throughout this book, it is possible for members of virtual communities to imagine themselves as part of a group, even as U.S. citizens imagine themselves as

Americans. In keeping with this, Philip Rosedale claims, "I'm not build-ing a game. I'm building a new country."[49]

Virtual worlds as countries, as imagined communities, can exert a pro-found pull upon residents. Players of *Uru*, a massively multiplayer online role-playing game (MMORPG) that continued the world and storyline of the classic 1990s personal computer (PC) game *Myst*, were so absorbed within their identity as members of that world–nation–community that when it was canceled they continued to migrate through other virtual worlds as a group.[50] Its players established *Uru* communities in other vir-tual worlds, such as *Second Life* and *World of Warcraft*, thereby retaining a sense of nationhood. Similarly, guilds often migrate from world to world or game to game,[51] and this happened en masse when *Star Wars: The Old Republic* replaced *Star Wars Galaxies* in 2011.

Virtual worlds are real places where real groups form. They are domains of life, real places where real individuals are, indeed, living.[52] The significance of people living in virtual spaces may turn out to be enor-mous, as many of their cheerleaders assert. Already, the economic impact of such worlds has been proven substantial;[53] it remains to be seen what other kinds of effects there will be on our everyday lives. Theologian Doug Estes claims that the virtual turn will equal the Protestant Reformation in its import for Christianity.[54] The new opportunities and challenges that Christians and other people of faith find in virtual worlds will allow them to rewrite their own traditions, and, if anything should prove historically significant about such environments, that will be a leading factor.

Whether virtual worlds will equal the Reformation or rewrite world politics, they will—without doubt—force new ways of being religious on us. All kinds of games are systems that open up a space of possibility, be they board games, video games, or even games that might not really be games, such as *Second Life*.[55] The possibilities thereby made available can be both within the game and even outside it. Both *World of Warcraft* and *Second Life* (whether or not we want to call this latter a game) open up enormous spaces of possibility—they enable vast ranges of behaviors and ways of thinking. And for both virtual worlds, the space of possibility includes religious thoughts, practices, and ways of being in the world.

Quite often, social commentary about virtual worlds is polarized: such worlds will save civilization, or they are the final sign of our decaying times. In this book, I have not sought to sail a middle line between this Scylla and Charybdis but have instead hoped to travel around these beasts. Rather than presenting a moral perspective (however balanced) that can direct our future philosophical and theological thinking, I have attempted to illuminate some of the ground on which such thinking will walk. Truly, we all too often find ourselves thinking about what it all means rather than noticing what any of it does. Virtual worlds are the homes to millions of users, and those people are real people, who do real things. To lesser or greater extent, they co-produce their virtual environments, and this reminds us that we are all actively shaping our conventional lives as well.

All religions are assemblages of human and nonhuman actors; virtual worlds, their designers, and their residents now participate in a wide variety of religious societies. They have become influential in particular religions by creating new ways of practicing, and they have become influential in our broader spiritual marketplace by creating new ways of being religious. The collaboration between worlds, designers, and residents is new to our religious landscape and of enormous import. As more people log on to virtual worlds, they will come into contact with new opportunities that sometimes replace and sometimes enlarge traditional religious involvement. *World of Warcraft* can be virtually sacred—it can provide communities, ethics, meaningful activity, and transcendent experiences. *Second Life* can do likewise, as in the transhumanist aspirations of many residents, or it can offer a new way of performing traditional religious obligations. Without doubt, these new worlds transfigure the practice of religion and give us ways of making life, itself, virtually sacred.

Appendix

ON METHOD IN THE STUDY OF VIRTUAL WORLDS

Virtual worlds are new, yet we are blessed with a variety of methodological tools for their study. Indeed, while game studies—the field most involved in the analysis of virtual worlds—is still young, it is already vibrant and fertile. Thanks to a century of relevant research and a burgeoning amount of new scholarship, we can indeed study virtual worlds even as pioneering work remains to be done. Throughout this book, I used three major methodological positions: history of religions; anthropology of role-playing games; and actor-network theory. In this Appendix, I would like to provide a bit more detail into each and also discuss the ways they combine to form my principle methodological position.

The most important theoretical contribution to the history of religions has been Jonathan Z. Smith's claim that "there is [sic] no data for religion."[1] What Smith means is that we cannot simply assert that some things are inherently religious; rather, we must actively work to establish a relationship between our theories and our data. When he calls for students of religion to be "relentlessly self-conscious,"[2] he demands that we know why we have chosen the examples we have and how they support the theories we assert. In this, his position is actually a reformulation of an old one: William Whewell's consilience of inductions. According to Whewell—who happens to have helped a young Charles Darwin gain the skills that would lead to one of the greatest such consiliences ever—a consilience of inductions is a relationship between theories and facts, where a theory explains facts and facts support a theory.[3] In this view, neither theories nor facts could have meaning on their own.

Grounded in Smith's meta-theoretical framework, the historian David Chidester has worked through the implications of secularism and religious practice. Religion, Chidester argues, "is the negotiation of what it means to be human with respect to the superhuman and subhuman."[4] This negotiation of the human person refers to the beliefs, practices, institutions, art, doctrines, morality, and more that help constitute personhood with respect to forces greater and lesser than humanity, such as gods, animals, or even other people who are considered subhuman, primitive, or savage. As discussed earlier in this work, Chidester describes a wide variety of secular practices that do religious work. He calls these authentic fakes. It is the classifying act that Chidester emphasizes, the way we establish meaningful lives by defining who we are as people. Thus, authentic fakes can offer a feeling of transcendence or meaningfulness, promote the establishment of communities and ethics, or present a path toward immortality.

To appreciate how virtual worlds operate as authentic fakes, I borrow from sociological and anthropological studies of role-playing games. In particular, I owe a heavy debt to Gary Fine, whose pioneering studies of pen-and-paper role-playing games (RPGs) in the 1980s worked through issues such as player–character identity and frames of reference.[5] Tabletop RPGs have been underexplored in academic research despite their substantial relevance in pop culture;[6] fortunately, however, they have not been entirely ignored. It was Fine who first noted that RPGs are cultural systems and that gamers use these systems to provide themselves with meaningful experiences.[7] As described in chapter 3, it is precisely because of the fluid movement between frames that a character's actions can profoundly affect the player. There is no magic circle, no true demarcation between virtual life and conventional life; rather, there are modes of being-in-the-world, and we manage to maintain several in sequence and even simultaneously.

Although Fine's communities of play would not fit in contemporary definitions of *virtual world*, which almost universally describe such worlds as digital, he clearly saw that role-players produce worlds of the imagination and was thus able to articulate important details of behavior within virtual worlds. To do this, Fine focused primarily on the virtual worlds established by J. R. R. Tolkien through his books and M. A. R. Barker through the Tekumel role-playing game world. Tolkien and Barker produced more than simple fantasy settings—they produced entire worlds in which activity takes place.[8] The fact that such activity takes place through role-play and imagination in no way diminishes its force, nor does it dismantle the worlds themselves, which are maintained through the shared culture of the group.[9]

In the years after Fine's work, other researchers have added to our capacity for appreciating virtual worlds. Many researchers now see the significance of virtual world studies, especially since video gaming and virtual worlds have grown in popularity and sophistication. Among many important scholars of games, I must single out William Bainbridge, Tom Boellstorff, Bonnie Nardi, and Celia Pearce for their ethnographic data and their deep efforts to appreciate the cultures that appear in and through virtual worlds.

Bainbridge reminds us of the significance of virtual worlds, including games like *World of Warcraft*, and grounds his descriptions in extensive personal observation and computer-based data accumulation. By combining sociological and anthropological methods, he firmly establishes the power of virtual worlds in contemporary life, going so far as to suggest that "digging beneath the surface of Azeroth reveals important truths about America."[10] In addition, he is responsible for showing that *World of Warcraft* is a culture in and of itself, not merely a cultural artifact. Mirroring Fine's interest in the cultures produced in game, Bainbridge argues that *World of Warcraft* "not only represents but also includes within itself a great culture.... It is so complex, and offers players so much scope for action, that it transcends the game category to become a virtual world."[11] Because Bainbridge sees both the culture of *World of Warcraft* and its engagement with conventional culture, he helps us analyze both the society of Azeroth and the ways that it reflects, refracts, and reformulates our traditional societies.

Boellstorff and Nardi have also followed in Fine's footsteps, but more than engaging the culture of role-play they have both explored the virtual cultures established by it. Boellstorff's thick description of *Second Life* offers an unparalleled glimpse into the world and also a standard to which future scholarship must live up.[12] In writing the first—and so far only—sustained ethnography of *World of Warcraft*, Nardi continues Fine's work by providing a powerful analysis of the cultural systems established in and by the game.[13] She describes the social and aesthetic environment of the game while also situating it within political contexts of gender, nationality, and personal experience. Although it came late into my own research work, Celia Pearce's *Communities of Play* includes an excellent methodological chapter, which should be required reading for all future students of virtual worlds and video games.[14]

Pearce offers the clearest account of what it means to be an ethnographer in a game, balancing the play of each role in the production of the ethnographer's sense of self. Because she does not want to lose the contributions that come from being in the game, she credits her avatar (Artemesia) with coauthorship of her work. While not all ethnographers will see the need to provide their avatars with this kind of independence, it is enormously important that all appreciate the ways their in-world activities shape their ethnographic projects. In addition, Pearce rightly observes that while there are many individual methods with which to study virtual worlds—from textual to sociological to ethnographic—a mixed method provides more points of view and more levels of detail.[15]

While the history of religions and game studies might appear too disparate to speak much to one another, a proper rendering of society reveals that, indeed, they intertwine in virtual worlds. Actor-network theorists such as Bruno Latour tell us that society is a network of agents, both human and nonhuman. Human agents can build, shape, or use nonhuman agents as the repositories of their will, but afterward such nonhumans are not passive—such entities actively shape human agents, often in unanticipated ways.[16] As a consequence, to fully appreciate modern life, we have to think about what kinds of motives, desires, fears, and interests operate on us and whether the agents of these forces are human or not. By multiplying the number of agents, exploring ever further, we get a better understanding of social outcomes, whether those outcomes are scientific, religious, political, commercial, or of any other type.

When we take an actor-network theorist look at religious life today, we see that a variety of new actors have joined the scene. Prominent among them are virtual worlds, their designers, and their residents. These two groups of human beings, and the nonhuman technical worlds they fabricate and use, work both consciously and unconsciously to change our religious landscape. They offer new opportunities that we cannot explore without attention to the scholars who have been building our knowledge of games.

Just as we cannot comprehend modern religion without appreciating the role of virtual worlds and video gaming in it, we need religious studies to understand the design, the use, and the appeal of virtual worlds. To assemble them in actor-network theory fashion, we cannot forsake the social and natural religious elements that help construct them. Video games are conduits, as Latour would have it, composed of material constructions, political and economic structures of empire,[17] an experience of worldhood and society,[18] possibly even the antidote to a broken society,[19] and certainly religious inclinations toward communities, ethics, meaning, transcendence, and even experiences of the divine. In the play of video games and the entrance into virtual worlds, objects play powerful roles in mediating human activity.[20] The religious interests incorporated into games that redirect or focus human attention have occupied me throughout this book, and I have sought to mobilize them in the pages of the work even as they direct real thoughts and real behaviors outside of it.

The mixing of methodologies, social scientific and humanistic, certainly raises important questions that must be addressed. My own strategy for integrating qualitative and quantitative data followed a basically linear structure: participant observation established a limited set of questions, which were engaged through surveys, and interviews then delved more deeply with matters of concern raised by the surveys. The advantage of this approach is that it relies on multiple streams of data; the input from each of the three can clarify the others. Surveys are abstract; they aggregate data. Interviews are concrete but are difficult to generalize from. Participant observation, then, is vital to orchestrating the two. It is through the observer's engagement and enculturation that he or she has the opportunity to think through the broad brushstrokes of surveys and the narrow details of interviews.

As has been previously indicated, the surveys used in this book were never intended to represent the final word on any of their subject matter. Rather, they enabled me to think about how individual game experiences might be part of the larger culture of *World of Warcraft*. Each of the surveys went through limited trial runs to refine the questions for maximal clarity and, as indicated elsewhere, was disseminated through a variety of Internet forums. Naturally, the surveys cannot promise to faithfully represent "the *World of Warcraft* community" or "the *Second Life* community," but at the same time there have been almost no surveys of virtual worlds that could hope to live up to such a goal.[21] Each of the surveys was of modest scope, with participation ranging from 57 respondents for the smallest survey set to 252 respondents to the largest (the surveys are described in chapter 1).

Obviously, it is ridiculous to assume without evidence that such numbers suffice to generalize to the enormous following of the virtual worlds studied here; nevertheless, several considerations make the surveys worth considering. First, data on the larger of the two *World of Warcraft* surveys can be considered reliable within the guilds to which it was distributed. Eighty-five people participated out of total guild membership that was (at that time) somewhat over one hundred individuals. Second, the data from the smaller survey of *World of Warcraft* users nearly always correspond with that taken from my guild survey (which implies that my guilds were relatively reflective of the random community garnered through the Penny Arcade website). Third, both respondents to the smaller *World of Warcraft* survey and to the *Second Life* survey arrived at the surveys through nonspecialist Internet forums. Respondents were not, for example, recruited from religious groups in *Second Life*; instead, the vast majority arrived from a link in the *New World Notes*, which is a general-interest blog about virtual worlds, especially *Second Life*. As such, the surveys may not perfectly represent the *World of Warcraft* or *Second Life* communities, but neither are the surveys the idiosyncratic perspective of one or another subculture within those communities. Following the surveys, interviews took place through website-facilitated email, standard email, and in-game chat (which could be preserved through screenshots and chat logs).

Interviews were crucial in considering the specifics of how players might derive religious and quasi-religious satisfaction from virtual world participation; they help drive this text and account for much of its theoretical value. Interviews allow us to give voice to the actual residents of virtual worlds, which is better than confining them within hermeneutical contexts of our own devising. It is from their voices that words like *success* and *meaning* must emerge, and it is their stories that provide us with insight into their worldviews. Although they miss out on the spontaneity and immediate feedback of in-person interviews, interviews through forums and email are also valuable. They can, on occasion, provide "more ethical, equal and, as a result, more in-depth research of players when compared to traditional face-to-face interviews."[22] Over the course of my research from 2007 to 2012, I conducted interviews via asynchronous interfaces such as email and Internet forums but also through in-game conversations and Skype.

World of Warcraft interviews all came from within my two guilds, which indicates that they could possibly represent a narrow interpretation of the game. Despite this, there was no uniform set of responses to interviews within the guilds that would indicate a clear subculture in the game, and the premise of this book has never been to establish that any one perspective is the only one at play in *World of Warcraft* or *Second Life*. Indeed, the purpose throughout this text has been to demonstrate ways virtual worlds *can be used* to do religious work, not how they automatically do so. While many players do join meaningful communities or acquire a meaningful purpose in *World of Warcraft*, this is not to say that all do so (though, indeed, it is probably the case that all players do participate in transcendent states of being merely by entering virtual worlds[23]). Internet forum postings taken from outside of my guilds, however, clearly demonstrate that the views expressed by interviewees are shared widely even if not universally in *World of Warcraft* culture. Perhaps it is worth pointing out that when I discuss *World of Warcraft* with other players and tell them about my research, they have universally found the fundamental claim—that the game can be used in a quasi-religious fashion—both interesting and intellectually compelling. It is quite a joy when a casual conversation with a friend's friend turns into an enthusiastic endorsement of the main arguments in chapters 1 through 3 of this book.

In *Second Life*, my interview data were collected over many years of involvement with transhumanist communities and from general discussions held in the world. Advertised discussions obviously tend to bring participants who are at least moderately interested in the topic, but this still does not mean that there was only one viewpoint on offer in those groups. Rather, lively discussions allowed different voices to emerge, including those of individuals who use *Second Life* in distinct ways. They also provide opportunities for individuals to reflect and come to consensus on issues. While this is not always the case, more than once residents expressed how they had not thought of issues from a particular perspective before and that this new viewpoint makes sense. Individual interviews with residents were almost always granted by individuals with whom I had contact over the years and were conducted in game and via email. In addition, it was helpful that several individuals present at Linden Lab in the early years of *Second Life* consented to interviews with me, carried out by email and Skype. Such interviews greatly expand the reach of analysis, as they provide insight into design intent that could otherwise be inferred only from observing the world itself.

My observation of *World of Warcraft* began, as stated in chapter 1, with my attendance at the conference "Convergence of the Real and Virtual: The First Scientific Conference in *World of Warcraft*," hosted by William Bainbridge and John Bohannon in May 2008. Joining *World of Warcraft* was an interesting experience, as I spent many years in my youth playing fantasy games such as *Dungeons & Dragons*, *Shadowrun*, and other tabletop RPGs. Indeed, researching *World of Warcraft* and writing this book contributed to a renaissance in my own interest in both the fantastic and gaming and led to the introduction of *Dungeons & Dragons* and other games into my parenting. As such, my status as researcher is inherently precarious: I am always a participant in gaming life even as I am a researcher, and I was one before the other.[24] Shortly after my first conference in *World of Warcraft*, I began creating characters on a different server to join the Dropped Stitches and Twisted Stitches guilds that gave me a home throughout the subsequent years of gaming. I did not play *World of Warcraft* continuously from 2008 to 2012, but I spent a minimum of five months of each year involved in the community.

My choice of guilds could not help but affect my experience in *World of Warcraft*. Guild membership, composed of knitters and their boyfriends and husbands (to my knowledge, there was only one male who knitted), shares a common interest that may color their interactions (knitting) and a preexistent community online (Ravelry) and has a different demographic profile than the overall *World of Warcraft* membership (as detailed in chapter 1). Several things, however, require particular note to clarify how the nature of my guilds affected my game play.

Dropped Stitches, in which I played most of my hours, is a casual guild with a core raiding group but with only a few players interested in player versus player (PvP) combat and battlegrounds. I participated in occasional raids but was never part of the core group and was not always sufficiently powerful to engage in the highest level of content. (I did not, for example, participate in the defeat of Deathwing in the Dragon Soul raid.) Rather, I substituted for other players when needed, but the nature of Dropped Stitches is such that no members of the guild demand such participation from one another. It is entirely voluntary. Along with members of the guild, I used the Random Dungeon Finder, but as with many of our members I much preferred using it with a group of my guildmates. We found that both in terms of competence and attitude our guildmates were preferable to the teammates acquired through the RDF, which can assemble a group based on their individual specialties but without regard to skill, preparation, or—most importantly—good manners and a sense of humor.

The demographics of Dropped Stitches and Twisted Stitches may well provide the clearest explanation for the collegial atmosphere that pervaded group dynamics. The guilds' memberships were composed almost entirely of adults from 20 to 60 years old (a few of us have had children participate, but the number of children can be counted on one hand). Although there was one significant altercation over the leadership of Twisted Stitches, political relations were generally very positive, and in-game relationships were extremely so. Many of us would drop whatever we happened to be doing to teleport to the location of a "guildie" who needed help with crafting a particular item or completing a quest. After one lengthy hiatus from the game, I returned and asked a question of the group on guild chat, only to have one of the senior members immediately post that he was on his way to help me. From this, I learned a valuable lesson and thereafter contributed to others' experiences by crafting for them, offering advice, and even purchasing expensive objects for those in need. This attitude is rampant in Dropped Stitches and Twisted Stitches, which unquestionably accounts for the strong loyalty within the group and likely also the greater frequency with which my guildmates expressed their enjoyment of the guild compared with the others surveyed. (This difference is briefly discussed in the notes to chapter 2). I should be clear that in these and other respects my guilds advocated supportiveness, collegiality, and fun in *World of Warcraft*, not competitiveness or aggression. Many other guilds emphasize the latter (often measured through guild player versus environment [PvE] or PvP rankings), and the experience of playing in a raiding guild or high-level PvP guild would not match my own.

As with many groups, both Dropped Stitches and Twisted Stitches enhanced the sense of community through in-game talk. Both guilds maintain a healthy amount of conversation, questions, and advice on the guild channel, and both use third-party software (Ventrilo and Mumble) to enable voice communication during dungeons and raids. Such conversations produce ongoing relationships: they establish and sustain insider jokes, allow geographically separated individuals to get to know one another and about one another's lives, and foster a sense of community through mutual support and recognition. Hearing others' voices during dungeons and raids is a particularly powerful way of bonding, and it adds substantially to the community even while it makes more strategic play possible.

In addition, the preexistent online community from which Dropped Stitches and Twisted Stitches emerged both enhanced the overall social structure and provided many opportunities for guild members to work and live together. The forum postings were social, practical, and philosophical, thus creating a wide arena for social behavior. Most comments on the forums were practical in nature, such as guild policies, how-tos, and information about various aspects of the game. But some threads and individual comments simply spoke to life—such as an individual's cares or concerns—and in others (including some cited in this book), players debated aspects of the game or discussed what they liked and disliked in the storyline or the structure of game play. I was generally an observer on the forums, though I did participate in the conversations from time to time. The Internet forum helps to stabilize the groups, providing additional modes of communication and standing in as a public notice board. As with guild chat and voice software, the forum webpage was thus a crucial place for the group, providing social coherence through the exchange of friendship online and creating a knowledge base for members of the guilds.[25]

It is certainly possible that my status as a researcher affected group dynamics, as previous scholarship indicates that a scholar's presence can reshape community goals and behaviors.[26] Nevertheless, many members of the guild either did not know or forgot that I was doing research and expressed surprise to hear that I had published a book in the past or that I was writing one in the present. Of those who did know, they never spoke directly to my identity as a researcher unless I brought up an issue explicitly under that guise. Occasionally, I would ask a question framed as being relevant to my book, and the ensuing chat comments reflected my identity; however, at no time did anyone specifically seek me out to provide insight that I could use for my research. In other words, I generally, and repeatedly, had to "out" myself as a researcher before anyone treated me as such. For the vast majority of time, I was simply a guild member of moderate standing, one who occasionally participated in dungeons or raids, who often joined in conversations and congratulations over guild chat, and who was better known for crafting or collecting pets than anything else.

In addition to my participation in the guild, I engaged in other standard *World of Warcraft* activities. I used the random dungeon finder to group with others and complete dungeons; I read and occasionally participated in the "trade" chat channel that everyone in a capital city can follow; and I worked for hire, crafting with engineering and alchemy when other players needed things I was capable of producing. Naturally, I also completed quests, gathered resources, sought after achievements, and engaged in the occasional PvP combat.

Participant observation is crucial to an effective study of virtual worlds, as it is an important way to explore how the worlds can act upon users. Virtual worlds are powerful objects, and the scenery, planned conversation, and available options help structure how the residents respond. In a very real sense, the virtual worlds must be given a voice, and this can happen only through a careful observation of them. Although I did not trace *World of Warcraft* through all of its possible iterations (there being more player race–class combinations than I had time to engage), I played a multitude of races and classes and worked my way through to endgame with my primary character. During this process, I took notes on a wide array of environmental and game play elements that contributed to the religious elements of *World of Warcraft*; many of these appear in the preceding pages, as descriptions of quests, non-player character (NPC) conversations, and other elements where the game provides players with ways of thinking.

In *Second Life*, unlike in *World of Warcraft*, I was almost always a researcher. Whether I hosted groups or interviewed others, my identity was always on display either through conversation or through a title that floated under my name: "SL Researcher" (denoting affiliation with others researching in *Second Life*). Of course, *Second Life* is not a game in the same sense that *World of Warcraft* is, so there was less scope for personal play in religious or transhumanist groups. I explored *Second Life*, seeing many wonderful creations by its residents and engaging in the world's social atmosphere of live music and conversational gathering, but my actual research acquisition on religion and on transhumanism was carried out as a separate enterprise. While I could be simply Soren Ferlinghetti at an Irish Pub or live music venue, I was Soren Ferlinghetti, SL Researcher, when on the job.

As an ethnographer, among other things, I have sought to appreciate how gaming cultures are distributed across many geographical spaces, both online and offline. George Marcus rightly points to the difficulties of doing anthropological fieldwork in contemporary life for the same reason that Latour indicates our need for a better method in sociology. "For ethnography...the world system is not the theoretically constituted holistic frame that gives context to the contemporary study of peoples or local subjects closely observed by ethnographers, but it becomes, in a piecemeal way, integral to and embedded in discontinuous, multi-sited objects of study," and therefore "strategies of quite literally following connections, associations, and putative relations are thus at the very heart of designing multi-sited ethnographic research."[27] Marcus rejects the holistic world system of earlier methodology[28] and favors instead a method of studying "the fractured, discontinuous plane of movement and discovery among sites as one maps an object of study and needs to posit logics of relationship, translation, and association among these sites."[29] The data gathered to study virtual worlds come from a vast array of actors, including the games' designers, content, players, critics, and social commentators. The actors include human agents, content within virtual worlds, the machines that run the worlds, and the worlds themselves. Good ethnography then, like good sociology, must work with actors who seem always to multiply themselves and must seek to identify those actors who do the work.

This book is about opportunities that exist for all members of the *World of Warcraft* and *Second Life* communities, though they are not adopted by all. The chapters on *World of Warcraft* are not just about my guildmates, though these were important in my understanding of what the game enables. The chapters on *Second Life* are not just about transhumanists or religiously affiliated residents, though my work with members of religious communities was crucial to how I perceived the worlds' technical and cultural affordances. The integration of survey data, individual interviews, and my own observations was designed to provide tools for appreciating not only what many players and residents in virtual worlds presently do but also what nearly all of them could do. And finally, that method aims to provide target areas where subsequent researchers may focus their inquiries.

The advantage of combining participant observation, quantitative surveys, and qualitative interviews should be obvious: it helps to provide a wide-ranging view of the subject and limits the extent to which one observer's beliefs can obfuscate reality. As Latour points out, social scientists have too often substituted their own words for their informants' and clouded empirical reality in a theoretical context. And scholars of virtual worlds have fallen into such traps in a variety of ways. Many scholars have, as Samuel Coavoux points out, generalized from their own points of view, presuming that all players engage *World of Warcraft* in the same way or ways that they do.[30] In virtual world ethnography, one's status as "being there" is always somewhat nebulous,[31] and this means that we must try to find ways of allowing actors to speak to their own presence while simultaneously evaluating that through ours.

This is not a book of predictions, although a few rather vague ones have been offered in previous chapters. Neither sociology nor anthropology should be hindered with the responsibility of establishing laws that permit future forecasting. As Boellstorff rightly points out, sometimes these cultural disciplines can identify something that looks like a law for predicting behavior, but sometimes it is our responsibility to eschew the elucidation of laws in favor of understanding a culture present to us.[32] Likewise, Latour points out that the point of sociology is to interpret culture, not transform it.[33] Just as Boellstorff worked to provide a sense for what *Second Life* is, rather than what it will become,[34] this book is about what kinds of religious activities are already with us and not so much about what they will become. By combining religious studies, the anthropology of games, and actor-network theory in my method, I hope that I have provided a glimpse into the many actors who make virtual worlds—at least potentially—virtually sacred.

Notes

1. I do feel obliged to point out that those who excoriate gamers often do so on entirely spurious grounds. For example, see Craig A. Anderson and Karen E. Dill, "Video Games and Aggressive Thoughts, Feelings, and Behavior in the Laboratory and in Life," *Journal of Personality and Social Psychology* 78 (2000); 772–790; Matthew Davis, "Christians Purge Video Game Demons," *BBC News*, May 24, 2005; Jon Frankel, "EverQuest or Evercrack?" *The Early Show*, CBSNews.com, May 28, 2002; Dan Mollman, "For Online Addicts, Relationships Float between Real, Virtual Worlds," *CNN.com*, January 29, 2008; Chris Morris, "The Greatest Story Never Played: Why Don't Religion and Video Games Mix? The Industry's Top Developers Ponder the Question," *CNN.com*, July 6, 2005; *Telegraph*, "Teenager Obsessed by World of Warcraft First to Attend US Internet Addiction Retreat," Telegraph.co.uk, August 21, 2009. Such attacks are in keeping with the tradition of moral panics over pop culture; see Bonnie Nardi, *My Life as a Night Elf Priest: An Anthropological Account of World of Warcraft* (Ann Arbor: Michigan University Press, 2010), 124–125; J. Patrick Williams, Sean Q. Hendricks, and W. Keith Winkler, "Introduction: Fantasy Games, Gaming Cultures, and Social Life," in *Gaming as Culture: Essays on Reality, Identity, and Experience in Fantasy Games*, ed. J. Patrick Williams, Sean Q. Hendricks, and W. Keith Winkler (Jefferson, NC: McFarland & Company, 2006), 8–9. Although there are problematic gamers who commit crimes of negligence or who squander their lives and resources in virtual worlds, these are few in number and in most cases bring their problems to the games. Given how many players there are in virtual worlds, we should be surprised not because there is an occasional maladjusted misfit but rather that there are not *more* such stories. Perhaps this evidence that the games can serve as a kind of therapy; see Dmitri Williams, Tracy

L.M. Kennedy, and Robert J. Moore, "Behind the Avatar: The Patterns, Practices, and Functions of Role Playing in MMOs," *Games and Culture* 6 (2011): 171–200. Players generally believe that fantasy games improve their social skills by helping them become more extroverted, more empathetic, and more committed to their communities; Florence Chee, Marcelo Vieta, and Richard Smith, "Online Gaming and the Interactional Self: Identity Interplay in Situated Practice," in Williams et al., *Gaming as Culture*, 159; Jane McGonigal, *Reality Is Broken: Why Games Make Us Better and How They Can Change the World* (New York: Penguin, 2011), 89–92; Heather L. Mello, "Invoking the Avatar: Gaming Skills as Cultural and Out-of-Game Capital," in Williams et al., *Gaming as Culture*, 189. So, while there are problem players, whose gaming can lead to serious consequences, the games themselves are unlikely to be the causes of those problems. In fact, it might even be possible to design video games that provide "inner peace" to players, thus alleviating problems for many; see Michael Highland and Gino Yu, "Communicating Inner Experience with Video Game Technology," *Online— Heidelberg Journal of Religions on the Internet* 3 (2008): 267–289. And there have been theological efforts to draw analogies between game play and spiritual fulfillment; see Craig Detweiler, "Introduction," in *Halos and Avatars: Playing Video Games with God*, ed. Craig Detweiler (Louisville, KY: Westminster John Knox Press, 2010), 2; Daniel White Hodge, "Role Playing: Toward a Theology for Gamers," in Detweiler, *Halos and Avatars*, 172. Sometimes gamers and game designers use the term *addiction* to describe a desirable state in which the player avidly immerses himself in the game. When gamers and designers do so, however, they are not usually aligning themselves with the critics who decry the addictive and dangerous properties of gaming. "Suffice it to say that the use of [the] term 'addiction,' when used by professionals in the game industry, does not describe medically pathological behavior. Instead, it refers to engaged and repeated play, to players that enjoy a game and therefore play it more than one time"; see Katie Salen and Eric Zimmerman, *Rules of Play: Game Design Fundamentals* (Cambridge, MA: MIT Press, 2004), 356. Online gaming is not a pathological retreat from the world but rather a form of escapism that maintains a long tradition in fantasy. As the great author J. R. R. Tolkien points out, in fantasy escape is not the same as desertion; see Tolkien, *The Tolkien Reader* (New York: Balantine Books), 79. Those immersed in good fantasy have not fled from the world but rather recognize the world for what it is, and patriotically resist what ought not be (81–84). Immersing oneself in a good story is an opportunity to resist the dangers and difficulties of life for a while and to be reminded that the problems in the world can be overcome. "It is the mark of a good fairy-story, of the higher and more complete kind, that however wild its events, however fantastic or terrible the adventures, it can give to child or man that hears it, when the 'turn' comes, a catch of the breath, a beat and lifting of the heart" (86). This transcendent experience also underlies the escapism of gaming.

2. *World of Warcraft* is a registered trademark of Blizzard Entertainment, Inc. *Second Life* is a registered trademark of Linden Research, Inc.

3. James Anthony, "God and Avatar," plenary lecture given at the Digital Religions conference at the University of Colorado, Boulder, January 14, 2012.

4. Ibid.

5. Mark W. Bell, "Toward a Definition of 'Virtual Worlds,'" *Journal of Virtual Worlds Research* 1 (2008): 2.

6. The extraordinary absence of religious themes could not be more apparent than in the otherwise effective history of video games from Mark J. Wolf, ed., *The Video Game Explosion: A History from Pong to Playstation and Beyond* (Westport, CT: Greenwood Press, 2008c), which completely lacks any reference to religious games or games with religious themes (though it does address morality). Early arcade games were almost uniformly shooters, space games, sporting games, or racing games (ibid.), and this naturally set the tone for subsequent development of console and PC games, which nevertheless branched out considerably. The absence of religious themes common throughout the game industry opened up opportunities for some game manufacturers, such as Wisdom Tree, which published *Bible Adventure* for the Nintendo Entertainment System in 1991 (six years after the launch of the NES). *Bible Adventure* serves as the exception that proves the rule; although games with Christian messages appeared for almost all gaming systems, they were not common. The more popular games tended to avoid explicitly religious narratives.

7. Mark Cameron Love, "Not-So-Sacred Quests: Religion, Intertextuality and Ethics in Video Games," *Religious Studies and Theology* 29 (2011): 192; see also Robert M. Geraci, "Theological Productions: The Role of Religion in Video Game Design," in *Cultural Perspectives of Video Games: From Designer to Player*, ed. Adam L. Brackin and Natacha Guyot (Oxford: Inter-Disciplinary Press, 2012a), 101–114.

8. I am deeply grateful to Vincent Gonzalez, a PhD candidate at the University of North Carolina at Chapel Hill, who introduced me to Christian video games and shared with me his understanding of them when we both attended the ARIL/*CrossCurrents* summer colloquium in July 2010.

9. See Vítek Šisler, "Digital Arabs: Representation in Video Games," *European Journal of Cultural Studies* 11 (2008): 203–219.

10. *Halopedia*, "Covenant Religion," http://www.halopedian.com/Covenant_religion, 2010.

11. Christopher Helland, "Popular Religion and the World Wide Web: A Match Made in (Cyber) Heaven," in *Religion Online: Finding Faith on the Internet*, ed. Lorne L. Dawson and Douglas E. Cowan (New York: Routledge, 2004), 33.

12. Ibid., 34.

13. See Stewart Hoover and Nabil Echchaibi, "The 'Third Spaces' of Digital Religion," *The Center for Media, Religion, and Culture,* http://cmrc.colorado.edu/the-natural-history-of-the-digital-religion-conference/, 2012.

14. We should certainly ask whether or not players receive optimal religious opportunities through games like *World of Warcraft,* but at the same time we ought to consider whether traditional religious systems are, themselves, providing anything near optimal social conditioning. I suspect that people are people and combine good motives and bad, whether they be gamers or not, religiously committed or not. Until such time as a significant measurement of social outcomes for particular religious systems is deployed (and I would question both the wisdom of such a deployment and the likelihood of its accuracy), we are no more able to assess the moral acceptability of religious gaming than of any other religious activity.

15. Tracy Fullerton, "The Night Journey," website comments, 2011.

16. Adam Rosenberg, "Indie Dev Builds 'Minecraft' Religion for GDC's Game Design Challenge," *MTV Multiplayer* blog, March 7, 2011.

17. Jason Fagone, "*Chain World* Videogame Was Supposed to be a Religion—Not a Holy War," *Wired,* July 15, 2011. Unfortunately, Rohrer's chosen successor, an audience member at the developer's conference named Jia Ji decided to make enormous changes to the ways the game was passed from player to player, igniting a controversy among game aficionados (ibid.) As of 2013, considerable confusion remains over the location of *Chain World*; even Rohrer does not know what happened to the game (see Geraci, "Theological Productions.")

18. The immersiveness of the *World of Warcraft* storyline probably accounts for why so few gamers also watch television. What could *Desperate Housewives* offer that they could want? Why spend three or four hours per day passively watching other people's generally dysfunctional lives when you can log on to *World of Warcraft* and become the hero you dreamt of being all through your childhood?

19. Our collective lack of imagination appears hilariously in 1960s through 1990s movies that depict the far future. While people may have learned to teleport or fly across vast interstellar distances, their computers still look like glorified typewriters or have graphics that resemble the capacity of 1970s-era computers.

20. Virtual worlds sustain our associations but also, in the case of disputation, dissolve them. Consider the religious games introduced earlier in this chapter. While playing *Catechumen* might help one user construct and sustain his or her Christian identity and love for all people, for another user it might do quite the opposite; the game might, for example, remind the player of Christian identity politics in either the ancient or the modern world and of an imperialist desire to see everyone else "on his knees." Neither association can be presumed; such ties emerge in and through the game and its play by specific individuals.

CHAPTER 1

1. Edward Hunter ("World of Warcraft Audience Grows in the Face of Increased Competition," Gamasutra.com, September 24, 2009) estimated that *World of Warcraft* surpassed thirteen million in late 2009. However, other sources place *World of Warcraft*'s peak subscribership at closer to 12 million; see BBC News, "World of Warcraft Suffers Subscriber Slump," BBC.co.uk, November 10, 2011; Joystiq, "*WoW* Subscriber Numbers," *WoW Insider*, 2012. While there has been a decline of subscribers, *World of Warcraft* continues to have more than nine million subscribers as of late 2012, and this is a remarkable achievement for an eight-year-old game; see John Walker, "World of Warcraft STILL Has 10 Million Subscribers!" *Rock, Paper Shotgun*, November 8, 2012. It is, in fact, testament to the commitment players have to the worldhood of *World of Warcraft*. They do not just play it as a game but also reside in it as a community.

2. Tom Boellstorff, *Coming of Age in Second Life: An Anthropologist Explores the Virtually Human* (Princeton, NJ: Princeton University Press, 2008), 21.

3. See, e.g., Peter Berger, *The Sacred Canopy: Elements of a Sociological Theory of Religion* (New York: Doubleday, [1967] 1990), 129; Sigmund Freud, *The Future of an Illusion*, trans. James Strachey (New York: W.W. Norton, [1927] 1961).

4. David Chidester, "Moralizing Noise," *Harvard Divinity Bulletin* 32 (2004): 17.

5. George L. Mosse, *The Nationalization of the Masses: Political Symbolism and Mass Movements in Germany from the Napoleonic Wars through the Third Reich* (New York: Howard Fertig, 1975).

6. Robert H. Nelson, *Economics as Religion: From Samuelson to Chicago and Beyond* (University Park: Pennsylvania State University Press, 2001).

7. David Chidester, "The Church of Baseball, the Fetish of Coca-Cola, and the Potlatch of Rock 'n' Roll: Theoretical Models for the Study of Religion in American Popular Culture," *Journal of the American Academy of Religion* 64 (1996a), 743–765.

8. David Chidester, *Savage Systems: Colonialism and Comparative Religion in Southern Africa* (Charlottesville: University of Virginia Press, 1996b).

9. Ninian Smart, *Dimensions of the Sacred: An Anatomy of the World's Beliefs* (Berkeley: University of California Press, 1996). Smart's list was under constant growth throughout his career. Eventually, he added two lesser dimensions (the political and the economic) to the seven he preferred as primary dimensions by the end of his career.

10. William Sims Bainbridge and Rodney Stark, *The Future of Religion: Secularization, Revival, and Cult Formation* (Los Angeles: University of California Press, 1985), 2.

11. I am aware of Dr. Chidester's preferred term from a public lecture given at the University of California, Santa Barbara, when I was a PhD student there in the early 2000s.

12. David Chidester, *Authentic Fakes: Religion and American Popular Culture* (Los Angeles: University of California Press, 2005), vii; see also Edward Bailey, "The Implicit Religion of Contemporary Society: An Orientation and Plea for Its Study," *Religion* 13 (1983): 69–83. In the middle of the twentieth century, Mircea Eliade noticed what we now call authentic fakes when he realized that modern art includes a religious aspiration toward transcendence; see Eliade, *Symbolism, the Sacred, and the Arts*, ed. Diane Apostolos-Cappadona (New York: Crossroad, 1985), 93–101. In his analysis of Constantin Brancusi, for example, Eliade argues that the "Endless Column" and the "Bird in Space" sculptures represent an ascent toward heaven without using explicitly religious language or iconography. He saw religion as camouflaged in modern art and believed that this is the inevitable result of the philosophical "death of god" (81–82). After all, if our religious impulses are innate, we must find some outlet for them even in a secular age.

13. William Sims Bainbridge, " Religion for a Galactic Civilization 2.0," Institute for Ethics & Emerging Technologies, August 20, 2009.

14. In Bainbridge and Stark's sociological model of religion, religion arises out of human exchange relationships in which particular goods cannot be provided by other human beings. Such goods, including eternal youth, perfect happiness, and others, can be had only through imaginary exchange partners, such as gods. See William Sims Bainbridge, *The Warcraft Civilization: Social Science in a Virtual World* (Cambridge, MA: MIT Press, 2010), 58–59 and Bainbridge and Stark, *Future of Religion*, 6–8. Religion, in Stark and Bainbridge's model, offers "compensators" rather than actual exchange items because it compensates for the lack of those items in everyday life; thus, while their model does not assume atheism, it explains how religion could arise even if there are no supernatural forces in the world. Bainbridge has even sought to recreate the origins of religion in artificial intelligence (AI) programs in which exchange between AIs takes place but where certain exchange items cannot be obtained from any of the actual AIs in the program. Williams Sims Bainbridge, "Neural Network Models of Religious Belief," *Sociological Perspectives* 38 (1995), 483–495.

15. William Sims Bainbridge, "Cognitive Technologies," in *Managing Nano-Bio-Info-Cogno Innovations: Converging Technologies in Society*, ed. Mihail Roco and William S. Bainbridge (Dordrecht, Netherlands: Springer, 2006), 208; Bainbridge, " Religion for a Galactic Civilization 2.0;" Bainbridge, *Warcraft Civilization*, 62.

16. Edward Castronova, *Exodus to the Virtual World: How Online Fun Is Changing Reality* (New York: Palgrave Macmillan, 2007), 69.

17. Frank Lantz, "Forward," in *Rules of Play: Game Design Fundamentals*, ed. Katie Salen and Eric Zimmerman (Cambridge, MA: MIT Press, 2004), xi.

18. For the sake of parity, I will refer to indefinite player characters as female and indefinite non-player characters as male. This is not merely acquiescing to

political correctness: in December 2008 approximately 40% of all U.S. *World of Warcraft* players were women; see Nielsen, "The State of the Video Gamer: PC Game and Video Game Console Usage Fourth Quarter 2008," 2009.

19. For a fee, players can move their characters from one realm to another. There are also "cross-realm" zones, where players from different servers can encounter one another.

20. There are considerable data on the time to acquire new levels as players advance and the amount of time that players tend to devote based on their levels of play; see Nicolas Ducheneaut, Nick Yee, Eric Nickell, and Robert J. Moore, "Building an MMO with Mass Appeal: A Look at Gameplay in World of Warcraft," *Games and Culture* 1 (2006), 281–317. When Blizzard released the *Cataclysm* expansion, it retooled the leveling process so that reaching 85 with a new character would take approximately the same time as reaching 60 would have in the original launch of the game. This was repeated with *Mists of Pandaria*.

21. Characters who participate in PvP battlegrounds earn "honor points" and "conquest points" that can be exchanged for equipment. Such equipment provides benefits for PvP play but is not ideal for raiders or questers. There are also "justice points" and "valor points" acquired through PvE activity, which are used to buy appropriate gear for such play.

22. For the sake of simplicity, I will collapse the distinction between *Dungeons & Dragons* and *Advanced Dungeons & Dragons*. While most players use the advanced version, they generally refer to it by the simpler name.

23. See Gary Fine, *Shared Fantasy: Role-Playing Games as Social Worlds* (Chicago: University of Chicago Press, 1983), 72–122.

24. For excellent sources on the history of RPGs and the computer games that overlap with them, see Richard A. Bartle, *Designing Virtual Worlds* (Berkeley, CA: New Riders, [2003] 2004); Brad King and John Borland, *Dungeons and Dreamers: The Rise of Computer Game Culture from Geek to Chic* (New York: McGraw-Hill/ Osborne, 2003); Lawrence Schick, *Heroic Worlds: A History and Guide to Role-Playing Games* (Amherst, NY: Prometheus Books, 1991).

25. See, e.g., Boellstorff, *Coming of Age*, 38; Edward Castronova, *Synthetic Worlds: The Business and Culture of Online Games* (Chicago: University of Chicago Press, 2005), 107–108; King and Borland, *Dungeons and Dreamers*, 21, 27; T.L. Taylor, *Play between Worlds: Exploring Online Game Culture* (Cambridge, MA: MIT Press, 2006), 21.

26. See, e.g., Bartle, *Designing Virtual Worlds*, 71–73; Ken Rolston, "My Story Never Ends," in *Third Person: Authoring and Exploring Vast Narratives*, ed. Pat Harrigan and Noah Wardrip-Fruin (Cambridge, MA: MIT Press, 2009), 119.

27. Quoted in Marty Cortinas, "The Story So Far: Inside the Mind of Blizzard's Creative Godfather, Chris Metzen," *World of Warcraft Official Magazine* 1 (2010): 24–26. The creators of *D&D*, Gary Gygax and Dave Arneson, used Tolkien's Middle-earth as the inspiration for their world, so as the *D&D* gamers

became video game designers they extended the reach of Tolkien into their new environment. See William Sims Bainbridge, "Introduction," in *Online Worlds: Convergence of the Real and the Virtual*, ed. William Sims Bainbridge (London: Springer, 2010), 205; Boellstorff, *Coming of Age*, 37–38; King and Borland, *Dungeons and Dreamers*, 106. Of course, Tolkien is not solely responsible for the production of *D&D* or its virtual offshoots. Jack Vance's *Dying Earth* (New York: Hillman Periodicals, 1950), for example, profoundly influenced *D&D* game mechanics, and it would be impossible to think about how virtual worlds have evolved without considering the influence of science fiction authors like Vernor Vinge, William Gibson, and Tad Williams, especially Gibson. See Bartle, *Designing Virtual Worlds*, 64; Castronova, *Exodus to the Virtual World*, 57, 62, 118, 167; Harrigan and Wardrip-Fruin, "Introduction," 3–4; King and Borland, *Dungeons and Dreamers*, 95; Allucquere Rosanne Stone, "Will the Real Body Please Stand Up?: Boundary Stories about Virtual Cultures," in *Cyberspace: First Steps*, ed. Michael Benedikt (Cambridge, MA: MIT Press, 1991), 99.

28. Boellstorff, *Coming of Age*, 61.

29. Ibid., 62.

30. Alex Goleb, "Being in the World (of Warcraft): Raiding, Realism, and Knowledge Production in a Massively Multiplayer Online Game," *Anthropological Quarterly* 83 (2010), 17–46.

31. Fine, *Shared Fantasy*.

32. Robert M. Geraci, *Apocalyptic AI: Visions of Heaven in Robotics, Artificial Intelligence and Virtual Reality* (New York: Oxford University Press, 2010), 72–105.

33. For a brief narrative about the Science guild and its conference activities, see Bainbridge (2010b), which chronicles the launch of the guild, the three sessions of its conference, and also the entertaining expeditions that followed the conference sessions.

34. Guild names are used with permission.

35. There was no particular method behind naming Argorr (it sounded "Orcish" to me), but Moravec is a tip of my hat to Hans Moravec, the roboticist whose apocalyptic ideas about the future of robot technology were the foundation for much of my early research. For example, Robert M. Geraci, "Robots and the Sacred in Science and Science Fiction: Theological Implications of Artificial Intelligence," *Zygon: Journal of Religion and Science* 42 (2007), 961–980; Geraci, "Apocalyptic AI: Religion and the Promise of Artificial Intelligence," *Journal of the American Academy of Religion* 76 (2008), 138–166; Geraci, *Apocalyptic AI*.

36. Odd though it may seem to a nongamer, one study indicates that the availability of virtual pets is a factor in players' decisions over which games to play. Yu-Ling Lin and Hong-Wen Lin, "A Study on the Goal Value for Massively Multiplayer Online Role-Playing Games Players," *Computers in Human Behavior* 27 (2011).

37. For a helpful review of raiding guilds, including differences among them, see Golub, "Being in the World," 31.

38. Robin Torres, "Drama Mamas: Much Ado about Funsuckers," *WoW Insider*, May 13, 2011.

39. Douglas Mandelkow, "Leveling Up into a Community: World of Warcraft as Authentic Fake," Undergraduate honors thesis at Manhattan College, 2011.

40. A colleague has suggested that this might be based on the average age of SL residents, who are a few years older on average than *World of Warcraft* players. Further research would need to differentiate between the ages of gamers and their respective religious commitments. In my survey of Ravelry players, however, nearly 70% spend no hours at all on religious practice (e.g., prayer, services) in any given week. As the Ravelry players range between twenty and sixty years old, it is not clear that age is, in fact, the deciding issue. Certainly more of them engage in religious activity than in the general group comprising the third survey, but not by a particularly large margin. Likewise, while the number of respondents in the Ravelry survey who claim to be religious is only a few percentage points fewer than those who claim not to be, the number of respondents who claim that they are "definitely not" religious is twice that of those who claim to "definitely" be religious.

41. Benjamin Čulig and Izvor Rukavina, "Psychosocial and Sociocultural Determinants of a Typology of Video Gamers," Paper presented at the 4th Annual Conference for Videogame Cultures and the Future of Interactive Entertainment, July 12, 2012.

42. Survey takers were cued as to the significance of their numerical choices: 1 was labeled "definitely not," 4 was labeled "neutral," and 7 was labeled "definitely."

43. In terms of their popularity, 73% of respondents listed Tolkien's books as significant to them, 42% listed Lewis, 35% listed Isaac Asimov, 27% listed Rowling, and 25% listed Gaiman.

44. See Keith Winkler, "The Business and Culture of Gaming," in *Gaming as Culture*, ed. J. Patrick Williams, Sean Q. Hendricks, and Keith Winkler (Jefferson, NC: McFarland & Company, Inc., 2006), 143.

45. J. R. R. Tolkien, *The Tolkien Reader* (New York: Ballantine, 1966), 60.

46. Ibid., 77–87.

47. Ibid., 77.

48. Ibid., 78.

49. Ibid., 83–84.

50. Clive S. Lewis, "On the Fairy Tale," Wedgewood Circle.

51. William Sims Bainbridge, *Dimensions of Science Fiction* (Cambridge, MA: Harvard University Press, 1986), 25.

52. Marek Oziewicz, *One Earth, One People: The Mythopoeic Fantasy Series of Ursula K. LeGuin, Lloyd Alexander, Madeleine L'Engle, and Orson Scott Card* (Jefferson, NC: McFarland & Company, 2008), 92.

53. Ibid., 85.

54. On the influence of fantasy in game design, see Bainbridge, "Introduction," 205; Bartle, *Designing Virtual Worlds*, 61–63; Boellstorff, *Coming of Age*, 37–38; King and Borland, *Dungeons & Dreamers*, 106. Likewise, cyberpunk and other forms of science fiction have been of vast importance. See Chapters 4–6 on the importance of William Gibson and Neal Stephenson, in particular.

55. Christopher McMahon, "Imaginative Faith: Apocalyptic, Science Fiction Theory, and Theology," *Dialog: A Journal of Theology* 47 (2008): 276.

56. On sci-fi and wonder, see Farah Mendlesohn, "Introduction," in *The Cambridge Companion to Science Fiction*, ed. Edward James and Farah Mendlesohn. *Cambridge Companions Online* (Cambridge: Cambridge University Press, 2003a), 3.

57. On the religious themes in sci-fi, see, e.g., Robert M. Geraci, "Robots and the Sacred;" Geraci, *Apocalyptic AI*, 49–55; Geraci, "There and Back Again: Transhumanist Evangelism in Science Fiction and Popular Science," *Implicit Religion* 14 (2009); Farah Mendlesohn, "Religion and Science Fiction," in James and Mendlesohn, *Cambridge Companion to Science Fiction* (Cambridge: Cambridge University Press, 2003b), 264–275.

58. See, e.g., Hugo De Garis, *The Artilect War: Cosmists vs. Terrans: A Bitter Controversy Concerning Whether Humanity Should Build Godlike Massively Intelligent Machines* (Palm Springs, CA: ETC Publications, 2005), 92.

59. Kevin M. Berry, "The Meaning of Artificial Life?" *Robot* 26 (January–February 2011): 27.

60. Bainbridge, *Dimensions of Science Fiction*, 214.

61. Nick Dyer-Witheford and Greig de Peuter, *Games of Empire: Global Capitalism and Video Games* (Minneapolis: University of Minnesota Press, 2009), 229.

62. Andy Kessler, "How Videogames Are Changing the Economy," *Wall Street Journal*, January 11, 2011. See also Brooke Gladstone, "Transcript of 'The Influence of Gaming,'" *On the Media*, December 31, 2010.

63. National Science Foundation, "On-line Gamers Succeed Where Scientists Fail, Opening Door to New AIDS Drug Design." Press Release 11–197.

64. William Sims Bainbridge and Wilma Alice Bainbridge, "Electronic Game Research Methodologies: Studying Religious Implications," *Review of Religious Research* 49 (2007): 36.

65. Ibid., 46.

66. S. Brent Plate, "Religion Is Playing Games: Playing Video Gods, Playing to Play," *Religious Studies and Theology* 29 (2010), 215–230.

CHAPTER 2

1. Florence Chee, Marcelo Vieta, and Richard Smith, "Online Gaming and the Interactional Self: Identity Interplay in Situated Practice," in *Gaming as Culture: Essays on Reality, Identity, and Experience in Fantasy Games*, ed. J. Patrick

Williams, Sean Q. Hendricks, and W. Keith Winkler (Jefferson, NC: McFarland & Company, 2006), 155.

2. Bruce Lincoln, *Discourse and the Construction of Society: Comparative Studies of Myth, Ritual, and Classification* (New York: Oxford University Press, 1989), 4–5.

3. Ibid., 6–7.

4. See Bruno Latour, *Reassembling the Social: An Introduction to Actor-Network-Theory* (New York: Oxford University Press, 2005), 63–86.

5. Tefillin are ritual phylacteries that house small parchments on which portions of the Torah are written. The tefillin have leather straps with which practitioners bind them to their foreheads and left arms while reciting the appropriate blessing.

6. Emile Durkheim, *The Elementary Forms of the Religious Life*, trans. Karen Fields (New York: Free Press, [1912] 1995), 217–219.

7. Ibid., 220.

8. David LaChapelle, *Rize* (Los Angeles: David LaChapelle Studios), 2005. Krumping is a twentieth and twenty-first century urban dance style characterized by wild, rapid, and often aggressive body movements. Performed solo and in concert with others, it emerged out of the Los Angeles clown dancing scene and has offered many impoverished participants socially redemptive alternatives to gang affiliation (see LaChapelle).

9. Myron Krueger quoted in Howard Rheingold, *Virtual Reality: The Revolutionary Technology of Computer-Generated Artificial Worlds—and How It Promises to Transform Society* (New York: Touchstone Books, 1991), 117.

10. Durkheim, *Elementary Forms*, 218.

11. Gary Fine, *Shared Fantasy: Role-Playing Games as Social Worlds* (Chicago: University of Chicago Press, 1983); Brad King and John Borland, *Dungeons and Dreamers: The Rise of Computer Game Culture from Geek to Chic* (New York: McGraw-Hill/Osborne, 2003).

12. Nick Yee, "The Gamer Habitat," *Daedalus Project* (2006).

13. Bonnie Nardi, *My Life as a Night Elf Priest: An Anthropological Account of World of Warcraft* (Ann Arbor: Michigan University Press, 2010), 179–181.

14. Edward Castronova, *Exodus to the Virtual World: How Online Fun Is Changing Reality* (New York: Palgrave Macmillan, 2007), 35.

15. Richard A. Bartle, *Designing Virtual Worlds* (Berkeley, CA: New Riders, [2003] 2004), 26.

16. Ibid., 55.

17. Jane McGonigal, *Reality Is Broken: Why Games Make Us Better and How They Can Change the World* (New York: Penguin, 2011), 272–273.

18. Nardi, *My Life*, 116; see also McGonigal, *Reality is Broken*, 89–92.

19. William Sims Bainbridge, *The Warcraft Civilization: Social Science in a Virtual World* (Cambridge, MA: MIT Press, 2010), 222; Edward Castronova, *Synthetic Worlds: The Business and Culture of Online Games* (Chicago: University of

Chicago Press, 2005), 161; Mia Consalvo, "There Is No Magic Circle," *Games and Culture* 4 (2009): 408–417; T.L. Taylor, *Play between Worlds: Exploring Online Game Culture* (Cambridge, MA: MIT Press, 2006), 152.

20. Robert D. Putnam, *Bowling Alone: The Collapse and Revival of American Community* (New York: Simon and Schuster, 2000).

21. Ray Oldenberg, *The Great Good Place: Cafés, Coffee Shops, Community Centers, Beauty Parlors, General Stores, Bars, Hangouts, and How They Get You Through the Day* (New York: Paragon House, 1989).

22. Ibid., 31.

23. Nicholas Ducheneaut, Robert J. Moore, and Eric Nickell, "Virtual 'Third Places': A Case Study of Sociability in Massively Multiplayer Games," *Computer Supported Cooperative Work* 16 (2007), 129–166; Dmitri Williams, "Why Game Studies Now?: Gamers Don't Bowl Alone," *Games and Culture* 1 (2006), 13–16.

24. See Julian Holland Oliver, "The Similar Eye: Proxy Life and Public Space in the MMORPG," in *Proceedings of Computer Games and Digital Cultures Conference*, ed. Frans Mäyrä, (Tampere: Tampere University Press, 2002), 171–184.

25. See Nicolas Ducheneaut and Robert J. Moore, "More Than Just 'XP': Learning Social Skills in Massively Multiplayer Online Games," *Interactive Technology and Smart Education* 2 (2005), 89–100; Taylor, *Play between Worlds*.

26. Nicolas Ducheneaut, Nick Yee, Eric Nickell, and Robert J. Moore, "Building an MMO with Mass Appeal: A Look at Gameplay in World of Warcraft," *Games and Culture* 1 (2006), 281–317.

27. A response of 5, 6, or 7 on a scale of 1–7, where 4 is neutral and 7 is very important.

28. Nicolas Ducheneaut, "The Chorus of the Dead: Roles, Identity Formation, and Ritual Processes Inside an FPS Multiplayer Online Game," in *Utopic Dreams and Apocalyptic Fantasies: Critical Approaches to Researching Video Game Play*, ed. J. Talmadge Wright, David G. Embrick, and András Lukács (New York: Lexington Books, 2010a), 214.

29. On rules, play, and culture as the constituents of game design, see Katie Salen and Eric Zimmerman, eds., *Rules of Play: Game Design Fundamentals* (Cambridge, MA: MIT Press, 2004).

30. Nardi, *My Life*, 63–65.

31. J. Patrick Williams, "Consumption and Authenticity in the Collectible Strategy Games Subculture," in *Gaming as Culture: Essays on Reality, Identity, and Experience in Fantasy Games*, ed. J. Patrick Williams, Sean Q. Hendricks, W. Keith Winkler (Jefferson, NC: McFarland & Company, 2006), 91.

32. Nardi, *My Life*, 57–58; Williams, "Consumption and Authenticity," 93.

33. This marks something of a difference between my own and others' observations of guild life. Nardi, *My Life*, 15, for example, states that guild chat in her guilds almost never addressed life outside the game. Dennis D. Waskul makes a similar point about tabletop RPGs; see Waskul, "The Role-Playing Game and

the Game of Role-Playing: The Ludic Self and Everyday Life," in *Gaming as Culture: Essays on Reality, Identity, and Experience in Fantasy Games*, ed. J. Patrick Williams, Sean Q. Hendricks, W. Keith Winkler (Jefferson, NC: McFarland & Company, 2006), 27. My own experience gaming, playing *Dungeons & Dragons* and other RPGs as a child and playing *World of Warcraft* as an adult researcher, does not mirror theirs. In my *World of Warcraft* guild, chat frequently revolves around people's jobs, health, and families, though this is, admittedly, quite small in frequency compared with the in-game chat about monsters, equipment, quests, and obnoxious groupmates from outside the guild. Likewise, everyday life was persistently a part of our youthful conversations during nights of *D&D* and other RPGs. Corroborating this, Heather Mello, who has surveyed gamers, finds that only 9.5% of respondents value other players for keeping "outside life separate." See Mello, "Invoking the Avatar: Gaming Skills as Cultural and Out-of-Game Capital," in *Gaming as Culture: Essays on Reality, Identity, and Experience in Fantasy Games*, ed. J. Patrick Williams, Sean Q. Hendricks, W. Keith Winkler (Jefferson, NC: McFarland & Company, 2006), 180.

34. Mikael Jakobsson and T.L. Taylor, "The Sopranos Meets EverQuest: Social Networking in Massively Multiplayer Online Games," presented at MelbourneDAC, the 5th International Digital Arts and Culture Conference, 2003.

35. Ibid., 87–88.

36. Mark G. Chen, "Communication, Coordination, and Camaraderie in World of Warcraft," *Games and Culture* 4 (2009), 47–73.

37. See Krista-Lee Malone, "Dragon Kill Points: The Economics of Power Gamers," *Games and Culture* 4 (2009), 296–316.

38. Chen, "Communication, Coordination, and Camaraderie."

39. The Looking for Raid feature introduced with *Mists of Pandaria* functions as a counterbalance to this. Although it cannot make up for the lost guild powers, it does provide players with ready access to raids that require large, coordinated groups. Rather than relying on a guild for raid membership, a solitary player may use the LFR feature to collaborate with others. In this, the game design puts individual achievement and transcendent experiences (discussed in chapter 3) in opposition to community formation as understood through the more established guild structure.

40. Nardi, *My Life*, 21.

41. Ibid., 194; see also McGonigal, *Reality Is Broken*, 78–80.

42. Respondents were allowed more than one answer to the question.

43. See, e.g., see Nardi, *My Life*, 22, 181.

44. Castronova, *Synthetic Worlds*, 121; see also Taylor, *Play between Worlds*, 3–5; Nardi, *My Life*, 194.

45. See Lorne L. Dawson, "Religion and the Quest for Virtual Community," in *Religion Online: Finding Faith on the Internet*, ed. Lorne L. Dawson and Douglas E. Cowan (New York: Routledge, 2004), 78.

46. *World of Warcraft Magazine*, "Raiding the Physical World," *World of Warcraft Official Magazine* 1 (2010), 58–63.

47. Jennifer Light, "Taking Games Seriously," *Technology and Culture* 49 (2008), 347–375.

48. See Douglas A. Gentile, Craig A. Anderson, Shintaro Yukawa, Nobuko Ihori, Muniba Saleem, Lim Kam Ming, Akiko Shibuya, Albert K. Liau, Angeline Khoo, Brad J. Bushman, L. Rowell Huesmann, and Akira Sakamoto, "The Effects of Prosocial Video Games on Prosocial Behaviors: International Evidence from Correlational, Longitudinal, and Experimental Studies," *Personality and Social Psychology Bulletin* 35 (2009), 752–763; Tobia Greitemeyer, Silvia Osswald, and Markus Brauer, "Playing Prosocial Video Games Increases Empathy and Decreases Schadenfreude," *Emotion* 10 (2010), 796–802; Tobias Greitemeyer and Silvia Osswald, "Effects of Prosocial Video Games on Prosocial Behavior." *Journal of Personality and Social Psychology* 98 (2010), 211–221; Greitemeyer and Osswald, "Playing Prosocial Video Games Increases the Accessibility of Prosocial Thoughts," *Journal of Social Psychology* 151 (2011), 121–128.

49. Kunal Puri and Rudy Pugliese, "Sex, Lies, and Video Games: Moral Panics or Uses and Gratifications," *Bulletin of Science, Technology & Society* 32 (2012): 349.

50. The cultural power of technology is obvious in the way it changes people's lives but is also simultaneously masked behind a pretense toward the social neutrality of science. Some time ago, Bruno Latour argues that new sources of power derive from laboratory work; see Latour, "Give Me a Laboratory and I Will Raise the World," in *Science Observed: Perspectives on the Social Study of Science*, ed. Karin Knorr-Cetina and Michael Mulkay (Beverley Hills, CA: SAGE, 1983), 141–170. Likewise Donna Haraway has presented science as a means of shaping and creating citizens; see Haraway, *Modest_Witness@Second_Millennium.Female_Man©_Meets_Oncomouse™* (New York: Routledge, 1997). Despite these and other efforts, somehow the idea that there is a direct connection between science, technology, and society has eluded many people. Yet technology, in particular, continues to lean on individuals, applying pressures that we rarely ignore. Cell phone ownership, for example, creates a vastly different communication environment, including new social expectations, than was present just a decade ago. Consequently, *World of Warcraft* can never be "just a game," unless by that we also accept that games are important in the constitution of our lived experience and thus are vitally important to culture.

51. Haraway, *Modest_Witness*.

52. See, e.g., Pippin Barr, Sky Marsen, and James Noble, "Oppositional Play: Gathering Negative Evidence for Computer Game Values," in *Proceedings of the Second Australasian Conference on Interactive Entertainment (IE2005)* (Sydney, Australia: Creativity & Cognition Studios Press, 2005).

53. Dominic Arsenault, "The Video Game as an Object of Controversy," in Mark J. Wolf, ed., *The Video Game Explosion: A History from Pong to Playstation and Beyond* (Westport, CT: Greenwood Press, 2008), 277.

54. Christoph Klimmt, Hannah Schmid, Andreas Nosper, Tilo Hartmann, and Peter Vorderer, "'Moral Management': Dealing with Moral Concerns to Maintain Enjoyment of Violent Video Games," in *Computer Games as a Sociocultural Phenomenon: Games without Frontiers, War without Tears*, ed. Andreas Jahn-Sudmann and Ralf Stockmann, (New York: Palgrave Macmillan, 2008), 108–118.

55. Ibid., 117–118.

56. See Mark Hayse, "*Ultima IV*: Simulating the Religious Quest," in *Halos and Avatars: Playing Video Games with God*, ed. Craig Detweiler (Louisville, KY: Westminster John Knox Press, 2010); Mark Cameron Love, "Not-So-Sacred Quests: Religion, Intertextuality and Ethics in Video Games," *Religious Studies and Theology* 29 (2011), 191–213; Kevin Newgren, "BioShock to the System: Smart Choices in Video Games," in *Halos and Avatars: Playing Video Games with God*, ed. Craig Detweiler (Louisville, KY: Westminster John Knox Press, 2010), 135–144; Kurt Squire, "From Content to Context: Videogames as Designed Experience," *Educational Researcher* 35 (2011), 19–29.

57. See Petri Lankoski, "Player Character Engagement in Computer Games," *Games and Culture* 6 (2011): 303–304.

58. Philip G. Zimbardo and Nikita Duncan, "'The Demise of Guys': How Video Games and Porn Are Ruining a Generation," *CNN.com*, May 23, 2012. Their essay is riddled with problems, especially its gross generalizations from a very limited number of examples and its total lack of empirical grounding.

59. José P. Zagal, "Ethically Notable Videogames: Moral Dilemmas and Gameplay," in *Breaking New Ground Innovation in Games, Play, Practice and Theory: Prodeedings of DiGRA 2009.* http://works.bepress.com/jose_zagal/3.

60. Bartle, *Designing Virtual Worlds*, 695. The ethics deployed in *World of Warcraft* reflect a historical relationship between excellence in gaming and the presumption of civic virtue; see Johann Huizinga, *Homo Ludens: A Study of the Play-Element in Culture* (London: Routledge, [1949] 2000), 64–66. Consider, for example, how upsetting the public finds it when a modern-day Olympian, home-run king, or Tour de France winner is proven to have used performance-enhancing drugs. Given this relationship between gaming and virtue, there may be nothing new in the fact that *World of Warcraft* is the product of ethical work on the part of its designers and a vehicle for the ethical action of its players. While most players recognize that the game has at least one internal ethical system, they do not necessarily believe that such ethics are meaningful outside of the game.

61. Salen and Zimmerman, *Rules of Play*, 605.

62. Quoted in McGonigal, *Reality Is Broken*, 301.

63. Jill Tarter and Will Wright, "Evolution, Creativity, and Future Life," in *Science Is Culture*, ed. Adam Bly (New York: Harper Perennial, 2010), 278.

64. McGonigal, *Reality Is Broken*, 302. Shortly after the publication of this book, Heather Chaplin, Heather Chaplin, "I Don't Want To Be a Superhero: Ditching Reality For a Game Isn't as Fun as It Sounds," *Slate.com*, March 29, 2011, criticized the "gamification" movement in *Slate*. Chaplin rejects the idea that we should use game structures to provide people with satisfaction from their otherwise banal lives, which is one of McGonigal's primary enterprises. According to Chaplin, "There are legitimate reasons why people feel they're achieving less. These include the boring literal truths of jobs shipped overseas, stagnant wages, and a taxation system that benefits the rich and hurts the middle class and poor. You want to transform peoples' [sic] lives into games so that the feel *as if* they're doing something worthwhile?... For McGonigal, Wikipedia is one of the most convincing gamification success stories.... Certainly there is nothing wrong with people volunteering to write encyclopedia entries. But to advocate this as a model to build on, explaining that 'positive emotions are the ultimate reward for participation,' is thoughtless at best and diabolical at worst. People might get off on points, but they need to be paid for their work." Essentially, Chaplin fears that laying a game on top of ordinary daily tasks could reduce people's incentive to struggle for more equitable living and working conditions.

65. See also Robert M. Geraci, "Theological Productions: The Role of Religion in Video Game Design," in *Cultural Perspectives of Video Games: From Designer to Player*, ed. Adam L. Brackin and Natacha Guyot (Oxford: Inter-Disciplinary Press, 2012a), 111–114.

66. Jordan Mechner, "*The Sands of Time*: Crafting a Video Game Story," in *Second Person: Role-Playing and Story in Games and Playable Media*, ed. Pat Harrigan and Noah Wardrip-Fruin (Cambridge, MA: MIT Press, 2007), 115.

67. Miguel Sicart, "The Ethics of Computer Game Design," presented at the Digital Games Research Association Conference, Vancouver, Canada, 2005.

68. Bainbridge, *Warcraft Civilization*, 14.

69. See Christopher Douglas, "Multiculturalism in World of Warcraft," *Electronic Book Review*, June 4, 2010; Jessica Langer, "The Familiar and the Foreign: Playing (Post)Colonialism in *World of Warcraft*," in *Digital Culture, Play, and Identity: A World of Warcraft Reader*, ed. Hilde G. Corneliussen and Jill Walker Rettberg, (Cambridge, MA: MIT Press, 2008), 87–108; Melissa J. Monson, "Race-Based Fantasy Realm: Essentialism in World of Warcraft," *Games and Culture* 7 (2012), 48–71. *World of Warcraft* is certainly not alone in presenting characters in stereotyped and possibly racist images. One study of game advertisements, for example, shows that game characters are very commonly portrayed in stereotypical fashion; see Paul R. Ketchum and B. Mitchell Peck, "Marketing Computer Games: Reinforcing or Changing Stereotypes?" in *Utopic Dreams and Apocalyptic Fantasies: Critical Approaches to Researching*

Video Game Play, edited by J. Talmadge Wright, David G. Embrick, and András Lukács, 125-142 (New York: Lexington Books, 2010). Additionally, as Nathaniel Poor describes, there is a long history of Elves in fantasy representing a racial other in dark and light terms; see Poor, "Digital Elves as a Racial Other in Video Games: Acknowledgment and Avoidance," *Games and Culture* 7 (2012), 375–396. This allows both thinking through racial otherness and prejudice and, unfortunately, an easy way to avoid doing so (ibid., 391–392).

70. WoWWiki, "Sargeras," http://www.wowwiki.com/Sargeras (2010)
71. Bainbridge, *Warcraft Civilization*, 109.
72. Esther MacCallum-Stewart, "Never Such Innocence Again: War and Histories in *World of Warcraft*," in Corneliussen and Rettberg, eds., *Digital Culture, Play, and Identity: A World of Warcraft Reader* (Cambridge, MA: MIT Press, 2008), 46–47.
73. Elsewhere, efforts to produce faction rivalries have provoked resistance from gamers. The designers of *Uru: Prologue* added a faction system and even paid actors to help foment dispute, but not everyone who played the game enjoyed the effort; see Celia Pearce and Artemesia, *Communities of Play: Emergent Cultures in Multiplayer Games and Virtual Worlds* (Cambridge, MA: MIT Press, 2009), 76, 135.
74. This bitterness between Horde and Alliance is problematized by members of each faction who engage in ethically problematic behavior. Some members of the Horde actively work against the interests of the other races, even within their own faction. For example, the blood elves' thirst for power reveals an ethical failing that endangers friend and foe alike, while members of the Forsaken hope to gain vengeance on all living creatures, including their fellow Horde races. Thrall, the spiritual leader and one-time war chief of the Horde, is unquestionably noble and seeks to lead the Horde into a better future, but this is undercut by blood elf and forsaken activities and the many evil members of all of the races, including orcs who continue serving demonic forces. Even a casual observer, however, will have no difficulty in seeing the internecine warfare as counterproductive and end up fully cognizant that the taurens, trolls, and orcs, at the very least, would be better served by an honorable arrangement with the Alliance. A history fraught with conflict, however, makes this difficult. Just as with the troublesome Horde races, the Alliance also regularly fails in its moral obligations. The failure of the human leaders to deal honorably with the masons who became the Defias brotherhood is one example of this. In addition, there are times when the human, dwarf, and gnome races appear to be "ecologically destructive, aggressive colonizers," especially when compared to the taurens; see MacCallum-Stewart, "Never Such Innocence Again," 43. The gnomes' technology has ruined their city, the dwarves dig up large archeological and mining sites (often with adverse results), and the human agriculture and

political expansion conflicts with other races' desire to live in harmony with the land (ibid.).

75. Miguel Sicart, "This War Is a Lie: Ethical Implications of Massively Multiplayer Online Game Design," in *Emerging Issues of Life in Virtual Worlds*, ed. Charles Wankel and Shaun Malleck, (Charlotte, NC: Information Age Publishing, 2010), 177–195.

76. Ibid., 192.

77. See, e.g., Timothy Rowlands, *Video Game Worlds: Working at Play in the Culture of* EverQuest (Walnut Creek, CA: Left Coast Press, 2012), 120; Will Slocombe, "Beyond Good and Evil: The Inhuman Ethics of *Redemption* and *Bloodlines*," in *Computer Games as a Sociocultural Phenomenon: Games without Frontiers, War without Tears*, ed. Andreas Jahn-Sudmann and Ralf Stockmann (New York: Palgrave Macmillan, 2008), 120–127. Some players make new stories out of the *World of Warcraft* mythos and out of *World of Warcraft* game play as a way to explore the ethics of interfactional politics. Jason Choi's *Edge of Remorse*, for example, is a machinima film published on *YouTube*, which explores the "destructive nature" of the Horde–Alliance conflict; see Henry Lowood, "*Warcraft* Adventures: Texts, Replay, and Machinima in a Game-Based Storyworld," in *Third Person: Authoring and Exploring Vast Narratives*, ed. Pat Harrigan and Noah Wardrip-Fruin (Cambridge, MA: MIT Press, 2009), 409. *Edge of Remorse* manages to show, without any characters speaking, the tragedy of Azeroth's war-stained politics through the dismay and death that occurs when two childhood friends find themselves on opposite sides of the conflict.

78. A full 26% of respondents indicate no preference between the Horde and Alliance, so the results are based on those respondents who do.

79. See Nick Dyer-Witheford and Greig de Peuter, *Games of Empire: Global Capitalism and Video Games* (Minneapolis: University of Minnesota Press, 2009); Eli Kosminksy, "Finding Adam Smith in Azeroth," in *World of Warcraft and Philosophy: Wrath of the Philosopher King*, ed. Luke Cuddy and John Norlinger (Chicago: Open Court, 2009); Scott Rettberg, "Corporate Ideology in *World of Warcraft*," in *Digital Culture, Play, and Identity: A World of Warcraft Reader*, ed. Hilde G. Corneliussen and Jill Wlaker Rettberg (Cambridge, MA: MIT Press), 19–38.

80. Bainbridge, *Warcraft Civilization*, 161.

81. S. Rettberg, "Corporate Ideology in *World of Warcraft*."

82. Bainbridge, *Warcraft Civilization*, 14.

83. Ibid., 32.

84. Ibid., 33.

85. In addition to the obvious ways Venture Company deforesting machinery reveals the problematic use of technology, the magical cravings of the blood elves may be seen as a warning about science and technology. Observers have long recognized that magic operates in primitive cultures much the

way that science and technology operate in our own. The famed anthropologist Bronislaw Malinowski, *Magic, Science and Religion, and Other Essays* (New York: Doubleday, [1948] 1954), 86–87, for example, argues that magic, like science, is a goal-oriented cultural technique: it follows definite principles of operation to achieve desired ends. While these principles seem faulty from our perspective, in *World of Warcraft* they are not. Bainbridge, *Warcraft Civilization*, 75, connects magic and technology in the game and observes that the blood elves' insatiable exploitation of magic parallels our own exploitation of science and technology, often at considerable cost.

86. Dyer-Witheford and de Peuter *Games of Empire*, xxiii.

87. Ibid.

88. Ibid., 185–214.

89. An answer of 5, 6, or 7 of 7, where 4 is "neutral/uncertain" and 7 is "definitely yes."

90. Interestingly, in a preliminary survey done with members of my own *World of Warcraft* guild and community, only 36% of respondents saw no ethical system in the game, and the percentage of respondents who gave positive answers was 49.4% rather than 40%. Whether this difference reflects a gendered understanding of the game (94% of guild respondents are female, as opposed to 34.5% of general survey respondents) or should be attributed to other factors is, at present, unclear.

91. See Bainbridge, "New World View," in *Online Worlds: Convergence of the Real and the Virtual*, ed. William Sims Bainbridge (London: Springer, 2010), 15.

92. David W. Simkins and Constance Steinkuehler, "Critical Ethical Reasoning and Role-Play." *Games and Culture* 3 (2008): 352.

93. Fine, *Shared Fantasy*, 210.

94. Peter, email interview with the author, August 3, 2010b.

95. Argoz, email interview with the author, December 6, 2011.

96. The precise meaning of these data is unclear. Among those who prefer a race for its ideology, orc and troll were the most popular responses (43.8% for each, where respondents could choose up to three preferred races). What precisely players like about these races' ideologies is less clear than it would be for respondents who chose tauren or night elf, as these latter show decided concerns for environmentalism. The orc race works to disengage itself from its prior corruption by demons but remains a warlike community. The trolls act as stereotypical Caribbean islanders with a penchant for Voodoo. Their civilization is in steep decline and requires revitalization. As with the question over beauty and aesthetics later in the chapter, this issue of preferring ideologies reflects a player desire to join a community with which he or she can philosophically identify but we need considerably more research to explore this issue.

97. Lucy, email interview with the author, August 2, 2010.

98. Peter, email interview with the author, August 2, 2010a.

99. Ibid.

100. Jill, email interview with the author, July 30, 2010.

101. Susan, Skype interview with the author, August 4, 2010. Susan likes her characters to have the mining profession in the game but differentiated her own mining from the Venture Company's. Whereas she simply removes mineral veins
at the surface of the ground, the company systematically demolishes areas in
their wood and mineral harvesting. To some extent conflating these two (ibid.),
Susan finds the company's mining activities repugnant. This conflation is
complex. Susan recognizes the difference between deforested and mined areas
and says that the deforesting does not always bother her because of her youth
growing up in a fire zone "where forest fires are an important part of the environment." Nevertheless, she mentions one of the Venture Company's mining
activities as being near the Charred Vale; in fact, the Venture Company engages
in deforesting, not mining, near the Charred Vale.

102. Guild, "Appalled at NPCs," thread on *Ravelry.com*, December 1, 2010a.

103. Jill, email interview.

104. Peter, email interview, 2010a.

105. Guild, "Wolves," thread on *Ravelry.com*, September 4, 2012b.

106. Responses were from 1 to 7, where one is "definitely not," 4 is "neutral/uncer-
tain," and 7 is "definitely." Negative responses, then, were answers of 1, 2, or 3. In
a related concern, when players have used *World of Warcraft* to develop their own
set of values, they have occasionally run into trouble within the game, as when
Blizzard rejected a peaceful protest of gnome warriors who were unhappy with
changes made to the warrior class; see Miguel Sicart, "A Flourishing Revolt," in
World of Warcraft and Philosophy: Wrath of the Philosopher King, ed. Luke Cuddy
and John Norlinger (Chicago: Open Court, 2009), 92–106.

107. See Robert Lemos, "Digital Plague Hits Online Game World of Warcraft,"
Security Focus, September 27, 2005.

108. Linda Dyson, "Teenage Girls 'Play House': The Cyber-Drama of *The Sims*,"
in *Computer Games as a Sociocultural Phenomenon: Games without Frontiers,
War without Tears*, ed. Andreas Jahn-Sudmann and Ralf Stockmann,
(New York: Palgrave Macmillan, 2008), 197–206.

109. Laura Sydell, "'Virtual' Virus Sheds Light on Real-World Behavior," *NPR*,
October 5, 2005.

110. Quoted in Kris Graft, "GDC 2011: An Epidemiologist's View of *World of Warcraft's*
Corrupted Blood Plague," *Gamasutra: The Art and Business of Making Games*
website, February 28, 2011.

111. In similar fashion, the PvP guild Serenity Now attacked and slaughtered players
from a rival guild while they held an in-game funeral march for a guild member
who had recently died in real life; see Monica Evans, "You Can Kill Your Friends
but You Can't Save Gnomeregan," in *World of Warcraft and Philosophy: Wrath
of the Philosopher King*, ed. Luke Cuddy and John Norlinger (Chicago: Open

Court, 2009), 3–4. This act of unnecessary violence sparked outrage among the mourners but was defended as simply "part of the game" by the perpetrators.

112. Angelica B. Ortiz de Gortari, Karin Aronsson and Mark D. Griffiths, "Game Transfer Phenomena in Video Game Playing: A Qualitative Interview Study," *International Journal of Cyber Behavior, Psychology and Learning* 1 (2011), 15–33.

113. Ibid., 28.

114. Gentile et al., "Effects of Prosocial Video Games," 754.

115. Robin S. Rosenberg, Shawnee L. Baughman, and Jeremy N. Bailenson, "Virtual Superheroes: Using Superpowers in Virtual Reality to Encourage Prosocial Behavior," *PLoS ONE* 8 (2013), 1–9.

116. Ibid.

117. Omri Gillath, Cade McCall, Phillip R. Shaver, and Jim Blascovich, "What Can Virtual Reality Teach Us about Prosocial Tendencies in Real and Virtual Environments?" *Media Psychology* 11 (2008), 259–282.

118. Gentile et al., "Effects of Prosocial Video Games."

119. See S. Brent Plate, "Religion Is Playing Games: Playing Video Gods, Playing to Play," *Religious Studies and Theology* 29 (2010): 221–222.

120. Tim Marsh, "Vicarious Experience: Staying There Connected with and through Our Own and Other Characters," in *Gaming as Culture: Essays on Reality, Identity and Experience in Fantasy Games*, ed. J. Patrick Williams, Sean Q. Hendricks, and W. Keith Winkler (Jefferson, NC: McFarland & Company, 2006), 206–209.

121. Ibid.

122. Simkins and Steinkuehler, "Critical Ethical Reasoning," 352.

123. See Larry Rosen, "Why Would Kids Who Spend More Time on Facebook Display More Empathy Online and in Real Life?" *Science and Religion Today*, August 25, 2011; Shirley Wang, "Could Those Hours Online Be Making Kids Nicer?" *Wall Street Journal*, August 16, 2011.

124. Bartle, *Designing Virtual Worlds*, 190.

125. In her study of *Guild Wars* players, Daniela Robles provides survey numbers that indicate that 69% of players regularly assist others by providing material goods or assistance on a quest; see Robles, "Dying to Play: How Death Mechanics Provide Meaningful Experiences in Guild Wars," in *Cultural Perspectives of Video Games: From Designer to Player*, ed. Adam L. Brackin and Natacha Guyot (Oxford: Inter-Disciplinary Press, 2012), 23–32.

126. In a widely distributed presentation for the nonprofit group Technology, Entertainment, Design (TED), game theorist Jane McGonigal argues that *World of Warcraft* play could be harnessed to make the world a better place; see McGonigal, "Gaming Can Make a Better World," presented at the TED 2010 Conference in Long Beach, CA. Something, she argues, must result from the 5.93 million person hours invested in *World of Warcraft* by players over the past decade. She concludes that all that time spent solving the problems of Azeroth could be used to solve the problems of Earth. McGonigal believes that the games

have four important ramifications for life that will help us make the world better: (1) urgent optimism; (2) a social fabric of trust and cooperation; (3) a blissful sense of productivity; and (4) a sense of epic meaning. All of these combined, she argues, make gamers super-powered hopeful individuals capable of changing the world. The only problem is that gamers are accustomed to seeing themselves empowered in their games only; McGonigal wants game design set up to help people see themselves as able to change the world outside of games also. Others, looking further out into the future, believe that *World of Warcraft* teaches lessons that will help us think through a technological Singularity: the hypothetical point in the future when machines become more intelligent than we and technology and culture thus evolve in completely unpredictable ways as technological progress accelerates toward infinite speed. As players engage the moral problems of Azeroth, perhaps they will "be ready to assume our rightful place, to advance the cause of life, to ensure wild freedom and endless possibility for ourselves and our species"; see Leon Spencer and Anna Janssen, "Future Pasts of Magic and Deceit," in *World of Warcraft and Philosophy: Wrath of the Philosopher King*, ed. Luke Cuddy and John Norlinger (Chicago: Open Court, 2009), 223. Games besides *World of Warcraft* might likewise be seen as preparing humanity for its future. Will Wright, the designer of the *Sim* franchise and *Spore* implies that the latter might help us prepare for a Singularity and posthuman life; Tarter and Wright, "Evolution, Creativity, and Future Life," 278–280.

127. Zhi-Jin Zhong, "The Effects of Collective MMORPG (Massively Multiplayer Online Role-Playing Games) Play on Gamers' Online and Offline Social Capital," *Computers in Human Behavior* 27 (2011): 2360.

128. Ibid., 2361.

129. SCA (2010) is "an international organization dedicated to researching and re-creating the arts and skills of pre-17th-century Europe." Its "'Known World' consists of 19 kingdoms, with over 30,000 members residing in countries around the world. Members, dressed in clothing of the Middle Ages and Renaissance, attend events which feature tournaments, royal courts, feasts, dancing, various classes & workshops, and more" (ibid.)

130. King and Borland, *Dungeons and Dreamers*, 50.

131. Peter, email interview, 2010a. Although video game play may certainly interfere with or be irrelevant to ethical development, there is no doubt that it can also be helpful. Effective game design should therefore take such processes into account. According to one study, *EverQuest* players explicitly claimed that their gaming activities help them to develop empathetic understandings of others, promoting more ethical treatment of them; Chee et. al., "Online Gaming," 189–190. A study of *Star Wars: The Old Republic* supports this, showing that the games' players believe playing helps them to appreciate just war and oppose unethical military tactics; Robert M. Geraci and Nat Recine, "A Moral Universe: Suffering and War in *Star Wars: The Old Republic*," forthcoming.

132. Salen and Zimmerman, *Rules of Play*, 522.

133. Mircea Eliade, *Symbolism, the Sacred, and the Arts*, ed. Diane Apostolos-Cappadona (New York: Crossroad, 1985).

CHAPTER 3

1. David Chidester, "Moralizing Noise," *Harvard Divinity Bulletin* 32 (2004): 17.

2. David Chidester, *Authentic Fakes: Religion and American Popular Culture* (Los Angeles: University of California Press, 2005).

3. Dmitri Williams, Tracy L.M. Kennedy, and Robert J. Moore, "Behind the Avatar: The Patterns, Practices, and Functions of Role Playing in MMOs," *Games and Culture* 6 (2011): 180.

4. Gary Fine, *Shared Fantasy: Role-Playing Games as Social Worlds* (Chicago: University of Chicago Press, 1983), 144–5. To illustrate the varying identities that one can experience in *World of Warcraft*, William Bainbridge begins every chapter of *The Warcraft Civilization* with an anecdote written from the first person perspective of one of his characters; see Bainbridge, *The Warcraft Civilization: Social Science in a Virtual World* (Cambridge, MA: MIT Press, 2010). Calling his characters "shards of self" (ibid., 187), Bainbridge describes each of them and their relationship to him personally, illustrating how the ties between player and character can vary immensely. Reviewing the range of investment that Bainbridge places in his characters easily recalls the varying degrees to which an individual might identify with any of his or her own.

5. Ibid., 113.

6. Fine, *Shared Fantasy*, 222.

7. Multi-User Dungeon, or MUD, was the first successful virtual world; see Richard Bartle, *Designing Virtual Worlds* (Berkeley, CA: New Riders, [2003] 2004), 4. It was a text-based world where players could earn powers over other players and the world by achieving sufficient expertise.

8. Ibid., 161.

9. Ibid.

10. Sherry Turkle, "Rethinking Identity through Virtual Community," in *Clicking In: Hot Links to a Digital Culture*, ed. Lynn Hershman Leeson (Seattle: Bay Press, 1996), 116–122.

11. Eyder Peralta, "In Second Life, the World Is Virtual. But the Emotions Are Real," *Houston Chronicle*, May 26, 2006; Turkle, "Rethinking Identity," 118.

12. Sherry Turkle, "What Are We Thinking about When We Are Thinking about Computers?" in *The Science Studies Reader*, ed. Mario Biagioli (New York: Routledge, 1999), 543–552.

13. Nicholas Ducheneaut, "Massively Multiplayer Online Games as Living Laboratories: Opportunities and Pitfalls," in *Online Worlds: Convergence of the Real and the Virtual*, ed. William S. Bainbridge (London: Springer, 2010b),144.

14. Celia Pearce and Artemesia, *Communities of Play: Emergent Cultures in Multiplayer Games and Virtual Worlds* (Cambridge, MA: MIT Press, 2009), 116.

15. Ibid., 115.

16. Reprinted from *Communities of Play: Emergent Cultures in Virtual Worlds and Multiplayer Gamers*; with permission from the author and Celia Pearce, published by The MIT Press (p. 118). Player–character identification is not just a feature of online games and virtual worlds but is part of a larger trend in gaming. Adam Smith, head of product development for Core, which released *Lara Croft: Tomb Raider*, says, "We wanted it to be a game where the player has more of an affinity for the character.... We wanted her to be as real a person as possible, so that people could really identify with the character"; quoted in Alison McMahan, "Video Game Stars: Lara Croft," in *The Video Game Explosion: A History from Pong to Playstation and Beyond*, ed. Mark J. Wolf (Westport, CT: Greenwood Press, 2008), 184. Identification with a character is part of the fun of gaming: it is part escapism, part self-realization, and profoundly immersive.

17. Richard Bartle, "Alice and Dorothy Play Together," in *Third Person: Authoring and Exploring Vast Narratives*, ed. Pat Harrigan and Noah Wardrip-Fruin (Cambridge, MA: MIT Press, 2009), 111.

18. Ibid., 116.

19. Thinkers, "Can MMORPGs Save the World?" transcript of Thinkers Discussion Group event posted at Mind Child's Musings weblog, October 12, 2010a.

20. John Lester, Skype interview with the author, December 6, 2011.

21. Erving Goffman, *The Presentation of Self in Everyday Life* (New York: Anchor Books, 1959); see also Fine, *Shared Fantasy*, 204; Dennis D. Waskul, "The Role-Playing Game and the Game of Role-Playing: The Ludic Self and Everyday Life," in *Gaming as Culture: Essays on Reality, Identity, and Experience in Fantasy Games*, ed. J. Patrick Williams, Sean Q. Hendricks, and W. Keith Winkler (Jefferson, NC: McFarland & Company, 2006), 22.

22. Fine, *Shared Fantasy*, 204.

23. Kutter Callaway, "Wii Are Inspirited: The Transformation of Home Video Gaming Consoles (and Us)," in *Halos and Avatars: Playing Video Games with God*, ed. Craig Detweiler (Louisville, KY: Westminster John Knox Press, 2010), 76

24. Edward Castronova, *Exodus to the Virtual World: How Online Fun Is Changing Reality* (New York: Palgrave Macmillan, 2007), 188.

25. Fine, *Shared Fantasy*, xiii.

26. Craig Detweiler, "Introduction," in *Halos and Avatars: Playing Video Games with God*, ed. Craig Detweiler (Louisville, KY: Westminster John Knox Press, 2010), 9.

27. Peter, email interview with the author, August 2, 2010a.

28. Susan, Skype interview with the author, August 4, 2010.

29. Susan, Skype interview with the author, December 20, 2011.

30. Sean Q. Hendricks, "Incorporative Discourse Strategies in Tabletop Fantasy Role-Playing Gaming," in *Gaming as Culture: Essays on Reality, Identity, and Experience in Fantasy Games*, ed. J. Patrick Williams, Sean Q. Hendricks, and W. Keith Winkler (Jefferson, NC: McFarland & Company, 2006), 44–46; Waskul, "Role-Playing Game," 29.

31. Chaim Gingold, "A Brief History of *Spore*," in *Third Person: Authoring and Exploring Vast Narratives*, ed. Pat Harrigan and Noah Wardrip-Fruin (Cambridge, MA: MIT Press, 2009), 135.

32. Emile Durkheim, *The Elementary Forms of the Religious Life*, trans. Karen Fields (New York: Free Press, [1912] 1995), 216–217.

33. Ibid., 217.

34. See Bonnie Nardi, *My Life as a Night Elf Priest: An Anthropological Account of World of Warcraft* (Ann Arbor: Michigan University Press, 2010), 95–97.

35. Bartle, *Designing Virtual Worlds*, 293. In *Second Life*, which is a closer approximation to conventional reality than *World of Warcraft*, players do take on fairly conventional economic activities (e.g., bar ownership), but the circumstances are unlikely to mimic those of conventional reality. For example, bar owners in Chicago are unlikely to go to *Second Life* and become bar owners. People who romanticize bar ownership and, in all likelihood, do not concern themselves with making a profit (because there will not be one), are the sort of people likely to end up owning a virtual bar. I did, in fact, become well acquainted with one bar owner in *Second Life*. She did not turn a profit but enjoyed running her "Irish Pub" anyway. She had a regular clientele of friends and a consistent line-up of live music performers, both of which she enjoyed very much.

36. Douglas Estes, *SimChurch: Being the Church in the Virtual Age* (Grand Rapids, MI: Zondervan, 2009), 52.

37. Lauren Langman and András Lukács, "Capitalism, Contradiction, and the Carnivalesque: Alienated Labor vs. Ludic Play," in *Utopic Dreams and Apocalyptic Fantasies: Critical Approaches to Researching Video Game Play*, ed. J. Talmadge Wright, David G. Embrick, and András Lukács (New York: Lexington Books, 2010a), 70.

38. Guild, "Farming (esp. Archeology)—the Good the Bad the Ugly," thread on *Ravelry.com*, February 20, 2011.

39. Ibid.

40. Katie Salen and Eric Zimmerman, eds., *Rules of Play: Game Design Fundamentals* (Cambridge, MA: MIT Press, 2004), 334.

41. Alison Gazzard and Alan Peacock, "Repetition and Ritual Logic in Video Games," *Games and Culture* 6 (2011): 509.

42. See also Nardi, *My Life*, 116.

43. Mia Consalvo, Timothy Dodd Alley, Nathan Dutton, Matthew Falk, Howard Fisher, Todd Harper, and Adam Yulish, "Where's My Montage? The Performance

of Hard Work and Its Reward in Film, Television, and MMOGs," *Games and Culture* 5 (2010): 381–402.

44. Thinkers, "Can MMORPGs Save the World?" It remains the case that games like *World of Warcraft*, unlike Durkheim's *corroboree*, have an economic element. Indeed, the lack of economics is precisely what guarantees a *corroboree's* religious nature. In game, however, there are powerful economic models at stake. People do find ways of making money within online games, and some people use the games to make money in the "conventional" world. Some individuals even make considerable amounts of money, as is the case with *Second Life's* Anshe Chung, the virtual world's first millionaire land speculator. Indeed, at one point *Second Life's* top ten business people averaged $200,000 per year in income; see *Economist*, "Living a *Second Life*," *Economist*, September 28, 2006. In 2010, John "Neverdie" Jacobs sold a virtual space station in the game *Entropia* for a record $635,000 and subsequently raised millions of investment dollars to produce an entire planet in the virtual world; see Oliver Chiang, "Meet the Man Who Just Made a Half Million from the Sale of Virtual Property," *Forbes.com*, November 13, 2010,. Clearly, money and virtual reality can go hand in hand. *World of Warcraft* players develop "professions" in which they craft objects (e.g., potions, armor, weaponry, food) and then sell these and other objects at auction in game. Some players, short on the time or skill to earn powerful characters through play, buy *World of Warcraft* gold through privately run websites, though this is against the game's licensing agreement. It may then be the case that the economics of capitalism are integral to game play (see Nick Dyer-Witheford and Greig de Peuter, *Games of Empire: Global Capitalism and Video Games* [Minneapolis: University of Minnesota Press, 2009], 132), but for the vast majority of players there is a distinct difference between their conventional economic life and their online economic life. Very few players join virtual worlds to make money; rather they generally spend money in order to enhance the value of play. One counterexample, obvious to even the most casual *World of Warcraft* player, is the supposedly ubiquitous "Chinese gold farmer." Some individuals, commonly in Asian countries, are employed to play MMORPGs and earn gold that is subsequently sold for conventional currencies over the Internet. These people are not, however, players—at least not properly speaking. Gold farmers (who are actually relatively rare despite the frequency of complaints against them) are employees of companies dedicated to making money off of video game worlds; they do not, therefore, count as countervailing evidence for my claim that the virtual worlds are held distinct from everyday, economic life.

45. Castronova, *Exodus to the Virtual World*, xvi.

46. Quoted in Lisa Swain, "*Myst* and *Halo*: A Conversation with Rand Miller and Marty O'Donnell," in *Halos and Avatars: Playing Video Games with God*, ed. Craig Detweiler (Louisville, KY: Westminster John Knox Press, 2010), 106.

47. Joystiq, "Bungie: 10 Billion Covenant Killed in Halo 3 . . . and Growing," *Joystiq. com*, April 14, 2009, emphasis added.

48. Greg Costikyan, "Games, Storytelling, and Breaking the String," in *Second Person: Role-Playing and Story in Games and Playable Media*, ed. Pat Harrigan and Noah Wardrip-Fruin (Cambridge, MA: MIT Press, 2007), 8.

49. Ibid., 10.

50. In fact, there are long narratives associated with many media, and the different styles of media enable different kinds of narratives. Tanya Krzywinska divides such narratives into "Arachne" styles and "Minerva" styles, where the former tend to be disjointed, amorphous, or polyvalent and the latter tend to be linear and precise in their meanings; see Tanya Krzywinska, "Arachne Challenges Minerva: The Spinning Out of Long Narrative in *World of Warcraft* and *Buffy the Vampire Slayer*," in *Third Person: Authoring and Exploring Vast Narratives*, ed. Pat Harrigan and Noah Wardrip-Fruin (Cambridge, MA: MIT Press, 2009), 385–398. She points out that *World of Warcraft* has an Arachne-inspired narrative but a Minervan world, where as the television show *Buffy the Vampire Slayer* works in the inverse, with a Minervan narrative and an Arachnid world (ibid.).

51. Joseph Laycock, "Myth Sells: Mattel's Commision of the Masters of the Universe Bible," *Journal of Religion and Popular Culture* 22 (2010). It has been suggested to me that Facebook games like *Farmville* belie this claim. Such a fact must be grounded in three ways (none of which is actually true): (1) that *Farmville* and similar games are immersive; (2) that narrative games are the only kinds of games; and (3) that *Farmville* has no narrative. This last issue is one of some obviousness; although the story doesn't go much of anywhere in particular, there is no question about the fact that developing a farm from its earliest stages into a complex system is narrative; see Salen and Zimmerman, *Rules of Play*, 396, on the narratives of game play; Bartle, "Alice and Dorothy Play Together," 106, on the inherent narrativity of all games. *Farmville* will, in all likelihood, lose its luster over the course of years as well, in part because it lacks a sophisticated narrative. As a counter to the second issue, I think we ought to look at *Tetris* rather than *Farmville* as a better example. *Tetris* has very little narrative (though since it can be told as a sequence of events, it certainly has one of some sort or another), but the game has remained significant for more than twenty years. Obviously, games can be designed with challenges that remain interesting to us. The question is whether playing such games provides any sense of meaning. They do so only a very limited extent because they do not try to do so and no one expects them to. For immersive games, in which the player must take on a role, story is a vital part of their appeal. A narrative arc is important for games that include a character with whom to identify, as opposed to a game like *Tetris*, which involves the manipulation of blocks but has no in-world characters. Games without stories just do not sell; see Chris Hansen, "From *Tekken* to *Kill Bill: The Future of Narrative Storytelling?*" in *Halos and Avatars: Playing Video*

Games with God, ed. Craig Detweiler (Louisville, KY: Westminster John Knox Press, 2010), 20. Hansen goes on to note that for "the average user, the story still reigns supreme" (ibid., 21); see also Daniel White Hodge, "Role Playing: Toward a Theology for Gamers," in *Halos and Avatars: Playing Video Games with God*, ed. Craig Detweiler (Louisville, KY: Westminster John Knox Press, 2010), 164. This may be connected to the short life expectancy of Facebook games. Consider *Zombies*, which was wildly popular for all of about a year before fading into the background, still played, but of considerably less significance than *Farmville* and others in 2009. As a result, the creators of *Zombies* attempted to make a MMORPG out of it as a way of revitalizing interest in the game. Story can even be so powerful that when Microsoft released its Xbox video game console it actually invented a mythology about the system's allegedly alien origins; see Dyer-Witheford and dePeuter, *Games of Empire*, 69.

52. McGonigal, *Reality Is Broken*, 97.

53. Robin D. Laws, "Intellectual Property Development in the Adventure Games Industry: A Practioner's View," in *Third Person: Authoring and Exploring Vast Narratives*, ed. Pat Harrigan and Noah Wardrip-Fruin (Cambridge, MA: MIT Press, 2009), 62. Purchased adventure modules are a clear exception to this in that they guide the players through particular stories. Even so, such modules are often cobbled together by a game master (GM) and interspersed with adventures of the GM's design. As such, even where players take advantage of developers' adventure modules, the overall story is one composed through the work and play of those at the table.

54. Krzywinksa, "Arachne Challenges Minerva," 388.

55. Quoted in Silvia Lindtner and Paul Dourish, "The Promise of Play: A New Approach to Productive Play," *Games and Culture* 6 (2011): 461.

56. Mechner, "*The Sands of Time*: Crafting a Video Game Story," 112.

57. Ibid., 120.

58. Castronova, *Exodus to the Virtual World*, 118.

59. Tanya Krzywinska, "World Creation and Lore: *World of Warcraft* as Rich Text," in *Digital Culture, Play, and Identity: A World of Warcraft Reader*, ed. Hilde G. Corneliussen and Jill Walker Rettberg (Cambridge, MA: MIT Press, 2008), 384.

60. Ibid., 395.

61. Castronova, *Exodus to the Virtual World*, 118. This is not just true of MMORPGs. In other video games the narrative can produce immersive game experiences as well, such as in the *Prince of Persia* console game franchise; see Drew Davidson, "Well Played: Interpreting *Prince of Persia: The Sands of Time*," *Games and Culture* 3 (2008): 370. Some fights in the game are evidently of such challenge and require so many attempts that for some players at least it is only the immersiveness of the story that will keep players engaged (ibid., 378).

62. Krzywinska "Arachne Challenges Minerva," 389.

63. Bonnie Nardi alleges that the visuals in *World of Warcraft* frequently overpower the lore in *World of Warcraft* (*My Life*, 89) but also importantly recognizes the fact that the lore requires considerable out-of-game attention. So whatever short-term attention players give to the visuals, in terms of time expenditure and careful thought, the lore clearly overshadows the graphics. In addition, according to my survey, more individuals enjoy participating in the storyline (36%) than enjoy exploring new regions (22%), which would seem like a approximation of the degree to which players enjoy the game's visual aesthetics. Empirical evidence thus undermines Nardi's initial claim that graphics matter more than lore.

64. Jill, email interview with the author, July 30, 2010.

65. Nain, *World of Warcraft* conversation with the author, January 1, 2012.

66. See Bartle, "Alice and Dorothy Play Together," 109.

67. At one point in time, achievements were character-bound, meaning that a player needed to earn the achievement with every character. As for the Mists of Pandaria expansion, however, achievements became account-bound, meaning that if a player accomplished something with one character, she need not do so with her other characters to have the titles, vanity items, or achievement listing with all of those other characters.

68. Lisa Poisso, "Breakfast Topic: Do Account-Wide Achievements Make Characters Too Interchangeable?" *WoW Insider*, December 17, 2012.

69. Digory, *World of Warcraft* interview with Nicholas Zachowski, March 2011.

70. The initial Wrath of the Lich King expansion did not include the Icecrown Citadel raid, which was part of patch 3.3.0. Delaying the release of content this way stretches out players' enjoyment over time, as simply leveling up characters can be done quite swiftly, but players must wait and improve their equipment if they hope to complete the highest level of content.

71. Caspian, *World of Warcraft* interview with Nicholas Zachowski, March 2011.

72. See Petri Lankoski, "Player Character Engagement in Computer Games," *Games and Culture* 6 (2011): 303–304

73. Guild, "The End of the World is TONIGHT!!!!" thread on Ravelry.com, November 22, 2010b.

74. Ibid.

75. Fine, *Shared Fantasy*, 80, 86.

76. See Lawrence Schick, *Heroic Worlds: A History and Guide to Role-Playing Games* (Amherst, NY: Prometheus Books, 1991), 11.

77. Will Hindmarch, "Storytelling Games as a Creative Medium," in *Second Person: Role-Playing and Story in Games and Playable Media*, ed. Pat Harrigan and Noah Wardrip-Fruin (Cambridge, MA: MIT Press, 2007), 48. To some extent, maybe it is true that "even in the most cutting-edge examples of the state of the art, it is not the players who tell the story, it is the game. Whether computer games with a narrative element, board games, card games, or face-to-face

role-playing games, the essential plot and structure of the narrative is predetermined before the game begins, and cannot be altered"; James Wallis, "Making Games that Make Stories," in *Second Person*, 69. Certainly, even in games like *D&D* there are constraints on what kinds of stories are told and how they are told; likewise, choices of the Dungeon Master who set up the environment limit the players' own contributions. Nevertheless, there is a considerable difference between the limits imposed in a game like *D&D* and those imposed by *World of Warcraft*.

78. Sean C. Duncan, "Remaking Azeroth," in *World of Warcraft and Philosophy: Wrath of the Philosopher King*, ed. Luke Cuddy and John Norlinger (Chicago: Open Court, 2009), 118.

79. Marty Cortinas, "The Story So Far: Inside the Mind of Blizzard's Creative Godfather, Chris Metzen," *World of Warcraft Official Magazine* 1 (2010): 24–26.

80. Perhaps sophisticated artificial intelligence programming will resolve the storytelling dilemma. If the AI could respond to players in real time, then games could be designed to permit and even promote interactive storytelling. For this reason, game designer Will Hindmarch claims that "interactive, electronic Storytellers are gaming's City of Gold;" "Storytelling Games," 55. Not only are increasing numbers of players engaged in electronic stories, but also even in conventional reality very good storytellers are hard to come by. If it were possible to create and subsequently market an AI that can do the work of an outstanding Dungeon Master, all computer players would have access to what only the luckiest of pen-and-paper players have. Although designers are presently at work on interactive storytelling systems, for the time being *World of Warcraft* and similar games must continue to restrict player options; see Christoph Klimmt, Christian Roth, Ivar Vermeulen, Peter Vorderer, and Franziska Susanne Roth, "Forecasting the Experience of Future Entertainment Technology: 'Interactive Storytelling' and Media Enjoyment," *Games and Culture* 7 (2012), 187–208.

81. Edward Burnett Tylor, *Primitive Culture* (New York: Harper Torchbooks, [1871] 1958), 12.

82. Lester, Skype interview, December 6, 2011.

83. Because players are there, contributing their words and deeds, various commentators (e.g., Taylor 2006, 159) have labeled MMORPGs co-creative. Nevertheless, compared to pen-and-paper RPGs they fail miserably in this.

84. Answers of 5, 6, or 7 out of 7, where 1 is "not at all" and 7 is "all of the time."

85. A response of 1 out of 7 was defined as "not at all."

86. Tanya Krzywinska, "Blood Scythes, Festivals, Quests, and Backstories: World Creation and Rhetorics of Myth in World of Warcraft," *Games and Culture* 1 (2006): 386.

87. Ibid., 386; see also Krzywinska, "World Creation and Lore," 127.

88. Tom Chilton, BlizzCast interview with Rob Simpson, BlizzCast episode 16, June 2011.

89. Dave Kosak, BlizzCast interview with Rob Simpson, BlizzCast episode 16, June 2011.

90. Quoted in McGonigal, *Reality Is Broken*, 59.

91. *WoWhead*, "Veteran of the Wrathgate—Achievement," comment by FranklinNoble, December 11, 2008.

92. Argoz, email interview with the author, December 6, 2011, emphasis added.

93. There are those who object to such practices on moral grounds. For example, in his examination of *EverQuest*, Jeffrey Cain suggests that "once *EQ* prevails as the home of mind and spirit, the world of RL and the individual human body begins to fade...as such, they are steadily refocused on the game, as opposed to RL"; Jeffrey P. Cain, "Another Bricolage in the Wall: Deleuze and Teenage Alienation," in *Computer Games as a Sociocultural Phenomenon: Games without Frontiers, War without Tears*, ed. Andreas Jahn-Sudmann and Ralf Stockmann (New York: Palgrave Macmillan, 2008), 62–63.

94. Susan, Skype interview with the author, August 4, 2010.

95. See Jill Walker Rettberg, "Quests in *World of Warcraft*: Deferral and Repetition," in *Digital Culture, Play, and Identity: A World of Warcraft Reader*, ed. Hilde G. Corneliussen and Jill Walker Rettberg (Cambridge, MA: MIT Press, 2008), 172–176.

96. Salen and Zimmerman, *Rules of Play*, 411.

97. Ibid.

98. Guild, "The End of the World Is TONIGHT!!!!"

99. See also Mark J. P. Wolf, "Morals, Ethics, and Video Games," in *The Video Game Explosion: A History from Pong to Playstation and Beyond*, ed. Mark J. P. Wolf (Westport, CT: Greenwood Press. 2008b), 285.

100. Schick, *Herioc Worlds*, 14, emphasis in original.

101. Not all players number themselves among the heroes of Azeroth, obviously. Though he pays close attention to the lore, Peter says it is "not 'me' or even my character who is performing these acts of heroism, it is collectively the 'Heroes of Azeroth' who are"; Peter, email interview, 2010a. There is undeniable nuance in Peter's position: on one hand he recognizes that a group that drives the story exists, but on the other he also sees that this group exists regardless of whether he plays the game. He is, therefore, realistic in his understanding of the story mechanics and his relationship to them.

102. Mircea Eliade, *The Myth of the Eternal Return: Or, Cosmos and History*, trans. Willard R. Trask (Princeton, NJ: Princeton University Press, [1954] 1991), xiv.

103. Max Weber, "Science as a Vocation," in *From Max Weber: Essays in Sociology*, ed. Hans Gerth and C. Wright Mills (Oxford: Oxford University Press, 1958).

104. Peter, email interview, 2010a.

105. Castronova, *Exodus to the Virtual World*, 207.

106. Quoted in Juan Carlos Pineiro-Escoriaza, *Second Skin*, Pure West Films, 2008.

107. Quoted in Rheingold, *Virtual Reality*, 385.

108. Langman and Lukács, "Capitalism, Contradiction, and the Carnivalesque."

109. Margaret Wertheim, *The Pearly Gates of Cyberspace: A History of Space from Dante to the Internet* (New York: W.W. Norton & Company, 1999).

110. Nardi, *My Life*, 51.

111. Ibid., 49–50.

112. S. Brent Plate, "Religion Is Playing Games: Playing Video Gods, Playing to Play," *Religious Studies and Theology* 29 (2010), 224–226.

113. Robert M. Geraci, "Theological Productions: The Role of Religion in Video Game Design," in *Cultural Perspectives of Video Games: From Designer to Player*, ed. Adam L. Brackin and Natacha Guyot (Oxford: Inter-Disciplinary Press, 2012a), 103.

114. See Robert M. Geraci, *Apocalyptic AI: Visions of Heaven in Robotics, Artificial Intelligence and Virtual Reality* (New York: Oxford University Press, 2010), 58–59.

115. Castronova, *Exodus to the Virtual World*, 189.

116. Quoted in Celia Pearce, "The Truth about Baby Boomer Gamers: A Study of Over-Forty Computer Game Players," *Games and Culture* 3 (2008): 172.

117. See, e.g., Bainbridge, *The Warcraft Civilization*, 214; Nardi, *My Life*, 86.

118. Hansen, "From *Tekken* to *Kill Bill*," 24.

119. This is not, of course, solely limited to *World of Warcraft*. There is a broad scope of virtual worlds and video games that "are persistent, commodified, and seamlessly integrated into everyday life" that "still represent episodic moments, times, and spaces where people can experience collective effervescence and empowerment" (Langman and Lukács, "Capitalism, Contradiction, and the Carnivalesque," 60).

120. 1 Corinthians 15:51; see also 2 Corinthians 5:1–4.

121. 1 Corinthians 15:53–54.

122. I have thoroughly engaged the connection between Jewish and Christian visions of glorified embodiment in prior work; Geraci, *Apocalyptic AI*, Robert M. Geraci, "Apocalyptic AI: Religion and the Promise of Artificial Intelligence," *Journal of the American Academy of Religion* 76 (2008), 138–166.

123. Quoted in Pineiro-Escoriaza, *Second Skin*.

124. Aravis, *World of Warcraft* conversation with the author, September 22, 2011.

125. Helen, *World of Warcraft* conversation with the author, September 22, 2011.

126. See Robert M. Geraci and Jovi Geraci, "Virtual Gender: How Men and Women Use Videogame Bodies," *Journal of Gaming and Virtual Worlds* 5 (2013), 329–348.

127. Nardi, *My Life*, 16.

128. It is clear that the *World of Warcraft* designers enjoy playing around with gender stereotypes in addition to the ways they reinscribe them. For example, during the Brewfest that happens in early October, a female gnome catcalls male characters as they pass by, shouting such things as, "You! The cute one! Would you like to go over to my place and look over my tool collection?" and "Ooo, walk by again, cutie! Your posterior muscles are very finely toned!" Bringing

the conversation back to conventional life and its gender expectations, she also asks, "Are you interested in a woman able to hold intelligent discourse and look attractive while doing so?" Clearly, by catcalling men and praising the possibility of women being attractive thanks to their intelligence rather than mute good looks, the designers want remind players that there are consequences to particular ways of thinking through beauty and treating those around us.

129. Anthony Little and David Perrett, "Putting Beauty Back in the Eye of the Beholder," *Psychologist* 15 (2002), 28–32; A.P. Møller and R. Thornhill, "Bilateral Symmetry and Sexual Selection: A Meta-Analysis," *American Naturalist* 151 (1998), 174–192.

130. Davendra Singh, "Adaptive Significance of Female Physical Attractiveness: Role of Waist-to-Hip Ratio," *Journal of Personality and Social Psychology* 65 (1993), 293–307.

131. Ibid.

132. See, e.g., Janine Hawkins, "Ophelia's Gaze: 3 Big Mistakes MMOs Make that Alienate Female Gamers," *New World Notes* Weblog, January 3, 2011; Andrea Rubenstein, "Idealizing Fantasy Bodies," *Iris Gaming Network* website, May 26, 2007.

133. T.L. Taylor, "Intentional Bodies: Virtual Environments and the Designers Who Shape Them," *International Journal of Engineering Education* 19 (2003), 25–34.

134. Geraci and Geraci, "Virtual Gender."

135. Pearce and Artemesia, *Communities of Play*, 21.

136. Guild, "Appalled at NPCs," thread on *Ravelry.com*, December 1, 2010.

137. Ibid.

138. Iris, "Can Any *WoW* Players Do Me a Favour?" *Iris Gaming Network* web forum, 2007.

139. Guild, "The 'Unloved' Races/Classes," thread on *Ravelry.com* (January 31, 2012a).

140. Iris, "Can Any *WoW* Players."

141. Each respondent was permitted to choose up to three answers from a list of seven.

142. See Bashiok, "4.3 Preview—Transmogrification," *World of Warcraft* official website, August 17, 2011.

143. Ibid.

144. Such desires are not unique to *World of Warcraft* but are important in other games as well. As Ken Rolston notes of Internet postings about *Daggerfall* characters: "It was a revelation to me when I saw all the Internet postings of *Daggerfall* characters posed in elegant green velvet garments, with harmoniously colored shields and weapons—all selected to complement to best advantage, for instance, the Argonian lizardman's lurid green, scaly skin. The game doesn't care how you dress, but the user does; Rolston..."My Story Never Ends," in *Third Person: Authoring and Exploring Vast Narratives*, ed. Pat Harrigan and Noah Wardrip-Fruin (Cambridge, MA: MIT Press), 122.

145. Anne Stickney, "Avengers Assemble! Transmogrify Your Own Superhero Team," *WoW Insider*, May 10, 2012.
146. See King and Borland, *Dungeons and Dreamers*, 15.
147. Nardi, *My Life*, 7.
148. See Maharishi, "TM-Sidhi Program and Yogic Flying," *Maharishi.org*, 2001.
149. Like so many of the issues in this chapter, the feeling of heroism is not unique to *World of Warcraft*: one *Halo* player writes, "*Halo* has always been a place where I feel loved…there is something profoundly warming in the reaction get from the marines when you stride (or bunny-hop) into view. They are genuinely pleased to see you. Genuinely buoyed by your presence. Being able to instill hope and confidence into people just [by] being near them sounds pretty heavenly to me"; Margaret Robertson, "One More Go: Why Halo Makes Me Want to Lay Down and Die," *Offworld—Boing Boing*, September 25, 2009).
150. Krzywinska, "World Creation and Lore," 390; see also Edward Castronova, *Synthetic Worlds: The Business and Culture of Online Games* (Chicago: University of Chicago Press, 2005), 119; McGonigal, *Reality Is Broken*, 3.
151. Nardi, *My Life*, 8. The experience of being the hero is not limited to MMORPGs like *World of Warcraft*. Game theorist Michael Nitsche, for example, writes of *Medal of Honor: Allied Assault* (2002): "once more I pick up the controller to win a war seemingly single-handed;" Nitsche, *Video Game Spaces: Image, Play, and Structure in 3D Game Worlds* (Cambridge, MA: MIT Press, 2008), 65. The feeling that he alone stands in the way of the Axis powers in World War II closely mirrors the feeling that *World of Warcraft* players get when they struggle against the demonic powers of the Burning Legion. One of the most delightful examples of how game design can produce a sense of heroism comes from the MMORPG *City of Heroes*, in which the "random fame string" causes NPCs to mention the hero as he or she walks nearby. Designer Matthew Miller writes, "The random fame string allowed us to put words in the mouths of the population. After a mission, you could walk down the street and hear a passing citizen make remarks like, 'Wow, it's Awesome Guy! I heard he rescued the mayor the other day!' With this little piece of dialogue, we now made it feel like Awesome Guy was making a difference in the everyday lives of the citizens of Paragon City"; Matthew P. Miller, "Storytelling in a Multiplayer Environment," in *Third Person: Authoring and Exploring Vast Narratives*, ed. Pat Harrigan and Noah Wardrip-Fruin (Cambridge, MA: MIT Press), 128.
152. Nardi, *My Life*, 13. *World of Warcraft* is not the only game in which players' work results in personal growth, of course. Richard Page, for example, argues that in the Chinese game *Zhengtu* "gamers construct an ethical selfhood that is coterminous with their actual world self, using the game not as an alternative reality but as a crucible for the heart'"; Richard Page, "Leveling Up: Playerkilling as Ethical Self-Cultivation," *Games and Culture* 7 (2012): 239. Similarly, Lindtner and Dourish quote a Chinese player of *Killer Game* averring that it "makes your

language more refined, more attractive…. This game makes you speak, and listen, others have to listen to you. That way, it will make you more open, and more self confident"; in Silvia Lindtner and Paul Dourish, "The Promise of Play: A New Approach to Productive Play," *Games and Culture* 6 (2011): 467.

153. Global Innovation Outlook, "Virtual Worlds, Real Leaders: Online Games Put the Future of Business Leadership on Display," distributed by IBM and Seriosity, Inc. (2007); Diana Rhoten and Wayne Lutters, "Virtual Worlds for Virtual Organizing," in *Online Worlds: Convergence of the Real and the Virtual*, ed. William Sims Bainbridge,(London: Springer, 2010), 265–278.

154. Margaret, email interview with the author, December 9, 2011.

155. Argoz, email interview with the author, December 6, 2011.

156. McGonigal, "Gaming Can Make a Better World"; McGonigal, *Reality Is Broken*, 248.

157. See Mikael Jakobsson, "The Achievement Machine: Understanding Xbox 360 Achievements in Gaming Practices," *Game Studies* 11 (2011).

158. Quoted in Pineiro-Escoriaza, *Second Skin*.

159. Mia Consalvo, "Achievement Deleted: The Challenges of Quantifying Gaming Capital," contribution to the 4th Flow Conference in Austin, TX, posted to Technoculture, Art and Games under the title "Gaming Capital and Flow," November 9, 2012.

160. Jakobbsson, "Achievement Machine."

161. In fact, as Jakobsson points out, some players even find that their achievement ambitions cause them emotional pain due to the grinding that some achievements cause (ibid.).

162. Jeffrey G. Snodgrass, H.J. François Denga II, Michael G. Lacy, Jesse Fagan, David Most, Michael Blank, Lahoma Howard, Chad R. Kershner, Gregory Kdrambeer, Alissa Leavitt-Reynolds, Adam Reynolds, Jessica Vyvial-Larson, Josh Whaley, and Benjamin WIntersteen, "Restorative Magical Adventure or Warcrack? Motivated MMO Play and the Pleasures and Perils of Online Experience," *Games and Culture* 7 (2012): 3–28.

163. Ibid.

164. Of course, social relationships that are tied specifically to the pursuit of achievements (e.g., hard-core raiding) lead to many negative situations, such as when raiding schedules interfere with conventional friends, family, and obligations (ibid., 21).

165. See especially Ray Kurzweil, *The Age of Spiritual Machines: When Computers Exceed Human Intelligence* (New York: Viking, 1999); Kurzweil, *The Singularity Is Near: When Humans Transcend Biology* (New York: Viking, 2005); Hans Moravec, "Today's Computers, Intelligent Machines and Our Future," *Analog* 99 (1978); Moravec, *Mind Children: The Future of Robot and Human Intelligence* (Cambridge, MA: Harvard University Press, 1988); Moravec, *Robot: Mere Machine to Transcendent Mind* (New York: Oxford University Press, 1999).

166. Geraci, *Apocalyptic AI*.

167. Castronova, *Synthetic Worlds*, 9; see also William Sims Bainbridge, "Introduction," in *Online Worlds: Convergence of the Real and the Virtual*, ed. William Sims Bainbridge (London: Springer, 2010), 6.

168. From my perspective, transhumanists are universally religious, though many resist this claim. Some, such as Giulio Prisco, recognize the religiosity of transhumanism ("Engineering Transcendence," blog post republished by the Institute for Ethics and Emerging Technologies, December 1, 2004), but others respond very negatively to this. Despite their reservations over the term, I believe that transhumanists are all religious; see Chapter 6 in this volume; Geraci, "Cyborgs, Robots, and Eternal Avatars: Transhumanist Salvation at the Interface of Brains and Machines," in *Routledge Companion to Religion and Science*, ed. James Haag, Gregory Peterson, and Michael Spezio, 578–590 (New York: Routledge, 2011a); Geraci, "There and Back Again: Transhumanist Evangelism in Science Fiction and Popular Science," *Implicit Religion* 14 (2009), 141–172. Of course, when I use the term religion, I do not use it perjoratively, but rather in keeping with the definitions previously offered.

169. Bainbridge, *Warcraft Civilization*, 62. Such a religion could circumvent the compensatory system that Bainbridge believes underpins religious life, demonstrably offering what religion can only claim to without proof. There are, however, problems with this kind of immortality, such as who can legally control an uploaded personality: unless the personality is given legal citizenship, then someone will "own" it. This leads to a host of possible ethical considerations; see Jeremy N. Bailenson and Kathryn Y. Segovia, "Virtual Doppelgangers: Psychological Effects of Avatars Who Ignore Their Owners," in *Online Worlds: Convergence of the Real and the Virtual*, ed. William Sims Bainbridge (London: Springer), 183–184.

170. Christopher Moriarty and Avelino J. Gonzelez, "Learning Human Behavior from Observation for Gaming Applications," *Proceedings of the 22nd International Florida Artificial Intelligence Research Society Conference* (FLAIRS-2009). I am grateful to Dr. Gonzalez for furnishing me with a copy of this paper.

171. Avelino J. Gonzalez, email correspondence with the author, September 14, 2009.

172. LifeNaut, official website, 2010; Terasem, official website, 2010.

173. See also Linda Geddes, "Immortal Brain: You Can Live Forever," *New Scientist* 206 (2010).

174. The Turing Church is a pun on the religiosity of transhumanism and the Turing-Church conjecture attributed to Alan Turing and Alonzo Church. The conjecture states that any process executed by a computer with infinite storage can be replicated by any other computer with infinite storage, regardless of the two computers' configuration. Use of the name reflects the desire to copy a

human mind in a computer, which quite obviously has a different architecture and material basis from a human body.

175. Order of Cosmic Engineers, "Order of Cosmic Engineers: Prospectus,", Order of Cosmic engineers website, 2008b.

176. Geraci, *Apocalyptic AI*, 101–104.

177. Giulio Prisco, email invitation to join the Turing Church, April 24, 2010d.

178. Jane McGonigal, "A Real Little Game," presented at the Digital Games Research Association Conference in Utrecht, 2003.

179. Turing Church, "First Question," email thread, April 26, 2010. This is a somewhat odd citation of McGonigal, whose primary thesis is that one must differentiate between actual belief and the performance of belief in commitments to games (e.g., a claim that "this is not a game"). If a transhumanist game led to only a performance of belief rather than actual belief, little successful conversion would take place.

180. See Robert M Geraci, "Video Games and the Transhuman Inclination," *Zygon: Journal of Religion and Science* 47 (2012), 735–756.

181. Castronova, *Synthetic Worlds*, 59.

182. Argoz, email interview with the author, December 6, 2011.

183. Margaret, email interview with the author, December 9, 2011.

184. Nardi, *My Life*, 120.

185. Bainbridge, *Warcraft Civilization*, 227.

186. Florence Chee, Marcelo Vieta, and Richard Smith, "Online Gaming and the Interactional Self: Identity Interplay in Situated Practice," in *Gaming as Culture: Essays on Reality, Identity, and Experience in Video Games*, ed. J. Patrick Williams, Sean Q. Hendricks, and W. Keith Winkler (Jefferson, NC: McFarland & Company, 2006), 154.

187. Langman and Lukács, "Capitalism, Contradiction, and the Carnivalesque," 71.

CHAPTER 4

1. Linden Lab, "What Is *Second Life*?" *Second Life* website (2010).

2. See, e.g., Tom Boellstorff, *Coming of Age in Second Life: An Anthropologist Explores the Virtually Human* (Princeton, NJ: Princeton University Press, 2008), 16–24.

3. See, e.g., Julien MacDougall and Wayne O'Brien, *Studying Video Games* (Leighton Buzzard: Auteur Press, 2008), 32.

4. See Mark J. P. Wolf, "Introduction," in *The Video Game Explosion: A History from Pong to Playstation and Beyond*, edited by Mark J.P. Wolf (Westport, CT: Greenwood Press, 2008a), pp. xiii–xv.

5. Wagner James Au, "Embracing *Second Life* as a Game Platform, Linden Lab Selects EA Exec & Game Developer Rod Humble as New CEO," *New World Notes*, December 23, 2010b; see also *Second Life*, "Games in *Second Life*," *YouTube* video, December 30, 2010.

6. Wagner James Au, "Linden to Add Game Mechanics to *Second Life*'s New User Experience," *New World Notes*, August 14, 2011a.

7. As I used a feminine pronoun for *World of Warcraft* players, I will use a male pronoun for *Second Life* residents.

8. Economic data on *Second Life*'s users is nearly impossible to acquire because, although Linden Lab releases quarterly reports, the data are universally clouded and thus reviled by those who pay attention. For example, in January 2011, Linden Lab reported that average monthly economic participants were up 4.3% from quarter four of 2009 but did not differentiate among "economic participants," some of whom who are useless in terms of measuring actual spending in-game (e.g., those who receive a stipend because they pay for premium accounts). Residents were quick to lambast Linden Lab for what they perceived to be the utterly deceptive economic reports; see Nelson Linden, "The Second Life Economy in Q4 2010," *Second Life* community forum, January 26, 2011.

9. It should be obvious, but by *contemporary life* I really mean something more like "contemporary American life" or "contemporary life in the developed world." *Second Life* in particular has pretty much nothing to do with how most people in developing nations think about or practice religion.

10. Frank Rose, "Lonely Planet," *Wired* 15 (2007); Rachel Rosmarin, "Virtual Fun and Games," *Forbes.com*, November 8, 2007.

11. Stephen D. O'Leary, "Utopian and Dystopian Possibilities of Networked Religion in the New Millennium," in *Religion and Cyberspace*, ed. Morten T. Højsgaard and Margit Warburg (New York: Routledge, 2005).

12. See Wagner James Au, "The Mystery of Second Life's Flat Growth in 2011—Despite 16K New Users Daily," *New World Notes*, December 28, 2011f; Au, "*Second Life* Forecast to Lose 10% of World's Private Sims This Year," *New World Notes*, June 6, 2012d.

13. Anonymous, comment on *Second Thoughts*, October 20, 2010.

14. Lag refers to the rate at which new information downloads to the user. A high lag rate will slow the users ability to interact with the world as people, objects, buildings, and even the landscape slowly "rez" (short for resolve) into view.

15. See Iggy O, "Failure to Disrupt: Why Second Life Failed," *Hypergrid Business*, February 8, 2011.

16. See Wagner James Au, "*Second Life* Still among Nielsen's Top 10 of PC Games in US," *New World Notes*, July 27, 2011c; Au, "*Second Life* Back on Nielsen's Latest Top 10 PC Game Ratings," *New World Notes*, June 26, 2012c.

17. Wagner James Au, "Philip Rosedale: Second Life Usage Surpasses 2 Billion Hours," *New World Notes* July 18, 2012b.

18. Jennifer Kahn, "The Visionary," *New Yorker* 87, 46–53, July 11, 2011.

19. Quoted in Cade Metz, "*Second Life* Will Dwarf the Web in Ten Years: So Says Linden Lab CEO," *Register*, August 1, 2007. It is worth noting that Lanier was a consultant to Linden Lab in the early days of *Second Life*.

20. See Rachel Wagner, *Godwired: Religion, Ritual and Virtual Reality* (New York: Routledge, 2012), 131.

21. Wagner James Au, "Embracing Second Life as a Game Platform, Linden Lab Selects EA Exec & Game Developer Rod Humble as New CEO," *New World Notes*, December 23, 2010b.

22. Wagner James Au, "NWN Exclusive: Interview with Rod Humble, Linden Lab's New CEO, on the Future of *Second Life*," *New World Notes* weblog, February 9, 2011b.

23. LamdaMOO is a text-based social world.

24. Seth Schiesel, "A Game to Make Zynga Nervous," *New York Times*, October 7, 2011.

25. Wagner James Au, "Shaker Gets $15 Million in Venture Funding, Renewing Valley Interest in Synchronous Avatar-Driven Socialization," *New World Notes*, October 10, 2011e.

26. Quoted in Wagner James Au, "*Myst* Co-Creator Rand Miller Thinks Worlds like *Second Life* & *Uru Live* Have a Future on Tablets," *New World Notes*, July 26, 2012a.

27. Giulio Prisco, email correspondence with the author, September 12, 2010g.

28. See Celia Pearce and Artemesia, "The Diasporic Game Community: Trans-Ludic Cultures and Latitudinal Research across Multiple Games and Virtual Worlds," in *Online Worlds: Convergence of the Real and the Virtual*, ed. William S. Bainbridge (London: Springer, 2010), 43–56.

29. Boellstorff, *Coming of Age*, 61.

30. Real-life name, used with permission.

31. Participation was garnered from a wide array of secular Internet media, ensuring a broad representation of *Second Life* users. I am especially grateful to Wagner James Au (http://nwn.blogs.com), Gweneth Llewellyn (http://www.gwynethllewelyn.net), and Akela Talamasca (http://Massively.com), who publicized the survey on their blogs. Additional support came from Zigi Bury of *SL'ang Life* magazine and Katt Kongo of the *Metaverse Messenger*.

32. Gregory Grieve, "Virtually Embodying the Field: Silent Online Buddhist Meditation, Immersion, and the Cardean Ethnographic Method," *Online—Heidelberg Journal of Religions on the Internet* 4 (2010): 37–38.

33. Ibid., 43.

34. Sophrosyne Stenvaag, "An Open Letter to My Augmentationist Friends," *Finding Sophrosyne* weblog (2008).

35. Virtual Temple, Discussion on Avatars as Persons (July 19) held at the Virtual Temple in *Second Life*, 2007a.

36. *Second Life* name, used with permission.

37. Extropia DaSilva, *Second Life* interview with the author, September 9, 2010c.

38. *Second Life* residents establish Facebook accounts to the consternation of the Facebook authorities, who cannot properly monetize their site without "real"

identification of users. The residents find Facebook's policy draconian and hope that Facebook and Google+ will accept their desire to remain anonymous.

39. DaSilva, *Second Life* interview, September 9, 2010c.

40. Extropia DaSilva, email correspondence with the author, September 7, 2010d, emphasis in original.

41. Extropia DaSilva, email correspondence with the author, September 10, 2010e.

42. Boellstorff, *Coming of Age*, 114.

43. This probably says something interesting about the "early adopters" of virtual worlds, who seem less inclined toward conventional religious practice than the later free account users. In 2006, there were very few religious buildings in *Second Life*, but there are now hundreds. According to my survey, approximately 25% of the *Second Life* population is atheist, and another 17.86% is agnostic; however, there is no way to correlate this to when the survey takers first joined because the latter issue was not included in the survey.

44. Kerstin Radde-Antweiler, "'Virtual Religion': An Approach to a Religious and Ritual Topography of *Second Life*," *Online—Heidelberg Journal of Religions on the Internet* 3 (2008), 174–211.

45. Timothy Hutchings, "Contemporary Religious Community and the Online Church," *Information, Communication, & Society* 14 (2011): 1125.

46. Kurt Lundby, "Patterns of Belonging in Online/Offline Interfaces of Religion," *Information, Communication, & Society* 14 (2011), 1219–1235.

47. See Hutchings, "Contemporary Religious Community," 1130.

48. Ibid.

49. The actual number for this is 49.6%, but 63 of the 103 people for whom earthly religious beliefs either "probably" or "definitely" do not affect the person's second lives are atheist or agnostic. I have culled these individuals from the data because it is not easy to imagine how atheism or agnosticism would powerfully affect one's second life as opposed to the influence one can imagine Roman Catholicism having on a person's choices.

50. Andrée Robinson-Neal found similar results in a similar, though smaller survey, as part of his research into the impact of virtual religious life on conventional practice; see "Enhancing the Spiritual Relationship: The Impact of Virtual Worship on the Real World Church Experience," *Online—Heidelberg Journal of Religions on the Internet* 3 (2008): 238.

51. Wagner James Au, "The Soul of *Second Life*," *New World Notes*, February 27, 2008c. At the time of Au's blog entry, survey numbers indicated nearly 20% of residents participated in monthly, weekly, or daily religious rituals in *Second Life*. As more individuals took the survey, the numbers went down somewhat, though it is important to note that these numbers probably do not include individuals who visit sites like Aslan's How, described in the next chapter, despite the fact that such visitors frequently engage in religious activity.

52. See Robin Pomeroy, "*Second Life* Raided by Catholic Missionaries," *News.com.au* (July 28, 2007).

53. Douglas Estes, *SimChurch: Being the Church in the Virtual Age* (Grand Rapids, MI: Zondervan, 2009), 123.

54. Rik Panganiban, "'Faces of Faith' Bringing Religious Leaders into *Second Life* July 29," *Click Heard Round the World*, July 18, 2007.

55. Estes, *SimChurch*, 85.

56. I return to this in Chapter 7.

57. It is worth considering whether virtual reality in general is presently amenable to or even encouraging of religious thought and practice, as Margaret Wertheim contends; see Wertheim, *The Pearly Gates of Cyberspace, A History of Space from Dante to the Internet* (New York: W.W. Norton & Company, 1999). For decades, participants in virtual reality have formed communities through activities that produce a feeling of what Emile Durkheim labels *collective effervescence*; on collective effervescence, see Durkheim, *The Elementary Forms of the Religious Life*, trans. Karen Fields (New York: Free Press, [1912] 1995). In an early experiment with virtual reality, researchers and artists at the University of Wisconsin–Madison created an environment in which the movement of people through the installation caused changes in lighting and sound, radically altering the environment and creating a different sense of reality from ordinary life. The project, GLOWFLOW, elicited precisely the kind of behavior that Durkheim expected from sacred gatherings among tribal people. Myron Krueger, a virtual reality pioneer who participated in the GLOWFLOW project, writes: "People had rather amazing reactions to the environment. Communities would form among strangers. Games, clapping, and chanting would arise spontaneously. The room seemed to have moods, sometimes being deathly silent, sometimes raucous and boisterous. Individuals would invent roles for themselves. One woman stood by the entrance and kissed each man coming in while he was still disoriented by the darkness"; quoted in Howard Rheingold, *Virtual Reality: The Revolutionary Technology of Computer-Generated Artificial Worlds—and How It Promises to Transform Society* (New York: Touchstone, 1991), 117. Paralleling many of the features of the *corroboree*, including nonstandard sexual activity, the story of GLOWFLOW shows how virtual environments can be turned into sacred spaces. Durkheim believed that participants in the *corroboree* perceived two "heterogeneous and incommensurable worlds.... In one world [a person] languidly carries on his daily life; the other is one that he cannot enter without abruptly entering into relations with extraordinary powers that excite him to the point of frenzy" (220). Durkheim has this backward: it is the frenzy that produces the extraordinary time, but his description is nonetheless apt. When the participants of GLOWFLOW walked through the doors of the installation, they collectively produced a radically different world, which would have been most obvious to the males as they were met by the young woman at the door but clear

enough to everyone clapping, chatting, or otherwise engaged in the creation of the environment and its ambiance.

58. Berkeley School of Journalism, "Faces of Faith in America: Live from *Second Life*," July 29, 2007.

59. Ibid.

60. O'Leary, "Utopian and Dystopian Possibilities," 44.

61. Triskele ceased as an active community in 2009, but many of the members migrated to similar role-play groups in *Second Life*. Role-play communities in *Second Life* suffer from a number of competing pressures that can tear them asunder: financial upkeep, appropriate cultural norms, adequate investment in learning about the relevant community, and overall projects of authenticity can be difficult to balance, especially with a group's missionary agenda; see Morgan Leigh, Mark Elwell, and Steven Cook, "Recreating Ancient Egyptian Culture in *Second Life*," in *Proceedings of the Third IEEE International Conference on Digital Game and Intelligent Toy Enhanced Learning* (2010).

62. Triskele, "Welcome to Triskele," *Second Life* note card (2008).

63. *Second Life* name, used with permission.

64. Wren Lilliehook, interview in *Second Life*, March 17, 2008a; Lillihook, interview in *Second Life*, March 31, 2008b.

65. Lilliehook, interview, 2008b.

66. See Morgan Leigh and Mark Elwell, "Authentic Theurgy: Ceremonial Magic in *Second Life*," in *Workshop Proceedings of the 18th International Conference on Computers in Education*, ed. Tsukasa Hirashima, Ahmad Fauzi Mohd Ayub, Lam-For Kwok, Su Luan Wong, Siu Cheung Kong, and Fu-Yun Yu (Putrajaya, Malaysia: Asia-Pacific Society for Computers in Education, 2010).

67. Morgan Leigh, email correspondence with the author, March 31, 2011b.

68. Lilliehook, interview, 2008a.

69. Ibid.

70. On occasion, this can go the opposite route. One member of Triskele who was a priest of Parlamay for a time told me that, as a Christian, he found his role-play to border on idolatry and felt it necessary that he diminish the significance of the goddess in his role as cleric; Benjamin Undercroft, electronic mail interview with the author, August 21, 2008).

71. Lilliehook, interview, 2008a. The similarity to St. Paul's claim that "now we see but a poor reflection as in a mirror; then we shall see face to face" (1 Corinthians 13:12) did not escape me, but she did not comment when I mentioned this. Wren claimed to feel the sacred power of nature more keenly when alone in nature in conventional reality, but in *Second Life* surrounded by her fellows she still feels "excitement" and a blurred communion with those sacred powers; Lilliehook, interview, 2008b. She thus expresses the power of both collective effervescence, as described by Durkheim, and the power of solitary, personal religion, which

Durkheim ignores; see E.E. Evans-Pritchard, *Nuer Religion* (New York: Oxford University Press, 1956), 313–320.

72. Stephen D. O'Leary, "Cyberspace as Sacred Space: Communicating Religion on Computer Networks," in *Religion Online: Finding Faith on the Internet*, ed. Lorne L. Dawson and Douglas E. Cowan (New York: Routledge, 2004), 54.

73. Ibid.

74. Real-life name, used with permission.

75. Leigh self-identifies as Hermetic Qabalist.

76. Morgan Leigh, email correspondence with the author, February 16, 2011a. The term *meatspace* derives from cyberpunk science fiction and refers—though with its own ideological baggage—to the conventional world.

77. Ibid.

78. Madeline Klink, "'I Type the Amens and Think the Rest': An Ethnographic Look at Religion in Virtual Reality," honors thesis written for the Division of Philosophy, Religion, Psychology and Linguistics at Reed College (2008), 48. I am grateful to Ms. Klink for providing me with a copy of her undergraduate thesis, which is a wonderfully well-done work.

79. Ibid., 50.

80. J.R.R. Tolkien, *The Tolkien Reader* (New York: Balantine, 1966), 89.

81. Stewart M. Hoover, *Religion in the Media Age* (New York: Routledge, 2006), 1.

82. Wade Clark Roof, *A Generation of Seekers: The Spiritual Journeys of the Baby Boom Generation* (San Francisco: Harper, 1994).

83. Christopher Helland, "Popular Religion and the World Wide Web: A Match Made in (Cyber) Heaven," in *Religion Online: Finding Faith on the Internet*, ed. Lorne L. Dawson and Douglas E. Cowan (New York: Routledge, 2004), 23.

84. Hoover, *Religion in the Media Age*, 9

85. Christopher Helland, "Online Religion/Religion Online and Virtual Communitas," in *Religion on the Internet: Research Prospects and Promises*, ed. Jeffrey K. Hadden and Douglas E. Cowan (London: JAI Press/Elsevier Science, 2000), 205–224.

86. Religious practitioners find the Internet a multivalent force based on who uses it and how. Tim Hutchings distinguishes among online media that are "author focused," which tend to disseminate one individual's position and, "network-focused" media, which permit a group's communal self-establishment; see Hutchings, "The Internet and the Church: An Introduction," *Expository Times* 122 (2010a): 14. Hutchings's distinction effectively bridges the shift into virtual worlds that occupies most of this book. Some, though far from all, of what Hutchings calls network-focused media includes virtual worlds like *Second Life*.

87. Brenda E. Brasher, *Give Me that Online Religion* (New Brunswick, NJ: Rutgers University Press, 2004), ix–xiv. The Internet enables decidedly different religious opportunities and challenges than those produced through older forms

of mass media. Lorne L. Dawson, and Douglas E. Cowan list five crucial differences between the two: the Internet is interactive, multimedial, hypertextual, cheap to enter and employ, and global in reach; see Dawson and Cowan, "Introduction," in *Religion Online: Finding Faith on the Internet*, ed. Lorne L. Dawson and Douglas E. Cowan (New York: Routledge), 10. In fact, anything that television can do, the Internet can also now do thanks to online TV broadcasting. In addition, the Internet has a host of other functions. If someone broadcasts video on the Internet, he will likely take advantage of all the other uses of the medium, adding to the broadcast a commentary, a place for comments, and ways to directly and easily link to social networking sites like Twitter or Facebook. Already, as soon as the Internet absorbs television, it does so within its own interactive, multimedial, and hypertextual approach.

88. See, e.g., see Helen A. Berger and Douglas Ezzy, "The Internet as Virtual Spiritual Community: Teen Witches in the United States and Australia," in *Religion Online: Finding Faith on the Internet*, ed. Lorne L. Dawson and Douglas E. Cowan (New York: Routledge, 2004), 175–188; Vítek Šisler, "European Courts' Authority Contested?: The Case of Marriage and Divorce Fatwas On-Line," *Masaryk University Journal of Law and Technology* 3 (2009), 51–78. Religious groups, especially New Religious Movements, suffer from the fact that the Internet permits interference by outside perspectives and links believers to apostates and outside friends and family; see Eileen Barker, "Crossing the Boundary: New Challenges to Religious Authority and Control as a Consequence of Access to the Internet," in *Religion and Cyberspace*, ed. Morten T. Høsgaard and Margit Warburg (New York: Routledge, 2005), 67–85. Meanwhile, even when the faithful attempt to use the Internet as a means of "plausibility alignment"—reconciling their faith to cultural conditions—they often fall into struggles between lay positions and those of the hierarchy; David Piff and Margit Warburg, "Seeking for Truth: Plausibility Alignment on a Baha'i Email List," in *Religion and Cyberspace*, ed. Morten T. Høsgaard and Margit Warburg (New York: Routledge, 2005), 86–101. And it is nearly impossible to censure individuals who can publish anonymously or semi-anonymously for heterodox teachings. The same conflict between traditional authority and instant expertise that confounds some commentators of Internet religious activity also plays out in *Second Life*. Because individual residents can establish groups for a minimal fee, they are free to create new religious organizations or affiliate themselves with traditional ones regardless of whether those groups would approve of the relationship. Some conventional religious groups eagerly establish *Second Life* branches, whereas others have been leery of getting involved. Just as there are both benefits and problems associated with instant expertise online, the freedom that *Second Life* offers could theoretically lead to conflict with established authority but also produce new ideas and traditions to the benefit of practitioners.

89. See Bruce Lincoln, *Discourse and the Construction of Society: Comparative Studies of Myth, Ritual, and Classification* (New York: Oxford University Press, 1989); Bruno Latour, *Reassembling the Social: An Introduction to Actor-Network-Theory* (New York: Oxford University Press), 63–86.

90. Paula Cheung, Shirlena Huang, and Jessie P.H. Poon, "Cultivating Online and Offline Pathways to Enlightenment," *Information, Communication & Society* 14 (2011), 1160–1180.

91. Dawson and Cowan, "Introduction," 10.

92. Helland, "Popular Religion," 25.

93. Heidi Campbell, "Who's Got the Power? Religious Authority and Internet," *Journal of Computer-Mediated Communication* 12 (2007).

94. Estes, *SimChurch*, 202.

95. Ibid., 155.

96. Brian D. McLaren, *A New Kind of Christianity: Ten Questions That Are Transforming the Faith* (New York: HarperCollins, 2010), 164, emphasis in original.

97. O'Leary, "Cyberspace as Sacred Space."

98. Charles S. Prebish, "The Cybersangha: Buddhism on the Internet," in *Religion Online: Finding Faith on the Internet*, ed. Lorne L. Dawson and Douglas E. Cowan (New York: Routledge, 2004), 135–148.

99. Grieve, "Virtually Embodying the Field."

100. Phyllis K. Herman, "Seeing the Divine through Windows: Online Darshan and Virtual Religious Experience," *Online—Heidelberg Journal of Religions on the Internet* 4 (2010), 151–178.

101. Nicole Karapanagiotis, "Vaishnava Cyber-*Pūjā*: Problems of Purity & Novel Ritual Solutions," *Online-Heidelberg Journal of Religions on the Internet* 4 (2010), 179-195.

102. Gary R. Bunt, "'Rip. Burn. Pray.'": Islamic Expression Online," in *Religion Online: Finding Faith on the Internet*, ed. Lorne L. Dawson and Douglas E. Cowan (New York: Routledge, 2004), 123–134.

103. Glenn Young, "Reading and Praying Online: The Continuity of Religion Online and Online Religion in Internet Christianity," in *Religion Online: Finding Faith on the Internet*, ed. Lorne L. Dawson and Douglas E. Cowan (New York: Routledge, 2004), 93–150.

104. Mark W. MacWilliams, "Virtual Pilgrimage to Ireland's Croagh Patrick," in *Religion Online: Finding Faith on the Internet*, ed. Lorne L. Dawson and Douglas E. Cowan (New York: Routledge, 2004).

105. Ibid., 231–235.

106. Paul Emerson Teusner, "New Thoughts on the Status of the Religious Cyborg," *Journal of Technology, Theology and Religion* 1 (2010), 1–18.

107. Simone Heidbrink, Nadja Miczek, and Kerstin Radde-Antweiler, "Contested Rituals in Virtual Worlds," in *Ritual, Media, and Conflict*, ed. Ronald L. Grimes,

Ute Hüsken, Udo Simon, and Eric Venbrux (New York: Oxford University Press, 2011), 165–187.

108. Ibid.

109. Heidi Campbell, "'This Is My Church': Seeing the Internet and Club Culture as Sacred Spaces," in *Religion Online: Finding Faith on the Internet*, ed. Lorne L. Dawson and Douglas E. Cowan (New York: Routledge, 2004), 107–121; Lorne L. Dawson, "Religion and the Quest for Virtual Community," in *Religion Online: Finding Faith on the Internet*, ed. Lorne L. Dawson and Douglas E. Cowan (New York: Routledge, 2004), 75–89; Prebish, "The Cybersangha: Buddhism on the Internet."

110. John P. Foley, "The Church and the Internet." Pontifical Council for Social Communications," www.vatican.va, February 28, 2002.

111. See, e.g., Benedict XVI, "Address of His Holiness Benedict XVI to Participants in the Congress Organized by the Pontifical Council for Social Communications," *www.vatican.va*, October 7, 2010.

112. Carmen Becker, "Muslims on the Path of the *Salaf al-Salih*: Ritual Dynamics in Chat Rooms and Discussion Forums," *Information, Communication & Society* 14 (2011), 1181–1203; Simone Heidbrink, "Exploring the Religious Frameworks of the Digital Realm: Offline-Online-Offline Transfers of Ritual Performance," *Masaryk University Journal of Law and Technology* 1 (2007), 175–184; Nadja Miczek, "Online Rituals in Virtual Worlds: Christian Online Services Between Dynamics and Stability," *Online—Heidelberg Journal of Religions on the Internet* 3 (2008),144–173; Kerstin Radde-Antweiler, "Rituals Online: Transferring and Designing Rituals," *Online—Heidelberg Journal of Religions on the Internet* 2 (2006), 54–72; Radde-Antweiler, "Cyber-Rituals in Virtual Worlds, Wedding-Online in *Second Life*," *Masaryk University Journal of Law and Technology* 1 (2007), 185–196. As questions explode over the authenticity of online religious activity, advances in technology are clarifying some issues in community and ritual practice. As the Internet has improved, graphically immersive technologies can give users an experience of "being there." The Clubbers Temple attempted to harness this early on, with a Flash website providing a two-dimensional nightclub atmosphere peopled with silhouetted figures who could discuss their Christian lives with one another; see Campbell, "This Is My Church." While that site failed to offer a particularly compelling environment, however, new technologies have opened new vistas for embodied participation in online religious life. The Internet marks a sensory revolution for religious practice. According to O'Leary, older media offer only limited sensory experiences but the Internet can offer something for nearly all of the five principal human senses; see "Cyberspace as Sacred Space." Smell and touch will be difficult to produce online (though some researchers have, indeed, tried), but text, pictures, videos, and sounds combine to form an impressive sensory experience for the faithful. This multisensory experience is growing

increasingly powerful. Where the Clubbers Temple failed, the Church of Fools succeeded, at least in part. Launched as a virtual world space embedded within the Ship of Fools website in May 2004, the Church of Fools was an immediate success, attracting 8,000 visitors per day and more than 41,000 in one twenty-four hour period; see Church of Fools, "41,000 Go to Church in One Day," *Church of Fools* website (2004a). Visitors chose cartoon avatars to enter the church and within it could perform the sign of the cross, chat, kneel, pray, and more. Planned as an experiment, the Church of Fools closed its virtual doors in September 2004, only to reopen for individual prayer and reflection, though not group worship in December of that year; see Church of Fools, "3D Church Reopens for Individual Visits Only," *Church of Fools* website (2004b). The Church of Fools was never intended to become a true replacement for local church, yet when it was shut down its members felt they had lost the one place they had online to pray and reflect. With its combination of serious theology and lightheartedness grounded in a mission of holy foolery, the Church of Fools "provokes a search for the sacred in the profane" of the Internet; see Randolph Kluver and Yanli Chen, "The Church of Fools: Virtual Ritual and Material Faith." *Online—Heidelberg Journal of Religions on the Internet* 3 (2008): 136. That search was sufficiently profound that members desired to continue the community and managed to keep the Church of Fools available in a limited capacity but also to launch a persistent online church at a new site, St. Pixel's. The Ship of Fools implemented its 3D church precisely because its community felt that church could not work in the chat room or online forums initially provided; creating the virtual space solved this. One of the church's founders writes, "We believed that running an act of worship online would need a greater sense of please than we had. We felt that the key difference would be to have somewhere that looked and felt like sacred space, and which gave a visible metaphor for people meeting together"; quoted in Simon Jenkins, "Rituals and Pixels: Experiments in Online Church," Online—Heidelberg Journal of Religions on the Internet 3 (2008): 96. After experimenting with a forty-day "ark," where twelve participants logged into a small virtual environment for one hour a day to interact, the ship launched the church. One fascinating way the designers maximized on the need to provide axes of orientation was to have speech bubbles appear when users chatted; the bubbles would subsequently float upward "toward heaven." It was his experience of such prayer that consolidated the founder's faith in the virtual church: "as the prayers started to appear on the screen—'Thank you God for this place'—I immediately knew that this not only felt like prayer, but was actually prayer. Even though it was being done in a virtual space, and we were separated by hundreds and even thousands of miles geographically, what we were doing was authentically praying together" (ibid., 105). Likewise, when congregants were invited to "lift up your hands towards the sanctuary" in a reading of Psalm 134, the service leader would watch as thirty avatars waved their air in unison (ibid., 109).

113. Hoover, *Religion in the Media Age*, 13.

114. Jason Shim, " 'Til Disconnection Do We Part: The Initiation and Wedding Rite in *Second Life*," in *Halos and Avatars: Playing Video Games with God*, edited by Craig Detweiler (Louisville, KY: Westminster John Knox Press, 2010), 162, emphasis added.

115. Hutchings, "The Internet and the Church," 16.

116. Bruce Epperly, "A Facebook Theology," *Patheos.com*, March 24, 2010.

117. Ibid.

118. Heidi Campbell, "Islamogaming: Digital Dignity via Alternative Storytellers," in *Halos and Avatars: Playing Video Games with God*, ed. Craig Detweiler (Louisville, KY: Westminster John Knox Press, 2010), 73.

119. See Latour, *Reassembling the Social*.

120. See Elena Larsen, "Cyberfaith: How Americans Pursue Religion Online," in *Religion Online: Finding Faith on the Internet*, ed. Lorne L. Dawson and Douglas E. Cowan (New York: Routledge, 2004), 17–20.

121. See Hutchings, "The Internet and the Church," 14–15.

122. Michael J. Laney, "Christian Web Usage: Motives and Desires," in *Religion and Cyberspace*, ed. Morten T. Høsgaard and Margit Warburg (New York: Routledge), 171.

123. In 2010, a U.S. Federal Appeals Court denied church status to an Internet ministry, asserting that it fails the associational test for such determinations; see Sheri Qualters, "Federal Circuit: Group's Internet and Radio Worship Does Not Meet IRS Definition of 'Church,'" *National Law Journal*, August 18, 2010. Whether regular associations in *Second Life* would, in fact, meet this test has yet to be questioned.

124. This name is a grateful acknowledgment to Jonathan Z. Smith, the famed historian of religions whose work has so deeply affected contemporary scholarship; see Smith, *Imagining Religion: From Babylon to Jonestown* (Chicago: University of Chicago Press, 1982).

CHAPTER 5

1. Quoted in Michael Rymaszewski, Wagner James Au, Mark Wallace, Catherine Winters, Cory Ondrejka, Benjamin Batstone-Cunningham, and *Second Life* residents from around the world, *Second Life: The Official Guide* (Indianapolis, IN: Wiley, 2007), 306.

2. Philip Rosedale, email correspondence with the author, April 7, 2011.

3. See Wagner James Au, "A Crisis of Faith," *New World Notes*, May 18, 2007.

4. Ibid.

5. Qyxxql Merlin, blog comment on Au, "Crisis of Faith."

6. Stephen Kaplan, *Different Paths, Different Summits: A Model for Religious Pluralism* (New York: Rowman & Littlefield, 2002). Kaplan's model addresses the possibility that more than one religion could truthfully make claims about what is true; it denies the possibility of including anything that a religion claims is false (17–18). Since accepting what one tradition labels as false would automatically exclude the possibility of another tradition's truths, then a model for pluralism cannot take seriously such claims.

7. The particular use to which Kaplan puts the hologram is in the relationship between its explicate and implicate domains, which refer to the stuff of the image and the interference waves recorded from light on a holographic film. Using that division, Kaplan illustrates how it can apply to several religious traditions, which all appear equally plausible interpretations (ibid., 117–158). He does, however, note, that the physical structure of a hologram is such that multiple holographic images may be stored on it and this is probably an important consideration to keep in mind.

8. Ibid., 95.

9. Ibid., 161.

10. See E. E. Evans-Pritchard, *Nuer Religion* (New York: Oxford University Press, 1956), 319.

11. Madeline Klink, "'I Type the Amens and Think the Rest': An Ethnographic Look at Religion in Virtual Reality," undergraduate honors thesis, Reed College, 2008).

12. Ibid., 23.

13. ibid., 21.

14. Mark Brown, "Christian Mission to a Virtual World," *www.brownblog.info* (2008).

15. Rupert Bursell, "Proposed Constitution for Anglicans of *Second Life*," Anglican Cathedral of *Second Life* weblog, July 13, 2010.

16. See Bruno Latour, *Reassembling the Social: An Introduction to Actor-Network-Theory* (New York: Oxford University Press, 2005), 27–42.

17. Similarly, one of the founders of the Church of Fools acknowledges as much when he writes that "it was good to be backed by real-life churches which had an interest in the virtual world, too. Although we were non-denominational, we wanted to be in the mainstream of Trinitarian orthodoxy"; see Simon Jenkins, "Rituals and Pixels: Experiments in Online Church," *Online—Heidelberg Journal of Religions on the Internet* 3 (2008): 101. Likewise, one participant in the ALM Cyberchurch in *Second Life* appreciated that the group's ministry leaders operate a ministry outside of the game as well; see Andreé Robinson-Neal, "Enhancing the Spiritual Relationship: The Impact of Virtual Worship on the Real World Church Experience," *Online—Heidelberg Journal of Religions on the Internet* 3 (2008): 236.

18. Timothy Hutchings, "The Politics of Familiarity: Visual, Liturgical and Organisational Conformity in the Online Church," *Online—Heidelberg Journal of Religions on the Internet* 4 (2010b): 77; Hutchings, "Contemporary Religious Community and the Online Church," *Information, Communication, & Society* 14 (2011): 1128.

19. Hutchings, "Contemporary Religious Community," 1131.

20. I am grateful to the Albany campus pastor, Eric Hodgkins, and his staff for welcoming me to their church in August 2010.

21. Polly is a pseudonym.

22. *LifeChurch.tv*, "Get Involved," *www.lifechurch.tv*, 2010a.

23. *LifeChurch.tv*, email correspondence with the author, September 14, 2010b.

24. Bobby Gruenewald, "The Ups and Downs of *Second Life*," *Swerve* weblog, April 20, 2007.

25. See Alex Murashko, "LifeChurch.tv Applies for Church Domain Name," *Christian Post*, June 15, 2012.

26. Real-life name, used with permission.

27. In *Second Life* Christianity, small churches can flourish. These groups are clearly more reminiscent of the house churches of the first century CE than of today's megachurches. Though fraught with their own concerns, such churches provide a comfort and familiarity that cannot be matched by a 10,000-seat auditorium (admittedly also without the energy that such auditoriums full of people provide).

28. Linden Lab, "LGBT Friendly," *Second Life* website, 2011.

29. Due to the inherently sloppy nature of text-based chat, I have cleaned up most misspellings and grammatical errors in my reporting of interviews and conversations in *Second Life*.

30. Kimberly Knight, interview in *Second Life*, August 22, 2010.

31. Kimberly Knight, "Sacred Space in Cyberspace," *Reflections* 96 (2009): 46.

32. Knight, interview in *Second Life*.

33. Knight, "Sacred Space in Cyberspace," 44.

34. Knight, interview in Second Life.

35. Ibid.

36. This term is my own and does not come from conversation with or essays by Ms. Knight.

37. Kimberly Knight, conversation in *Second Life*, March 22, 2008.

38. Brian D. McLaren, *A New Kind of Christianity: Ten Questions That Are Transforming the Faith* (New York: HarperCollins, 2010),168–170.

39. Ibid.

40. Ibid., 171.

41. Knight, conversation in *Second Life*; Knight, interview in *Second Life*.

42. Knight, interview in *Second Life*.

43. Ibid.

44. Knight, Skype interview with the author, June 20, 2012.
45. Ibid.
46. Ibid.
47. Aslan's How, "Welcome to Aslan's How," notecard delivered in *Second Life*, August 15, 2010.
48. Ligonier Ministries, "What Is Reformed Theology?" *Ligonier.org*, 2010.
49. Real-life name, used with permission. In *Second Life*, Londy's avatar is Ridge Cronon.
50. Larry Londy, interview in *Second Life*, August 26, 2010.
51. See Jonathan H. Ebel, "Jesus Freak and the Junkyard Prophet: The School Assembly as Evangelical Revival," *Journal of the American Academy of Religion* 77 (2009), 16–54.
52. Londy, interview in *Second Life*.
53. Ibid.
54. See, e.g., Michael Ward's excellent book on the influence of seven-planet cosmology on the Chronicles of Narnia; Ward, *Planet Narnia: The Seven Heavens in the Imagination of C.S. Lewis* (New York: Oxford University Press, 2008).
55. Londy, interview in *Second Life*.
56. *Second Life* name, used with permission.
57. Simone Lyvette, *Second Life* conversation with the author, February 13, 2011.
58. *Second Life* name, used with permission.
59. Annabelle Lykin, email communication with the author, February 14, 2011.
60. Ibid.
61. Real-life name, used with permission.
62. Maciej Kijowski, conversation in *Second Life*, February 20, 2011.
63. Ibid.
64. Ibid.
65. Londy, interview in *Second Life*.
66. Practical considerations can intervene. For example, the hajj is not mandatory for those who lack the financial means to undertake the travel. In addition, restrictions on the number of hajjis placed by Saudi Arabia as a means of crowd control mean that not all Muslims could possibly attend in their lifetimes.
67. Ibrahim is known as Abraham to Jews and Christians.
68. Mohammad Yahia, "IOL Virtual Hajj in *Second Life*," *IslamOnline.net*, December 6, 2007.
69. Quoted in Yahia, "IOL VIrtual Hajj."
70. Ruuh Cassini, email communication with the author, September 7, 2010.
71. Mark W. MacWilliams, "Virtual Pilgrimage to Ireland's Croagh Patrick," in *Religion Online: Finding Faith on the Internet*, ed. Lorne L. Dawson and Douglas E. Cowan (New York: Routledge, 2004), 223–238.
72. Cassini clearly means "enforced" rather than "attractive" by his use of "compelling."

73. Cassini, email.

74. Ibid.

75. *Second Life* name, used with permission.

76. Gaber Crystal, *Second Life* interview with the author, November 8, 2010.

77. Ibid.

78. Ibid.

79. Cassini, email.

80. Ibid.

81. Larissa Vacano, *Second Life* interview with the author, September 2, 2010.

82. *Second Life* name, used with permission.

83. Vacano, *Second Life* interview.

84. Quoted in Wagner James Au, "Muslims and the Metaverse: Can Second Life Improve US-Islamic Relations?" *New World Notes*, February 11, 2008b.

85. Rose Springvale, "Introduction," Land Covenant for Al-Andalus region of *Second Life*, August 30, 2009.

86. Rose Springvale, "Al Andalus in *Second Life*: The Al Andalus Magic Carpet Guided Tour Text," Al Andalus in *Second Life* weblog, March 8, 2008.

87. Quoted in Ethan Gilsdorf, "A Virtual World that Breaks Real Barriers," *www.csmonitor.com*, September 10, 2010.

88. Ibid.

89. Quoted in Joshua Fouts, "Al-Andalus 2.0," *Saudi Aramco World* 61 (2010).

90. Ibid.

91. Rita J. King and Joshua S. Fouts, *Digital Diplomacy: Understanding Islam through Virtual Worlds* (New York: Carnegie Council for International Affairs, 2008).

92. Rose Springvale, comment on the Virtual Democracy of Al Andalus Facebook page, June 6, 2012.

93. Virgilio Elizondo, *Galilean Journey: The Mexican-American Promise* (Maryknoll, NY: Orbis Books, 1983), 64; Elizondo, *The Future is Mestizo: Life Where Cultures Meet*, revised edition (Boulder: University of Colorado Press, 2000), 102; Gustavo Gutiérrez, *A Theology of Liberation: History, Politics, and Salvation* (Maryknoll, NY: Orbis Books, [1971] 1988), 56.

94. A community of believers can produce a powerful theology. Orlando O. Espín documents the power of popular religion among Latino Catholics, who come into conflict with their hierarchy not over theological matters but generally over concern for power; *The Faith of the People: Theological Reflections on Popular Catholicism* (Maryknoll, NY: Orbis Books, 1997), 3. Despite the fact that theological differences are apparent, Espín believes that the people and the hierarchy are generally in agreement rather than discord (ibid.). But while this may be close to true with regard to major issues of doctrine, it is certainly untrue with regard to strategy. In a popular religion, the needs of the community trump those of the hierarchy. While a powerful organization such as the Roman Catholic Church must make many decisions based on the need to sustain itself,

a community of believers will make decisions based on their existential and emotional needs. These can come into conflict.

95. Christopher Helland, "Popular Religion and the World Wide Web: A Match Made in (Cyber) Heaven," in *Religion Online: Finding Faith on the Internet*, ed. Lorne L. Dawson and Douglas E. Cowan (New York: Routledge, 2004), 23–35.

96. For unknown reasons, seventy respondents did not answer this question. Accordingly, the percentages are taken from the 176 respondents who did.

97. Londy, interview.

98. Edward Castronova, *Synthetic Worlds: The Business and Culture of Online Games* (Chicago: University of Chicago Press, 2005), 148.

99. Alvin Toffler, *The Third Wave* (New York: Bantam, 1980).

100. See Robinson-Neal, "Enhancing the Spiritual Relationship," 239.

101. See David Piff and Margit Warburg, "Seeking for Truth: Plausibility Alignment on a Baha'i Email List," in *Religion and Cyberspace*, ed. Morten T. Højsgaard and Margit Warburg (New York: Routledge, 2005), 88.

102. Ibid., 99.

103. T.L. Taylor, *Play between Worlds: Exploring Online Game Culture* (Cambridge, MA: MIT Press, 2006), 53.

104. They also provide opportunities for institutions in that while *Second Life* real estate is not exactly cheap, it comes with far less overhead than a brick-and-mortar building. This is what enables individuals to start their own churches, but it also could conceivably be an opportunity for traditional institutions.

105. Wade Clark Roof, *A Generation of Seekers: The Spiritual Journeys of the Baby Boom Generation* (San Francisco: Harper, 1994).

106. Charles Henderson, untitled presentation at the summer colloquium of the Association for Religion in Intellectual Life, July 22, 2010.

107. John W. Morehead, "Cybersociality: Connecting Fun to the Play of God," in *Halos and Avatars: Playing Video Games with God*, ed. Craig Detweiler (Louisville, KY: Westminster John Knox Press, 2010), 188.

108. Ibid., 189, emphasis in original.

109. Chris Hansen, "From *Tekken* to *Kill Bill*," in *Halos and Avatars: Playing Video Games with God*, ed. Craig Detweiler (Louisville, KY: Westminster John Knox Press, 2010), 31–32.

110. Klink, "'I Type the Amens.'"

111. *LMU Magazine* Staff, "Satisfying Relationships: Real vs. Virtual," *LMU Magazine*, July 7, 2010.

CHAPTER 6

1. William Gibson, *Neuromancer* (New York: Ace, 1984); Neal Stephenson, *Snow Crash* (New York: Bantam, 1992).

2. It is worth noting that Vernor Vinge's novella, *True Names*, in *True Names and the Opening of the Cyberspace Frontier*, ed. James Frenkel (New York: Tor [1981] 2001), 239–330, revolves around activity within cyberspace also, called by the rather less catchy name the Other Plane, and emerged alongside Gibson's first short stories, though before the novels of either Gibson or Stephenson. Nevertheless, while his work earned him some notoriety, *True Names* did not have the revolutionary impact of either *Neuromancer* or *Snow Crash*. Vinge did, however, advocate mind uploading in his book, and there is some reason to believe that this work deeply influenced roboticist Hans Moravec and his students at Carnegie Mellon University; see Olin Shivers, "Stunning Achievement: A Review of Vernor Vinge's True Names and the Opening of the Cyberspace Frontier, *Amazon.com*, 1999.

3. Like Tolkien, cyberpunk authors produced entire worlds in their writings. Tolkien is widely recognized for accomplishing what few, if any, people before him had managed: he created an entire world with people, places, and a mythos, a worldview; see Gary Fine, *Shared Fantasies: Role-Playing Games as Social Worlds*, Chicago: University of Chicago Press, p. 133. Although none of the cyberpunks developed their world as thoroughly as did Tolkien, taken as a whole they manage a similar feat. The cyberpunk aesthetic, though used and abused by pretenders and marketers, was nevertheless all-consuming; it was a way of seeing the world, a new world itself; see Tom Maddox, "After the Deluge: Cyberpunk in the '80s and '90s," in *Thinking Robots, An Aware Internet, and Cyberpunk Librarians: The 1992 LITA President's Program*, ed. R. Bruce Miller and Milton T. Wolf (Chicago: Library and Information Technology Association, 1992).

4. William Gibson, *Neuromancer* (New York: Ace, 1984), 6.

5. Neal Stephenson, *Snow Crash* (New York: Bantam, 1992), 63.

6. See Allucquere Rosanne Stone, "Will the Real Body Please Stand Up?: Boundary Stories about Virtual Cultures," in *Cyberspace: First Steps*, ed. Michael Benedikt (Cambridge, MA: MIT Press, 1991), 81–118.

7. See Julian Lombardi and Marilyn Lombardi, "Opening the Metaverse," in *Online Worlds: Convergence of the Real and the Virtual*, ed. William S. Bainbridge (London: Springer, 2010), 111–113,

8. Wagner James Au, *The Making of Second Life: Notes from the New World* (New York: HarperCollins, 2008a), 16; Thomas M. Malaby, *Making Virtual Worlds: Linden Lab and Second Life* (Ithaca, NY: Cornell University Press, 2009), 51.

9. Malaby, *Making Virtual Worlds*, 51, 147.

10. Richard Childers, "A Virtual Mars," in *Online Worlds: Convergence of the Real and the Virtual*, ed. William S. Bainbridge (London: Springer, 2010), 102.

11. See, e.g., Extropia DaSilva, "CTRL-ALT-R: Rebake Your Reality," *Gwen's Home* weblog, May 18, 2008; Malaquias DeCuir, "Metalife," *SL'ang Life: Real Information at Home* 5 (2008): 16–17.

12. David Chidester, *Authentic Fakes: Religion and American Popular Culture* (Los Angeles: University of California Press, 2005). See also Chapter 1, note 11.

13. J.B.S. Haldane, Daedalus, Or Science and the Future. Presented to the Heretics Society, Cambridge, UK, February 4, 1923.

14. Julian Huxley, *New Bottles for New Wine* (New York: Harper and Brothers, 1957a), 14.

15. Ibid., 17

16. Julian Huxley, *Religion without Revelation* (New York: Harper & Row, 1957b), preface (unpaginated).

17. Ibid. For Huxley, the modern world does not simply enable, it actually demands the development of a scientific religion. Religion, he argues, is essential for the majority of human beings (176) and will always be part of culture, so as culture evolves so should religion: "twentieth-century man, it is clear, needs a new organ for dealing with destiny, a new system of religious beliefs and attitudes adapted to the new situation in which his societies now have to exist" (188). The newly evolved religious outlook should help mankind "cope with his knowledge and his creative possibilities; and this implies the capacity to meet, inspire and guide change" (ibid.). Such a goal maps precisely onto late twentieth- and early twenty-first century transhumanist agendas, including those that deny the religious nature of it. The most recent and thorough attempt to fulfill Huxley's vision is Ben Goertzel's *Cosmist Manifesto: Practical Philosophy for the Posthuman Age* (Los Angeles: Humanity + Press, 2010). Goertzel, the founder and chief executive officer of Novamente, a company devoted to the development of artificial general intelligence, and former director of research for the Singularity Institute, has been active in transhumanist communities since the early 2000s, was a founding member of the OCE, and is a member of the Turing Church. Goertzel's manifesto aims toward a "practical philosophy" that expresses a vision encompassing science fiction enthusiasm and spiritual vision; Goertzel, *Cosmist Manifesto*, ix–x. Drawing on some of Prisco's contributions to the OCE (9–11), Goertzel seeks a worldview and value system that can shape decision making (2). His effort to make Cosmism practical and to develop it for human use in human life marks a radical step forward, one that Huxley would have appreciated. Goetzel's Cosmism accepts the religious promises of transhumanism and, though it never quite acknowledges its own religiosity, the *Cosmist Manifesto* repeatedly comes into contact with religion. Goertzel seems to define Cosmism as nonreligious (21), yet he acknowledges that it does the work of a religion (ibid., 10) and makes religious claims, such as when he asserts "there is quite likely some meaningful sense in which the 'universe as a whole' (an unclear concept!) has a form of awareness" (24; see also 87). Likewise, Goertzel argues against a Cartesian subject with free will, preferring to see consciousness and will as part of cosmic interactions. Any given willful act is an "'intentional' action on the part of the Cosmos, or a large hunk

thereof, manifested in a way that focuses on one mind's deliberative, reflective consciousness (perhaps among other focii [*sic*])" (79). Certainly, there are many religious individuals who agree with this whole-heartedly. Likewise, his belief that compassion is a "critical principle of the universe" (24) appears to draw on his acknowledged youthful readings in Buddhism (x). The most religious of Goertzel's claims revolve around technology. First, Goertzel believes that technology (drawing on a Cosmist philosophy) can circumvent contemporary moral problems such as those addressing abortion or vegetarianism by "obsoleting the dilemma" (117–123). Second, the dilemmas most in need of being made obsolete are human mortality and limitations: "helping with life extension research is one of the most important things any person can do today" (216). Unfortunately, this kind of technoenthusiasm always misses a key deficiency in technological solutions: by avoiding the real problem, they often create new ones. For example, "obsoleting the dilemma" of flammable buildings by putting asbestos in them ends up damaging the inhabitants of the building in far more widespread (if less dramatic) ways. This is not to say that making death obsolete would, by definition, create considerable harm, only that doing so *may well* cause historical harm. Goertzel's version of Cosmism clearly reflects a religious vision in line with Huxley's evolutionary humanism (later renamed transhumanism). Goertzel believes we might "level jump" through information hierarchies to attain control over our universe if, as Hans Moravec first suggested, it is a simulation carried out by higher beings (50). Huxley called it humankind's destiny "to realize new possibilities for the whole terrestrial sector of the cosmic process, to be the instrument of further evolutionary progress on this planet;" *Religion without Revelation,* 193. For Huxley, such control is not just an opportunity; it is a "sacred duty" (194; see also 201). We *ought* to use our technoscientific knowledge to master our cosmic environment and make it more amenable to our existential needs. Huxley also believed that as part of our transcendence we should protect Earth's flora and fauna as well as conserve resources (201–202).

18. Arthur C. Clarke described a cosmic evolution into an "Overmind," clearly borrowing from the Jesuit anthropologist Pierre Teilhard de Chardin; see Clarke, *Childhood's End* (New York: Balantine Books, 1953b). The Vatican finally lifted its interdict against Teilhard de Chardin after his death, thus permitting the publication of his first book, a hybrid of theology and popular science describing cosmic evolution into a super-consciousness unified with Jesus; see Teilhard de Chardin, *The Phenomenon of Man,* trans. Bernard Wall (New York: Harper & Brothers Publishers, [1955] 1959). The concept of such evolution had already gained traction with authors familiar with Teilhard's work, such as Clarke, who describes an astronaut who travels to an alien civilization and comes back a galactic powerhouse, having evolved into his new state through advanced technology; see Clarke, *2001: A Space Odyssey* (New York: New American Library, 1968).

19. In *The City and the Stars,* first published in 1956, Clarke describes uploading human minds into a machine so that they could be downloaded into cloned bodies; Clarke, *The City and the Stars* and *The Sands of Mars* (New York: Warner Books, 2001). *The City and the Stars* is a revised version of *Against the Fall of Night* (New York: Gnome Press, 1953a), which was first published in an edition of the science fiction magazine, *Startling Stories* 18 (November, 1948), pp. 11–70. *Against the Fall of Night,* however, does not include the mind transfer and cloning technology of *The City and the Stars.* Other science fiction authors also explored mind-uploading themes in the middle to late twentieth century, including Frederick Pohl, "The Tunnel under the World," in *The Best of Frederik Pohl,* ed. Lester del Rey (Garden City, NY: Nelson Doubleday, 1975; and Roger Zelazny, *Lord of Light* (Garden City, NY: Doubleday, 1967).

20. Robert Heinlein, *Methuselah's Children* (New York: New American Library, 1958); Heinlein, *Time Enough for Love: The Lives of Lazarus Long* (New York: G.P. Putnam's Sons, 1973).

21. See Robert M. Geraci, "There and Back Again: Transhumanist Evangelism in Science Fiction and Popular Science," *Implicit Religion* 14 (2011b), 141–172.

22. See Max More, "Principles of Extropy: Version 3.11." *Extropy.org* (2003).

23. FM-2030, *Are You a Transhuman? Monitoring and Stimulating Your Personal Rate of Growth in a Rapidly Changing World* (New York: Warner Books, 1989).

24. Hans Moravec, *Mind Children: The Future of Robot and Human Intelligence* (Cambridge, MA: Harvard University Press, 1988).

25. Chip Walker, "You, Robot," *Scientific American* 292 (2005): 36.

26. Moravec, "Today's Computers, Intelligent Machines and Our Future," *Analog* 99 (1978), 59–84. To the best of my knowledge, the first prediction of mind uploading by an actual scientist, as opposed to a science fiction author, is that of the biogerontologist George Martin; but his claim is not so much a road map of such a technological salvation as an assertion of its future feasibility; see Martin, "Brief Proposal on Immortality: An Interim Solution," *Perspectives in Biology and Medicine* 14 (1971), 339–340.

27. Moravec, *Mind Children.*

28. Ibid., 117.

29. Hans Moravec, *Robot: Mere Machine to Transcendent Mind* (New York: Oxford University Press, 1999), 167.

30. For example, see William Sims Bainbridge, "Introduction," In *Online Worlds: Convergence of the Real and the Virtual,* ed. William Sims Bainbridge (London: Springer, 2008a), 1–6; Goertzel, *A Cosmist Manifesto;* Ray Kurzweil, *The Age of Spiritual Machines: When Computers Exceed Human Intelligence* (New York: Viking, 1999); Kurzweil, *The Singularity is Near: When Humans Transcend Biology* (New York: Viking, 1999); Marvin Minsky, "Will Robots Inherit the Earth?" *Scientific American* (October, 1994); Giulio Prisco, "Engineering Transcendence." Institute for Ethics and Emerging Technologies

website (2004); Prisco, "Transcendent Engineering," presented at the *Second Life* Seminar on Transhumanism and Engineering, April 27, 2007.

31. Robert M. Geraci, "There and Back Again: Transhumanist Evangelism in Science Fiction and Popular Science," *Implicit Religion* 14 (2009), 141–172. See also William S. Bainbridge, *Dimensions of Science Fiction* (Cambridge, MA: Harvard University Press, 1986),197; Farah Mendlesohn, "Religion and Science Fiction," in *The Cambridge Companion to Science Fiction*, ed. Edward James and Farah Mendlesohn (Cambridge University Press, 2003b), 264–275.

32. See Stanislaw Ulam, "Tribute to John von Neumann," *Bulletin of the American Mathematical Society* 64 (1958): 5.

33. Vernor Vinge, "Technological Singularity" ([1993] 2003), http://www.rohan.sdsu.edu/faculty/vinge/misc/WER2.html.

34. The growth of transhumanism, however, has not been uncontroversial. The reactionary opposition to modern biotechnology in the 1970s and 1980s led transhumanists to stake out a public advocacy of technoscientific progress based on its potentially salvific powers. Publicity surrounding recombinant DNA technology, early developments in cloning, and the patenting of a bacterium genome approved by the U.S. Supreme Court case *Diamond v. Chakrabarty* in 1980 led to widespread religious opposition to biotechnology later adopted by conservative political pundits; see John G. Whitesides, "Religion, Genetics, and the Evolving American Experiment with Bioethics," *Masaryk University Journal of Law and Technology* 3 (2009). Subsequently, leading conservatives such as Jeremy Rifkin, Leon Kass, and Francis Fukuyama made fear a constant presence in political conversations surrounding biotechnology; see Francis Fukuyama, *Our Posthuman Future: Consequences of the Biotechnology Revolution* (New York: Farrar, Straus and Giroux, 2002); President's Council of Bioethics, *Beyond Therapy: Biotechnology and the Pursuit of Happiness—A Report of the President's Council on Bioethics* (Washington, DC: President's Council on Bioethics, 2003); Jeremy Rifkin, *Algeny*, in collaboration with Nicanor Perlas (New York: Viking, 1983). Transhumanists, especially the subgroup of "life extensionists" who sought long life spans through vitamin and diet regimens, believed that federal obstruction of biotechnology was tantamount to murder. Saul Kent's Life Extension Foundation even likened biotech regulation to genocide by establishing a display at its headquarters alleging that the U.S. Food and Drug Administration (FDA) is responsible for a "Holocaust"; see Brian Alexander, *Rapture: How Biotech Became the New Religion* (New York: Basic Books, 2003), 3. Just as life extensionists decried FDA obstruction of supplement and hormone regimens they considered vital for their long-term health, transhumanists have resented any religious or political opposition to stem cell, cloning, or bioengineering research.

35. Kevin Kelly, "Nerd Theology," *Technology in Society* 21 (1999).

36. See, Bartle, *Designing Virtual Worlds* (Berkeley, CA: New Riders, [2003] 2004), 247; Stefan Helmreich, *Silicon Second Nature: Culturing Artificial Life in a Digital World* (Los Angeles: University of California Press, [1998] 2000), 83–85, 193.

37. Bartle, *Designing Virtual Worlds*, 61.

38. Fred Turner, *From Counterculture to Cyberculture: Stewart Brand, the Whole Earth Network, and the Rise of Digital Utopianism* (Chicago: University of Chicago Press, 2006), 173.

39. Turner, *From Counterculture to Cyberculture, passim.*

40. See, Giulio Prisco, "Future Evolution as Virtual Worlds as Communication Environments," in *Online Worlds: Convergence of the Real and the Virtual*, ed. William S. Bainbridge (London: Springer, 2010e), 288; Natasha Vita-More, "Epoch of Plasticity: The Metaverse as a Vehicle for Cognitive Enhancement," *Metaverse Creativity* 1 (2010), 69–80.

41. See Feridoun Esfandiary, *Up-Wingers: A Futurist Manifesto* (New York: Popular Library Press, [1973] 1977), 121, 156.

42. More, "Principles of Extropy."

43. Ibid.

44. While transhumanists generally decry religion and distance their own move- ment from it, transhumanism is, in fact, a religion. Its believers claim that perfect health, unfettered happiness, and even immortality are within the pur- view of modern technoscience. Advancements in gene therapy, for example, could eliminate illness and aging, whereas nanotechnology and cloning might enable the reconstruction of injured bodies. Finally, many transhumanists have professed faith in the eventual uploading of human minds into machine bod- ies and virtual reality. The transhumanist commitment to supernatural enti- ties (be these vastly enhanced human beings or "godlike" machines) and the practices and institutions that can bring such entities into existence clearly belie any claim that rejects its religiosity. Transhumanism has, as Amarnath Amarasingam puts it, "charismatic leaders, authoritative texts, mystique, and a fairly complete vision of salvation. [It] is, in effect, a new religious move- ment"; Amarasingam, "Transcending Technology: Looking at Futurology as a New Religious Movement," *Journal of Contemporary Religion* 23 (2008): 2. Hope for salvation is but one aspect of the larger religious picture of trans- humanism. Religion "is the negotiation of what it means to be human with respect to the superhuman and the subhuman"; David Chidester, "Moralizing Noise," *Harvard Divinity Bulletin* 32 (2004): 17. This means that practices and beliefs that establish values, identities, and meanings for human life against other values, identities, and meanings perceived as superior to or inferior to human life are religious. Transhumanism, conceiving of a superhuman state free of illness, unhappiness and death, defines value and meaning for indi- viduals in the here and now; it is therefore religious. Given that transhuman- ism is unquestionably religious, it behooves other religious communities to

enter into dialogue with them, as has been recognized by the Catholic journalist Bernard Daly; see Daly, "Transhumanism," *America: The National Catholic
Weekly*, October 25, 2004. Other small groups, such as the Society for Universal
Immortalism (SUI) and the Morman Transhumanist Association appreciate
the religious underpinnings of transhumanism. Borrowing from immortalist
literature such as Michael Perry's *Forever for All: Moral Philosophy, Cryonics, and
the Scientific Prospects for Immortality* (Boca Raton: Universal Publishers, 2000),
the SUI asserts on its webpage that it is "a progressive religion that holds rationality, reason, and the scientific method as central tenets of our faith"; Society
of Universal Immortalism website, 2008; see also Gregory Jordan, "Apologia
for Transhumanist Religion," *Journal of Evolution & Technology* 15 (2006), 55–72.
The Order of Cosmic Engineers, which included a number of very well-known
transhumanists among its founding members, accepted that using virtual
worlds as the destinations for mind uploading is part of a spiritual vision;
OCE, "Order of Cosmic Engineers: Prospectus" www.cosmeng.org (2008b).
However, that group essentially imploded within a few years.

45. R.U. Sirius, "Digital Polytheism (on the Event of Timothy Leary's 90th
    Birthday)," *H+ Magazine*, October 20, 2010.

46. Ben Goertzel, "Technological Transcendence: An Interview with Giulio Prisco,"
    H+ Magazine, February 8, 2011. Prisco and other religious transhumanists have
    noticeably affected their peers. Samantha Atkins suggests, for example, "that
    the extensive life blogs and other recordings…are essential parts of our own
    'salvation'/immortality," and comments, "pity we can't wrap a religion around
    that" (Atkins, email contribution to the Cosmic Engineers listserv, September
    20, 2010). To this, Prisco immediately responded "Why not? Martine [Rothblatt]
    is wrapping a religion around that. Perhaps her approach is the way to go"
    (Prisco, email contribution to the Cosmic Engineers listserv, September 20,
    2010a, emphasis in original). Elsewhere, Prisco claims that "transhumanism
    IS a religion, it has always been one, and it doesn't (want to) know it is a reli-
    gion…. Transhumanism is meant to answer the same questions of religion"
    (email contribution to the Heirohacking listserv, November 8, 2010b). While
    the Order of Cosmic Engineer's original plan to homestead virtual worlds and
    create a full-fledged "UNreligion" never matured, the approach impressed oth-
    ers with the potential for creating explicitly spiritual visions of transhumanist
    beliefs. The Turing Church is a philosophical divergence from the OCE, neces-
    sitated by the latter's diffusion, internal strife, and, in the end, ineffectualness.

47. Extropia DaSilva, *Second Life* interview with the author, September 9, 2010c.

48. DaSilva, Facebook communication with the author, January 5, 2011; DaSilva,
    "Holy Singularity," *H+ Magazine*, July 5, 2012.

49. Prisco, "Engineering Transcendence."

50. Ibid. Like Prisco after him, Huxley (*Religion without Revelation*, 209) also
    believed that there could be rituals, priesthoods, temples, and so forth for

transhumanism, though these could not be guessed in advance of their advent. The influence of August Comte's Religion of Humanity is decisive here.

51. See Chapter 3, note 24.

52. Prisco, email contribution to the Turing Church listserv, June 15, 2010c, emphasis in original. Ambivalence over whether transhumanism is religious does exist within transhumanist communities, which are not always completely polarized. The Order of Cosmic Engineers, for example, rather ambiguously calls itself an UNreligion. The group claims to be "not a religion, not a faith, not a belief, not a church, not a sect, not a cult. We are not a faith-based organization. We are a *convictions-based organization*"; Order of Cosmic Engineers, "Prospectus," 2008, emphasis in original. The difference between a faith-based organization and a convictions-based organization is, of course, more than a little vague, but this is because some members of the OCE oppose religion in its entirety on account of their dislike for certain traditional religions while others are comfortable with establishing a religion that is based in scientific rationality. The target of this dislike is clearly visible in the group's reference to "an imaginary, indifferent, and biblically tyrannical and threatening god" (ibid.). The "one and only label the OCE will not contest is that of being a so-called 'UNreligion'" (ibid.), though it also acknowledges itself to be "a spiritual movement"; Order of Cosmic Engineers, "Order of Cosmic Engineers: About" www.cosmeng.org (2008a). After a time, controversy erupted within the OCE over whether the group could or should be associated with religion, even as an UNreligion. This opposition is grounded in fundamental dislike of religious institutions, which are taken by one member to be "fatally tainted and...to be avoided like the plague"; Order of Cosmic Engineers, "Restart OCE," email delivered through the Order of Cosmic Engineers GoogleGroup (2010)—the author's identity and the date of the email are withheld for reasons of privacy. The very use of the term UNreligion was, however, a consequence of one founder's belief that transhumanism is religious and could fulfill the spiritual longings of humankind. Despite conceptual resistance to religion, the OCE's prospectus describes religious work. The prospectus, among other things, advocates (1) building virtual worlds "suitable for ultimate permanent living," (2) mind uploading to live in those worlds, (3) the establishment of a cosmic "meta-mind society," and (4) answering *"the ultimate questions* of the origin, nature, purpose and destiny of reality"; Order of Cosmic Engineers, "Prospectus," emphasis in original. That little effort has been made among OCE members to fulfill these desires does not change the fact that the desire to create heaven, to attain immortality in a cosmically meaningful superhuman state, and to subsequently explain all questions of meaning and purpose cannot possibly be taken for anything but a religious perspective. A lack of clear leadership—a consequence of the non-hierarchical aspirations of many members—allowed opinions to diverge until they no longer appeared relevant to one another. As a consequence, the OCE's

original intent to advocate, design, and homestead synthetic realities dissolved and its activity as of 2011 is limited to occasional email listserv posts. Though it was eventually derailed from the project, the Order of Cosmic Engineers originally used virtual worlds as a platform for advancing its (religious) aims. The group advocated conversations about the future of humanity in *World of Warcraft* and intended to hold discussions about the future of technology in *Second Life*. When the group was active, virtual worlds were the evangelical zone for the OCE and also its sacred space, though many would probably contest this latter claim. Reports in conventional media also explain the group's aims; see, e.g., John Bohannon, "Courting Controversy: Out of the Mainstream," *Science Careers*, July 11, 2008. However, these do not often carry the emotional punch that participation in virtual worlds already provides. Visitors to *World of Warcraft* and *Second Life* can be captivated by them, providing ready ground for evangelical work. New groups have had to fill the gap left when many members of the OCE stopped communicating with one another and those who were left could no longer agree on their focus or practical steps forward. Prisco reflects on this problem; he has "kind of lost interest in the OCE because [he thinks] it cannot be more than a discussion list: there are too wide of differences in personal opinions to achieve the synthesis between science and religion that was originally planned;" email correspondence with the author, August 31, 2010f. Despite the apparent death of the OCE, religious transhumanism remains a vibrant, if small community that can continue to draw on the resources of wider transhumanist networks. The growing relevance of transhumanist communities in academic circles shows the growing significance of transhumanism as a contemporary religious movement (as represented, for example, in the development of a Transhumanism and Religion Group in the Annual Meeting for the American Academy of Religion). Despite the religion bashing common among many transhumanists, many of the movement's leading figures make religious promises and are comfortable with religious labels; see Kurzweil, *The Singularity Is Near*; Moravec, *Robot*; Prisco, "Engineering Transcendence;" Sirius, "Digital Polytheism." If transhumanists wish to continue the growth of their community, they might do well to accept that their hopes and fears are religious ones and, as Prisco has suggested, take advantage of that fact.

53. See Michael Fitzgerald, "How I Did It: Philip Rosedale, CEO, Linden Lab and *Second Life*," *Inc.com*, February 1, 2007.

54. Ibid.

55. Quoted in Wagner James Au, *The Making of Second Life: Notes from the New World* (New York: HarperCollins, 2008a), 16–17.

56. Ibid., 16.

57. Rosedale, email correspondence with the author, April 7, 2011.

58. Ibid.

59. This seems to be a common strategy among major tech advocates. Neither Moravec nor Kurzweil, for example, shows any interest in working on technologies that would *actually* enable something like mind uploading, preferring to believe that their other work, along with that of others, will somehow produce the desired ends of its own accord. For example, when I sought out Moravec in the writing of my first book, he replied he was "too busy making the plan happen to want to spend time talking about it"; Moravec, email communication with the author, June 25, 2007. By this he evidently meant that building robots that can navigate factory floors will produce massively intelligent robots and allow human mind uploading. Perhaps he is correct, though I have my doubts.

60. Quoted in Au, *The Making of Second Life*, 233.

61. Ibid., 15.

62. Ibid., 15.

63. Philip Rosedale, email correspondence with the author, April 7, 2011.

64. Au, *The Making of Second Life*, 232.

65. Ibid., 232.

66. Ibid., 231.

67. Ibid., 231.

68. Ibid., 233.

69. Tim Guest, *Second Lives: A Journey through Virtual Worlds* (New York: Random House, 2007), 273.

70. Michael Rymaszewski, Wagner James Au, Mark Wallace, Catherine Winters, Cory Ondrejka, Benjamin Batstone-Cunningham, and *Second Life* residents from around the world, *Second Life: The Official Guide* (Indianapolis, IN: Wiley, 2007), 7.

71. For a while, at least, Kurzweil also mentioned *Second Life* nearly every time he discussed the future of virtual reality; see, e.g., Big Think, "Ray Kurzweil Explores the Next Phase of Virtual Reality," *BigThink.com*, April 28, 2009; EarthSky, "Ray Kurzweil's Vision of the Future," *EarthSky.com*, August 7, 2008.

72. Philip Rosedale, email correspondence with the author, April 7, 2011.

73. John Lester, Skype interview with the author, December 6, 2011.

74. Ibid.

75. Ibid. Of course, all technologies that augment human powers are, for the transhumanists, transhumanist technologies and not all transhumanists advocate mind uploading. So in some sense Lester's differentiation of his own position and theirs is a semantic opposition, but it also reflects differing end goals. Even as he pursues a more modest transhumanist agenda, Lester is not working toward immortality, regardless of whether it could happen through technology.

76. Wagner James Au, email to the author, September 6, 2011d.

77. Quoted in Au, *Making of Second Life*, 234.

78. Guest, *Second Lives*, 275. All employees are given the last name Linden for their avatars and are thenceforth known as "Lindens." Linden Lab's pendants have the *Second Life* logo on them.

79. Ibid., 275.

80. Quoted in Guest, *Second Lives*, 275.

81. Quoted in ibid., emphasis in original. Guest persistently questions the beneficence of *Second Life* in his book, raising the dark side of cults and revealing some of the problems that assailed his mother's commune, which he took to possibly foreshadow *Second Life*'s own fate.

82. Lawrence Schick, *Heroic Worlds: A History and Guide to Role-Playing Games* (Amherst, NY: Prometheus Books, 1991), 13.

83. Ibid., 13.

84. See Robert M. Geraci, "Video Games and the Transhuman Inclination," *Zygon: Journal of Religion and Science* 47 (2012b): 735–756.

85. Katie Salen and Eric Zimmerman, *Rules of Play: Game Design Fundamentals* (Cambridge, MA: MIT Press, 2004), 5–6.

86. See Tom Boellstorff, *Coming of Age in Second Life: An Anthropologist Explores the Virtually Human* (Princeton, NJ: Princeton University Press, 2008), 118–150.

87. Ibid., 136.

88. Guest, *Second Lives*, 277.

89. Ibid., 277.

90. These experiences indicate that Linden Lab has, indeed, successfully promoted an "ideal of agency for its users that accords with...technoliberal promise" (Malaby, *Making Virtual Worlds*, 59).

91. Quoted in Malaby, *Making Virtual Worlds*, 110.

92. Gtec, "Second Life with BCI," *YouTube* video, 2011.

93. See Goertzel, "Technological Transcendence."

94. See Au, *Making of Second Life*, 235.

95. See Maria Beatrice Bittarello, "Another Time, Another Space: Virtual Worlds: Myths and Imagination," *Online—Heidelberg Journal of Religions on the Internet* 3 (2008): 244-266.

96. Geraci, "Video Games and the Transhuman Inclination."

97. Philip Rosedale, email correspondence with the author, April 7, 2011. "It is," for example, "less likely that other people can harm you or restrict your ability to live a fulfilling life."

98. Guest, *Second Lives*, 21.

99. Moravec, "Today's Computers;" Moravec, *Mind Children*; Moravec, *Robot*.

100. Kurzweil, *Age of Spiritual Machines*, 142.

101. Kurzweil, *Singularity Is Near*, 375.

102. Quoted in Guest, *Second Lives*, 274.

103. Quoted in Au, *Making of Second Life*, 234–235. In case *Second Life* fails (or refuses) to become sentient itself, however, Rosedale has also set about producing an

artificial intelligence that he hopes will "think and dream" in *Second Life*; Wagner James Au, "Philip Rosedale Attempting to Create Sentient Artificial Intelligence that Thinks and Dreams in Second Life!" *New World Notes*, February 3, 2010c.

104. It might seem likely that game designers would be removed from the sacred experience of online worlds. As influential game designer Richard Bartle puts it, "Magic isn't magic when you know how the trick is done. *That's* why most players aren't good at design. They still sense the magic;" Bartle, *Designing Virtual Worlds*, 123. Bartle believes there's a noticeable difference between players and designers, but that difference is belied by the multitude of virtual world designers who express belief in the magical aspects of such worlds.

105. Jane McGonigal, *Reality Is Broken: Why Games Make Us Better and How They Can Change the World* (New York: Penguin, 2011).

106. Quoted in Eric Davis, "Osmose," *Wired* 4 (1996).

107. Nicole Stengers, "Mind Is a Leaking Rainbow," *Cyberspace: First Steps*," ed. Michael Benedikt (Cambridge, MA: MIT Press), 52.

108. Quoted in Stef Aupers and Dick Houtman, "'Reality Sucks': On Alienation and Cybergnosis," *Concilium: International Journal of Theology* (2005), 81–89. The desire for angelic bodies is a common Judeo-Christian motif. Indeed, it was apparently out of his desire to join the heavenly host that Origen, one of the Church Fathers, chose to castrate himself. Jews and Christians who have believed in the resurrection of the dead almost universally agreed that such resurrection would be bodily. Given that our present bodies are implicated in the sinfulness of mortal life, our resurrected bodies must be different and better. The saved "shall be made equal to the stars" (2 Baruch 51:10; see also Mark 12:25, Luke 20:35–36, and 1 Corinthians 15:42–54).

109. Boellstorff, *Coming of Age*, 121.

110. Extropia DaSilva, "If the Singularity Is Not Happening," *Mind Child's Musings* weblog, August 3, 2010a.

111. Natasha Vita-More, email correspondence with the author, September 22, 2011.

112. Vita-More, "Epoch of Plasticity," 71.

113. Rymaszewski, et al., *Second Life*, 194.

114. Vita-More, "Epoch of Plasticity," 71.

115. Ibid., 76.

116. Vita-More, email correspondence with the author, September 22, 2011.

117. Merlin, blog comment.

118. *Second Life* name, used with permission. Elsewhere, Seraph will be referred to by her real-life name, Samantha Atkins. Ms. Atkins expressed a preference for having me use her *Second Life* avatar's name (Serendipity Seraph) in reference to *Second Life* activities and her legal name in reference to activity outside of *Second Life*.

119. Seraph would like to import Fulfillment to the Bay Area, where she resides in conventional life.

120. Serendipity Seraph, email correspondence with the author, November 13, 2010.
121. Ibid.
122. Fulfillment, "Cosmist or Terran voting results from Fulfillment meeting in *Second Life*," May 22, 2010a.
123. Giulio Prisco, email correspondence with the author, September 12, 2010g.
124. Extropia DaSilva, "Ray Kurzweil and the Conquest of Mount Improbable," *H+ Magazine*, November 23, 2009; DaSilva, "Lanier's Singularity," *H+ Magazine*, May 5, 2010b.
125. See Esfandiary, *Up-Wingers*, on the transhumanist term "upwing."
126. Khannea Suntzu, email correspondence with the author, September 10, 2010b.
127. Ibid.
128. Huxley, *Religion without Revelation*, 33.
129. Giulio Prisco, "Transcendent Engineering."
130. see Robert M. Geraci, *Apocalyptic AI: Visions of Heaven in Robotics, Artificial Intelligence, and Robotics* (New York: Oxford University Press), 99.
131. Extropia Core, "Extropia: History," *Extropiacore.net*, 2010.
132. Stenvaag's good-byes were at one time available on her blog, which has been removed. Another digital person, Botgirl Questi, has eulogized Stenvaag and other departed digital persons; Botgirl Questi, "The Death of the Digital Person in *Second Life*: An Old School Botgirl Rant," *Botgirl's Second Life Diary* weblog, May 23, 2010.
133. Prisco has largely abandoned *Second Life*; he established a new place for transhumanists to congregate for business, though not social purposes. The TeleXLR8 (pronounced tel-accelerate) Project was a virtual location using Teleplace software to host meetings and individual talks where he held a conference that took place jointly in Teleplace and in Milan, Italy. Atkins expressed concern about the vastly weaker social interaction enabled by Teleplace, but given the flux in *Second Life* transhumanist sites Prisco's project had as much chance as any to become a key virtual location for transhumanists. Financial difficulties put TeleXLR8 on hiatus from January to August 2011, before it reopened on an open software platform. As Humanity+ moved to communications through *Second Life* at the same time, however, the latter platform seems to have more traction than TeleXLR8 or any other.
134. J.Z. Smith, *To Take Place: Toward Theory in Ritual* (Chicago: University of Chicago Press, 1988), 54.
135. Thinkers, "This Could Be Heaven?" transcript of May 25 Thinkers Discussion Group event posted at Mind Child's Musings weblog, June 14, 2010c.
136. Serendipity Seraph, email correspondence with the author, November 13, 2010.
137. Vita-More, "Epoch of Plasticity," 76.
138. Interestingly, the vigorous debates that led to declaring the OCE an "UNreligion" rather than officially a religion are simmering down, and transhumanists in *Second Life* are increasingly accepting a religious vision. Prisco, who has long

disagreed with transhumanists who deny the religiosity of the group, finds that more and more have come to agree with him; see Goertzel, "Technological Transcendence." The end of the OCE may actually be helping to produce this. In addition to the Thinkers group events cited above, the Fulfillment group in *Second Life* also engages religion and spirituality. In email correspondence with me, Seraph said that the founding the group was a reaction to the implosion of the OCE and now offers a meaningful opportunity for shared group identity. She wants "to elicit a coherent shared near term future vision and get us moving toward it;" Seraph, email correspondence with the author.

139. Fulfillment, "Spirituality and Fulfillment," Chat log from *Second Life* Fulfillment meeting in *Second Life*, September 10, 2010b. Likewise, at another discussion event a resident said, "we're all pretty spiritual here"; Thinkers, "Sacred Cyberspace," transcript of July 20 Thinkers Discussion Group event posted at Mind Child's Musings weblog, July 21, 2010b.

140. Fulfillment, "Spirituality and Fulfillment."

141. Ibid.

142. Ibid.

143. Seraph, email correspondence with the author, November 13, 2010.

144. Kurzweil, *Singularity Is Near*, 375.

145. Eric Steinhart, email to the author, April 12, 2011; Steinhart, email to the author, March 8, 2013.

146. See Goertzel, "Technological Transcendence." The task of creating a scientific-religious worldview is the goal of the Turing Church, despite the fact that it is a discussion group and not a full-fledged church. After all, writes one member of the OCE, Turing Church and Hierohacking e-mail lists, "religion is an early expression of transhumanism"; Heirohacking, email contribution to the listerv, November 2, 2010. Prisco launched the Turing Church with the question of "how to define a memetically strong meta-religion, as outlined below, *without* falling into strongly normative and coercive prescriptions? Is it possible at all?"; Prisco, email contribution to the Turing Church listserv, June 15, 2010c, emphasis in original. Prisco's work on the Turing Church promises to engage Huxley's hope and seek its fulfillment. The Turing Church, he writes in an email invitation to possible members, "will be a virtual place of contemplation, discussion and learning, and a community of scientifically minded persons who are also open to and interested in spiritual and religious visions, compatible with science"; Prisco, email invitation, 2010d. The direct correspondence between this and Huxley's aspirations in *Religion without Revelation* is clear, though Prisco remains embroiled in the difficult task of shaping the transhumanist religion and making it powerfully evangelical. Discussions among the participants have engaged how to create strong belief structures without simultaneously becoming totalitarian and how to produce ritual structures that can lead toward a transhumanist religion.

147. DaSilva, *Second Life* interview.

148. See Max Weber, *On Charisma and Institution Building: Selected Papers* (Chicago: University of Chicago Press, 1968).

149. Corin, email contribution to the Cosmic Engineers listserv, November 5, 2010.

150. Cor, email contribution to the Cosmic Engineers listserv, November 6, 2010.

151. Lune, email contribution to the Cosmic Engineers listserv, November 7, 2010.

152. Terasem Project, "Terasem Rituals," *terasemfaith.net* (2011).

153. Martine Rothblatt, "Brains Are to Minds as Birds Are to Flight," presentation at TransVision 2010 Conference, October 23.

154. See, e.g., Suntzu, email contribution to the Cosmic Engineers listserv, September 20, 2010a; Remi Sussan, email contribution to the Turing Church listserv, April 26, 2010.

155. In a cascade of similarities, the near anarchy among transhumanists in *Second Life* is evident also in Linden Lab, which rejected corporate authoritarianism in both its own operations and, allegedly, in its governance of *Second Life*; see Malaby, *Making Virtual Worlds*.

156. DaSilva, *Second Life* interview with the author, September 9, 2010.

157. In 2006, the Extropy Institute declared its fundamental and primary mission "essentially completed"; Natasha Vita-More, "Extropy Institute Strategic Plan," *extropy.org*, 2006. It thus closed its doors while advocating that members remain active in its e-mail listserv and elsewhere. That mission was to develop a transhumanist philosophy, engage in debate about it, and produce a community committed to it. For reasons discussed in its 2006 strategic plan (ibid.), the Extropy Institute declared this mission complete.

158. Geraci, *Apocalyptic AI*.

159. See also Colin Milburn, "Atoms and Avatars: Virtual Worlds as Massively-Multiplayer Laboratories," *Spontaneous Generations* 2 (2008), 63–89.

160. Suntzu, email contribution, 2010a.

161. Remi Sussan, email contribution to the Turing Church listserv, April 26, 2010.

162. See Geraci, "Video Games and the Transhuman Inclination."

163. Olvin, respondent to online survey on transhumanism and video games, 2012.

164. I am grateful to the Order of Cosmic Engineers and the Turing Church for allowing me access to their digital communities. They have been gracious hosts, allowing me to monitor email conversations and to use material gleaned from my observations. For the most part, such communication has been left anonymous, with exceptions made only for the users who have public profiles in transhumanist circles or who gave me explicit permission to quote them.

165. Le Corbusier, *Towards a New Architecture*, trans. Frederick Etchells (New York: Praeger, 1946), 17.

166. Huxley, *Religion without Revelation*, 208.

167. Huxley, *Religion without Revelation*, 212.

168. Kurzweil, *The Singularity is Near*, 374–375.

169. Virtual Temple, discussion on "Religion and Virtual Reality," February 1, 2007b, held at the Virtual Temple in *Second Life*.

CHAPTER 7

1. José Zagal, Clara Fernández-Vara, and Michael Mateas, "Rounds, Levels, and Waves: The Early Evolution of Gameplay Segmentation," *Games and Culture* 3 (2008), 176–198. The ways video games also rework conventional time and space through the play and its pause are yet another way players use games as a form of orienteering; see Samuel Tobin, "Time and Space in Play: Saving and Pausing with the Nintendo DS," *Games and Culture* 7 (2012), 127–141. However, in this case the time and space navigated is a juxtaposition of game and non-game territories and times.

2. Timothy Crick, "The Game Body: Toward a Phenomenology of Contemporary Video Gaming," *Games and Culture* 6 (2011): 261.

3. Ibid., 263.

4. Ibid., 265–267.

5. Mircea Eliade, *The Sacred and the Profane: The Nature of Religion*, trans. Willard Trask (Orlando, FL: Harcourt Inc, [1957] 1987), 20–21.

6. Though subsequent research has justly criticized the essentialism Mircea Eliade's research program, the famed historian does show how important orientation in space and time is for religious practice, and thus remains a vital resource for contemporary scholarship into virtual religion. There is no doubt that Eliade's own work was all too commonly apolitical and acontextual and, therefore, disentangled from religious reality as Kurt Rudolph attests; see "Mircea Eliade and the 'History' of Religions," *Religion* 19 (1989), 101–127. Calling himself an historian, Eliade was nevertheless unable to truly engage the historical realities of his subject matter; he persistently decontextualized rituals and myths, comparing them to others that were far divorced in space and time and attempting to see equivalence among them. This approach led Eliade into a number of significant interpretive problems. There are no historical actors in Eliade's work: no one ever does or says anything, and, in consequence, Eliade misinterprets both myths and rituals; Jonathan Smith, e.g., dismantles Eliade's interpretation of religious phenomena, such as the Hainuwele myth and the Akitu ritual in ancient Babylonia; *Imagining Religion: From Babylon to Jonestown* (Chicago: University of Chicago Press, 1982), 90–101. For Eliade's own interpretation of these, see Eliade, *The Myth of the Eternal Return: Or, Cosmos and History*, trans. Willard Trask (Princeton, NJ: Princeton University Press, [1954] 1991) and *The Quest: History and Meaning in Religion* (Chicago: University of Chicago Press, 1969). Despite the validity of criticisms leveled against him, Eliade nevertheless offers important theoretical tools for religious studies. By rectifying the problems from which he suffers, subsequent scholars have found

considerable value in thinking about contemporary religious life from within aspects of his theoretical paradigm.

7. Smith, *Imagining Religion*, 55–56.
8. Bruno Latour, *Reassembling the Social: An Introduction to Actor-Network-Theory* (New York: Oxford University Press).
9. Eliade, *Sacred and the Profane*, 22, emphasis in original.
10. Ibid.,12.
11. See Bruno Latour, "Give Me a Laboratory and I Will Raise the World," in *Science Observed: Perspectives on the Social Study of Science*, ed. Karin Knorr-Cetina and Michael Mulkay, 141–170 (Beverly Hills, CA: Sage, 1983).
12. Stephen Kaplan, "Grasping at Ontological Straws: Overcoming Reductionism in the Advaita Vedānta—Neuroscience Dialogue," *Journal of the American Academy of Religion* 77 (2009), 238–274.
13. Louise Connelly, "Virtual Buddhism: An Analysis of Aesthetics in Religion to Religious Practice," *Online—Heidelberg Journal of Religions on the Internet* 4 (2010): 17–18.
14. Ibid., 31.
15. See Eliade, *Myth of the Eternal Return, passim*.
16. Eliade, *Myth of the Eternal Return*, 4.
17. Ibid., 34.
18. Ibid., 103–104.
19. Ibid., 107.
20. Players ensure Thrall's safety by going backward in time in the Caverns of Time instance.
21. Daniel White Hodge, "Role Playing: Toward a Theology for Gamers," in *Halos and Avatars: Playing Video Games with God*, ed. Craig Detweiler (Louisville, KY: Westminster John Knox Press), 174.
22. Bruno Latour, *We Have Never Been Modern*, trans. Catherine Porter (Cambridge, MA: Harvard University Press, [1991] 1993).
23. Latour, *Reassembling the Social*, 1.
24. Of course, the Lysenko affair does illustrate that social factors affect how science is done, and yet quite often scientists at the time avoided engaging political debates over it for fear of endangering their colleagues in the USSR. In *The Lysenko Affair* (Cambridge, MA: Harvard University Press, 1970), David Joravsky offers a classic interpretation of the political and scientific issues at stake. For a more recent summary of the affair, see Oren Harman, "C.D. Darlington and the British and American Reaction to Lysenko and the Soviet Conception of Science." *Journal of the History of Biology* 36 (2003): 309–352. For a discussion of the asymmetry between explanations of truth and error, see Bruno Latour, *Science in Action* (Cambridge, MA: Harvard University Press, 1987), 179–213; and Latour, "For David Bloor...and Beyond: A Reply to David Bloor's 'Anti-Latour,'" *Studies in History and Philosophy of Science* 30 (1999a): 113–129.

25. For example, see the classic collection of essays by Barry Barnes, David Bloor, and John Henry, *Scientific Knowledge: A Sociological Analysis* (Chicago: University of Chicago Press, 1996). It is important to note that this work is a classic representation of the "Strong Programme" in the sociology of science, and that Latour and his actor-network theory colleagues differentiate themselves from it in important ways.

26. Bruno Latour, *Aramis: Or the Love of Technology*, trans. Catherine Porter (Cambridge, MA: Harvard University Press, [1993] 1996), 33.

27. Smith, *Imagining Religion*, xi.

28. Latour, *Reassembling the Social*, 4–5.

29. Latour, *We Have Never Been Modern*, 51.

30. Bruno Latour, *Pandora's Hope: Essays on the Reality of Science Studies* (Cambridge, MA: Harvard University Press, 1999b), 123.

31. Latour, *Reassembling the Social*, 59.

32. Ibid., 71.

33. Ibid., 217.

34. Ibid., 5, emphasis in original.

35. Ibid., 10, emphasis in original.

36. Kenneth Hite, "Multicampaign Setting Design for Role-Playing Games," in *Third Person: Authoring and Exploring Vast Narratives*, ed. Pat Harrigan and Noah Wardrip-Fruin (Cambridge, MA: MIT Press, 2009), 69.

37. I use association here to denote a relationship between two things, as it operates in actor-network theory, not just as a grouping of human beings.

38. Latour, *Reassembling the Social*, 70.

39. Ibid, 72.

40. See, e.g., Kerstin Radde-Antweiler, "'Virtual Religion': An Approach to a Religious and Ritual Topography of *Second Life*," *Online—Heidelberg Journal of Religions on the Internet* 3 (2008), 174–211.

41. Video games have become so real that first the Boy Scouts of America (BSA) and subsequently the Girl Scouts have adopted them into their merit system. Young Scouts can earn both video games belt loops and academic pins for engaging responsible game play; Boy Scouts of America, "Video Games," *scouting.org*, 2010. A firestorm of criticism and support poured in after the BSA announced this in December 2010, and it is not my intention to evaluate the relative merits of adding video games to the list of things that Boy Scouts ought to understand and enjoy. Obviously, this move is the sort of thing decried by critics, but support has been found among parents, who hope that the awards will promote actual conversations about video games and their appropriate uses; see the comments on a *Huffington Post* article about the BSA decision for both criticism of and support for the awards in Bianca Bosker, "Boy Scouts 'Video Game' Badge Introduced," *Huffington Post*, April 28, 2010. At some point, whether we approve of the BSA decision or not, however, we simply must acknowledge that

video games are a part of modern life. The BSA appears to be pushing for management, rather than repression, as an approach to them. Subsequent to this, both the BSA and the Girl Scouts of Greater Los Angeles announced badges earned by studying game design as a bridge to both future careers and advancing knowledge in science and technology; GG AngelThanatos, "Exclusive: Women in Games International & Girl Scouts Creating Video Game Patch," *GirlGamer. com*, April 18, 2013; Angela Moscaritolo, "Boy Scouts Introduce Badge for Game Design," *PCMag.com*, March 13, 2013. Video games have thus infiltrated venerable cultural institutions and are now found in children's leisure activities twice over: both as games and as activities employing or about games. This kind of pervasiveness makes video gaming one of the most substantial influences on daily life today.

42. I am grateful to Wagner James Au, who pointed out this project to me. He has written about its potential for *Second Life* and gaming on his blog, "3D World Breakthrough: Warcraft Played with Kinect Using Open Source Software Available to All!," *New World Notes*, December 28, 2010a.

43. Evan Suma, "World of Warcraft with Microsoft Kinect," *YouTube* video, 2010.

44. See, e.g., Richard Childers, "A Virtual Mars," in *Online Worlds: Convergence of the Real and the Virtual*, ed. William Sims Bainbridge (London: Springer, 2010), 108.

45. Roger Scruton, "Hiding behind the Screen," *New Atlantis* 28 (2010): 52.

46. Ibid., 51.

47. See Wagner James Au, *The Making of Second Life: Notes from the New World* (New York: HarperCollins, 2008a), 202–207.

48. Benedict Anderson, *Imagined Communities: Reflections on the Origin and Spread of Nationalism* (New York: Verso, [1983] 1991).

49. Quoted in Au, *Making of Second Life*, 136.

50. Pearce and Artemesia, "The Diasporic Game Community: Trans-Ludic Cultures and Latitudinal Research across Multiple Games and Virtual Worlds," in *Online Worlds: Convergence of the Real and the Virtual*, ed. William S. Bainbridge, 43–56 (New York: Springer).

51. See Douglas Mandelkow, "Leveling Up into a Community: World of Warcraft as Authentic Fake," Undergraduate honors thesis, Manhattan College (2011).

52. Edward Castronova, *Exodus to the Virtual World: How Online Fun is Changing Reality* (New York: Palgrave Macmillan, 2007), 12.

53. Edward Castronova, *Synthetic Worlds: The Business and Culture of Online Games* (Chicago: University of Chicago Press, 2005); Castronova, *Exodus to the Virtual World*.

54. Douglas Estes, *SimChurch: Being the Church in the Virtual Age* (Grand Rapids, MI: Zondervan, 2009), 222.

55. Katie Salen and Eric Zimmerman, *Rules of Play: Game Design Fundamentals* (Cambridge, MA: MIT Press, 2004), 66–67.

APPENDIX

1. Jonathan Z. Smith, *Imagining Religion: From Babylon to Jonestown* (Chicago: University of Chicago Press, 1982), xi.
2. Ibid., xi.
3. On facts and theories, see William Whewell, *Novum Organon Renovatum* (London: J.W. Parker and Son, 1858), 71–78.
4. David Chidester, "Moralizing Noise," *Harvard Divinity Bulletin* 32 (2004), 17.
5. Gary Fine, *Shared Fantasy: Role-Playing Games as Social Worlds* (Chicago: University of Chicago Press, 1983).
6. Pat Harrigan and Noah Wardrip-Fruin, "Introduction," in *Third Person: Authoring and Exploring Vast Narratives*, ed. Pat Harrigan and Noah Wardrip-Fruin (Cambridge, MA: MIT Press), 7.
7. Fine, *Shared Fantasy*, 223–241.
8. Ibid., 76.
9. Ibid., *passim*.
10. William Sims Bainbridge, *The Warcraft Civilization: Social Science in a Virtual World* (Cambridge, MA: MIT Press, 2010c), 32.
11. Ibid., 4.
12. Tom Boellstorff, *Coming of Age in Second Life: An Anthropologist Explores the Virtually Human* (Princeton, NJ: Princeton University Press, 2008).
13. Bonnie Nardi, *My Life as a Night Elf Priest: An Anthropological Account of World of Warcraft* (Ann Arbor: University of Michigan Press, 2010).
14. Celia Pearce and Artemesia, *Communities of Play: Emergent Cultures in Multiplayer Games and Virtual Worlds* (Cambridge, MA: MIT Press, 2009), 195–211.
15. Ibid.
16. Bruno Latour, *Reassembling the Social: An Introduction to Actor-Network-Theory* (New York: Oxford University Press, 2005).
17. Nick Dyer-Witheford and Greig de Peuter, *Games of Empire: Global Capitalism and Video Games* (Minneapolis: University of Minnesota Press, 2009).
18. Boellstorff, *Coming of Age*.
19. Jane McGonnigal, *Reality Is Broken: Why Games Make Us Better and How They Can Change the World* (New York: Penguin, 2011).
20. e.g. Emma Witkowski, "On the Digital Playing Field: How We 'Do Sport' with Networked Computer Games," *Games and Culture* 7 (2012): 367–368.
21. see Samuel Coavoux, " The Quantitative-Qualitative Antinomy in Virtual World Studies," in *Utopic Dreams and Apocalyptic Fantasies: Critical Approaches to Researching Video Game Play*, ed. J. Talmadge Wright, David G. Embrick, and András Lukács (New York: Lexington Books, 2010), 234.
22. Hanna Wirman, "Email Interviews in Player Research: The Case of the Sims 2 Skinners," *Westminster Papers in Communication and Culture* 9 (2012): 156.

23. For more on the connection between transhumanism and virtual worlds/video games, see Robert M. Geraci, "Video Games and the Transhuman Inclination" *Zygon: Journal of Religion and Science* 47 (2012b), 735–756.

24. On the benefits of this position, see Greg Gillespie and Darren Crouse, "There and Back Again: Nostalgia, Art, and Ideology in Old School Dungeons and Dragons," *Games and Culture* 7 (2012): 442–443.

25. In fact, Ravelry members who did not join Dropped Stitches and Twisted Stitches but who also played *World of Warcraft* also used the Ravelry forums. There were, however, specific forum groups for members of the guilds, and these were largely used only by guild members.

26. Latour, *Reassembling the Social*, 135; Pearce and Artemesia, *Communities of Play*, 198–199.

27. George Marcus, "Ethnography in/of the World System: The Emergence of Multi-Sited Ethnography," *Annual Review of Anthropology* 24 (1995): 97.

28. Ibid., 99.

29. Ibid., 102.

30. Coavoux, "Quantitative-Qualitative Antinomy," 237.

31. Nicholas Ducheneaut, "The Chorus of the Dead: Roles, Identity Formation, and Ritual Processes Inside an FPS Multiplayer Online Game," in *Utopic Dreams and Apocalyptic Fantasies: Critical Approaches to Researching Video Game Play*, ed. J. Talmadge Wright, David G. Embrick, and András Lukács (New York: Lexington Books), 202.

32. Tom Boellstorff, "A Typology of Ethnographic Scales for Virtual Worlds," in *Online Worlds: Convergence of the Real and the Virtual*, ed. William Sims Bainbridge, 123–133 (London: Springer, 2010).

33. Latour, *Reassembling the Social*, 42.

34. See Boellstorff, *Coming of Age*.

References

Alexander, Brian. 2003. *Rapture: How Biotech Became the New Religion.* New York: Basic Books.

Amarasingam, Amarnath. 2008. "Transcending Technology: Looking at Futurology as a New Religious Movement." *Journal of Contemporary Religion* 23 (1): 1–16.

Anderson, Benedict. [1983] 1991. *Imagined Communities: Reflections on the Origin and Spread of Nationalism.* New York: Verso.

Anderson, Craig A., and Karen E. Dill. 2000. "Video Games and Aggressive Thoughts, Feelings, and Behavior in the Laboratory and in Life." *Journal of Personality and Social Psychology* 78 (4): 772–790.

AngelThanatos, G. G. 2013. "Exclusive: Women in Games International & Girl Scouts Creating Video Game Patch." *GirlGamer.com* (April 18). http://www.girl-gamer.com/zine/article/2677/ (accessed April 21, 2013).

Anonymous. 2010. Comment on the *Second Thoughts* weblog (October 20). http://secondthoughts.typepad.com/second_thoughts/2010/10/philip-rosedale-the-long-view.html (accessed March 12, 2011).

Anthony, James. 2012. "God and Avatar." Plenary lecture at the Digital Religions conference at the University of Colorado, Boulder (January 14).

Aravis. 2011. *World of Warcraft* conversation with the author (September 22).

Argoz. 2011. Email interview with the author (December 6).

Arsenault, Dominic. 2008. "The Video Game as an Object of Controversy." In *The Video Game Explosion: A History from Pong to Playstation and Beyond*, edited by Mark J. P. Wolf, pp. 277–281. Westport, CT: Greenwood Press.

Aslan's How. 2010. "Welcome to Aslan's How." Notecard delivered in *Second Life* (August 15, 2010).

Atkins, Samantha. 2010. Email contribution to the Cosmic Engineers listserv (September 20).

Au, Wagner James. 2007. "A Crisis of Faith." *New World Notes* weblog (May 18). http://nwn.blogs.com/nwn/2007/05/avatars_of_unch.html (accessed May 20, 2007).

———. 2008a. *The Making of Second Life: Notes from the New World.* New York: HarperCollins.

———. 2008b. "Muslims and the Metaverse: Can *Second Life* Improve US–Islamic Relations?" *New World Notes* weblog (February 11). http://nwn.blogs.com/nwn/2008/02/muslims-and-the.html (accessed September 5, 2010).

———. 2008c. "The Soul of *Second Life*." *New World Notes* weblog (February 27). http://nwn.blogs.com/nwn/2008/02/the-soul-of-sec.html (accessed August 3, 2008).

———. 2010a. "3D World Breakthrough: Warcraft Played with Kinect Using Open Source Software Available to All!" *New World Notes* weblog (December 28). http://nwn.blogs.com/nwn/2010/12/wow-with-kinect-.html (accessed December 31, 2010).

———. 2010b. "Embracing *Second Life* as a Game Platform, Linden Lab Selects EA Exec & Game Developer Rod Humble as New CEO." *New World Notes* weblog (December 23). http://nwn.blogs.com/nwn/2010/12/linden-lab-new-ceo-rod-humble.html.

———. 2010c. "Philip Rosedale Attempting to Create Sentient Artificial Intelligence that Thinks and Dreams in *Second Life!*" *New World Notes* weblog (February 3). http://nwn.blogs.com/nwn/2010/02/philip-rosedale-ai.html#more (accessed February 5, 2011).

———. 2011a. "Linden to Add Game Mechanics to SL's New User Experience." *New World Notes* weblog (August 14). http://nwn.blogs.com/nwn/2011/08/linden-lab-to-add-game-mechanics-to-new-sl-user-experience.html (accessed August 14, 2011).

———. 2011b. "NWN Exclusive: Interview with Rod Humble, Linden Lab's New CEO, on the Future of *Second Life*." *New World Notes* weblog (February 9). http://nwn.blogs.com/nwn/2011/02/rod-humble-linden-lab-ceo-second-life-inteview.html (accessed February 10, 2011).

———. 2011c. "*Second Life* Still among Nielsen's Top 10 of PC Games in US." *New World Notes* weblog (July 27). http://nwn.blogs.com/nwn/2011/07/top-pc-games-may-2011-nielsen-second-life.html (accessed August 17, 2011).

———. 2011d. Email to the author (September 6).

———. 2011e. "Shaker Gets $15 Million in Venture Funding, Renewing Valley Interest in Synchronous Avatar-Driven Socialization." *New World Notes* weblog (October 10). http://nwn.blogs.com/nwn/2011/10/shaker-gets-15-million-funding.html (accessed October 10, 2011).

———. 2011f. "The Mystery of *Second Life*'s Flat Growth in 2011—Despite 16K New Users Daily." *New World Notes* weblog (December 28). http://nwn.blogs.com/nwn/2011/12/second-life-absolute-growth-in-2011-remains-flat.html (accessed June 12, 2012).

———. 2012a. "*Myst* Co-Creator Rand Miller Thinks Worlds like *Second Life* & *Uru Live* Have a Future on Tablets." *New World Notes* weblog (July 26). http://nwn.blogs.com/nwn/2012/07/future-of-virtual-worlds-on-tablets.html (accessed July 27, 2012).

——. 2012b. "Philip Rosedale: *Second Life* Usage Surpasses 2 Billion Hours." *New World Notes* weblog (July 18). http://nwn.blogs.com/nwn/2012/07/second-life-2-billion-user-hours.html (accessed July 20, 2012).

——. 2012c. "*Second Life* Back on Nielsen's Latest Top 10 PC Game Ratings." *New World Notes* weblog (June 26). http://nwn.blogs.com/nwn/2012/06/second-life-back-on-nielsens-latest-top-10-ratings.html (accessed June 26, 2012).

——. 2012d. "SL Forecast to Lose 10% of World's Private Sims This Year." *New World Notes* weblog (June 6). http://nwn.blogs.com/nwn/2012/06/second-life-losing-10-private-land.html (accessed June 12, 2012).

Aupers, Stef, and Dick Houtman. 2005. "'Reality Sucks': On Alienation and Cybergnosis." *Concilium: International Journal of Theology* 2005 (1): 81–89.

Bacon, Francis. 1951. *The Advancement of Learning and New Atlantis*. London: Oxford University Press.

Bailenson, Jeremy N., and Kathryn Y. Segovia. 2010. "Virtual Doppelgangers: Psychological Effects of Avatars Who Ignore Their Owners." In *Online Worlds: Convergence of the Real and the Virtual*, edited by William Sims Bainbridge, pp. 175–186. London: Springer.

Bailey, Edward. 1983. "The Implicit Religion of Contemporary Society: An Orientation and Plea for Its Study." *Religion* 13 (1): 69–83.

Bainbridge, William Sims. 1986. *Dimensions of Science Fiction*. Cambridge, MA: Harvard University Press.

——. 1995. "Neural Network Models of Religious Belief." *Sociological Perspectives* 38 (4): 483–495.

——. 2006. "Cognitive Technologies." In *Managing Nano-Bio-Info-Cogno Innovations: Converging Technologies in Society*, edited by Mihail Roco and William S. Bainbridge, pp. 203–226. Dordrecht, Netherlands: Springer.

——. 2007. "The Scientific Research Potential of Virtual Worlds." *Science* 317 (July 27): 472–476.

——. 2009. " Religion for a Galactic Civilization 2.0." Institute for Ethics & Emerging Technologies website (August 20). http://ieet.org/index.php/IEET/more/bainbridge20090820/ (accessed August 21, 2009).

——. 2010a. "Introduction." In *Online Worlds: Convergence of the Real and the Virtual*, edited by William Sims Bainbridge, pp. 1–6. London: Springer.

——. 2010b. "New World View." In *Online Worlds: Convergence of the Real and the Virtual*, edited by William Sims Bainbridge, pp. 7–20. London: Springer.

——. 2010c. *The Warcraft Civilization: Social Science in a Virtual World*. Cambridge, MA: MIT Press.

Bainbridge, William Sims, and Rodney Stark. 1985. *The Future of Religion: Secularization, Revival, and Cult Formation*. Los Angeles: University of California Press.

Bainbridge, William Sims, and Wilma Alice Bainbridge. 2007. "Electronic Game Research Methodologies: Studying Religious Implications." *Review of Religious Research* 49 (1): 35–53.

Barker, Eileen. 2005. "Crossing the Boundary: New Challenges to Religious Authority and Control as a Consequence of Access to the Internet." In *Religion and Cyberspace*, edited by Morten T. Højsgaard and Margit Warburg, pp. 67–85. New York: Routledge.

Barnes, Barry, David Bloor, and John Henry. 1996. *Scientific Knowledge: A Sociological Analysis.* Chicago: University of Chicago Press.

Barr, Pippin, Sky Marsen, and James Noble. 2005. "Oppositional Play: Gathering Negative Evidence for Computer Game Values." In *Proceedings of the Second Australasian Conference on Interactive Entertainment (IE2005)*, pp. 3–10. Sydney, Australia: Creativity & Cognition Studios Press.

Bartle, Richard A. [2003] 2004. *Designing Virtual Worlds.* Berkeley, CA: New Riders.

——. 2009. "Alice and Dorothy Play Together." In *Third Person: Authoring and Exploring Vast Narratives*, edited by Pat Harrigan and Noah Wardrip-Fruin, pp. 105–117. Cambridge, MA: MIT Press.

Bashiok. 2011. "4.3 Preview—Transmogrification." *World of Warcraft* official website (August 17). http://us.battle.net/wow/en/blog/3309048 (accessed October 10, 2011).

BBC News. 2011. "World of Warcraft Suffers Subscriber Slump." *BBC News online* (November 10, 2011). http://www.bbc.co.uk/news/technology-15672416 (accessed April 4, 2013).

Becker, Carmen. 2011. "Muslims on the Path of the Salaf al-Salih: Ritual Dynamics in Chat Rooms and Discussion Forums." *Information, Communication & Society* 14 (8): 1181–1203.

Bell, Mark W. 2008. "Toward a Definition of 'Virtual Worlds.'" *Journal of Virtual Worlds Research* 1 (1): 2–5.

Benedict XVI. 2010. "Address of His Holiness Benedict XVI to Participants in the Congress Organized by the Pontifical Council for Social Communications" (October 7). http://www.vatican.va/holy_father/benedict_xvi/speeches/2010/october/documents/hf_ben-xvi_spe_20101007_pccs_en.html (accessed February 23, 2011).

Benson, Timothy O. (ed). 2001. *Expressionist Utopias: Paradise, Metropolis, Architectural Fantasy.* Los Angeles: University of California Press.

Berger, Peter. [1967] 1990. *The Sacred Canopy: Elements of a Sociological Theory of Religion.* New York: Doubleday.

Berger, Helen A., and Douglas Ezzy. 2004. "The Internet as Virtual Spiritual Community: Teen Witches in the United States and Australia." In *Religion Online: Finding Faith on the Internet*, edited by Lorne L. Dawson and Douglas E Cowan, pp. 175–188. New York: Routledge.

Berkeley School of Journalism. 2007. "Faces of Faith in America: Live from *Second Life*." Conference hosted in *Second Life* (July 29).

Berry, Kevin M. 2011. "The Meaning of Artificial Life?" *Robot* 26 (January–February): 26–28.

Big Think. 2009. "Ray Kurzweil Explores the Next Phase of Virtual Reality." BigThink. com (April 28). http://bigthink.com/ideas/14533 (accessed March 14, 2011).

Bittarello, Maria Beatrice. 2008. "Another Time, Another Space: Virtual Worlds: Myths and Imagination." *Online—Heidelberg Journal of Religions on the Internet* 3 (1): 246–266.

Boellstorff, Tom. 2008. *Coming of Age in Second Life: An Anthropologist Explores the Virtually Human.* Princeton, NJ: Princeton University Press.

——. 2010. "A Typology of Ethnographic Scales for Virtual Worlds." In *Online Worlds: Convergence of the Real and the Virtual,* edited by William Sims Bainbridge, pp. 123–133. London: Springer.

Bohannon, John. 2008. "Courting Controversy: Out of the Mainstream." *Science Careers* (July 11). http://sciencecareers.sciencemag.org/career_development/ previous_issues/articles/2008_07_11/caredit_a0800103 (accessed August 16, 2008).

Bosker, Bianca. 2010. "Boy Scouts 'Video Game' Badge Introduced." *Huffington Post* (April 28). http://www.huffingtonpost.com/2010/04/28/boy-scouts-video-g ame-bad_n_555085.html (accessed December 31, 2010).

Boy Scouts of America. 2010. "Video Games." http://www.scouting.org/scout- source/cubscouts/cub%20scouts/uniformsandawards/sanda/video_games. aspx (accessed December 31, 2010).

Brasher, Brenda E. 2004. *Give Me that Online Religion.* New Brunswick, NJ: Rutgers University Press.

Brown, Mark. 2008. "Christian Mission to a Virtual World." http://brownblog. info/wp-content/.../Christian_Mission_to_a_Virtual_World.pdf (accessed April 15, 2010).

Bunt, Gary R. 2004. "'Rip. Burn. Pray.'": Islamic Expression Online." In *Religion Online: Finding Faith on the Internet,* edited by Lorne L. Dawson and Douglas E. Cowan, pp. 123–134. New York: Routledge.

Bursell, Rupert. 2010. "Proposed Constitution for Anglicans of *Second Life.*" Anglican Cathedral of *Second Life* weblog by Helene Milena. http://slangcath.wordpress. com/2010/07/13/proposed-constitution-of-aosl/#more-2318 (accessed August 19, 2010).

Bruns, Axel. 2008. *Blogs, Wikipedia, Second Life, and Beyond: From Production to Produsage.* New York: Peter Lang.

Cain, Jeffrey P. 2008. "Another Bricolage in the Wall: Deleuze and Teenage Alienation." In *Computer Games as a Sociocultural Phenomenon: Games with- out Frontiers, War without Tears,* edited by Andreas Jahn-Sudmann and Ralf Stockmann, pp. 56–65. New York: Palgrave Macmillan.

Callaway, Kutter. 2000. "Wii Are Inspirited: The Transformation of Home Video Gaming Consoles (and Us)." In *Halos and Avatars: Playing Video Games with God,* edited by Craig Detweiler, pp. 75–88. Louisville, KY: Westminster John Knox Press.

Campbell, Heidi. 2004. "'This Is My Church': Seeing the Internet and Club Culture as Sacred Spaces." In *Religion Online: Finding Faith on the Internet*, edited by Lorne L. Dawson and Douglas E. Cowan, pp. 107–121. New York: Routledge.

———. 2007. "Who's Got the Power? Religious Authority and Internet." *Journal of Computer-Mediated Communication* 12 (3). http://jcmc.indiana.edu/vol12/issue3/campbell.html (accessed August 8, 2008).

———. 2010. "Islamogaming: Digital Dignity via Alternative Storytellers." In *Halos and Avatars: Playing Video Games with God*, edited by Craig Detweiler, pp. 63–74. Louisville, KY: Westminster John Knox Press.

Cantor, Geoffrey. 2011. *Religion and the Great Exhibition of 1851*. New York: Oxford University Press.

Capra, Fritjof. 1975. *The Tao of Physics*. Berkeley, CA: Shambhala Publications.

Caspian. 2011. *World of Warcraft* interview with Nicholas Zachowski (March). Used with permission.

Cassini, Ruuh. 2010. Email communication with the author (September 7).

Castronova, Edward. 2005. *Synthetic Worlds: The Business and Culture of Online Games*. Chicago: University of Chicago Press.

———. 2007. *Exodus to the Virtual World: How Online Fun is Changing Reality*. New York: Palgrave Macmillan.

Chaplin, Heather. 2011. "I Don't Want To Be a Superhero: Ditching Reality For a Game Isn't as Fun as It Sounds." *Slate.com* (March 29). http://www.slate.com/id/2289302 (accessed April 8, 2011).

Chee, Florence, Marcelo Vieta, and Richard Smith. 2006. " Online Gaming and the Interactional Self: Identity Interplay in Situated Practice." In *Gaming as Culture: Essays on Reality, Identity, and Experience in Fantasy Games*, edited by J. Patrick Williams, Sean Q. Hendricks, and W. Keith Winkler, pp. 154–174. Jefferson, NC: McFarland & Company.

Chen, Mark G. 2009. "Communication, Coordination, and Camaraderie in World of Warcraft." *Games and Culture* 4 (1): 47–73.

Cheung, Paula, Shirlena Huang, and Jessie P. H. Poon. 2011. "Cultivating Online and Offline Pathways to Enlightenment." *Information, Communication & Society* 14 (8): 1160–1180.

Chiang, Oliver. 2010. "Meet the Man Who Just Made a Half Million from the Sale of Virtual Property." *Forbes.com* (November 13). http://blogs.forbes.com/oliver-chiang/2010/11/13/meet-the-man-who-just-made-a-cool-half-million-from-the-sale-of-virtual-property/ (accessed February 17, 2011).

Chidester, David. 1996a. "The Church of Baseball, the Fetish of Coca-Cola, and the Potlatch of Rock 'n' Roll: Theoretical Models for the Study of Religion in American Popular Culture." *Journal of the American Academy of Religion* 64 (4): 743–765.

———. 1996b. *Savage Systems: Colonialism and Comparative Religion in Southern Africa*. Charlottesville: University of Virginia Press.

——. 2004. "Moralizing Noise." *Harvard Divinity Bulletin* 32 (3): 17.

——. 2005. *Authentic Fakes: Religion and American Popular Culture.* Los Angeles: University of California Press.

Childers, Richard. 2010. "A Virtual Mars." In *Online Worlds: Convergence of the Real and the Virtual,* edited by William Sims Bainbridge, pp. 101–109. London: Springer.

Chilton, Tom. 2011. BlizzCast Interview with Rob Simpson. *BlizzCast* episode 16 (June). http://us.blizzard.com/en-us/community/blizzcast/archive/episode16.html.

Choi, Jason. 2006. *Edge of Remorse.* Riot Films (http://filmsriot.com/).

Church of Fools. 2004a. "41,000 Go to Church in One Day." *Church of Fools.* http://churchoffools.com/news-stories/03_41000.html (accessed November 3, 2010).

Church of Fools. 2004b. "3D Church Reopens for Individual Visits Only." *Church of Fools.* http://churchoffools.com/news-stories/05_3D_reopens.html (accessed November 3, 2010).

Clarke, Arthur C. 1948. *Against the Fall of the Night.* In *Startling Stories* 18 (November): 11-70.

-------- 1953a. *Against the Fall of the Night.* New York: Gnome Press.

-------- 1953b. *Childhood's End.* New York: Balantine Books.

——. 1968. *2001: A Space Odyssey.* New York: New American Library.

——. 2001. *The City and the Stars and The Sands of Mars.* New York: Warner Books.

Coavoux, Samuel. 2010. " The Quantitative-Qualitative Antinomy in Virtual World Studies." In *Utopic Dreams and Apocalyptic Fantasies: Critical Approaches to Researching Video Game Play,* edited by J. Talmadge Wright, David G. Embrick, and András Lukács, pp. 223–244. New York: Lexington Books.

Connelly, Louise. 2010. "Virtual Buddhism: An Analysis of Aesthetics in Religion to Religious Practice." *Online—Heidelberg Journal of Religions on the Internet* 4 (1): 12–34.

Consalvo, Mia. 2009. "There Is No Magic Circle." *Games and Culture* 4 (4): 408–417.

——. 2012. "Achievement Deleted: The Challenges of Quantifying Gaming Capital." Contribution to the 4th Flow Conference in Austin, TX. Posted to *Technoculture, Art and Games* weblog under the title "Gaming Capital and Flow" (November 9). http://tag.hexagram.ca/blog/gaming-capital-and-flow/ (accessed November 22, 2012).

Consalvo, Mia, Timothy Dodd Alley, Nathan Dutton, Matthew Falk, Howard Fisher, Todd Harper, and Adam Yulish. 2010. "Where's My Montage? The Performance of Hard Work and Its Reward in Film, Television, and MMOGs." *Games and Culture* 5 (4): 381–402.

Cor. 2010. Email contribution to the Cosmic Engineers listserv (November 6). Author listed pseudonymously.

Corin. 2010. Email contribution to the Cosmic Engineers listserv (November 5). Author listed pseudonymously.

Cortinas, Marty. 2010. "The Story So Far: Inside the Mind of Blizzard's Creative Godfather, Chris Metzen." *World of Warcraft Official Magazine* 1 (3): 22–33.

Costikyan, Greg. 2007. "Games, Storytelling, and Breaking the String." In *Second Person: Role-Playing and Story in Games and Playable Media*, edited by Pat Harrigan and Noah Wardrip-Fruin, pp. 5–14. Cambridge, MA: MIT Press.

Crick, Timothy. 2011. "The Game Body: Toward a Phenomenology of Contemporary Video Gaming." *Games and Culture* 6 (3): 259–269.

Crystal, Gaber. 2010. *Second Life* interview with the author (November 8).

Čulig, Benjmain, and Izvor Rukavina. 2012. "Psychosocial and Sociocultural Determinants of a Typology of Video Gamers." Presented at the 4th Annual Conference for Videogame Cultures and the Future of Interactive Entertainment, Oxford, UK (July 12).

Daly, Bernard M. 2004. "Transhumanism." *America: The National Catholic Weekly* (October 25). http://www.americamagazine.org/content/article.cfm?article_id=3826 (accessed April 1, 2011).

DaSilva, Extropia. 2008. "CTRL-ALT-R: Rebake Your Reality." *Gwen's Home*. http://gwynethllewelyn.net/2008/05/18/ctrl-alt-r-rebake-your-reality-an-essay-by-extropia-dasilva/ (accessed February 17, 2011).

——. 2009. "Ray Kurzweil and the Conquest of Mount Improbable." *H+ Magazine* (November 23). http://www.hplusmagazine.com/articles/ai/ray-kurzweil-and-conquest-mount-improbable (accessed September 7, 2010).

——. 2010a. "If the Singularity Is Not Happening." *Mind Child's Musings* weblog (August 3) http://extropiadasilva.wordpress.com/2010/08/03/if-the-singularity-is-not-happening/ (accessed August 3, 2010).

——. 2010b. "Lanier's Singularity." *H+ Magazine* (May 5). http://hplusmagazine.com/articles/ai/lanier's-singularity (accessed September 7, 2010).

——. 2010c. *Second Life* interview with the author (September 9).

——. 2010d. Email correspondence with the author (September 7).

——. 2010e. Email correspondence with the author (September 10).

——. 2011. Facebook communication with the author (January 5).

——. 2012. "Holy Singularity." *H+ Magazine* (July 5). http://hplusmagazine.com/2012/07/05/holy-singularity/ (accessed July 6, 2012).

Davidson, Drew. 2008. "Well Played: Interpreting Prince of Persia: The Sands of Time." *Games and Culture* 3 (3–4): 356–386.

Davis, Eric. 1996. "Osmose." *Wired* 4.08 (August). http://www.wired.com/wired/archive/4.08/osmose.html (accessed February 20, 2008).

Davis, Matthew. 2005. "Christians Purge Video Game Demons." BBC News (May 24). http://news.bbc.co.uk/2/hi/americas/4534835.stm (accessed July 19, 2010).

Dawson, Lorne L. 2004. "Religion and the Quest for Virtual Community." In *Religion Online: Finding Faith on the Internet*, edited by Lorne L. Dawson and Douglas E. Cowan, pp. 75–89. New York: Routledge.

Dawson, Lorne L., and Douglas E. Cowan. 2004. "Introduction." In *Religion Online: Finding Faith on the Internet*, edited by Lorne L. Dawson and Douglas E. Cowan, pp. 1–16. New York: Routledge.

De Garis, Hugo. 2005. *The Artilect War: Cosmists vs. Terrans: A Bitter Controversy Concerning Whether Humanity Should Build Godlike Massively Intelligent Machines.* Palm Springs, CA: ETC Publications.

DeCuir, Malaquias. 2008. "Metalife." *SL'ang Life: Real Information at Home* 5: 16–17.

Dery, Mark. *Escape Velocity: Cyberculture at the End of the Century.* New York: Grove Press.

Detweiler, Craig. 2010. "Introduction." In *Halos and Avatars: Playing Video Games with God,* edited by Craig Detweiler, pp. 1–18. Louisville, KY: Westminster John Knox Press.

Digory. 2011. *World of Warcraft* interview with Nicholas Zachowski (March). Used with permission.

Douglas, Christopher. 2010. "Multiculturalism in World of Warcraft." *Electronic Book Review* (June 4). http://www.electronicbookreview.com/thread/firstperson/ intrinsically (accessed April 28, 2012).

Ducheneaut, Nicolas. 2010a. "The Chorus of the Dead: Roles, Identity Formation, and Ritual Processes Inside an FPS Multiplayer Online Game." In *Utopic Dreams and Apocalyptic Fantasies: Critical Approaches to Researching Video Game Play,* edited by J. Talmadge Wright, David G. Embrick, and András Lukács, pp. 199–222. New York: Lexington Books.

———. 2010b. "Massively Multiplayer Online Games as Living Laboratories: Opportunities and Pitfalls." In *Online Worlds: Convergence of the Real and the Virtual,* edited by William Sims Bainbridge, pp. 135–145. London: Springer.

Ducheneaut, Nicolas, and Robert J. Moore. 2005. "More than Just 'XP': Learning Social Skills in Massively Multiplayer Online Games." *Interactive Technology and Smart Education* 2: 89–100.

Ducheneaut, Nicholas, Robert J. Moore, and Eric Nickell. 2007. "Virtual 'Third Places': A Case Study of Sociability in Massively Multiplayer Games." *Computer Supported Cooperative Work* 16: 129–166.

Ducheneaut, Nicolas, Nick Yee, Eric Nickell, and Robert J. Moore. 2006. "Building an MMO with Mass Appeal: A Look at Gameplay in World of Warcraft." *Games and Culture* 1: 281–317.

Duncan, Sean C. 2009. "Remaking Azeroth." In *World of Warcraft and Philosophy: Wrath of the Philosopher King,* edited by Luke Cuddy and John Norlinger, pp. 117–127. Chicago: Open Court.

Durkheim, Emile. [1912] 1995. *The Elementary Forms of the Religious Life.* Translated by Karen Fields. New York: Free Press.

Dyer-Witheford, Nick, and Greig de Peuter. 2009. *Games of Empire: Global Capitalism and Video Games.* Minneapolis: University of Minnesota Press.

Dyson, Linda. 2008. "Teenage Girls 'Play House': The Cyber-drama of The Sims." In *Computer Games as a Sociocultural Phenomenon: Games without Frontiers, War without Tears,* edited by Andreas Jahn-Sudmann and Ralf Stockmann, pp. 197–206. New York: Palgrave Macmillan.

EarthSky. 2008. "Ray Kurzweil's Vision of the Fugure." *EarthSky.com* (August 7). http://earthsky.org/human-world/ray-kurzweils-vision-of-the-future (accessed March 14, 2011).

Ebel, Jonathan H. 2009. "Jesus Freak and the Junkyard Prophet: The School Assembly as Evangelical Revival." *Journal of the American Academy of Religion* 77 (1): 16–54.

Economist. 2006. "Living a *Second Life.*" *Economist.* http://www.economist.com/displaystory.cfm?story_id=7963538. September 28 (accessed October 31, 2006).

Eliade, Mircea. [1954] 1991. *The Myth of the Eternal Return: Or, Cosmos and History.* Translated by Willard R. Trask. Princeton, NJ: Princeton University Press.

——. [1957] 1987. *The Sacred and the Profane: The Nature of Religion.* Translated by Willard Trask. Orlando, FL: Harcourt Inc.

——. 1969. *The Quest: History and Meaning in Religion.* Chicago: University of Chicago Press.

——. 1985. *Symbolism, the Sacred, and the Arts.* Edited by Diane Apostolos-Cappadona. New York: Crossroad.

Elizondo, Virgilio. 1983. *Galilean Journey: The Mexican-American Promise.* Maryknoll, NY: Orbis Books.

——. 2000. *The Future Is Mestizo: Life Where Cultures Meet* (rev. ed.). Boulder: University of Colorado Press.

Epperly, Bruce. 2010. "A Facebook Theology." *Patheos.com* (March 24). http://www.patheos.com/Resources/Additional-Resources/Facebook-Theology.html?cnn=yes (accessed February 23, 2011).

Esfandiary, Feridouin M. [1970] 1978. *Optimism One.* New York: Popular Library.

——. [1973] 1977. *Up-Wingers: A Futurist Manifesto.* New York: Popular Library Press.

Espín, Orlando O. 1997. *The Faith of the People: Theological Reflections on Popular Catholicism.* Maryknoll, NY: Orbis Books.

Estes, Douglas. 2009. *SimChurch: Being the Church in the Virtual Age.* Grand Rapids, MI: Zondervan.

Ettinger, Robert. 1964. *The Prospect of Immortality.* New York: Doubleday & Company.

——. 1972. *Man into Superman.* New York: Avon.

Evans, Monica. 2009. "You Can Kill Your Friends but You Can't Save Gnomeregan." In *World of Warcraft and Philosophy: Wrath of the Philosopher King,* edited by Luke Cuddy and John Nordlinger, pp. 3–12. Chicago: Open Court.

Evans-Pritchard, E. E. 1956. *Nuer Religion.* New York: Oxford University Press.

Extropia Core. 2010. "Extropia: History." *Extropia.* http://core.extropiacore.net/History (accessed September 13, 2010).

Fagone, Jason. 2011. "Chain World Videogame Was Supposed To Be a Religion—Not a Holy War." *Wired* (July 15). http://www.wired.com/magazine/2011/07/mf_chainworld/all/1?pid=6413&viewall=true (accessed August 28, 2011).

Fine, Gary. 1983. *Shared Fantasy: Role-Playing Games as Social Worlds.* Chicago: University of Chicago Press.

Fitzgerald, Michael. 2007. "How I Did It: Philip Rosedale, CEO, Linden Lab and *Second Life*." *Inc.com* (February 1). http://www.inc.com/magazine/20070201/hidi-rosedale.html (accessed March 31, 2011).

FM-2030. 1989. *Are You a Transhuman? Monitoring and Stimulating Your Personal Rate of Growth in a Rapidly Changing World.* New York: Warner Books.

Foley, John P. 2002. "The Church and the Internet." Pontifical Council for Social Communications. http://www.vatican.va/roman_curia/pontifical_councils/pccs/documents/rc_pc_pccs_doc_20020228_church-internet_en.html (accessed April 8, 2010).

Fouts, Joshua. 2010. "Al-Andalus 2.0." *Saudi Aramco World* 61 (4): 10–15. http://www.saudiaramcoworld.com/issue/201004/al-andalus.2.0.htm (accessed September 25, 2010).

Frankel, Jon. 2002. "EverQuest or Evercrack?" *The Early Show,* CBSNews.com. http://wwww.cbsnews.com/stories/2002/05/28/earlyshow/living/caught/main510302.shtml (accessed July 14, 2010).

Freud, Sigmund. [1927] 1961. *The Future of an Illusion.* Translated by James Strachey. New York: W.W. Norton.

Fukuyama, Francis. 2002. *Our Posthuman Future: Consequences of the Biotechnology Revolution.* New York: Farrar, Straus and Giroux.

Fulfillment. 2010a. "Cosmist or Terran Voting Results from Fulfillment Meeting in *Second Life*" (May 22). http://soft-transcend.org/Fulfillment/Brain/#-170.

Fulfillment. 2010b. "Spirituality and Fulfillment." Chat log from *Second Life* Fulfillment meeting in *Second Life* (September 10). http://www.thefulfillment.org/chatlogs/100910_SpiritualityAndFulfillment.htm (accessed November 8, 2010).

Fullerton, Tracy. 2011. "The Night Journey." *Tracy Fullerton, Game Design.* http://tracyfullerton.com/projects/the_night_journey.html (accessed December 25, 2011).

Gartner Group. 2007. "Gartner Says 80 Percent of Active Internet Users Will Have a '*Second Life*' in the Virtual World by the End of 2011." *Gartner.com* (April 24). http://www.gartner.com/it/page.jsp?id=503861 (accessed January 10, 2008).

Gazzard, Alison, and Alan Peacock. 2011. "Repetition and Ritual Logic in Video Games." *Games and Culture* 6 (6): 499–512.

Geddes, Linda. 2010. "Immortal Brain: You Can Live Forever." *New Scientist* 206 (2763): 28–31.

Gentile, Douglas A., Craig A. Anderson, Shintaro Yukawa, Nobuko Ihori, Muniba Saleem, Lim Kam Ming, Akiko Shibuya, Albert K. Liau, Angeline Khoo, Brad J. Bushman, L. Rowell Huesmann, and Akira Sakamoto. 2009. "The Effects of Prosocial Video Games on Prosocial Behaviors: International Evidence from Correlational, Longitudinal, and Experimental Studies." *Personality and Social Pyschology Bulletin* 35 (6): 752–763.

Geraci, Robert. 2006. "Spiritual Robots: Religion and Our Scientific View of the Natural World." *Theology and Science* 4 (3): 229–246.

——. 2007. "Robots and the Sacred in Science and Science Fiction: Theological Implications of Artificial Intelligence." *Zygon: Jounral of Religion and Science* 42 (4): 961–980.

——. 2008. "Apocalyptic AI: Religion and the Promise of Artificial Intelligence." *Journal of the American Academy of Religion* 76 (1): 138–166.

——. 2010. *Apocalyptic AI: Visions of Heaven in Robotics, Artificial Intelligence and Virtual Reality.* New York: Oxford University Press.

——. 2010. "Popular Appeal of Apocalyptic AI." *Zygon: Journal of Religion and Science* 45 (4): 1003–1020.

——. 2011a. "Cyborgs, Robots, and Eternal Avatars: Transhumanist Salvation at the Interface of Brains and Machines." In *Routledge Companion to Religion and Science*, edited by James Haag, Gregory Peterson, and Michael Spezio, pp. 578–590. New York: Routledge.

——. 2011b. "There and Back Again: Transhumanist Evangelism in Science Fiction and Popular Science." *Implicit Religion* 14 (2): 141–172.

——. 2012a. "Theological Productions: The Role of Religion in Video Game Design." In *Cultural Perspectives of Video Games: From Designer to Player*, edited by Adam L. Brackin and Natacha Guyot, pp. 101–114. Oxford: Inter-Disciplinary Press.

——. 2012b. "Video Games and the Transhuman Inclination." *Zygon: Journal of Religion and Science* 47 (4): 735–756.

Geraci, Robert M., and Jovi Geraci. 2013. "Virtual Gender: How Men and Women Use Videogame Bodies." *Journal of Gaming and Virtual Worlds* 5(3): 329–348.

Geraci, Robert M., and Nat Recine. Forthcoming. "A Moral Universe: Suffering and War in *Star Wars: The Old Republic*." *Religion Dispatches*.

——. In review. "Enlightening the Galaxy: How Players Experience Political Philosophy in Star Wars: The Old Republic."

Gibson, William. 1984. *Neuromancer*. New York: Ace.

——. 1986. *Count Zero*. New York: Ace.

Gillath, Omri, Cade McCall, Phillip R. Shaver, and Jim Blascovich. 2008. "What Can Virtual Reality Teach Us about Prosocial Tendencies in Real and Virtual Environments?" *Media Psychology* 11 (2): 259–282.

Gillespie, Greg, and Darren Crouse. 2012. "There and Back Again: Nostalgia, Art, and Ideology in Old School Dungeons and Dragons." *Games and Culture* 7 (6): 441–470.

Gilsdorf, Ethan. 2010. "A Virtual World that Breaks Real Barriers." *Christian Science Monitor* (September 10). http://www.csmonitor.com/The-Culture/Arts/2010/0910/A-virtual-world-that-breaks-real-barriers (accessed September 23, 2010).

Gingold, Chaim. 2009. "A Brief History of Spore." In *Third Person: Authoring and Exploring Vast Narratives*, edited by Pat Harrigan and Noah Wardrip-Fruin, pp. 131–136. Cambridge, MA: MIT Press.

Gladstone, Brooke. 2010. "Transcript of 'The Influence of Gaming.'" *On the Media* website (December 31). http://www.onthemedia.org/transcripts/2010/12/31/01 (accessed March 4, 2011).

Global Innovation Outlook. 2007. "Virtual Worlds, Real Leaders: Online Games Put the Future of Business Leadership on Display." IBM and Seriosity, Inc. http://www.seriosity.com/leadership.html.

Goertzel, Ben. 2010. *A Cosmist Manifesto: Practical Philosophy for the Posthuman Age.* Los Angeles: Humanity + Press.

———. 2011. "Technological Transcendence: An Interview with Giulio Prisco." *H+ Magazine* (February 8). http://hplusmagazine.com/2011/02/08/technological-transcendence-an-interview-with-giulio-prisco/ (accessed February 8, 2011).

Goffman, Erving. 1959. *The Presentation of Self in Everyday Life.* New York: Anchor Books.

Goleb, Alex. 2010. "Being in the World (of Warcraft): Raiding, Realism, and Knowledge Production in a Massively Multiplayer Online Game." *Anthropological Quarterly* 83 (1): 17–46.

Gonzalez, Avelino J. 2009. Email correspondence with the author (September 14).

Graft, Kris. 2011. "GDC 2011: An Epidemiologist's View of *World of Warcraft*'s Corrupted Blood Plague." *Gamasutra: The Art and Business of Making Games* website (February 28). http://www.gamasutra.com/view/news/33276/gdc_2011_an_epidemiologists_view_.php (accessed October 12, 2011).

Greitemeyer, Tobias, and Silvia Osswald. 2010. "Effects of Prosocial Video Games on Prosocial Behavior." *Journal of Personality and Social Psychology* 98 (2): 211–221.

———. 2011. "Playing Prosocial Video Games Increases the Accessibility of Prosocial Thoughts." *Journal of Social Psychology* 151 (2): 121–128.

Greitemeyer, Tobias, Silvia Osswald, and Markus Brauer. 2010. "Playing Prosocial Video Games Increases Empathy and Decreases Schadenfreude." *Emotion* 10 (6): 796–802.

Grieve, Gregory. 2010. "Virtually Embodying the Field: Silent Online Buddhist Meditation, Immersion, and the Cardean Ethnographic Method." *Online— Heidelberg Journal of Religions on the Internet* 4 (1): 35–62.

Gruenewald, Bobby. 2007. "The Ups and Downs of *Second Life*." *Swerve* weblog (April 20). http://swerve.lifechurch.tv/2007/04/20/the-ups-and-downs-of-second-life/ (accessed September 25, 2010).

Gtec. 2011. "*Second Life* with BCI." *YouTube* video. http://www.youtube.com/watch?v=Y8TEsoti3EI&feature=player_embedded (accessed September 5, 2011).

Guest, Tim. 2007. *Second Lives: A Journey through Virtual Worlds.* New York: Random House.

Guild. 2010a. "Appalled at NPCs." Thread on *Ravelry.com* (December 1).

———. 2010b. "The End of the World Is TONIGHT!!!!" Thread on *Ravelry.com* (November 22).

———. 2011. "Farming (Esp. Archeology)—The Good the Bad the Ugly." Thread on *Ravelry.com* (February 20).

———. 2012a. "The 'Unloved' Races/Classes." Thread on *Ravelry.com* (January 31).

———. 2012b. "Wolves." Thread on *Ravelry.com* (September 4).

Gutiérrez, Gustavo. [1971] 1988. *A Theology of Liberation: History, Politics, and Salvation*. Maryknoll, NY: Orbis Books.

Haldane, J. B. S. 1923. "Daedalus, or Science and the Future." Presented to the Heretics Society, Cambridge, UK (February 4). http://www.cscs.umich.edu/~crshalizi/Daedalus.html.

Halopedia. 2010. "Covenant Religion." http://www.halopedian.com/Covenant_religion (accessed December 30, 2010).

Hansen, Chris. 2010. "From *Tekken* to *Kill Bill*: The Future of Narrative Storytelling?" In *Halos and Avatars: Playing Video Games with God*, edited by Craig Detweiler, pp. 19–33. Louisville, KY: Westminster John Knox Press.

Haraway, Donna. 1997. *Modest_Witness@ Second_Millennium.Female_Man©_Meets_Oncomouse™*. New York: Routledge.

Harman, Oren Solomon. 2003. "C. D. Darlington and the British and American Reaction to Lysenko and the Soviet Conception of Science." *Journal of the History of Biology* 36 (2): 309–352.

Harrigan, Pat, and Noah Wardrip-Fruin. 2009. "Introduction." In *Third Person: Authoring and Exploring Vast Narratives*, edited by Pat Harrigan and Noah Wardrip-Fruin, pp. 1–9. Cambridge, MA: MIT Press.

Hawkins, Janine. 2011. "Ophelia's Gaze: 3 Big Mistakes MMOs Make that Alienate Female Gamers." *New World Notes* weblog (January 3). http://nwn.blogs.com/nwn/2011/01/3-mistakes-that-alienate-female-gamers.html (accessed January 3, 2011).

Hayse, Mark. 2010. "Ultima IV: Simulating the Religious Quest." In *Halos and Avatars: Playing Video Games with God*, edited by Craig Detweiler, pp. 34–46. Louisville, KY: Westminster John Knox Press.

Hefner, Philip. 2009. "The Animal that Aspires To Be an Angel: The Challenge of Transhumanism." *Dialog: A Journal of Theology* 48 (2): 164–173.

Heidbrink, Simone. 2007. "Exploring the Religious Frameworks of the Digital Realm: Offline-Online-Offline Transfers of Ritual Performance." *Masaryk University Journal of Law and Technology* 1 (2): 175–184.

Heidbrink, Simone, Nadja Miczek, and Kerstin Radde-Antweiler. 2011. "Contested Rituals in Virtual Worlds." In *Ritual, Media, and Conflict*, edited by Ronald L. Grimes, Ute Hüsken, Udo Simon, and Eric Venbrux, pp. 165–187. New York: Oxford University Press.

Heinlein, Robert. 1958. *Methuselah's Children*. New York: New American Library.

———. 1973. *Time Enough for Love: The Lives of Lazarus Long*. New York: G.P. Putnam's Sons.

Heirohacking. 2010. Email contribution to the listerv (November 2).

Helen. 2011. *World of Warcraft* conversation with the author (September 22).

Helland, Christopher. 2000. "Online Religion/Religion Online and Virtual Communitas." In *Religion on the Internet: Research Prospects and Promises*, edited by Jeffrey K. Hadden and Douglas E. Cowan, pp. 205–224. London: JAI Press/ Elsevier Science.

——. 2004. "Popular Religion and the World Wide Web: A Match Made in (Cyber) Heaven." In *Religion Online: Finding Faith on the Internet*, edited by Lorne L. Dawson and Douglas E. Cowan, pp. 23–35. New York: Routledge.

Helmreich, Stefan. [1998] 2000. *Silicon Second Nature: Culturing Artificial Life in a Digital World*. Los Angeles: University of California Press.

Henderson, Charles. 2010. Untitled presentation at the summer colloquium of the Association for Religion in Intellectual Life, New York City, USA (July 22).

Hendricks, Sean Q. 2006. "Incorporative Discourse Strategies in Tabletop Fantasy Role-Playing Gaming." In *Gaming as Culture: Essays on Reality, Identity, and Experience in Fantasy Games*, edited by J. Patrick Williams, Sean Q. Hendricks, and W. Keith Winkler, pp. 39–56. Jefferson, NC: McFarland & Company.

Herman, Phyllis K. 2010. "Seeing the Divine through Windows: Online Darshan and Virtual Religious Experience." *Online—Heidelberg Journal of Religions on the Internet* 4 (1): 151–178.

Highland, Michael, and Gino Yu. 2008. "Communicating Inner Experience with Video Game Technology." *Online—Heidelberg Journal of Religions on the Internet* 3 (1): 267–289.

Hindmarch, Will. 2007. "Storytelling Games as a Creative Medium." In *Second Person: Role-Playing and Story in Games and Playable Media*, edited by Pat Harrigan and Noah Wardrip-Fruin, pp. 47–55. Cambridge, MA: MIT Press.

Hite, Kenneth. 2009. "Multicampaign Setting Design for Role-Playing Games." In *Third Person: Authoring and Exploring Vast Narratives*, edited by Pat Harrigan and Noah Wardrip-Fruin, pp. 67–75. Cambridge, MA: MIT Press.

Hodge, Daniel White. 2010. "Role Playing: Toward a Theology for Gamers." In *Halos and Avatars: Playing Video Games with God*, edited by Craig Detweiler, pp. 163–175. Louisville, KY: Westminster John Knox Press.

Hof, Robert D. 2006. "My Virtual Life." *Business Week* 3982 (May 1): 72–75.

Hoover, Stewart M. 2006. *Religion in the Media Age*. New York: Routledge.

Hoover, Stewart, and Nabil Echchaibi. 2012. "The 'Third Spaces' of Digital Religion." *The Center for Media, Religion, and Culture*. http://cmrc.colorado.edu/ the-natural-history-of-the-digital-religion-conference/ (accessed February 2012).

Huizinga, Johann. [1949] 2000. *Homo Ludens: A Study of the Play-Element in Culture*. London: Routledge.

Hunter, Edward. 2009. "World of Warcraft Audience Grows in the Face of Increased Competition." *Gamasutra.com* (September 24). http://www.gamasutra.com/ blogs/EdwardHunter/20090924/3179/World_Of_Warcraft_Audience_Grows_ In_The_Face_Of_Increased_Competition.php (accessed March 25, 2013).

Hutchings, Timothy. 2010a. "The Internet and the Church: An Introduction." *Expository Times* 122 (1): 11–19.

——. 2010b. "The Politics of Familiarity: Visual, Liturgical and Organisational Conformity in the Online Church." *Online—Heidelberg Journal of Religions on the Internet* 4 (1): 63–86.

——. 2011. "Contemporary Religious Community and the Online Church." *Information, Communication, & Society* 14 (8): 1118–1135.

Huxley, Julian. 1957a. *New Bottles for New Wine.* New York: Harper and Brothers.

——. 1957b. *Religion without Revelation.* New York: Harper & Row.

Iris. 2007. "Can Any WoW Players Do Me a Favour?" *Iris Gaming Network* Web forum. http://forums.theirisnetwork.org/viewtopic.php?t=308 (accessed March 4, 2011).

Jakobsson, Mikael. 2011. "The Achievement Machine: Understanding Xbox 360 Achievements in Gaming Practices." *Game Studies* 11 (1). http://gamestudies.org/1101/articles/jakobsson (accessed November 22, 2012).

Jakobsson, Mikael, and T. L. Taylor. 2003. "The Sopranos Meets EverQuest: Social Networking in Massively Multiplayer Online Games." Presented at MelbourneDAC, the 5th International Digital Arts and Culture Conference. http://hypertext.rmit.edu.au/dac/papers/Jakobsson.pdf (accessed July 12, 2010).

Jenkins, Simon. 2008. "Rituals and Pixels: Experiments in Online Church." *Online—Heidelberg Journal of Religions on the Internet* 3 (1): 95–115.

Jill. 2010. Email interview with the author (July 30). Listed pseudonymously.

Joravsky, David. 1970. *The Lysenko Affair.* Cambridge, MA: Harvard University Press.

Jordan, Gregory. 2006. "Apologia for Transhumanist Religion." *Journal of Evolution & Technology.* 15 (1): 55–72.

Joystiq. 2009. "Bungie: 10 Billion Covenant Killed in Halo 3…and Growing." *Joystiq.com* (April 14). http://www.joystiq.com/2009/04/13/bungie-10-billion-covenant-killed-in-halo-3-and-growing/ (accessed April 10, 2011).

Joystiq. 2012. "WoW Subscriber Numbers." *WoW Insider.* http://wow.joystiq.com/tag/wow-subscriber-numbers/ (accessed April 4, 2013).

Kahn, Jennifer. 2011. "The Visionary." *New Yorker* 87 (July 11): 46–53.

Kaplan, Stephen. 2002. *Different Paths, Different Summits: A Model for Religious Pluralism.* New York: Rowman & Littlefield.

——. 2009. "Grasping at Ontological Straws: Overcoming Reductionism in the Advaita Vedānta—Neuroscience Dialogue." *Journal of the American Academy of Religion* 77 (2): 238–274.

Karapanagiotis, Nicole. 2010. "Vaishnava Cyber-Pūjā: Problems of Purity & Novel Ritual Solutions." *Online-Heidelberg Journal of Religions on the Internet* 4 (1): 179–195.

Kelly, Kevin. 1999. "Nerd Theology." *Technology in Society* 21 (4): 387–392.

Kessler, Andy. 2011. "How Videogames Are Changing the Economy." *Wall Street Journal* (January 11). http://online.wsj.com/article/SB10001424052970203418804576040103609214400.html (accessed January 20, 2011).

Ketchum, Paul R., and B. Mitchell Peck. 2010. "Marketing Computer Games: Reinforcing or Changing Stereotypes?" In *Utopic Dreams and Apocalyptic Fantasies: Critical Approaches to Researching Video Game Play*, edited by J. Talmadge Wright, David G. Embrick, and András Lukács, pp. 125–142. New York: Lexington Books.

Kijowski, Maciej. 2011. Conversation in *Second Life* (February 20).

King, Brad, and John Borland. 2003. *Dungeons and Dreamers: The Rise of Computer Game Culture from Geek to Chic*. New York: McGraw-Hill/Osborne.

King, Rita J., and Joshua S. Fouts. 2008. "Digital Diplomacy: Understanding Islam through Virtual Worlds." New York: Carnegie Council for International Affairs. http://dancinginkproductions.com/projects/understanding-islam-through-virtual-worlds/.

Klimmt, Christoph, Hannah Schmid, Andreas Nosper, Tilo Hartmann, and Peter Vorderer. 2008. "'Moral Management': Dealing with Moral Concerns to Maintain Enjoyment of Violent Video Games." In *Computer Games as a Sociocultural Phenomenon: Games without Frontiers, War without Tears*, edited by Andreas Jahn-Sudmann and Ralf Stockmann, pp. 108–118. New York: Palgrave Macmillan.

Klimmt, Christoph, Christian Roth, Ivar Vermeulen, Peter Vorderer, and Franziska Susanne Roth. 2012. "Forecasting the Experience of Future Entertainment Technology: 'Interactive Storytelling' and Media Enjoyment." *Games and Culture* 7 (3): 187–208.

Klink, Madeline. 2008. "'I Type the Amens and Think the Rest': An Ethnographic Look at Religion in Virtual Reality." Honors Thesis written for the Division of Philosophy, Religion, Psychology and Linguistics at Reed College.

Kluver, Randolph, and Yanli Chen. 2008. "The Church of Fools: Virtual Ritual and Material Faith." *Online—Heidelberg Journal of Religions on the Internet* 3 (1): 116–143.

Knight, Kimberly. 2008. Conversation in *Second Life* (March 22).

——. 2009. "Sacred Space in Cyberspace." *Reflections* 96 (2): 43–46.

——. 2010. Interview in *Second Life* (August 22).

——. 2012. Skype interview with the author (June 20).

Kosak, Dave. 2011. "Interview with Rob Simpson." *BlizzCast* episode 16 (June). http://us.blizzard.com/en-us/community/blizzcast/archive/episode16.html.

Kosminksy, Eli. 2009. "Finding Adam Smith in Azeroth." In *World of Warcraft and Philosophy: Wrath of the Philosopher King*, edited by Luke Cuddy and John Norlinger, pp. 17–26. Chicago: Open Court.

Krzywinska, Tanya. 2006. "Blood Scythes, Festivals, Quests, and Backstories: World Creation and Rhetorics of Myth in World of Warcraft." *Games and Culture* 1 (4): 383–396.

——. 2008. "World Creation and Lore: World of Warcraft as Rich Text." In *Digital Culture, Play, and Identity: A World of Warcraft Reader*, edited by Hilde G. Corneliussen and Jill Walker Rettberg, pp. 123–142. Cambridge, MA: MIT Press.

———. 2009. "Arachne Challenges Minerva: The Spinning Out of Long Narrative in World of Warcraft and Buffy the Vampire Slayer." In *Third Person: Authoring and Exploring Vast Narratives*, edited by Pat Harrigan and Noah Wardrip-Fruin, pp. 385–398. Cambridge, MA: MIT Press.

Kurzweil, Ray. 1990. *The Age of Intelligent Machines*. Cambridge, MA: MIT Press.

———. 1999. *The Age of Spiritual Machines: When Computers Exceed Human Intelligence*. New York: Viking.

———. 2005. *The Singularity Is Near: When Humans Transcend Biology*. New York: Viking.

LaChapelle, David. 2005. *Rize*. Los Angeles: David LaChapelle Studios.

Laney, Michael J. 2005. "Christian Web Usage: Motives and Desires." In *Religion and Cyberspace*, edited by Morten T. Højsgaard and Margit Warburg, pp. 166–179. New York: Routledge.

Langer, Jessica. 2008. "The Familiar and the Foreign: Playing (Post)Colonialism in World of Warcraft." In *Digital Culture, Play, and Identity: A World of Warcraft Reader*, edited by Hilde G. Corneliussen and Jill Walker Rettberg, pp. 87–108. Cambridge, MA: MIT Press.

Langman, Lauren, and András Lukács. 2010. "Capitalism, Contradiction, and the Carnivalesque: Alienated Labor vs. Ludic Play." In *Utopic Dreams and Apocalyptic Fantasies: Critical Approaches to Researching Video Game Play*, edited by J. Talmadge Wright, David G. Embrick, and András Lukács, pp. 59–72. New York: Lexington Books.

Lanier, Jaron. 2010. *You Are Not a Gadget: A Manifesto*. New York: Knopf.

Lankoski, Petri. 2011. "Player Character Engagement in Computer Games." *Games and Culture* 6 (4): 291–311.

Lantz, Frank. 2004. "Forward." In *Rules of Play: Game Design Fundamentals*, edited by Katie Salen and Eric Zimmerman, pp. ix–xi. Cambridge, MA: MIT Press.

Larsen, Elena. 2004. "Cyberfaith: How Americans Pursue Religion Online." In *Religion Online: Finding Faith on the Internet*. Edited by Lorne L. Dawson and Douglas E. Cowan, pp. 17–20. New York: Routledge.

Latour, Bruno. 1983. "Give Me a Laboratory and I Will Raise the World." In *Science Observed: Perspectives on the Social Study of Science*, edited by Karin Knorr-Cetina and Michael Mulkay, pp. 141–170. Beverley Hills, CA: SAGE.

———1987. *Science in Action*. Cambridge, MA: Harvard University Press.

———. [1991] 1993. *We Have Never Been Modern*. Translated by Catherine Porter. Cambridge, MA: Harvard University Press.

———. [1993] 1996. *Aramis: Or the Love of Technology*. Translated by Catherine Porter. Cambridge, MA: Harvard University Press.

———. 1999a. "For David Bloor... and Beyond: A Reply to David Bloor's 'Anti-Latour.'" *Studies in History and Philosophy of Science* 30 (1): 113–129.

———. 1999b. *Pandora's Hope: Essays on the Reality of Science Studies*. Cambridge, MA: Harvard University Press.

———. 2005. *Reassembling the Social: An Introduction to Actor-Network-Theory.* New York: Oxford University Press.

Laws, Robin D. 2009. "Intellectual Property Development in the Adventure Games Industry: A Practioner's View." In *Third Person: Authoring and Exploring Vast Narratives*, edited by Pat Harrigan and Noah Wardrip-Fruin, pp. 59–65. Cambridge, MA: MIT Press.

Laycock, Joseph. 2010. "Myth Sells: Mattel's Commision of the Masters of the Universe Bible." *Journal of Religion and Popular Culture* 22 (2).

Le Corbusier. 1946. *Towards a New Architecture.* Translated by Frederick Etchells. New York: Praeger.

Leigh, Morgan. 2011a. Email correspondence with the author (February 16).

———. 2011b. Email correspondence with the author (March 31).

Leigh, Morgan, and Mark Elwell. 2010. "Authentic Theurgy: Ceremonial Magic in Second LIfe." In *Workshop Proceedings of the 18th International Conference on Computers in Education*, edited by Tsukasa Hirashima, Ahmad Fauzi Mohd Ayub, Lam-For Kwok, Su Luan Wong, Siu Cheung Kong, and Fu-Yun Yu, pp. 260–267. Putrajaya, Malaysia: Asia-Pacific Society for Computers in Education.

Leigh, Morgan, Mark Elwell, and Steven Cook. 2010. "Recreating Ancient Egyptian Culture in *Second Life*." In *Proceedings of the Third IEEE International Conference on Digital Game and Intelligent Toy Enhanced Learning* (held April 12–16 at the National Science and Technology Museum, Kaohsiung, Taiwan). New York: Institute of Electrical and Electronics Engineers.

Lemos, Robert. 2005. "Digital Plague Hits Online Game World of Warcraft." *Security Focus* website (September 27). http://www.securityfocus.com/news/11330 (accessed October 12, 2011).

Lester, John. 2011. Skype interview with the author (December 6).

Lewis, Clive S. 1956. "On the Fairy Tale." *Wedgewood Circle.* http://wedgwoodcircle. com/news/articles/sometimes-fairy-stories-may-say-best-whats-to-be-said/ (accessed August 15, 2010).

LifeChurch.tv. 2010a. "Get Involved." http://www.lifechurch.tv/who-we-are/ get-involved (accessed August 22, 2010; no longer available).

———. 2010b. Email correspondence with the author (September 14). Name of *LifeChurch.tv* representative kept anonymous.

LifeNaut. 2010. "How It Works." http://lifenaut.com/Mind-How.html (accessed July 18, 2010).

Light, Jennifer. 2008. "Taking Games Seriously." *Technology and Culture* 49 (2): 347–375.

Ligonier Ministries. 2010. "What Is Reformed Theology?" http://www.ligonier.org/ learn/series/what_is_reformed_theology/ (accessed August 18, 2010).

Lilliehook, Wren. 2008a. Interview in *Second Life* (March 17).

———. 2008b. Interview in *Second Life* (March 31).

Lin, Yu-Ling, and Hong-Wen Lin. 2011. "A Study on the Goal Value for Massively Multiplayer Online Role-Playing Games Players." *Computers in Human Behavior* 27: 2153–2160.

Lincoln, Bruce. 1989. *Discourse and the Construction of Society: Comparative Studies of Myth, Ritual, and Classification.* New York: Oxford University Press.

Linden, Nelson. 2011. "The *Second Life* Economy in Q4 2010." *Second Life* community forum (January 26). http://community.secondlife.com/t5/Featured-News/The-Second-Life-Economy-in-Q4–2010/ba-p/674618 (accessed March 12, 2011).

Linden Lab. 2010. "What Is *Second Life*?" *Second Life* website. http://secondlife.com/whatis/?lang=en-US (accessed September 5, 2010).

Linden Lab. 2011. "LGBT Friendly." *Second Life* website. http://secondlife.com/destinations/gay/2 (accessed March 15, 2011.

Lindtner, Silvia, and Paul Dourish. 2011. "The Promise of Play: A New Approach to Productive Play." *Games and Culture* 6 (5): 453–478.

Little, Anthony, and David Perrett. 2002. "Putting Beauty Back in the Eye of the Beholder." *Psychologist* 15 (1): 28–32.

LMU Magazine Staff. 2010. "Satisfying Relationships: Real vs. Virtual." *LMU Magazine* (July 7). http://magazine.lmu.edu/archive/2010/satisfying-relationships-real-vs-virtual.

Lombardi, Julian, and Marilyn Lombardi. 2010. "Opening the Metaverse." In *Online Worlds: Convergence of the Real and the Virtual*, edited by William Sims Bainbridge, pp. 111–122. London: Springer.

Londy, Larry. 2010. Interview in *Second Life* (August 26).

Love, Mark Cameron. 2011. "Not-So-Sacred Quests: Religion, Intertextuality and Ethics in Video Games." *Religious Studies and Theology* 29 (2): 191–213.

Lowood, Henry. 2009. "Warcraft Adventures: Texts, Replay, and Machinima in a Game-Based Storyworld." In *Third Person: Authoring and Exploring Vast Narratives*, edited by Pat Harrigan and Noah Wardrip-Fruin, pp. 407–427. Cambridge, MA: MIT Press.

Lucy. 2010. Email interview with the author (August 2). Listed pseudonymously.

Lundby, Kurt. 2011. "Patterns of Belonging in Online/Offline Interfaces of Religion." *Information, Communication, & Society* 14 (8): 1219–1235.

Lune. 2010. Email contribution to the Cosmic Engineers listserv (November 7). Author listed pseudonymously.

Lykin, Annabelle. 2011. Email communication with the author (February 14).

Lyvette, Simone. 2011. *Second Life* conversation with the author (February 13).

MacCallum-Stewart, Esther. 2008. "Never Such Innocence Again: War and Histories in World of Warcraft." In *Digital Culture, Play, and Identity: A World of Warcraft Reader*, edited by Hilde G. Corneliussen and Jill Walker Rettberg, pp. 39–62. Cambridge, MA: MIT Press.

MacDougall, Julien, and Wayne O'Brien. 2008. *Studying Video Games.* Leighton Buzzard: Auteur Press.

MacWilliams, Mark W. 2004. "Virtual Pilgrimage to Ireland's Croagh Patrick." In *Religion Online: Finding Faith on the Internet*, edited by Lorne L. Dawson and Douglas E. Cowan, pp. 223–238. New York: Routledge.

Maddox, Tom. 1992. "After the Deluge: Cyberpunk in the '80s and '90s." In *Thinking Robots, An Aware Internet, and Cyberpunk Librarians: The 1992 LITA President's Program*, edited by R. Bruce Miller and Milton T. Wolf, pp. 107–112. Chicago: Library and Information Technology Association.

Maharishi. 2001. "TM-Sidhi Program and Yogic Flying." *Maharishi.org*. http://www.maharishi.org/sidhi/ (accessed April 14, 2013).

Malaby, Thomas M. 2009. *Making Virtual Worlds: Linden Lab and Second Life*. Ithaca, NY: Cornell University Press.

Malinowski, Bronislaw. [1948] 1954. *Magic, Science and Religion, and Other Essays*. New York: Doubleday.

Malone, Krista-Lee. 2009. "Dragon Kill Points: The Economics of Power Gamers." *Games and Culture* 4 (3): 296–316.

Mandelkow, Douglas. 2011. "Leveling Up into a Community: World of Warcraft as Authentic Fake." Undergraduate honors thesis, Manhattan College.

Marcus, George. 1995. "Ethnography in/of the World System: The Emergence of Multi-Sited Ethnography." *Annual Review of Anthropology* 24: 95–117.

Margaret. 2011. Email interview with the author (December 9).

Marsh, Tim. 2006. "Vicarious Experience: Staying There Connected with and through Our Own and Other Characters." In *Gaming as Culture: Essays on Reality, Identity and Experience in Fantasy Games*, edited by J. Patrick Williams, Sean Q. Hendricks, and W. Keith Winkler, pp. 196–214. Jefferson, NC: McFarland & Company, Inc.

Martin, George. 1971. "Brief Proposal on Immortality: An Interim Solution." *Perspectives in Biology and Medicine* 14 (2): 339–340.

Martínková, Libuse. 2007. "GSM Technology and Its Use in Religious Life: A Preliminary Inquiry." *Masaryk University Journal of Law and Technology* 1 (2): 231–240.

McLaren, Brian D. 2010. *A New Kind of Christianity: Ten Questions that Are Transforming the Faith*. New York: HarperCollins.

McMahan, Alison. 2008. "Video Game Stars: Lara Croft." In *The Video Game Explosion: A History from Pong to Playstation and Beyond*, edited by Mark J. P. Wolf, pp. 183–185. Westport, CT: Greenwood Press.

McMahon, Christopher. 2008. "Imaginative Faith: Apocalpytic, Science Fiction Theory, and Theology." *Dialog: A Journal of Theology* 47 (3): 271–276.

McGonigal, Jane. 2003. "A Real Little Game." Presented at the Digital Games Research Association Conference in Utrecht (November).

——. 2010. "Gaming Can Make a Better World." Presented at the TED 2010 Conference in Long Beach, CA. http://blog.ted.com/2010/03/gaming_can_make.php (accessed July 19, 2010).

———. 2011. *Reality Is Broken: Why Games Make Us Better and How They Can Change the World*. New York: Penguin.

Mechner, Jordan. 2007. "The Sands of Time: Crafting a Video Game Story." In *Second Person: Role-Playing and Story in Games and Playable Media*, edited by Pat Harrigan and Noah Wardrip-Fruin, pp. 111–120. Cambridge, MA: MIT Press.

Mello, Heather L. 2006. "Invoking the Avatar: Gaming Skills as Cultural and Out-of-Game Capital." In *Gaming as Culture: Essays on Reality, Identity, and Experience in Fantasy Games*, edited by J. Patrick Williams, Sean Q. Hendricks, W. Keith Winkler, pp. 175–195. Jefferson, NC: McFarland & Company.

Mendlesohn, Farah. 2003a. "Introduction." In *The Cambridge Companion to Science Fiction*, edited by Edward James and Farah Mendlesohn, pp. 1–12. Cambridge, UK: Cambridge University Press.

———. 2003b. "Religion and Science Fiction." In *The Cambridge Companion to Science Fiction*, edited by Edward James and Farah Mendlesohn, pp. 264–275. Cambridge, UK: Cambridge University Press.

Merlin, Qyxxql. 2007. "Blog comment, May 20, 'A Crisis of Faith,' by W. James Au," *New World Notes* weblog (May 18). nwn.blogs.com/nwn/2007/05/avatars_of_unch.html (accessed June 5, 2007).

Metz, Cade. 2007. "*Second Life* Will Dwarf the Web in Ten Years: So Says Linden Lab CEO." *Register*, August 1. www.theregister.co.uk/2007/08/01/second_life_to_dwarf_web_in_ten_years/ (accessed August 14, 2007).

Miczek, Nadja. 2008. "Online Rituals in Virtual Worlds: Christian Online Services between Dynamics and Stability." *Online—Heidelberg Journal of Religions on the Internet* 3 (1): 144–173.

Midgley, Mary. 1992. *Science as Salvation*. New York: Routledge.

Milburn, Colin. 2008. "Atoms and Avatars: Virtual Worlds as Massively-Multiplayer Laboratories." *Spontaneous Generations* 2 (1): 63–89.

Miller, Matthew P. 2009. "Storytelling in a Multiplayer Environment." In *Third Person: Authoring and Exploring Vast Narratives*, edited by Pat Harrigan and Noah Wardrip-Fruin, pp. 125–130. Cambridge, MA: MIT Press.

Minsky, Marvin. 1994. "Will Robots Inherit the Earth?" *Scientific American* (October). http://web.media.mit.edu/~minsky/papers/sciam.inherit.html (accessed June 14, 2007).

Møller, A. P., and R. Thornhill. 1998. "Bilateral Symmetry and Sexual Selection: A Meta-Analysis." *American Naturalist* 151 (2): 174–192.

Mollman, Dan. 2008. "For Online Addicts, Relationships Float between Real, Virtual Worlds." *CNN.com* (January 29). http://edition.cnn.com/2008/BUSINESS/01/29/digital.addiction (accessed January 29, 2008).

Mona, Erik. 2007. "From the Basement to the Basic Set: The Early Years of Dungeons & Dragons." In *Second Person: Role-Playing and Story in Games and Playable Media*, edited by Pat Harrigan and Noah Wardrip-Fruin, pp. 25–30. Cambridge, MA: MIT Press.

Monson, Melissa J. 2012. "Race-Based Fantasy Realm: Essentialism in World of Warcraft." *Games and Culture* 7 (1): 48–71.

Moravec, Hans. 1978. "Today's Computers, Intelligent Machines and Our Future." *Analog* 99 (February): 59–84. http://www.frc.ri.cmu.edu/~hpm/project.archive/general.articles/1978/analog.1978.html (accessed August 5, 2007).

——. 1988. *Mind Children: The Future of Robot and Human Intelligence.* Cambridge, MA: Harvard University Press.

——. 1999. *Robot: Mere Machine to Transcendent Mind.* New York: Oxford University Press.

——. 2007. Email communication with the author (June 25).

More, Max. 2003. "Principles of Extropy: Version 3.11." *Extropy.* http://www.extropy.org/principles.htm (accessed October 4, 2008).

Morehead, John W. 2010. "Cybersociality: Connecting Fun to the Play of God." In *Halos & Avatars: Playing Video Games with God,* edited by Craig Detweiler, pp. 176–189. Louisville, KY: Westminster John Knox Press.

Moriarty, Christopher, and Avelino J. Gonzalez. 2009. "Learning Human Behavior from Observation for Gaming Applications." In *Proceedings of the 22nd International Florida Artificial Intelligence Research Society Conference* (FLAIRS-2009, held May 19–21, 2009 at Sanibel Island, Florida). Palo Alto: AAAI Press.

Morris, Chris. 2005. "The Greatest Story Never Played: Why Don't Religion and Video Games Mix? The Industry's Top Developers Ponder the Question." *CNN.com* (July 6). http://money.cnn.com/2005/07/06/commentary/game_over/column_gaming/index.htm (accessed July 19, 2010).

Moscaritolo, Angela. 2013. "Boy Scouts Introduce Badge for Game Design." *PCMag.com* (March 13). http://www.pcmag.com/article2/0,2817,2416360,00.asp (accessed April 21, 2013).

Mosse, George L. 1975. *The Nationalization of the Masses: Political Symbolism and Mass Movements in Germany from the Napoleonic Wars Through the Third Reich.* New York: Howard Fertig.

Murashko, Alex. 2012. "LifeChurch.tv Applies for Church Domain Name." *Christian Post* (June 15). http://www.christianpost.com/news/lifechurch-tv-applies-for-church-domain-name-76696/ (accessed June 20, 2012).

Nardi, Bonnie. 2010. *My Life as a Night Elf Priest: An Anthropological Account of World of Warcraft.* Ann Arbor: University of Michigan Press.

Nain. 2012. *World of Warcraft* conversation with the author (January 1). Listed pseudonymously.

National Science Foundation. 2011. "On-Line Gamers Succeed Where Scientists Fail, Opening Door to New AIDS Drug Design." Press Release 11–197 (September 19). http://nsf.gov/news/news_summ.jsp?cntn_id=121680&org=NSF&from=news (accessed September 19, 2011).

Neilsen. 2009. "The State of the Video Gamer: PC Game and Video Game Console Usage Fourth Quarter 2008." http://blog.nielsen.com/nielsenwire/wp-content/uploads/2009/04/stateofvgamer_040609_fnl1.pdf (accessed October 10, 2011).

Nelson, Robert H. 2001. *Economics as Religion: From Samuelson to Chicago and Beyond.* University Park: Pennsylvania State University Press.

Newell, Allen. 1990. "Fairy Tales." In *The Age of Intelligent Machines*, edited by Raymond Kurzweil, pp. 420–423. Cambridge, Mass.: MIT Press.

Newgren, Kevin. 2010. "BioShock to the System: Smart Choices in Video Games." In *Halos and Avatars: Playing Video Games with God*, edited by Craig Detweiler, pp. 135–144. Louisville, KY: Westminster John Knox Press.

Nitsche, Michael. 2008. *Video Game Spaces: Image, Play, and Structure in 3D Game Worlds*. Cambridge, MA: MIT Press.

Noble, David F. 1999. *The Religion of Technology: The Divinity of Man and the Spirit of Invention*. New York: Penguin.

Nye, David E. 2003. *America as Second Creation: Technology and Narratives of a New Beginning*. Cambridge, MA: MIT University Press.

O, Iggy. 2011. "Failure to Disrupt: Why *Second Life* Failed." *Hypergrid Business* (February 8). http://www.hypergridbusiness.com/2011/02/failure-to-disrupt-why-second-life-failed/ (accessed February 8, 2011).

O' Leary, Stephen D. 2004. "Cyberspace as Sacred Space: Communicating Religion on Computer Networks." In *Religion Online: Finding Faith on the Internet*, edited by Lorne L. Dawson and Douglas E. Cowan, pp. 37–58. New York: Routledge.

——. 2005. "Utopian and Dystopian Possibilities of Networked Religion in the New Millennium." In *Religion and Cyberspace*, edited by Morten T. Højsgaard and Margit Warburg, pp. 38–49. New York: Routledge.

Oldenberg, Ray. 1989. *The Great Good Place: Cafés, Coffee Shops, Community Centers, Beauty Parlors, General Stores, Bars, Hangouts, and How They Get You Through the Day*. New York: Paragon House.

Oliver, Julian Holland. 2002. "The Similar Eye: Proxy Life and Public Space in the MMORPG." In *Proceedings of Computer Games and Digital Cultures Conference*, edited by Frans Mäyrä, pp. 171–184. Tampere: Tampere University Press.

Olvin. 2012. "Respondent to Online Survey on Transhumanism and Video Games."

Order of Cosmic Engineers (OCE). 2008a. "Order of Cosmic Engineers: About." http://www.cosmeng.org/index.php/Order_of_Cosmic_Engineers:About (accessed August 16, 2008; link no longer active).

——. 2008b. "Order of Cosmic Engineers: Prospectus." http://www.cosmeng.org/index.php/Order_of_Cosmic_Engineers:Prospectus (accessed August 16, 2008; link no longer active).

——. 2010. "Restart OCE." Email delivered through the Order of Cosmic Engineers GoogleGroup. The author's identity and the date of the email are withheld for reasons of privacy.

Ortiz de Gortari, Angelica B., Karin Aronsson, and Mark D. Griffiths. 2011. "Game Transfer Phenomena in Video Game Playing: A Qualitative Interview Study." *International Journal of Cyber Behavior, Psychology and Learning* 1 (3): 15–33.

Oziewicz, Marek. 2008. *One Earth, One People: The Mythopoeic Fantasy Series of Ursula K. LeGuin, Lloyd Alexander, Madeleine L'Engle, and Orson Scott Card*. Jefferson, NC: McFarland & Company.

Page, Richard. 2012. "Leveling Up: Playerkilling as Ethical Self-Cultivation." *Games and Culture* 7 (3): 238–257.

Panganiban, Rik. 2007. "'Faces of Faith' Bringing Religious Leaders into *Second Life* July 29." *The Click Heard Round the World* blog. http://www.rikomatic.com/blog/2007/07/faces-of-faith-.html (accessed July 18, 2007).

Pearce, Celia. 2008. "The Truth about Baby Boomer Gamers: A Study of Over-Forty Computer Game Players." *Games and Culture* 3 (2): 142–174.

Pearce, Celia, and Artemesia. 2009. *Communities of Play: Emergent Cultures in Multiplayer Games and Virtual Worlds*. Cambridge, MA: MIT Press.

———. 2010. "The Diasporic Game Community: Trans-Ludic Cultures and Latitudinal Research Across Multiple Games and Virtual Worlds." In *Online Worlds: Convergence of the Real and the Virtual*, edited by William S. Bainbridge, pp. 43–56. New York: Springer.

Peralta, Eyder. 2006. "In *Second Life*, the World Is Virtual. But the Emotions Are Real." *Houston Chronicle*, May 26. www.chron.com/disp/story.mpl/ent/389953.html (accessed October 31, 2006).

Perry, R. Michael. 2000. *Forever for All: Moral Philosophy, Cryonics, and the Scientific Prospects for Immortality*. Boca Raton: Universal Publishers.

Pesce, Mark. 2001. "True Magic." In *True Names and the Opening of the Cyberspace Frontier*, edited by James Frankel, pp. 221–238. New York: Tor.

Peter. 2010a. Email interview with the author (August 2). Listed pseudonymously.

———. 2010b. Email interview with the author (August 3). Listed pseudonymously.

Piff, David, and Margit Warburg. 2005. "Seeking for Truth: Plausibility Alignment on a Baha'i Email List." In *Religion and Cyberspace*, edited by Morten T. Højsgaard and Margit Warburg, pp. 86–101. New York: Routledge.

Pineiro-Escoriaza, Juan Carlos. 2008. *Second Skin*. Long Island City: Pure West Films.

Plate, S. Brent. 2010. "Religion Is Playing Games: Playing Video Gods, Playing to Play." *Religious Studies and Theology* 29 (2): 215–230.

Pohl, Frederik. [1955] 1975. The Tunnel under the World. In *The Best of Frederik Pohl*, edited by Lester del Rey, pp. 8–35. Garden City, NY: Nelson Doubleday.

Poisso, Lisa. 2012. "Breakfast Topic: Do Account-Wide Achievements Make Characters Too Interchangeable?" *WoW Insider* (December 17). http://wow.joystiq.com/2012/12/17/breakfast-topic-do-account-wide-achievements-make-characters-to/ (accessed April 26, 2013).

Pomeroy, Robin. 2007. "*Second Life* Raided by Catholic Missionaries." *News.com.au* (July 28). http://www.news.com.au/story/0,23599,22148187-2,00.html (accessed August 3, 2008).

Poor, Nathaniel. 2012. "Digital Elves as a Racial Other in Video Games: Acknowledgment and Avoidance." *Games and Culture* 7 (5): 375–396.

Postrel, Virgina. 1998. *The Future and Its Enemies: The Growing Conflict over Creativity, Enterprise, and Progress*. New York: Touchstone.

Prebish, Charles S. 2004. "The Cybersangha: Buddhism on the Internet." In *Religion Online: Finding Faith on the Internet*, edited by Lorne L. Dawson and Douglas E. Cowan, pp. 135–148. New York: Routledge.

President's Council of Bioethics. 2003. *Beyond Therapy: Biotechnology and the Pursuit of Happiness—A Report of the President's Council on Bioethics*. Washington, DC: President's Council on Bioethics.

Prisco, Giulio. 2004. "Engineering Transcendence." Original blog post republished by the Institute for Ethics and Emerging Technologies. http://ieet.org/index.php/IEET/more/prisco20041201/.

——. 2007. "Transcendent Engineering." Presented at the *Second Life* Seminar on Transhumanism and Engineering (April 27).

——. 2008. "Transhumanist Religions." Presented at the Future of Religions/ Religions of the Future conference held in Extropia and Al-Andalus in *Second Life* (June 4–5).

——. 2010a. Email contribution to the *Cosmic Engineers* listserv (September 20).

——. 2010b. Email contribution to the *Heirohacking* listserv (November 8).

——. 2010c. Email contribution to the Turing Church listserv (June 15).

——. 2010d. Email invitation to join the Turing Church (April 24).

——. 2010e. "Future Evolution as Virtual Worlds as Communication Environments." In *Online Worlds: Convergence of the Real and the Virtual*, edited by William Sims Bainbridge, pp. 279–288. London: Springer.

——. 2010f. Email correspondence with the author (August 31).

——. 2010g. Email correspondence with the author (September 12).

Putnam, Robert D. 2000. *Bowling Alone: The Collapse and Revival of American Community*. New York: Simon and Schuster.

Qualters, Sheri. 2010. "Federal Circuit: Group's Internet and Radio Worship Does Not Meet IRS Definition of 'Church.'" *National Law Journal* (August 18). http://www.law.com/jsp/article.jsp?id=1202470154549&rss=newswire&slreturn=1&hbxlogin=1 (accessed March 15, 2011).

Questi, Botgirl. 2010. "The Death of the Digital Person in *Second Life*: An Old School Botgirl Rant." *Botgirl's Second Life Diary* weblog (May 23). http://botgirl.blogspot.com/2010/05/death-of-digital-person-in-second-life.html (accessed September 13, 2010).

Radde-Antweiler, Kerstin. 2006. "Rituals Online: Transferring and Designing Rituals." *Online—Heidelberg Journal of Religions on the Internet* 2 (1): 54–72.

——. 2007. "Cyber-Rituals in Virtual Worlds, Wedding-Online in *Second Life*." *Masaryk University Journal of Law and Technology* 1 (2): 185–196.

——. 2008. "'Virtual Religion': An Approach to a Religious and Ritual Topography of *Second Life*." *Online—Heidelberg Journal of Religions on the Internet* 3 (1): 174–211.

Rettberg, Jill Walker. 2008. "Quests in World of Warcraft: Deferral and Repetition." In *Digital Culture, Play, and Identity: A World of Warcraft Reader*, edited by Hilde G. Corneliussen and Jill Walker Rettberg, pp. 167–184. Cambridge, MA: MIT Press.

Rettberg, Scott. 2010. "Corporate Ideology in World of Warcraft." In *Digital Culture, Play, and Identity: A World of Warcraft Reader*, edited by Hilde G. Corneliussen and Jill Walker Rettberg, pp. 19–38. Cambridge, MA: MIT Press.

Rheingold, Howard. 1991. *Virtual Reality: The Revolutionary Technology of Computer-Generated Artificial Worlds—and How It Promises to Transform Society*. New York: Touchstone Books.

Rhoten, Diana, and Wayne Lutters. 2010. "Virtual Worlds for Virtual Organizing." In *Online Worlds: Convergence of the Real and the Virtual*, edited by William Sims Bainbridge, pp. 265–278. London: Springer.

Rifkin, Jeremy. 1983. *Algeny* (in collaboration with Nicanor Perlas). New York: Viking.

Robertson, Margaret. 2009. "One More Go: Why Halo Makes Me Want to Lay Down and Die." *Offworld—Boing Boing* website (September 25). http://www.offworld. com/2009/09/one-more-go-why-halo-makes-me.html (accessed March 4, 2011).

Robinson-Neal, Andreé. 2008. "Enhancing the Spiritual Relationship: The Impact of Virtual Worship on the Real World Church Experience." *Online—Heidelberg Journal of Religions on the Internet* 3 (1): 228–245.

Robles, Daniela. 2012. "Dying to Play: How Death Mechanics Provide Meaningful Experiences in Guild Wars." In *Cultural Perspectives of Video Games: From Designer to Player*, edited by Adam L. Brackin and Natacha Guyot, pp. 23–32. Oxford: Inter-Disciplinary Press.

Rolston, Ken. 2009. "My Story Never Ends." In *Third Person: Authoring and Exploring Vast Narratives*, edited by Pat Harrigan and Noah Wardrip-Fruin, pp. 119–124. Cambridge, MA: MIT Press.

Roof, Wade Clark. 1994. *A Generation of Seekers: The Spiritual Journeys of the Baby Boom Generation*. San Francisco: Harper.

Rose, Frank. 2007. "Lonely Planet." *Wired* 15 (August): 140–144.

Rosedale, Philip. 2011. Email correspondence with the author (April 7).

Rosmarin, Rachel. 2007. "Virtual Fun and Games." *Forbes.com* (November 8). http://www.forbes.com/technology/2007/11/08/virtual-world-ga mes-technology-cx_rr_1108world.html (accessed December 21, 2007).

Rosen, Larry. 2011. "Why Would Kids Who Spend More Time on Facebook Display More Empathy Online and in Real Life?" *Science and Religion Today* weblog (August 25). http://www.scienceandreligiontoday.com/2011/08/25/why-would-kids-who-s pend-more-time-on-facebook-display-more-empathy-online-and-in-real-life/ (accessed August 25, 2011).

Rosenberg, Adam. 2011. "Indie Dev Builds 'Minecraft' Religion for GDC's Game Design Challenge." *MTV Multiplayer* blog (March 7). http://multiplayerblog.mtv. com/2011/03/07/minecraft-religion-gdc/ (accessed March 18, 2011).

Rosenberg, Robin S., Shawnee L. Baughman, and Jeremy N. Bailenson. 2013. "Virtual Superheroes: Using Superpowers in Virtual Reality to Encourage Prosocial Behavior." *PLoS ONE* 8 (1): 1–9.

Rothblatt, Martine. 2010. "Brains Are to Minds as Birds Are to Flight." Presentation at TransVision 2010 Conference, Milan, Italy and via Teleplace (October 23).

Rowlands, Timothy. 2012. *Video Game Worlds: Working at Play in the Culture of EverQuest.* Walnut Creek, CA: Left Coast Press.

Rubenstein, Andrea. 2007. "Idealizing Fantasy Bodies." *Iris Gaming Network* website. http://theirisnetwork.org/2007/05/26/idealizing-fantasy-bodies/ (accessed January 3, 2011).

Rudolph, Kurt. 1989. "Mircea Eliade and the 'History' of Religions." *Religion* 19 (2): 101–127.

Rymaszewski, Michael, Wagner James Au, Mark Wallace, Catherine Winters, Cory Ondrejka, Benjamin Batstone-Cunningham, and *Second Life* residents from around the world. 2007. *Second Life: The Official Guide.* Indianapolis, IN: Wiley.

Salen, Katie, and Eric Zimmerman. 2004. *Rules of Play: Game Design Fundamentals.* Cambridge, MA: MIT Press.

Schaffer, Simon. 2002. "The Devices of Iconoclasm." *Iconoclash: Beyond the Image Wars in Science, Religion, and Art*, edited by Bruno Latour and Peter Weibel, pp. 498–515. Cambridge, MA: MIT Press and ZKM Center for Art and Media.

Schick, Lawrence. 1991. *Heroic Worlds: A History and Guide to Role-Playing Games.* Amherst, NY: Prometheus Books.

Schiesel, Seth. 2011. "A Game to Make Zynga Nervous." *New York Times* (October 7). http://www.nytimes.com/2011/10/08/arts/video-games/sims-social-is-an-astonishing-success-on-facebook.html?nl=todaysheadlines&emc=tha26 (accessed October 7, 2011).

Scruton, Roger. 2010. "Hiding behind the Screen." *New Atlantis* 28: 48–60. Available online: http://www.thenewatlantis.com/publications/hiding-behind-the-screen.

Second Life. 2010. "Games in *Second Life*." *YouTube* video (December 30). http://www.youtube.com/watch?v=xJSkApWFo3c (accessed December 31, 2010).

Seraph, Serendipity. 2010. Email correspondence with the author (November 13).

Shim, Jason. 2010. "'Til Disconnection Do We Part: The Initiation and Wedding Rite in *Second Life*." In *Halos and Avatars: Playing Video Games with God*, edited by Craig Detweiler, pp. 149–162. Louisville, KY: Westminster John Knox Press.

Shivers, Olin. 1999. "Stunning Achievement: A Review of Vernor Vinge's True Names and the Opening of the Cyberspace Frontier." *Amazon.com* (March 23). http://www.amazon.com/True-Names-Opening-Cyberspace-Frontier/dp/0312862075/ref=cm_cr-mr-title/103-0096591-9331054 (accessed April 17, 2007).

Sicart, Miguel. 2005. "The Ethics of Computer Game Design." Presented at the Digital Games Research Association Conference, Vancouver, Canada. http://miguelsicart.net/papers/DIGRA_05_Ethics.pdf (accessed June 20, 2010).

——. 2009. "A Flourishing Revolt." In *World of Warcraft and Philosophy: Wrath of the Philosopher King*, edited by Luke Cuddy and John Norlinger, pp. 92–106. Chicago: Open Court.

——. 2010. "This War Is a Lie: Ethical Implications of Massively Multiplayer Online Game Design." In *Emerging Issues of Life in Virtual Worlds*, edited by Charles

Wankel and Shaun Malleck, pp. 177–195. Charlotte, NC: Information Age Publishing.

Simkins, David W., and Constance Steinkuehler. 2008. "Critical Ethical Reasoning and Role-Play." *Games and Culture* 3 (3): 335–355.

Singh, Devendra. 1993. "Adaptive Significance of Female Physical Attractiveness: Role of Waist-to-Hip Ratio." *Journal of Personality and Social Psychology* 65 (2): 293–307.

Sirius, R.U. 2010. "Digital Polytheism (on the Event of Timothy Leary's 90th Birthday." *H+ Magazine* (October 20). http://hplusmagazine.com/editors-blog/digital-polytheism-event-timothy-learys-90th-birthday (accessed November 8, 2010).

Šisler, Vítek. 2008. "Digital Arabs: Representation in Video Games." *European Journal of Cultural Studies* 11 (2): 203–219.

———. 2009. "European Courts' Authority Contested?: The Case of Marriage and Divorce Fatwas On-Line." *Masaryk University Journal of Law and Technology* 3 (1): 51–78.

Slocombe, Will. 2008. "Beyond Good and Evil: The Inhuman Ethics of Redemption and Bloodlines. In *Computer Games as a Sociocultural Phenomenon: Games without Frontiers, War without Tears*, edited by Andreas Jahn-Sudmann and Ralf Stockmann, pp. 119–130. New York: Palgrave Macmillan.

Smart, Ninian. 1996. *Dimensions of the Sacred: An Anatomy of the World's Beliefs*. Berkeley: University of California Press.

Smith, Jonathan Z. 1982. *Imagining Religion: From Babylon to Jonestown*. Chicago: University of Chicago Press.

———. 1987. *To Take Place: Toward Theory in Ritual*. Chicago: University of Chicago Press.

Snodgrass, Jeffrey G., H. J. François Denga II, Michael G. Lacy, Jesse Fagan, David Most, Michael Blank, Lahoma Howard, Chad R. Kershner, Gregory Kdrambeer, Alissa Leavitt-Reynolds, Adam Reynolds, Jessica Vyvial-Larson, Josh Whaley, and Benjamin WInsteen. 2012. "Restorative Magical Adventure or Warcrack? Motivated MMO Play and the Pleasures and Perils of Online Experience." *Games and Culture* 7 (1): 3–28.

Society for Creative Anachronism. 2010. "Homepage." http://www.sca.org/ (accessed July 10, 2010).

Society for Universal Immortalism. 2008. "Homepage." http://www.universalim-mortalism.org/index.html (accessed August 16, 2008).

Spencer, Leon, and Anna Janssen. 2009. "Future Pasts of Magic and Deceit." In *World of Warcraft and Philosophy: Wrath of the Philosopher King*, edited by Luke Cuddy and John Norlinger, pp. 215–223. Chicago: Open Court.

Springvale, Rose. 2008. "Al Andalus in *Second Life*: The Al Andalus Magic Carpet Guided Tour Text." Al Andalus in *Second Life* weblog (March 8). http://alanda-lusinsecondlife.blogspot.com/2008/03/al-andalus-magic-carpet-guided-tour.html (accessed June 14, 2012).

———. 2009. "Introduction." Land Covenant for Al-Andalus region of *Second Life* (August 30).

———. 2012. Comment on the Virtual Democracy of Al Andalus Facebook page (June 6).

Sproul, Robert C. 1985. *The Holiness of God*. Wheaton, IL: Tyndale House Publishers.

Squire, Kurt. 2011. "From Content to Context: Videogames as Designed Experience." *Educational Researcher* 35 (8): 19–29.

Stark, Rodney, and William S. Bainbridge. 1985. *The Future of Religion: Secularization, Revival, and Cult Formation*. Los Angeles: University of California Press.

Steinhart, Eric. 2011. Email to the author (April 12).

———. 2013. Email to the author (March 8).

Stengers, Nicole. 1994. "Mind Is a Leaking Rainbow." *Cyberspace: First Steps*, edited by Michael Benedikt, pp. 49–58. Cambridge, MA: MIT Press.

Stenvaag, Sophrosyne. 2008. "An Open Letter to My Augmentationist Friends." *Finding Sophrosyne* weblog. http://sophrosyne-sl.livejournal.com/50673.html (accessed March 14, 2011).

Stephenson, Neal. 1992. *Snow Crash*. New York: Bantam.

Stickney, Anne. 2012. "Avengers Assemble! Transmogrify Your Own Superhero Team." *WoW Insider*. http://wow.joystiq.com/2012/05/10/avengers-assemble-transmogrify-your-own-superhero-team/ (accessed June 7, 2012).

Stock, Gregory. 2003. *Redesigning Humans: Choosing Our Genes, Changing Our Future*. New York: Houghton Mifflin Company.

Stone, Allucquere Rosanne. 1991. "Will the Real Body Please Stand Up?: Boundary Stories about Virtual Cultures." In *Cyberspace: First Steps*, edited by Michael Benedikt, pp. 81–118. Cambridge, MA: MIT Press.

Suma, Evan. 2010. "World of Warcraft with Microsoft Kinect," *YouTube* video. http://www.youtube.com/watch?v=62wj8eJoFHw&feature=player_embedded (accessed December 31, 2010).

Suntzu, Kheanna. 2010a. Email contribution to the *Cosmic Engineers* listserv (September 20).

———. 2010b. Email correspondence with the author (September 10).

Susan. 2010. Skype interview with the author (August 4). Listed pseudonymously.

———. 2011. Skype interview with the author (December 20). Listed pseudonymously.

Sussan, Remi. 2010. Email contribution to the Turing Church listserv (April 26).

Swain, Lisa. 2010. "*Myst* and *Halo*: A Conversation with Rand Miller and Marty O'Donnell." In *Halos and Avatars: Playing Video Games with God*, edited by Craig Detweiler, pp. 91–107. Louisville, KY: Westminster John Knox Press.

Sydell, Laura. 2005. "'Virtual' Virus Sheds Light on Real-World Behavior." *NPR* (October 5). http://www.npr.org/templates/story/story.php?storyId=4946772 (accessed October 12, 2011).

Tarter, Jill, and Will Wright. 2010. "Evolution, Creativity, and Future Life." In *Science Is Culture*, edited by Adam Bly, pp. 269–282. New York: Harper Perennial.

Taylor, Mark C. 1993. *Disfiguring: Art, Architecture, Religion*. Chicago: University of Chicago Press.

Taylor, T. L. 2003. "Intentional Bodies: Virtual Environments and the Designers Who Shape Them." *International Journal of Engineering Education* 19 (1): 25–34.

———. 2006. *Play between Worlds: Exploring Online Game Culture.* Cambridge, MA: MIT Press.

Teilhard de Chardin, Pierre. [1955] 1959. *The Phenomenon of Man.* Translated by Bernard Wall. New York: Harper & Brothers Publishers.

Telegraph.co.uk. 2009. "Teenager Obsessed by World of Warcraft First to Attend US Internet Addiction Retreat." *Telegraph.co.uk* (August 21). http://www.telegraph.co.uk/news/worldnews/northamerica/usa/6068807/Teenager-obsessed-by-World-of-Warcraft-first-to-attend-US-internet-addiction-retreat.html (accessed July 18, 2010).

Teusner, Paul Emerson. 2010. "New Thoughts on the Status of the Religious Cyborg." *Journal of Technology, Theology and Religion* 1 (2): 1–18.

Terasem Project. 2010. "Welcome to the CyBeRev Project." http://www.cyberev.org/ (accessed July 18, 2010).

———. 2011. "Terasem Rituals." *Terasem Faith.* http://terasemfaith.net/rituals (accessed March 14, 2011).

Thinkers. 2010a. "Can MMORPGs Save the World?" Transcript of October 12 Thinkers Discussion Group event posted at Mind Child's Musings weblog (October 13). http://extropiadasilva.wordpress.com/2010/10/13/thinkers-october-12-2010-can-mmorpgs-save-the-world/ (accessed October 13, 2010).

———. 2010b. "Sacred Cyberspace." Transcript of July 20 Thinkers Discussion Group event posted at Mind Child's Musings weblog (July 21). http://extropiadasilva.wordpress.com/2010/07/21/thinkers-july-20-2010-sacred-cyberspace/ (accessed March 14, 2011).

———. 2010c. "This Could Be Heaven?" Transcript of May 25 Thinkers Discussion Group event posted at Mind Child's Musings weblog (June 14). http://extropiadasilva.wordpress.com/2010/06/14/thinkers-may-25-2010-this-could-be-heaven/ (accessed March 14, 2011).

Tobin, Samuel. 2012. "Time and Space in Play: Saving and Pausing with the Nintendo DS." *Games and Culture* 7 (2): 127–141.

Toffler, Alvin. 1980. *The Third Wave.* New York: Bantam Books.

Tolkien, J. R. R. 1966. *The Tolkien Reader.* New York: Balantine Books.

Torres, Robin. 2011. "Drama Mamas: Much Ado about Funsuckers." *WoW Insider* (May 13). http://wow.joystiq.com/2011/05/13/drama-mamas-much-ado-about-funsuckers-friday/#continued (accessed June 4, 2011).

Triskele. 2008. "Welcome to Triskele." *Second Life* notecard.

Turing Church. 2010. "First Question," electronic mail thread (April 26).

Turkle, Sherry. 1996. "Rethinking Identity through Virtual Community." In *Clicking In: Hot Links to a Digital Culture,* edited by Lynn Hershman Leeson, pp. 116–122. Seattle: Bay Press.

———. 1999. "What Are We Thinking about When We Are Thinking about Computers?" In *The Science Studies Reader,* edited by Mario Biagioli, pp. 543–552. New York: Routledge.

Turner, Fred. 2006. *From Counterculture to Cyberculture: Stewart Brand, the Whole Earth Network, and the Rise of Digital Utopianism.* Chicago: University of Chicago Press.

Tylor, Edward Burnett. [1871] 1958. *Primitive Culture.* New York: Harper Torchbooks.

Ulam, Stanislaw. 1958. "Tribute to John von Neumann." *Bulletin of the American Mathematical Society* 64 (3, pt. 2): 1–49.

Undercroft, Benjamin. 2008. Email interview with the author (August 21).

Vacano, Larissa. 2010. *Second Life* interview with the author (September 2).

Vance, Jack. 1950. *The Dying Earth.* New York: Hillman.

Vinge, Vernor. [1981] 2001. *True Names.* In *True Names and the Opening of the Cyberspace Frontier,* edited by James Frenkel, pp. 239–330. New York: Tor.

——. [1993] 2003. "Technological Singularity" (rev. ed.). http://www.rohan.sdsu.edu/faculty/vinge/misc/WER2.html (accessed August 29, 2009). (Originally presented at the VISION-21 Symposium sponsored by NASA Lewis Research Center and the Ohio Aerospace Institute, March 30–31, 1993.)

Virtual Temple. 2007a. Discussion on Avatars as Persons (July 19) held at the Virtual Temple in *Second Life.*

——. 2007b. Discussion on Religion and Virtual Reality (February 1) held at the Virtual Temple in *Second Life.*

Vita-More, Natasha. 2006. "Extropy Institute Strategic Plan." *Extropy.* http://www.extropy.org/strategicplan.htm (accessed August 13, 2010).

——. 2010. "Epoch of Plasticity: The Metaverse as a Vehicle for Cognitive Enhancement." *Metaverse Creativity* 1 (1): 69–80.

——. 2011. Email correspondence with the author (September 22).

Wagner, Rachel. 2012. *Godwired: Religion, Ritual and Virtual Reality.* New York: Routledge.

Wald, Stephen. 2002. "The Technological New Jerusalem: Machines and Millennial Visions in Protestant America, 1880–1915." Master's thesis in history, University of Wisconsin–Madison.

Walker, Chip. 2005. "You, Robot." *Scientific American* 292: 36–37.

Walker, John. 2012. "World of Warcraft STILL Has 10 Million Subscribers!" *Rock, Paper Shotgun* (November 8). http://www.rockpapershotgun.com/2012/11/08/world-of-warcraft-still-has-10-million-subscribers/ (accessed April 4, 2013).

Wallis, James. 2007. "Making Games that Make Stories." In *Second Person: Role-Playing and Story in Games and Playable Media,* edited by Pat Harrigan and Noah Wardrip-Fruin, pp. 69–80. Cambridge, MA: MIT Press.

Wang, Shirley. 2011. "Could Those Hours Online Be Making Kids Nicer?" *Wall Street Journal* (August 16), p. D1.

Ward, Michael. 2008. *Planet Narnia: The Seven Heavens in the Imagination of C.S. Lewis.* New York: Oxford University Press.

Waskul, Dennis D. 2006. "The Role-Playing Game and the Game of Role-Playing: The Ludic Self and Everyday Life." In *Gaming as Culture: Essays on Reality, Identity, and*

Experience in Fantasy Games, edited by J. Patrick Williams, Sean Q. Hendricks, W. Keith Winkler, pp. 19–38. Jefferson, NC: McFarland & Company.

Weber, Max. 1958. "Science as a Vocation." In *From Max Weber: Essays in Sociology*, edited by Hans Gerth and C. Wright Mills, pp. 129–156. Oxford: Oxford University Press.

———. 1968. *On Charisma and Institution Building: Selected Papers*. Chicago: University of Chicago Press.

Wertheim, Margaret. 1999. *The Pearly Gates of Cyberspace: A History of Space from Dante to the Internet*. New York: W.W. Norton & Company.

Whewell, William. 1858. *Novum Organon Renovatum*. London: J.W. Parker and Son.

Whitesides, John G. 2009. "Religion, Genetics, and the Evolving American Experiment with Bioethics." *Masaryk University Journal of Law and Technology* 3 (1): 7–32.

Williams, Dmitri. 2006. "Why Game Studies Now?: Gamers Don't Bowl Alone." *Games and Culture* 1 (1): 13–16.

Williams, Dmitri, Tracy L. M. Kennedy, and Robert J. Moore. 2011. "Behind the Avatar: The Patterns, Practices, and Functions of Role Playing in MMOs." *Games and Culture* 6 (2): 171–200.

Williams, J. Patrick. 2006. "Consumption and Authenticity in the Collectible Strategy Games Subculture." In *Gaming as Culture: Essays on Reality, Identity, and Experience in Fantasy Games*, edited by J. Patrick Williams, Sean Q. Hendricks, W. Keith Winkler, pp. 77–99. Jefferson, NC: McFarland & Company.

Williams, J. Patrick, Sean Q. Hendricks, W. Keith Winkler. 2006. "Introduction: Fantasy Games, Gaming Cultures, and Social Life." In *Gaming as Culture: Essays on Reality, Identity, and Experience in Fantasy Games*, edited by J. Patrick Williams, Sean Q. Hendricks, W. Keith Winkler, pp. 1–18. Jefferson, NC: McFarland & Company.

Winkler, Keith. 2006. "The Business and Culture of Gaming." In *Gaming as Culture*, edited by J. Patrick Williams, Sean Q. Hendricks, and Keith Winkler. Jefferson, NC: McFarland & Company, Inc.

Wirman, Hanna. 2012. "Email Interviews in Player Research: The Case of the Sims 2 Skinners." *Westminster Papers in Communication and Culture* 9 (1): 153–170.

Witkowski, Emma. 2012. "On the Digital Playing Field: How We 'Do Sport' with Networked Computer Games." *Games and Culture* 7 (5): 349–374.

Wolf, Mark J. P. 2008a. "Introduction." In *The Video Game Explosion: A History from Pong to Playstation and Beyond*, edited by Mark J. P. Wolf, pp. xiii–xv. Westport, CT: Greenwood Press.

———. 2008b. "Morals, Ethics, and Video Games." In *The Video Game Explosion: A History from Pong to Playstation and Beyond*, edited by Mark J. P. Wolf, pp. 283–291. Westport, CT: Greenwood Press.

———, ed. 2008c. *The Video Game Explosion: A History from Pong to Playstation and Beyond*. Westport, CT: Greenwood Press.

World Council of Churches. 2006. "Towards 2010—Mission for the 21st Century." http://www.oikoumene.org/resources/documents/wcc-programmes/unity-mission-evangelism-and-spirituality/mission-and-unity/towards-2010-mission-for-the-21st-century.html (accessed August 15, 2010).

World of Warcraft Magazine. 2010. "Raiding the Physical World." *World of Warcraft Official Magazine* 1 (3): 58–63.

WoWhead. 2008. "Veteran of the Wrathgate—Achievement." Comment by FranklinNoble (December 11). http://www.wowhead.com/achievement=547/veteran-of-the-wrathgate#comments:40 (accessed September 8, 2011).

WoWWiki. 2010. "Sargeras." http://www.wowwiki.com/Sargeras (accessed July 10, 2010).

Yahia, Mohammad. 2007. "IOL Virtual Hajj in *Second Life*." *IslamOnline.net* (December 6). http://www.islamonline.net/servlet/Satellite?c=Article_C&pagename=Zone-English-News/NWELayout&cid=1196786035497 (accessed September 5, 2010).

Yee, Nick. 2006. "The Gamer Habitat." *Daedalus Project* website. http://www.nick-yee.com/daedalus/archives/001518.php?page=3 (accessed March 4, 2011).

Young, Glenn. 2004. "Reading and Praying Online: The Continuity of Religion Online and Online Religion in Internet Christianity." In *Religion Online: Finding Faith on the Internet,* edited by Lorne L. Dawson and Douglas E. Cowan, pp. 93–105. New York: Routledge.

Zagal, José P. 2009. "Ethically Notable Videogames: Moral Dilemmas and Gameplay." *Breaking New Ground Innovation in Games, Play, Practice and Theory: Prodeedings of DiGRA 2009.* http://works.bepress.com/jose_zagal/3/ (accessed March 10, 2012).

Zagal, José P., Clara Fernández-Vara, and Michael Mateas. 2008. "Rounds, Levels, and Waves: The Early Evolution of Gameplay Segmentation." *Games and Culture* 3 (2): 176–198.

Zelazny, Roger. 1967. *Lord of Light.* Garden City, NY: Doubleday.

Zhong, Zhi-Jin. 2011. "The Effects of Collective MMORPG (Massively Multiplayer Online Role-Playing Games) Play on Gamers' Online and Offline Social Capital." *Computers in Human Behavior* 27: 2352–2363.

Zimbardo, Philip G., and Nikita Duncan. 2012. "'The Demise of Guys': How Video Games and Porn Are Ruining a Generation." *CNN.com.* http://www.cnn.com/2012/05/23/health/living-well/demise-of-guys/index.html (accessed May 27, 2012).

Zukav, Gary. 1979. *The Dancing Wu Li Masters: An Overview of the New Physics.* New York: William Morrow and Company.

Index